The Sixties in America

The Sixties in America

Volume III

School Desegregation — Zappa, Frank

Editor

Carl Singleton

Fort Hays State University

Project Editor

Rowena Wildin

Salem Press, Inc.

Pasadena, California

Hackensack, New Jersey

Managing Editor: Christina J. Moose
Project Editor: Rowena Wildin   *Production Editor:* Janet Long
Research Supervisor: Jeffry Jensen   *Research Assistant:* Jun Ohunki
Acquisitions Editor: Mark Rehn   *Graphics and Design:* James Hutson
Photograph Editor: Karrie Hyatt   *Layout:* William Zimmerman

Title page photo: London Daily Express/Archive Photos

Library of Congress Cataloging-in-Publication Data

The Sixties in America / editor, Carl Singleton ; project editor, Rowena Wildin.
    p. cm.
    Includes bibliographical references and index.
    ISBN 0-89356-982-8 (set : alk. paper). — ISBN 0-89356-983-6 (v. 1 : alk. paper). — ISBN 0-89356-984-4 (v. 2 : alk. paper). — ISBN 0-89356-985-2 (v. 3 : alk. paper)
    1. United States — History — 1961-1969 — Encyclopedias.
    I. Singleton, Carl. II. Wildin, Rowena, 1956-   .

E841.S55   1999
973.92—dc21   98-49255
                                                                                      CIP

Fifth Printing

■ Contents

■ Alphabetical List of Entries

Volume I

Volume II

Volume III

The Sixties in America

■ School Desegregation

The process of eliminating segregated, or dual, schools. School desegregation, one of the most controversial social and political issues of the 1960's, was originally directed at the southern states but would later have national implications.

Before the Civil War, African Americans were prohibited from getting an education in most of the United States. After the Civil War, schools were established for black education but strictly on a segregated basis. For African Americans in the South, where 90 percent of the U.S. black population lived in 1900, education, if available at all, was usually only up to the fifth or sixth grade. High schools for African Americans were rarely available except in the largest cities of the South, and curricula were limited to the trades for boys and home economics for girls.

In 1896, the United States Supreme Court reviewed a Louisiana law calling for the "equal but separate accommodation for the white and colored race" on the railroads. In a seven-to-one decision, *Plessy v. Ferguson*, the Supreme Court upheld the Louisiana law and established the doctrine of "separate but equal." This doctrine of "separate but equal" provided the legal justification for segregated schools for the next sixty years.

Led by the National Association for the Advancement of Colored People (NAACP), African Americans were ready by the 1950's to attempt overturning the "separate but equal" doctrine contending that separate race schools could never be equal. According to the NAACP, separate schools violated the "equal protection" clause of the Fourteenth Amendment to the United States Constitution. The United States Supreme Court agreed with the NAACP in its 1954 *Brown v. Board of Education of Topeka, Kansas* decision. Chief Justice Earl Warren, in delivering a unanimous Supreme Court decision, declared that segregated schools, even if they provided equal facilities, deprived African Americans of "equal educational opportunity."

Even though the "separate but equal" doctrine was invalidated by the Supreme Court and dual schools were no longer legal, the battle for school integration was just beginning. A policy of "massive resistance" was quickly implemented throughout the South. Massive resistance meant the South

would do almost anything to prevent the integration of public schools. Most southern states passed "interposition and nullification" laws declaring the Brown decision null and void. Some cities, such as Little Rock, Arkansas, and Norfolk, Virginia, closed their public schools rather than integrate.

The 1960's was the turning point for school desegregation in the United States. The massive resistance of the 1950's was followed by "token compliance" in the early 1960's and massive desegregation by the end of the decade. Token compliance meant that a few African American students were admitted to traditionally white schools. By admitting one or two black students to traditionally white schools, the southern states hoped to convince the country that they were in compliance with the Brown decision.

During the 1959-1960 school year, only .01 percent of black students in the South were attending school with white students. By the 1964-1965 school year, a full decade after *Brown*, only 2.2 percent of blacks were attending schools with whites. The pace of school desegregation was so slow that two political scientists calculated that at the current pace it would take 3,180 years to fully integrate southern schools.

Two main factors influenced the slow pace of school desegregation. First, the Supreme Court can render decisions, but it has no power to enforce them. Second, the Supreme Court, realizing the enormous impact the *Brown* decision would have in arousing the emotions of southerners, wanted the states with segregated schools to implement desegregation on their own without interference from the Court. The Court was willing to let southern states determine what "all deliberate speed" meant when desegregating their schools.

However, the patience of the Supreme Court was not limitless. In two different decisions in 1964, the Court indicated its displeasure with the slow pace of desegregation. In a Virginia case, the Court ruled that "there has been entirely too much deliberation and not enough speed" in desegregation. Likewise, in a Tennessee decision, the Court observed that "deliberate speed" did not mean indefinite delay in desegregation. Congress also tried to accelerate the pace of school desegregation. Title VI of the 1964 Civil Rights Act provided federal assistance to desegregating districts and also authorized the denial of federal education funds to school districts refusing to desegregate. This carrot-and-stick approach by the federal government was responsible, in part, for a substantial increase in school desegregation. By 1966, 17 percent of African Americans in the South were attending integrated schools.

Two Supreme Court decisions in the late 1960's put an end to token compliance and helped bring about the complete desegregation of public schools in America. In a 1968 decision, *Green v. New Kent County, Virginia,* the Supreme Court struck down "freedom of choice" plans that allowed pupils to choose the school they wished to attend. Under these plans, no whites requested enrollment in black schools, and few blacks were bold enough to request enrollment in white schools. In striking down "freedom of choice" plans, the Supreme Court ruled that school boards were "charged with the affirmative duty to take whatever steps might be necessary to convert to a unitary system in which racial discrimination would be eliminated 'root and branch.'"

The following year, the Supreme Court struck the final blow to "token compliance." A number of Mis-

sissippi school districts requested additional time to implement school desegregation plans and, for the first time, the executive branch agreed with Mississippi's request for additional time to desegregate. The Court refused any further delay. In *Alexander v. Holmes County, Mississippi, Board of Education,* the Court declared that "the obligation of every school district is to terminate dual schools at once and to operate now and hereafter only unitary schools." Dual, or segregated, schools would no longer be permitted, while unitary, or integrated, schools became the new standard. By the beginning of the 1970 school year, 79 percent of African Americans in the South were attending desegregated schools.

Impact The primary tool used to integrate the millions of public school students in accordance with the Court's ruling was busing. The use of busing to achieve integrated schools caused numerous problems in the 1970's and 1980's; however, most states

In May, 1962, demonstrators gather on the steps of a high school in Englewood, New Jersey, which was to be opened as an experiment in integration. (National Archives)

complied with federal mandates. Critics of busing maintain that it led to the abandonment of neighborhood schools, which accelerated the decline in a sense of community. Parents complained that busing impeded their ability to attend parent-teacher meetings, and students complained that busing made it more difficult for them to participate in extracurricular activities. Increasingly, African Americans questioned busing as a tool for desegregation. In most school districts, the burden of busing falls on minority pupils. A far higher percentage of minorities are bused for desegregation, and they are bused for many more years than are white students.

School desegregation was perhaps the most important, visible goal of the Civil Rights movement. Although desegregation of public transportation, housing, and restaurants and other businesses along with the securing of voting rights were all vital, it was in public schools that blacks and whites would actually spend several hours together each day. Desegregation of schools was also significant for both real and symbolic reasons because it was the nation's youth, the children, who were growing up in biracial and multiracial school systems. Leaders and parents on both sides of the issue clearly realized that the integration of schools would have a lasting influence on the relations between whites and African Americans.

Subsequent Events By the mid-1970's, resegregation of the schools was a common phenomenon. Although the Supreme Court declared dual schools unconstitutional, the courts have not been able to control the social and demographic changes that have taken place in the United States and have led to resegregation. Public schools in Chicago, Detroit, Philadelphia, Boston, and New York City, as well as most other large U.S. cities, are overwhelmingly populated by minorities. The movement of whites to the suburbs has meant that inner-city schools have fewer white pupils. In addition, concerns about the quality of public schools or the subjects taught or not taught (sex education, evolution, creationism) have led wealthier, often white, parents to enroll their children in private schools.

Since the 1960's, the composition of the Supreme Court has changed, and the justices have different views about busing and school desegregation. For example, in *Pasadena v. Spangler* (1976), the Court ruled that once a school district has adopted a ra-

cially neutral plan, it need not continue to assign students to meet racial balance. Also, in *Oklahoma City v. Dowell* (1991), the Court ruled that school districts could be released from federal supervision if they have shown good faith and have eliminated past practices of intentional segregation—even if it results in a return to single-race schools.

Additional Information The best single volume on school desegregation is Richard Kluger's *Simple Justice* (1975). Two other excellent sources are *The Burden of Brown* (1984), by Raymond Wolters, and *From Brown to Bakke: The Supreme Court and School Integration, 1954-1978* (1979), by J. Harris Wilkinson. For opposing views on busing see Gary Orfield's, *Must We Bus?* (1978) and Lino Graglia's *Disaster by Decree* (1976).

Darryl Paulson

See also Busing; Civil Rights Act of 1964; Education; Holmes, Hamilton, and Charlayne Hunter; Malone, Vivian; National Association for the Advancement of Colored People (NAACP).

■ Schwerner, Goodman, and Chaney Deaths

Date June 21, 1964

Three civil rights workers murdered by members of the Ku Klux Klan in Mississippi. The outrage over their murders brought unprecedented publicity and pressure for the federal government to enforce civil rights of African Americans in the southern states.

Origins and History The Civil Rights movement reached the high-water mark in 1964. A number of Supreme Court decisions had forced racial integration in the South, and on July 2, 1964, President Lyndon B. Johnson signed the Civil Rights Act, which, along with the Voting Rights Act of 1965, did more to ensure the political rights of African Americans than anything since the Emancipation. However, actions by the federal government were only a part of the civil rights struggle of the 1960's. Thousands of civil rights activists from both the North and South fought, and sometimes gave their lives, for equality of all citizens under the law, regardless of race.

One group in the forefront of the civil rights struggle was the Council of Federated Organizations (COFO), an umbrella group of affiliated civil

The burned remains of the station wagon that three civil rights activists—Michael Schwerner, Andrew Goodman, and James Chaney—were riding in when they disappeared June 21 was found three days later, but their bodies were not found until August 4. (AP/Wide World Photos)

rights organizations including the National Association for the Advancement of Colored People (NAACP), the Student Nonviolent Coordinating Committee (SNCC), and the Congress for Racial Equality (CORE). The COFO's main activity for 1964 was the Mississippi Summer Project, designed to bring hundreds of northern college students to the southern states to help register African American voters and run "freedom schools," which taught southern African Americans their legal and constitutional rights and basic reading and writing in areas where schools were lacking.

The COFO expected a violent reaction to its efforts in the South. To prepare the volunteers who would serve in the South during the summer of 1964, the COFO held a training camp at the Western College for Women in Oxford, Ohio. The volunteers were taught techniques such as nonviolent resistance, how best to protect themselves against police batons, and how to travel in groups for safety.

It was at this training camp that twenty-four-year-old Michael Schwerner, a recent graduate of Cornell University, met fellow New Yorker Andrew Goodman, a twenty-year-old student at Queens College. By the middle of June, they were assigned to work in Neshoba County, Mississippi, where they met twenty-one-year-old James Chaney, a local NAACP activist. Chaney, the only African American of the three, had grown up in the area and served as a local contact who could guide them through what was essentially foreign territory.

On Sunday, June 21, Schwerner, Chaney, and Goodman were in Longdale, a rural part of the county where, a week earlier, the local Ku Klux Klan had burned down a church and attacked and beaten many of its leaders. The three activists were investigating the attack with the idea of helping track down the perpetrators and offering their assistance in rebuilding the church. Schwerner had spoken at the church the previous Memorial Day, and the Klan attack sent a clear message about the welcome civil rights workers would receive in Neshoba County. After surveying the burnt-out church and speaking with church leaders, the three began to drive back to their headquarters in Meridian, Mississippi, about thirty miles away. Their training had taught them it was not safe to be out in rural Mississippi after dark.

The Murders At about 4:00 P.M., Neshoba County Deputy Sheriff Cecil Ray Price stopped the car carrying Schwerner, Goodman, and Chaney, ostensibly for speeding. The local police and Klan were well aware that the station wagon belonged to civil rights organizers, and the speeding charge may have been a pretext for Price, a Klansman, to arrest and harass the three men. In any event, the three were locked up in Neshoba County Jail—a dangerous situation, they realized, since civil rights workers had previously been severely beaten by the police in southern jails. They were released unharmed, however, at about 10:00 that evening. While they were being detained at the jail, Price alerted a number of local Klansmen and their sympathizers that he had detained the three civil rights activists. The Klansmen arranged to intercept the trio on their way out of Neshoba County. Just before Schwerner, Chaney, and Goodman were to cross the county line, Price, followed by two other carloads of a self-selected "posse," caught up with them. Price pulled the civil rights workers' car over, as he had earlier that day, but this time he ordered the three into the back seat of his police cruiser, striking Chaney across the back of his head when he did not move fast enough.

The Klansmen drove the three terrified civil rights workers to an isolated meadow. When the caravan of cars stopped, one of the lynch mob, Wayne Roberts, opened the rear door of Price's cruiser and pulled Schwerner out, yelling, "Are you that nigger-lover?," then shot him point-blank in the heart. He then grabbed Goodman and shot him in the chest. Another member of the lynch mob, James Jordan, pulled Chaney from the other side of the police cruiser, and he and Roberts both shot him in the abdomen. After Chaney fell, Roberts shot Chaney again, in the back of the head.

The killers loaded the three bodies into the station wagon and drove to a nearby farm where an earthen dam was being constructed. They threw the bodies at the foot of the dam and bulldozed earth over them. They arranged to have the station wagon torched and pushed into a swamp. The burnt-out hulk of the car was found within a few days, but the decomposed bodies of Schwerner, Chaney, and Goodman lay undiscovered until August 4.

Impact The disappearance of the three civil rights workers caused a national sensation. Journalists from the national media and Federal Bureau of Investigation (FBI) agents descended on Neshoba County in droves. For forty-four days, the nation followed the search in the newspapers and on television. President Lyndon B. Johnson obtained regular updates from FBI director J. Edgar Hoover and personally phoned the news to the families of the missing men.

The immense publicity surrounding the disappearance of the three activists brought home to the nation like never before the violent nature of the resistance to the Civil Rights movement in the South. Some African American southerners bitterly noted that hundreds of African Americans had been lynched in the South during the previous half century, but it took the murders of two white Northern students for national attention to be focused on the South's vicious and illegal resistance to their efforts to obtain civil rights.

On October 20, 1967, an all-white Mississippi jury found seven men, including Deputy Sheriff Price and Roberts, guilty of murder. The jury could not agree on charges against or acquitted a number of other defendants, including the sheriff of Neshoba County, Lawrence Rainey. This marked the first time a Mississippi jury ever found a white person guilty of crimes perpetrated on a black person or civil rights worker. After exhausting their appeals, the guilty men all served lengthy prison sentences at various federal penitentiaries.

Additional Information A well-written story of the incident, set in the broader background of the Civil Rights movement, is Seth Cagin and Phillip Dray's *We Are Not Afraid: The Story of Goodman, Schwerner, Chaney, and the Civil Rights Campaign for Mississippi* (1988); a more focused and immediate account by a journalist covering the civil rights struggle in Mississippi is William Bradford Huie's *Three Lives for Mississippi* (1965).

Christopher Berkeley

See also Civil Rights Act of 1964; Civil Rights Movement; Congress of Racial Equality (CORE); Ku Klux

Klan (KKK); National Association for the Advancement of Colored People (NAACP); Student Nonviolent Coordinating Committee (SNCC); Voting Rights Legislation.

■ Science and Technology

The 1960's saw scientific breakthroughs, including a lunar landing, that altered scientists' view of nature on large and small scales and the development of medical technology and electronics that improved the standard of living.

In 1957, the Soviet Union launched Sputnik 1 into orbit, and Americans reacted with horror, thinking that proof of a Soviet lead in technology and science had suddenly appeared overhead. The reaction was unwarranted. Although the United States' early space program suffered embarrassing failures, science was robust in nearly all fields; U.S. scientists, many of whom were naturalized European refugees, increasingly won prestigious prizes and announced major new discoveries throughout the 1950's.

The United States had once been a scientific backwater, but World War II changed that. Before the war, France, Germany, and England dominated physics, chemistry, mathematics, and engineering; only in astronomy and biology, genetics especially, was the United States Europe's equal. Americans seemed not to care much about science, and funding for it was low. In the 1930's, however, European refugees, including Albert Einstein, immigrated to the United States to escape persecution in their homelands, and the country assembled a formidable scientific expertise, especially in physics. During the war, that expertise, concentrated in the Manhattan Project, built the first atomic bomb. Americans also contributed to the development of radar and improved radio communications and designed advanced aircraft and submarines. Most of the European scientists stayed in U.S. academia after the war, expanding the indigenous talent and training a new generation of researchers.

The fevered pace of achievement in both theoretical and applied sciences hardly slackened during the late 1940's and 1950's, as the Cold War created a rivalry and lent urgency to research and development, particularly of armaments. However, the public perception that the United States was in second place, and therefore militarily vulnerable, persisted into the 1960's and intensified when Soviet astronaut Uri Gagarin became the first man in space in 1961. International politics was behind President John F. Kennedy's vow on May 26, 1961, to put an American on the Moon by the end of the decade, increases in government research grants and scholarships in all the natural sciences, and a new emphasis on science education in public schools. Nevertheless, many noteworthy scientific achievements of the 1960's were independent of politics.

Astronomy In 1960, Allan Sandage of Mount Palomar Observatory spotted the source of some strong radio-frequency emissions. The exotic object had a strange glow and baffling spectrum, but he did not fully appreciate what he had found and called it a quasi-stellar object (or quasar). Three years later, Maarten Schmidt found that such objects were receding at extremely high speeds. Astronomers concluded that the quasars marked the edge of the observable universe and their light was billions of years old. These findings suggested that the universe was expanding, which fit a cosmological theory that the universe originated in an primeval explosion, or "big bang." The theory predicted that an afterglow from the explosion should still exist at microwave frequencies, and in 1964, Arno A. Pensias and Robert W. Wilson discovered cosmic microwave background radiation while they were seeking the source of static in an experimental antenna. Their discovery, hailed as among the most important in twentieth century science, made the big bang the standard model in cosmology.

Astronomers also detected astonishingly strong sources of X rays among the stars, some of them the first evidence of black holes, a term coined by Princeton University's John A. Wheeler in 1968. Meanwhile, Cornell University astronomers put radar to use by mapping the surface of Venus, invisible to optical telescopes because of its thick cloud cover.

Biology Microbiology grew into a dynamic subspecialty, and from it came the first techniques of genetic engineering. Specifically, biologists learned how the deoxyribonucleic acid (DNA) of cell nuclei and proteins interact; the knowledge promised to lead to control of the process. In 1960, U.S. scientists parsed the sequence of 124 amino acids in ribonuclease, an enzyme involved in the chemical action of ribonucleic acid (RNA). The following year, Marshall W. Warren deciphered the RNA code for the

Science Milestones

1960	American physicists Arthur L. Schawlow and Charles H. Townes create the first laser in the United States.
	The United States launches Tiros 1, an experimental weather satellite that takes thousands of pictures of Earth's cloud cover.
	The first felt-tip pen, the Pentel; pans coated with Teflon, a nonstick coating; and the first electronic wristwatch, the Bulova Accutron tuning-fork watch, are introduced.
	The Xerox 914, which can handle nine-by-fourteen-inch paper, initiates a revolution in document copying.
1962	The first commercial communications satellite, the Telstar, is launched and used to transmit the first live television programming between England and the United States.
	The first commerical nuclear reactor, Jersey Central Power and Light's Oyster Creek Plant, has the capacity to compete with traditional power plants.
	The first direct-dial long distance telephone service goes into operation.
	The world's first nuclear-powered ship, the *Savannah*, completes its first voyage from Yorktown, Virginia, to Savannah, Georgia.
1963	Astronomer Maarten Schmidt discovers the nature of quasars, or quasi-stellar objects.
	The first touch-tone telephones are introduced in Pennsylvania by American Telephone and Telegraph.

Continued on next page

amino acid phenylalanine in eggs and milk—the first genetic decoding. In 1963, scientists described the spiral and circular forms that DNA can assume, and in 1964, Carl Yanofsky showed that the sequence of nucleotides, the "letters" of the genetic code, line up with the order of amino acids in proteins. Yanofsky's discovery helped scientists understand how proteins are assembled in the nucleus. Further understanding of synthesis occurred in 1965 when Robert W. Holley determined the molecular structure of transfer RNA. In 1969, the first amino acid sequence of an immunoglobulin was found, and Harvard scientists discovered the gene responsible for sugar metabolism in bacteria. Among the most significant events was the synthesis of ribonuclease, which plays a part in cutting RNA nucleotides and, therefore, became a tool in genetic engineering. The first trans-species cells, hybrids whose chromo-somes came from both humans and mice, were grown in 1967 and became another tool for genetic engineering. James D. Watson awoke the public to the excitement of such discoveries with his best-selling popular science book *The Double Helix* (1968), which recounted the discovery of DNA's structure.

Other areas of biology, particularly those related to the environment, saw advances. Robert H. MacArthur and Edward O. Wilson published the equilibrium theory of species distribution, which helped explain how species fill ecological niches. New strains of wheat increased crop yields dramatically, part of the Green Revolution in food production. However, warnings of dangers to the food supply and the environment captured the widest attention. In 1962, Rachel Carson worried consumers and angered pesticide manufacturers with her book, *Silent Spring*, which explained how pesticides were harm-

Science Milestones (continued)

1964	The big bang theory for the creation of the universe gains support when Arno A. Pensias and Robert W. Wilson discover cosmic microwave background radiation.
	The longest suspension bridge, the Verrazano-Narrows Bridge, between Staten Island and Brooklyn, opens.
1965	Dartmouth College's John Kemeny and Thomas Kurt create a new, simple computer programming language, Beginner's All-purpose Symbolic Instructional Code, or BASIC.
	Biologists develop pheromones, artificial sex attractants, for some insects.
1966	Robert Ardrey publishes a book theorizing that humans, like animals, are territorial.
	Kodak introduces a small, disposable four-shot flashcube for cameras.
1967	Jocelyn Bell, a graduate student at Cambridge University, discovers pulsars, clocklike radio pulses from space.
1968	American geologists, including W. Jason Morgan, develop the theory of plate tectonics, the idea that Earth's outer shell is made up of rigid plates sliding past or under each other.
	Physicists Jerome Friedman, Henry Kendell, and Richard Taylor discover quarks, the foundation of protons and neutrons.
	Physicist John Wheeler first uses the term "black hole" to refer to the aftermath of a stellar collapse.
1969	Scientists at Merck Laboratories and Rockefeller University announce the synthesis of the enzyme ribonuclease.
	Astronaut Neil A. Armstrong becomes the first human to step on the surface of the Moon.

ing people and animals. She helped create a popular sentiment against pesticides that, in turn, led to a government ban on the insecticide DDT (dichloro-diphenyl-trichloroethane) in 1969. During the same year, the government banned or restricted some food additives, such as cyclamates, because research had associated them with cancer.

Chemistry In 1960, Robert B. Woodward synthesized chlorophyll, the chemical involved in plant photosynthesis, and the next year, scientists created lawrencium, a radioactive element that does not exist naturally. In 1965, chemists produced the first compound that included a noble, or inert, gas, xenon platinum hexaflouride. Like other noble gases such as helium and neon, xenon had long been thought incapable of forming compounds. Techno-

logical advances aided chemical processing and investigation. Gas chromatography first succeeded in separating rare-earth complexes—rare earths are elements with atomic numbers 58 through 71—in 1965, and by 1967, the scanning electron microscope was perfected for practical use. It could produce three-dimensional images of objects as small as ten nanometers wide.

Computers and Electronics The invention of transistors and the integrated circuit in the 1950's dramatically expanded the number of electronic devices available to the public while reducing their size. These solidstate electronics included stereos, televisions, and communications equipment; however, the ubiquitous transistor radio symbolized the decade's infatuation with technology.

Patenting of the silicon chip by Texas Instruments in 1961, commercial availability of semiconductor diodes after 1963, and the invention of bubble memory in 1969 contributed to the growing computing power and miniaturization of computers through the decade. Meanwhile, computer languages, such as COBOL (*CO*mmon *B*usiness *O*riented *L*anguage) and BASIC (*B*eginning *A*ll-purpose *S*ymbolic *In*struction *C*ode), simplified programming. In 1964, International Business Machines (IBM) marketed the Magnetic Tape/Selectric Typewriter, the first word processor.

Geology That continents could slowly drift over Earth's surface had been proposed in 1912, but most geologists dismissed the idea. By the end of the 1960's, however, this concept had become part of a new theory. In 1960, Harry Hess suggested that seafloors spread and, in doing so, push continents. Evidence gathered at Columbia University's Lamont Geological Observatory and elsewhere confirmed seafloor spreading, and geologists had reason to think that continents were the exposed parts of huge plates on Earth's surface, sliding past each other or diving under one another. In 1967, W. Jason Morgan named the theory "plate tectonics," and it steadily gained acceptance.

Medicine As new materials and electronic technologies improved the living standard of Americans, new medical treatments offered hope of healthier and longer lives. During the 1960's, vaccines were introduced to combat hepatitis B, German measles, and meningitis. New operations corrected some disabilities such as deafness and curvature of the spine. Lasers were used in eye surgery, and in 1967, Irving S. Cooper successfully used cryosurgery to treat Parkinson's disease. However, the most dramatic new medical procedures involved organ transplants. The development of immunosuppressant drugs that checked the body's natural rejection of foreign tissue made organ transplants much more successful. Surgeons were able to transplant livers and lungs for the first time in 1963. The first heart transplantation took place in South Africa, but in the United States, Denton A. Cooley implanted an artificial heart, made of Dacron and silicon rubber, for the first time in 1969. Michael De Bakey had already used an artificial heart to keep a patient alive during cardiac surgery in 1963 and in 1965 tested the implantation of plastic arteries. Also in 1965, a plastic mesh became available that allowed surgeons to join large sections of body tissue without incurring a rejection reaction.

Physicians made wider use of machines. For example, improvements in incubators increased the survival rate of prematurely born infants. Portable units made it possible to perform kidney dialysis in a patient's home. Thermography helped physicians map temperature variations in the body and thereby detect cancers, especially breast cancer, and ultrasonic imaging improved in quality during the decade until it became a standard tool for examining the body's interior.

Public health benefited from announcements by the American Lung Association (1960) and the U.S. Surgeon General (1964) linking cigarette smoking and lung cancer. After 1964, all tobacco companies were required to print warnings of the health risk on cigarette packages.

Military Technology At the same time, a host of developments in military hardware produced new threats to life. The deadliest developments were in nuclear arms. In 1960, the U.S. Navy deployed the first submarine-launched ballistic missile, the Polaris, capable of delivering a nuclear warhead far inland; by the end of the decade, even longer ranged Poseidon missiles were on some of the United States' seventy-four nuclear-powered submarines. These missiles expanded the nation's strategic choices— military doctrine had hitherto relied on bombers and land-based missiles—and intensified the arms race. In 1963, a new type of nuclear weapon, the neutron bomb, was tested, although it was not deployed. Also in 1963, a treaty with the Soviet Union and Great Britain stopped nuclear testing above ground or in or under water, but in the United States, tests continued underground. To watch for threats to U.S. security, the military launched dozens of spy satellites.

Physics The decade was momentous for physics and its technological spin-offs. In 1960, Robert V. Pound and Glen A. Rebka confirmed a key prediction of Albert Einstein's general theory of relativity when they showed that gravity shifts light waves toward the red end of the spectrum. New theories helped explain the unexpected abundance of new elementary particles that were being detected at particle accelerators, including the Stanford Linear Accelerator Center (SLAC), opened in 1965. In

1961, Murray Gell-Mann announced a classification scheme, called the "Eightfold Way," which explained particles' relations; his ideas were confirmed by experiments in 1964. Also in 1961, Richard Hofstadter unveiled the basic structure of protons and neutrons. In 1965, Gell-Mann and George Zweig argued that the structure of protons and neutrons indicated they were made up of even smaller particles, dubbed quarks; researchers at SLAC confirmed the existence of quarks in 1968. In 1965, Moo-Young Han and Yoichiro Nambu added a crucial property, color, to the theory of quarks, which became known as quantum chromodynamics. Another new theory emerged in 1967. Steven Weinberg and Sheldon Glashow (with Pakistani physicist Abdus Salam) explained how electromagnetism and the weak nuclear interaction are aspects of the same fundamental force. Their electroweak theory marked the first advance in unifying the forces of nature since the theory of electromagnetism in the nineteenth century.

Nuclear power grew steadily through the decade: In 1962, two hundred atomic reactors were already in operation. However, the technical marvel of the era—to popular science writers and their readers—was the laser. Theodore H. Maiman fired up the first pulse laser in 1960, and continuous-beam lasers soon followed. Although they did not turn into the death-rays that some writers predicted, lasers gradually found applications in materials processing, surgery, communications, and instrumentation.

Space Science The space age developed rapidly during the 1960's as the National Aeronautics and Space Administration (NASA) undertook space exploration, the most ambitious and expensive engineering project of modern times. Although probes to other planets and manned spaceflight grabbed most of the headlines, satellites affected Americans' lives profoundly by providing improved communications and the new science of remote sensing. The first communications satellite, Echo 1, went into orbit in 1960; it reflected radio signals. Telstar, which could amplify radio and television signals, began service in 1962. The first commercial satellite, Early Bird, began transmitting telephone and television signals in 1965, and many NASA or commercial satellites of greater sophistication followed. The chief purpose of remote sensing satellites was weather forecasting. The ten satellites in the Television Infra-Red Observation Satellites program from 1960 to 1965 and the Environmental Science Services Administration satellite of 1966 began the continuous photographing of Earth's cloud cover that has revolutionized meteorology. The six Orbiting Geophysical Observatory satellites launched between 1964 and 1969 returned information about Earth's atmosphere, magnetic field, and radiation belts.

The first U.S. space probe to reach another planet was Mariner 2, which was launched in 1962 and passed within 34,800 kilometers of Venus later the same year. In 1964, Mariner 4 sent back the first close-up photos of Mars—from less than 10,000 kilometers. More Mariner probes visited Venus and Mars later in the decade, producing ever sharper photographs and gathering data. The first close-up of the Moon came from Ranger 7 in 1964. The Lunar Orbiter mapped large portions of the Moon with photographs in 1966, and Surveyor 1, the first U.S. probe to land softly, sent back images of the surface during the same year. More Surveyor and Ranger probes followed to study the Moon in preparation for a visit by astronauts.

Meanwhile, manned spaceflight programs practiced the skills necessary for the trip to the Moon. Project Mercury, 1958 to 1963, put the first American in space with Alan B. Shepard, Jr.'s fifteen-minute suborbital flight on May 5, 1961; John Glenn was the first American to orbit Earth in 1962. Mercury's six manned missions tested how humans adapt to launch and spaceflight. Mercury's successor, the Gemini program—ten missions from 1961 to 1966—gave pairs of astronauts practice walking in space, maneuvering for rendezvous and docking, and adjusting to long-duration flights. The final technological step toward a lunar landing began in 1964 with the Apollo program. However, the effort suffered a tragic setback when three astronauts died during a ground test of the Apollo 1 command module; manned flights were postponed until the capsule was redesigned. In 1968, James A. Lovell, Frank Borman, and William A. Anders circled the moon in Apollo 8. On July 20, 1969, fulfilling President Kennedy's vow, Neil A. Armstrong stepped from the lunar landing module, *Eagle*, onto the Moon's surface, the first human to visit another heavenly body; Edwin E. "Buzz" Aldrin soon followed him, while command module pilot Michael Collins orbited overhead. They returned with lunar rock samples, as did the Apollo 12 crew during their voyage three months later.

Transportation Although the United States trailed Europe and Japan in development of high-speed trains, transportation otherwise became safer, more versatile, and faster. Expansion of the interstate highway system shortened long-distance driving times, and engineering improvements generally made automobiles more powerful and reliable—but not reliable enough: Ralph Nader's indictment of automobile safety, *Unsafe at Any Speed* (1965), awoke public concern and moved Congress to create the National Highway Traffic Safety Administration, which later effected such safety measures as standard seat belts.

Air traffic steadily increased during the decade. New, smaller commercial jet aircraft, such as the DC-9, opened passenger service to many more destinations with short flights that had been uneconomical using larger planes. Meanwhile, aircraft manufacturers were developing jumbo jets, such as Boeing's 747, which first flew in 1970, to carry large groups long distances at reduced cost.

Impact Armstrong's first steps on the Moon produced a national euphoria. It looked as if U.S. scientists could achieve anything that they wanted, an attitude summed up by an often repeated joke: "If they can send a man to the Moon, why can't they cure the common cold?" New discoveries in astronomy, physics, and biology maintained the leadership of the United States in scientific research and in big experimental projects, such as those conducted at the Fermi National Accelerator Laboratory near Chicago, founded in 1968 and operational in 1972. The pace of research and development for technology quickened.

However, powerful social countercurrents brought criticism of science and technology. Because of public disgust over the Vietnam War and the arms race, the military and its technology came under attack. The cost of big government science projects, such as the Apollo program, also displeased many taxpayers. Furthermore, creationism and research based upon biblical revelations challenged the authenticity of some scientific theories. Most of all, however, after the heady days of Apollo, the nation had no obvious, easily understandable goal in science and technology, and although Americans continued to benefit from new products, particular those developed from research in physics, biology, and medicine, their enthusiasm abated.

Additional Information Detailed information can be gleaned from histories of scientific specialties. For astronomy, see John North's *The Norton History of Astronomy and Cosmology* (1995); for physics, *The Second Creation* (1986), by Robert P. Crease and Charles C. Mann; for biology, Lois N. Magner's *A History of the Life Sciences* (1994); for geology; William Glen's *The Road to Jaramillo* (1982); and for technology, Donald Cardwell's *The Norton History of Technology* (1995). Clark A. Elliott provides a handy reference tool in *History of Science in the United States: A Chronological and Research Guide* (1996).

Roger Smith

See also Arms Race; Cancer; Carson, Rachel; Communications; Computers; Cyclamates; Genetics; Heart Transplants; Lasers; Medicine; Nader, Ralph; Nuclear Reactors; Nuclear Test Ban Treaties; Pulsating Radio Waves; Quasars, Discovery of; Space Race; Telecommunications Satellites; Weather Satellites.

■ *Scorpion* Disappearance

Date May 22, 1968

The second U.S. nuclear submarine lost at sea during the 1960's. On its way to Norfolk, Virginia, from the Mediterranean Sea, the submarine sank with ninety-nine men aboard four hundred miles southwest of the Azores.

Origins and History Following the loss of the USS *Thresher* in 1963, the U.S. Navy had initiated a major program to improve the safety of its nuclear submarines. The USS *Scorpion* was originally scheduled to receive these safety improvements during its maintenance period at Norfolk Naval Shipyard in 1967, but tight schedules mandated a change of plans. The work performed on *Scorpion* was drastically reduced in order to get it back to sea more quickly. Because the exact cause of the sinking is not known, this reduction in repair work may not have caused the disaster, but the Navy will always wonder if it acted prudently in returning the *Scorpion* to sea.

The Sinking After a maintenance period at Norfolk Naval Shipyard, the USS *Scorpion* left for the Mediterranean Sea in February, 1968. The ship completed its mission and sailed for home in mid-May, 1968. The *Scorpion* was last seen off Rota, Spain, the night of May 16, and the ship's last radio message was received on May 21.

The death throes of *Scorpion* were apparently detected by the Navy's hydrophone listening system on the floor of the Atlantic Ocean. Analysis of these sound signals suggests that some event occurred with the ship at a depth of about two hundred and fifty feet. This unspecified event caused rapid flooding and led to the sinking of the submarine.

After a five-month search, the Navy located the wreckage of the *Scorpion* in eleven thousand feet of water about four hundred miles southwest of the Azores. The wreck has been extensively photographed by underwater cameras carried by the *Trieste II*, a deep-diving research submarine. Careful review of the photographs has failed to reveal the cause of the sinking. Early theories that a torpedo exploded either inside or outside the submarine have been discounted, and enemy action and sabotage have been ruled out.

Subsequent Events In addition to its two nuclear reactors, the *Scorpion* carried two nuclear torpedoes. None of the nuclear material has been recovered from the wreck, but careful monitoring has revealed no radioactive leakage decades after the event.

Impact The crew left behind sixty-four widows, some pregnant, and ninety-nine children. Sailors represented twenty-five states, Puerto Rico, and the Philippines. Most of the twelve officers and eighty-seven enlisted men who perished were younger than twenty-five. The Navy's Court of Inquiry concluded, "The evidence does not establish that the loss of *Scorpion* and deaths of those embarked were caused by the intent, fault, negligence, or inefficiency of any person or persons in the naval service or connected therewith." The ship's disappearance gave rise to speculation that the submarine had been sunk

The USS Scorpion, *a nuclear-powered submarine shown entering a British port in 1960, sank in May, 1968, killing all ninety-nine men aboard.* (Library of Congress)

through enemy action or sabotage, and many Americans feared nuclear contamination of the ocean. Although these rumors and fears later proved groundless, the disaster, with its large loss of life, still shocked many Americans.

Additional Information In his 1984 book *Lost at Sea*, A. A. Hoehling devotes almost thirty pages, including underwater photographs, to the *Scorpion* disaster.

Edwin G. Wiggins

See also Nuclear Reactors; *Thresher* Disaster; *Trieste* Dive; *Triton* Submarine.

■ SCUM Manifesto

Published 1968
Author Valerie Solanas (1936-1988)

An early second-wave feminist document that captures women's rage against men. The manifesto calls for women to wage a violent revolution to eliminate men and create a women's world.

The Work In the *SCUM (Society for Cutting Up Men) Manifesto*, Valerie Solanas, a playwright who was the founder and sole member of the society, argues that men are biological accidents, that the Y gene is an incomplete X, making men incomplete women. To compensate for their deficiency, men have constructed all of Western civilization and a host of social evils such as war, religion, marriage, money, violence, disease, and death. Furthermore, men have projected their own passivity onto women, defining themselves as active, and set out to prove their manhood by compulsive sexual encounters. However, men are indeed passive and actually want to be women, so they spend their lives attempting to complete themselves by becoming female through usurping women's creativity, energy, and vitality. Solanas's solution is for SCUM to take over the country by sabotage and kill all men who are not in the SCUM Men's Auxiliary. Solanas vowed that SCUM, unlike other organizations within the women's movement, would not picket or strike but would operate on a criminal basis, not to change the system but to destroy it.

Impact Solanas wrote *SCUM Manifesto* in 1967, mimeographed two thousand copies, and sold them on the streets of Greenwich Village in New York. Solanas had accepted an advance to write a book for publisher Maurice Girodias, but when she was un-

able to complete the manuscript, he accepted the *SCUM Manifesto* instead. Solanas had also been trying to get pop artist Andy Warhol to produce a play she had written. When repeated attempts to retrieve the play from Warhol failed, she began to accuse him of appropriating her ideas. In June, 1968, she entered Warhol's studio and shot him and one of his assistants, turning herself in to a rookie cop later that day. *SCUM Manifesto* was published after the shooting and became a focal document for segments of the women's movement. Ti-Grace Atkinson, elected president of the New York chapter of National Organization for Women in 1967, publicly supported Solanas in the aftermath of the shooting, though Atkinson's radicalism eventually put her at odds with the organization, which she left in October, 1968. Roxanne Dunbar, founder of the radical women's liberation group, Cell 16, considered the *SCUM Manifesto* to be "the essence of feminism," and purportedly Cell 16 read the document as their first order of business. Dunbar created controversy when she read excerpts from the *SCUM Manifesto* at a meeting of radical women in Sandy Springs, Maryland, in 1968. Many in the women's movement did not agree with Solanas's views, and her increasing mental instability allowed many people to trivialize the document because of its outrageous nature. Others saw the document as a form of political satire in the style of Jonathan Swift's "A Modest Proposal." Nonetheless, Solanas's *SCUM Manifesto* did fuel debate in the women's movement, and it did give expression to the rage many women felt toward patriarchy.

Related Work The 1996 film, *I Shot Andy Warhol*, provides a look at Solanas's life and includes excerpts from *SCUM Manifesto*.

Additional Information In 1990, Alice Echols published a book-length study of radical feminism in the United States entitled *Daring to Be Bad: Radical Feminism in America, 1967-1975*; the book discusses both the *SCUM Manifesto* and the attempt on Warhol's life.

Susan M. Shaw

See also *Feminine Mystique, The*; Feminist Movement; Women's Identity.

■ Sealab

A pioneering undersea living experiment by the U.S. Navy. Teams of men lived days and weeks on the ocean floor at depths as low as six hundred feet.

Deep-sea work has always been limited by the time-consuming process of decompression. As long as divers must return to the surface to eat and rest, their work time is limited by the time required to accommodate pressure changes in the body during each descent and ascent. Sealab was conceived as a way for divers to live and work beneath the ocean without returning to the surface for days or even months and as an underwater laboratory to observe and experiment with the effects of prolonged submersion.

The Sealab series of experiments began in 1964 as part of the U.S. Navy's Deep Submergence Systems Project. *Sealab I*, a forty-by-ten-foot pressurized steel chamber, was submerged 193 feet below the water off the coast of Bermuda. Four men lived in the station for ten days, getting air and electricity through an "umbilical supply line" from a barge on the surface. A hatch in the floor allowed divers to make daily excursions into the surrounding waters for maintenance and experiments. In 1965, *Sealab II* was submerged 205 feet below the water off the coast of La Jolla, California, and inhabited by three teams for weeks at a time. Commander Scott Carpenter stayed underwater continuously for thirty days. The Sealab program came to an abrupt end in 1969 when aquanaut Berry Cannon died of carbon dioxide poisoning just outside *Sealab III* because of a missing carbon dioxide scrubber in his rebreather.

Impact The Sealab experiments produced a wealth of information on the psychological and physiological effects of prolonged submersion in close quarters, underwater construction, marine biology, geology studies, sonic work, and evaluation of thermal protection. This information led to the Navy's development of saturation diving, in which divers are pressurized in a chamber and transported to depths as low as one thousand feet, primarily for work in offshore oil fields. Instead of staying underwater as in the Sealab model, however, these divers return to the surface inside their pressurized capsules, remaining inside for repeated trips until their work is completed.

Subsequent Events When the Sealab project began, scientists hoped that divers would be able to adjust to depths of about twenty thousand feet. Peter Benett, a British submarine researcher, discovered that divers become incapacitated below about two thousand feet. Researchers also hoped that underwater habitats for humans would soon become com-

monplace, but by the late 1990's, only three existed: a small hotel at a depth of thirty feet in Key Largo, Florida; an educational lab for Scott Carpenter's Man-in-the-Sea program; and a scientific lab run by the National Oceanic and Atmospheric Administration at a depth of sixty feet, which accommodates five scientists and a crew member for ten-day missions to study corals.

Additional Information *Project Sealab: The Story of the United States Navy's Man-in-the-Sea Program* (1966), by Terry Shannon and Charles Payzant, offers many photographs and details of daily life in *Sealab II*. A complete history of undersea exploration from earliest times to the construction of *Sealab III* can be found in *Exploring the Ocean World: A History of Oceanography* (1969), edited by C. P. Idyll.

Jean McKnight

See also *Trieste* Dive.

■ Seattle World's Fair

Date April 21-October 21, 1962

Opened by President John F. Kennedy using remote control in Palm Beach, Florida, on April 21, 1962. The fair recorded 9.6 million visitors and became the first single-year fair in history to make a profit.

Origins and History Seattle business leaders campaigned for the world's fair as early as 1955 as a commemorative event that would outshine the 1909 Alaska-Yukon-Pacific Exhibition. The city and state pledged $20 million, local businesses raised $4.5 million, and the federal government contributed $9 million. Joseph E. Gandy was successful in a request to the Bureau of International Expositions to designate Seattle as the only recognized international fair in the United States for the decade.

The Fair Century 21, as the fair was known, highlighted the space age and technological advancements. The futuristic fair was set on seventy-four acres and linked by a 1.2-mile monorail to Seattle's business district. The Space Needle, the fair's signature structure, hosted almost twenty thousand visitors per day. Seventy-two U.S. industries exhibited their products, and forty-nine nations showcased their respective technological advances.

Impact The six-building science complex formed the nucleus of the Seattle Center, which opened with an eight-hundred seat playhouse, an opera house, a sports coliseum, an international fountain, the Science Center, and a lasting landmark, the Space Needle, towering six hundred feet in the air.

Additional Information Peter T. White and photographer Winfield Parks published a photoessay on the fair entitled "Seattle Fair Looks to the Twenty-first Century" in the September, 1962, issue of *National Geographic.*

Karan A. Berryman

See also New York World's Fair; Science and Technology.

■ Sgt. Pepper's Lonely Hearts Club Band

Released 1967
Performers The Beatles

The quintessential and groundbreaking Beatles album. It revolutionized rock and set new standards for popular music worldwide.

The Work *Sgt. Pepper's Lonely Hearts Club Band,* conceived by the Beatles as an album by a mythical band, was the first concept rock album. It consisted of thirteen tracks, including some of the group's best-known songs. An impression of thematic conti-

The six-hundred-foot-high Space Needle rises over the 1962 Seattle World's Fair, a showcase for space age technology. (Library of Congress)

The Beatles celebrate the release of their latest album, Sgt. Pepper's Lonely Hearts Club Band, *in May, 1967.* (Archive Photos)

nuity is achieved by musical arrangements unlike those on any other pop record at the time. The title song, which begins the album, segues into "With a Little Help from My Friends," and is reprised at the end of the album. The sense of continuity is furthered by an ingenious fusing of two unrelated but complimentary songs to form "A Day in the Life." The music and lyrics were highly complex and innovative for the 1960's; in making the album, the group employed studio techniques and engineering intricacies impossible to re-create or perform live.

Innovation was not limited to the music; the album cover was a monumental breakthrough in conceptual pop art. It featured the Beatles, center set, dressed in brightly colored military-type uniforms and holding brass and woodwind instruments. The foreground spelled out the group's name in flowers, and the background was a dense collage of celebrities and lesser-known characters. In addition, the album was the first to devote the entire back of the album cover to the record's tightly printed lyrics.

Impact Undoubtedly, *Sgt. Pepper's Lonely Hearts Club Band* is one of the most recognizable and influential albums of popular music. It featured a rich and divergent sound coupled with a depth of lyricism unheard of before 1967. Its impact was immediate and staggering: In the United States, the album sold more than two and half million copies within three months and occupied the number-one spot on the music charts for nineteen consecutive weeks. It also won four Grammy Awards, including the prestigious Best Album award. Apart from its financial and critically acclaimed success, the album revolutionized and galvanized the youth movement of the 1960's. It encapsulated the scope of the "psychedelic" generation's aspirations for universal love and heightened spiritual and social consciousness. Both musically and lyrically, it personified and unified a community that had been ideologically scattered. In this sense, *Sgt. Pepper's Lonely Hearts Club Band* became the central anthem visually and musically for the hippies of the late 1960's. The album's lyrics were widely debated and analyzed, particularly by the group's detractors, who pointed to the album's alleged hints and references to drugs. For example, the track "Lucy in the Sky with Diamonds" was said to be about LSD (lysergic acid diethylamide) because its title could be shortened to the same acronym. Despite these minor controversies, *Sgt. Pepper's Lonely Hearts Club Band* proved to be an astounding and unparalleled leap in the quality and creativity of popular music in the 1960's.

Related Work *Sgt. Pepper's Lonely Hearts Club Band* (1978), directed by Michael Schultz, was Hollywood's fanciful yet disastrous film interpretation of the album.

Additional Information *The Love You Make: An Insider's Story of the Beatles* (1983), by Peter Brown and Steven Gaines, provides a comprehensive view of the Beatles.

Gary Juliano

See also Beatles, The; Hippies; Music; Summer of Love.

■ *Sex and the Single Girl*

Published 1962
Author Helen Gurley Brown (1922-   )

A book that promoted sexuality among single women. The book, according to author Brown, is not a "study on how to get married but how to stay single—in superlative style."

The Work Helen Gurley Brown wrote *Sex and the Single Girl*, her first book, at the encouragement of her husband, motion picture producer David Brown, to whom the book is dedicated. The thirteen chapters offer information and advice, based on Brown's thirty-seven years of being single, for single women in their late twenties through their thirties. Brown says her book is for women who may remain single but who are "not necessarily planning to join a nunnery." She contends, citing the father of psychoanalysis Sigmund Freud, that the two most important things in life are work and love. Based on that premise, she devotes chapters to validating the single life, finding men, attracting men, managing

money, succeeding at a career, keeping in shape, dressing attractively, decorating an apartment tastefully, entertaining (right down to the recipes), and—the most controversial—having an affair. Her core message, summed up in the final words of the book, is for single women to "live life" and not to "miss any of it." In the tradition of the American myth of the self-made man, Brown tells single women that they are in control of their own lives and careers, that they have to do it themselves. *Sex and the Single Girl* was the first of Brown's four books, three of which made best-seller lists.

Impact *Sex and the Single Girl*, an instant best-seller made into a hit film of the same name, encouraged single women to live the life of the Cosmo (*Cosmopolitan* magazine) girl, a type of young woman described in the January 29, 1996, issue of *Time* magazine as "sexually bold, if socially conventional." The book encouraged single women to realize that, like men, they could engage in "recreational sex," with both single and married partners. The success of the book and film launched Brown's career. At age forty-three, she became editor of *Cosmopolitan* magazine, a position she held for thirty-one years, after which she became editor in chief of *Cosmopolitan*'s almost thirty international editions. Brown's voice influenced the sexual revolution of the 1960's and 1970's and, ultimately, influenced the voice of other women's magazines such as *Glamour*, *Allure*, *Mademoiselle*, and *American Woman*. As a result of *Sex and the Single Girl*, Brown's views permeated the values of single career women for the next three decades.

Related Work *Sex and the New Single Girl* (1970), Brown's second book, also a best-seller, updates Brown's advice to single women.

Additional Information For Brown's reflections on *Sex and the Single Girl*, see "Bad Girl," an interview with Brown in *Psychology Today*, March/April, 1994. For an overview and analysis of Brown's career, see "Was Helen Gurley Brown the Silliest Editor in America—or the Smartest?" in *Playboy*, March, 1997.

Carol Franks

See also Sexual Revolution; Women's Identity.

■ **Sex-Change Operations**

Surgical procedures in which a person's gender is changed to that of the opposite sex. These operations received wide-

spread popular and academic attention, particularly after Christine Jorgensen's surgery in 1952 and the opening of a gender clinic at The Johns Hopkins University in 1966.

In articles published 1955-1957, John Money, Joan Hampton, and John Hampton identified "sex of rearing" rather than biological factors to be the main determinant of what they termed "gender role." Their ideas about an individual's "psychological sex" laid the foundation for understanding transsexuals, who believe they are one sex trapped in the body of another.

Christine Jorgensen, an American and former private in the U.S. Army (born George Jorgensen), was the first transsexual to publicly announce that she had undergone a sex-change operation. The surgery was performed in Denmark in November, 1952, by noted endocrinologist Christian Hamburger. Both Hamburger and Jorgensen received a barrage of attention and publicity, particularly in the United States. In the year following the surgery, Hamburger received more than one thousand letters from transsexuals around the world. Operations such as the one Hamburger performed were made possible because of the hormone therapy and plastic surgery techniques that had been developed and the increasing acceptance of cosmetic surgery, which has no physiological purpose.

Specialists such as endocrinologist Harry Benjamin and psychologist Money wrote and spoke extensively on their work with transsexuals, who are physically normal but deeply unhappy with their apparent gender, especially the genitals. Their unhappiness is manifested as anguish, depression, and even attempts at self-mutilation or suicide. Benjamin adamantly proclaimed that these individuals either refused psychotherapy or failed to benefit from it. Male transsexualism was far more prevalent than female. A 1968 estimate was one transsexual for every one hundred thousand people in the United States.

Men accepted for surgery first underwent hormone therapy to enlarge their breasts and redistribute body fat. The genital surgery involved castration, removal of the penis, construction of a vagina and clitoris, and shortening of the urethra. Many men also had electrolysis to remove facial and body hair, silicone breast implants, and surgery on the nose and Adam's apple. Women had hormone therapy to cease menstruation, cause growth of facial and body hair, and deepen their voices. Their surgery was usually limited to mastectomy (removal of the breasts) and a total hysterectomy (removal of the reproductive organs); however, penis and scrotum construction were sometimes included.

The Johns Hopkins Gender Clinic, whose December, 1966, announcement of its first sex-change operation received worldwide attention, was the first reputable U.S. hospital to perform the surgery. The Johns Hopkins team, composed of psychiatrists, plastic surgeons, gynecologists, urologists, and endocrinologists, was a model for other clinics.

Benjamin and others helped transsexuals cope with a variety of problems associated with a sex change. Patients were required by gender clinics to live and dress as the opposite sex for several months before surgery. They were often unfairly arrested for female impersonation or disorderly conduct. Surgeons and clinics sometimes declined to perform the operation for fear of prosecution under state mayhem statutes, which forbade willful and permanent deprivation or mutilation of a bodily part. Patients endured legal battles to change their name and sex on public papers such as birth certificates.

Impact Strong interest in sex-change operations continued into the 1970's. *Newsweek* magazine estimated that by 1976, three thousand operations had been performed and ten thousand people viewed themselves as candidates. Accurate statistics were difficult to obtain, partly because those denied surgery in the United States could have it performed in Mexico, Morocco, or Japan. By the early 1980's, forty gender-identity clinics were in operation in the Western Hemisphere.

Though transsexuals welcomed the advent of this operation, many in the general public were less accepting. Many opposed the surgery for religious or philosophical reasons, and others found it disturbing or distasteful. Full social acceptance of those who had undergone a sex change was lacking, even among many people who favored the operations.

Subsequent Events From the 1970's through the 1990's, sex reassignment surgery was further refined, and academics explored transsexualism, some of them questioning of the benefits of the surgery. Some researchers and writers wondered if the pioneering specialists who wrote widely about the surgery's benefits helped create demand by heightening the expectations of self-diagnosed transsexuals.

Indeed, the surgery became central to the identity of the transsexual. Ideological studies of transsexualism asserted that the surgery hindered the movement to eliminate sex-role stereotyping and oppression.

In 1973, an American Psychological Association (APA) committee recommended hormones and surgery, rather than psychotherapy, as the preferred treatment for transsexuals. By the 1980's, follow-up reports on patients who had received surgery revealed a less than completely positive outcome. Patients sometimes showed marginal social adjustment or were found to have serious psychopathology that was not helped by the surgery. Some writers asserted that gender clinics had few personnel trained in the kinds of psychotherapy best suited for transsexuals. Others suggested that transsexuals might not devote serious effort to psychotherapy until they had seen that their problems were not completely resolved by anatomical changes.

Additional Information Benjamin's *The Transsexual Phenomenon* (1966) is a readable, sympathetic overview of the differences among transvestites, homosexuals, and transsexuals. It discusses the possible causes of transsexualism, the sex-change operation, and the legal aspects of sex changes. Richard Green and Money's *Transsexualism and Sex Reassignment* (1969) examines the assessment, diagnosis, and treatment of transsexuals in a more academic and clinical style.

Glenn Ellen Starr

See also Medicine; Sexual Revolution; Silicone Injections.

■ Sexual Revolution

Changes in sexual mores in the United States, fueled by a mixture of idealism and lust. The sexual revolution was intended to enable more people to enjoy more sex with less guilt and fewer undesired consequences, but some saw it as a selfish attack upon morality or women.

In the 1950's, two major constraints enforcing traditional sexual morality were weakening. Antibiotics had made syphilis and gonorrhea easily and painlessly treatable, and improved contraceptive technology was making unwanted pregnancy significantly less likely. In addition, Alfred Kinsey's published studies, *Sexual Behavior in the American Male* (1948) and *Sexual Behavior in the Human Female*

(1953), had not only broken through the taboo on discussing sex but also suggested that much more sex, and more varied sex, was occurring than was widely believed. Barriers were falling in other areas as well; a series of court cases was beginning to legalize the sale of books that had long been banned as pornographic.

Science and Sex In May, 1960, the Food and Drug Administration approved the first contraceptive pill; by 1966, six million women in the United States were taking it. The pill's inventor, John Rock, was a Roman Catholic physician who hoped that his church would find his creation acceptable. He hoped that an effective oral contraceptive would allow married women to limit the number of children they bore so that they would not be worn out by year after year of childbirth and to space their children so that they could give each one enough attention; indeed, it did just that for many women. However, it was obvious that the pill would work just as well for unmarried women. Secular prohibitions against discussion of birth control methods crumbled. In *Griswold v. Connecticut* (1964), the Supreme Court affirmed the right of individuals to have access to contraceptive information.

Moving further in the territory charted by Kinsey, a team of scientists led by William H. Masters and Virginia E. Johnson studied the physiology of sexual intercourse, viewing and even filming and measuring volunteers in the act. In 1966, they published their first study, *Human Sexual Response*. Despite its scientific and technical nature, the book caused an immediate sensation. The idea that people would willingly copulate in a laboratory was shocking to many, and the study's results offered further surprises, notably the finding that the supposed distinction between the mature vaginal orgasm and the immature clitoral one, a keystone of the Freudian approach to female sexuality, was not supported by experimental evidence. Masters and Johnson continued their research, attempting to apply their results to sexual dysfunction and employing "surrogates" whose work included having sex with people who had sexual problems.

The Arts and Sex The sexual revolution was also waged in the arts. Although there were a few obscenity convictions (such as that of Ralph Ginzburg in 1963, found guilty as much for the pandering tone of his advertising as for the erotic content of the

Three members of the Sexual Freedom League, an organization designed to promote the legalization of nudity on beaches, test the waters at Aquatic Park in San Francisco. The sexual revolution ushered in a period of experimentation and changes in sexual mores. (Library of Congress)

material), the trend toward allowing printed matter to be sold regardless of its sexual content continued and escalated. In 1964, the Supreme Court announced that Henry Miller's notorious *Tropic of Cancer* was covered by the First Amendment, and two years later, the Court extended the same protection to William S. Burroughs's *Naked Lunch* (1962)—a literary work that, although not erotic, had a high density of "forbidden" words—and to an anonymous bit of pulp fiction called *The Sex Life of a Cop*. In 1968, Maurice Girodias, who had been operating Olympia Press in Paris to publish "dirty books" that U.S. tourists would then smuggle home, moved his base of operations to the United States. By the end of the decade, the Supreme Court had indicated that any book with "redeeming social importance" (liberally interpreted) was lawful, and in *Stanley v. Georgia* (1969), it asserted the right of individuals to own and use pornographic materials in the privacy of their own homes.

This new freedom led to the publication of books that would probably have been banned in earlier

times, such as Gore Vidal's *Myra Breckenridge* (1968), which openly presented homosexuality and transsexualism; Philip Roth's *Portnoy's Complaint* (1969), whose narrator discourses at length upon his masturbatory practices; and the increasingly explicit and erotic work of John Updike, notably *Couples* (1968), a look at suburban adultery. In addition, the 1960's saw the publication of idealistic works such as Robert A. Heinlein's *Stranger in a Strange Land* (1961) and Robert H. Rimmer's *The Harrad Experiment* (1966), which attractively presented alternatives to traditionally monogamous arrangements.

In other arts, the results were more mixed. Early in the decade, Lenny Bruce's nightclub act led to obscenity charges on several occasions (though some maintained that his negative attitudes toward the police and organized religion had more to do with the arrests than the words he used). His death in 1966 kept the matter from going to the Supreme Court. That same year, Carol Doda bared her silicone-enhanced breasts on stage in a San Francisco bar. She was arrested, as were others who followed her, but within a few years, topless performances had become acceptable in many cities.

On the Broadway stage, the use of phrases such as "hump the hostess" in Edward Albee's *Who's Afraid of Virginia Woolf?* (1962) was considered daring in its time, but by the end of the decade, audiences were being treated to full frontal nudity in *Oh, Calcutta!* (1968) and *Hair* (1969). In popular music, songs became more openly sexual. In 1965, the Rolling Stones' "Let's Spend the Night Together" was too suggestive for many radio stations, and when they appeared on *The Ed Sullivan Show*, they had to change the lyrics to "Let's spend some time together." By the end of the decade, the Beatles were asking, "Why Don't We Do It in the Road?"

Before the 1960's, the sexual content of films playing in the United States was rigidly monitored. The studios submitted their productions to the Catholic Legion of Decency and rarely proceeded without that group's approval. In the 1950's, a few films dared to utter such words as "virgin" and "seduction," thus failing to get the coveted seal of approval. In 1965, *The Pawnbroker*, a serious treatment of themes such as race relations and the Holocaust, became the first U.S. film to show bare breasts. By 1968, U.S. Customs had grudgingly admitted *I Am Curious—Yellow*, a Swedish film showing apparent sexual intercourse, and before long, actual unmistakable sex would appear on film.

Sex and Idealism In the mid-1960's, the hippie movement sprang up. The hippies, taking advantage of the progress in contraception and disease control, followed the free-love ideals advocated by earlier generations of bohemians. They felt that the sexual revolution could be both personally and socially transformative. Some, for instance, believed that all violence, including war, was merely misdirected sexual energy; therefore, sexual freedom would bring peace. The hippies offered relief from gender stereotyping, at least for males, who blossomed forth with long hair and bright clothing. Some hippies tried communal living and other alternatives to the nuclear family, and although many communes collapsed immediately, a few, such as Jud Presmont's Kerista, remained in operation more than thirty years later.

Among the more settled members of the community, particularly in the suburbs, sexual experimentation took the form of what was first called "wife swapping" and then, when the sexist and proprietarian connotations of that term became too obvious, was renamed "swinging." This usually took the form of a few couples getting together and rearranging the partnerships, sometimes by random methods such as picking car keys out of a hat. The theory behind swinging was that sexual experimentation without romantic or emotional involvement would offer excitement without destabilizing the original marriage.

Almost as soon as the term "sexual revolution" was heard, charges arose that the whole thing was nothing more than a ploy by men to obtain more sex. Those who felt that way were by no means entirely mistaken, but that oversimplification left out the revolution's genuine dimension of idealism. Idealistic sexual revolutionaries attacked the double standard whereby a man with a rich and varied sex life was to be envied, but a woman with the same number of partners was a slut. The idealists believed, with some justification, that many women wanted the freedom to experiment sexually and some would never want monogamy, though the numbers of both of these were probably overestimated.

Sex and Controversy An issue of great importance to many in the sexual revolution was abortion, illegal everywhere in the United States through most of the 1960's. In 1962, Paul Krassner, whose magazine *The Realist* tested the limits of expression in sex, politics, and religion, published an anonymous interview with an abortionist, a Pennsylvania doctor who had been performing the illegal operation for forty years. The reaction to this interview led Krassner to set up an abortion referral service. As the sexual revolution gained momentum, legalized abortion became one of its primary issues, with demonstrations and an abortion underground that connected desperate pregnant women with doctors.

In 1960, homosexual relations were illegal in all states except Illinois, and although these laws were rarely enforced when the behavior was entirely private, the police in many jurisdictions took advantage of vaguely written "vagrancy" and "disorderly person" laws to harass suspected gays; police were frequently assigned to public restrooms, either attempting to entrap men into making sexual offers or looking through peepholes to catch homosexuals in the act. (The arrest of an aide to President Lyndon B. Johnson during the 1964 presidential election drew attention to these practices.) Most heterosexuals who considered themselves part of the sexual revolution opposed these uses of police power.

Impact As the women's movement grew in the late 1960's, some of its members criticized the sexual revolution because they felt men were pressuring reluctant women to have sex to demonstrate that they were part of the revolution. At the same time, many feminists praised the sexual revolution for making it possible for women to have an active sex life without being stigmatized socially. Many women considered the Masters and Johnson results regarding vaginal and clitoral orgasm as an important step toward letting women define their own sexuality, and the right to abortion became an essential element in most definitions of feminism.

Opposition also came from the Roman Catholic Church. In 1968, Pope Paul VII wrote the encyclical *Humanae Vitae,* condemning the contraceptive pill and all other methods of birth control except "natural" methods such as abstinence and the rhythm method and thus drawing a battle line between himself and those who wanted to enjoy sex without worrying about unwanted pregnancies. Other social conservatives joined in the condemnation. In 1969, there was a brief flurry of decency rallies, which often opposed not only the sexual revolution but also other aspects of the counterculture such as recreational drugs and antiwar activism.

Subsequent Events The sexual revolution fell from favor for a number of reasons, including reversals in two areas where progress had helped bring it about. The contraceptive pill turned out to be neither as foolproof nor as free from side effects as its proponents had hoped. Also, the spread of incurable sexually transmitted diseases such as genital herpes and AIDS returned sex to its former role as an activity fraught with peril, in which an encounter with the wrong person could have lifelong or life-threatening consequences. However, it is generally agreed that the pendulum has not swung all the way back. The nation's courts hear few pornography trials, and almost none of those involve the written word; sex laws have been liberalized in many jurisdictions; and a nonstandard sexual lifestyle is more likely to gain the attention of a television talk show host than that of the police. Improvements in contraceptive and disease-control technology could presage a new sexual revolution.

Additional Information *What Wild Ecstasy* (1997), by John Heidenry, tells the story of the sexual revolution from the 1960's through the 1990's. *No More Nice Girls* (1992), by Ellen Willis, and *Sexing the Millennium* (1994), by Linda Grant, offer sympathetic yet critical feminist perspectives. Edward de Grazia's *Girls Lean Back Everywhere* (1992) presents an in-depth look at the censorship battles.

Arthur D. Hlavaty

See also Abortion; Birth Control; Censorship; Communes; Feminist Movement; Free Love; Gay Liberation Movement; Hippies; *Human Sexual Response*; Pill, The.

■ Sheppard, Sam

One of the most publicized criminal trial appeals of the decade and the probable inspiration behind the popular 1960's television drama The Fugitive. *In overturning Sheppard's 1954 murder conviction, the Supreme Court redefined the boundaries between the right of freedom of speech and the right to a fair trial.*

On July 4, 1954, Marilyn Reese Sheppard, four months pregnant, was found stabbed to death in her bed in a western suburb of Cleveland, Ohio. Local police and the Cleveland police department quickly gathered evidence against her husband, Sam Sheppard, a doctor of osteopathy who worked in his family-owned hospital. Sheppard insisted that an intruder had murdered his wife and then attacked him when he came to his wife's aid.

Throughout the highly publicized police investigation, indictment, and criminal trial, the *Cleveland Press* and its editor, Louis Seltzer, led local news media in a relentless assault on Sheppard and his family. Inflammatory headlines, editorials, and non-objective reporting criticized the Sheppard family's wealth and questioned Sheppard's marital fidelity. Despite the defense team's attempts to move the trial elsewhere, Judge Edward Blythin denied the attorneys' motions and allowed newspeople to sit within the bar of the courtroom, only three feet from the jury box. In one of the longest-running criminal trials of that era, amid what was described as a "carnival" atmosphere, Sheppard was convicted of murder and sentenced to life in prison without parole.

Initial appeals were rejected by both the county and state, and the case was refused review by the United States Supreme Court. Almost ten years after his conviction, Sheppard retained twenty-nine-year-old Boston attorney F. Lee Bailey, who, in 1964, convinced Judge Carl A. Weinman of the United States District Court of Southern Ohio that Blythin had failed to grant a change of venue or postpone the trial, had failed to disqualify himself for suspected lack of impartiality, and had permitted the improper introduction of lie-detector testimony and unauthorized communications with the jury during deliberations. Reversed by the Sixth Circuit Court of Appeals in May, 1965, Weinman's decision was sustained by the United States Supreme Court in June, 1966, which then instructed Weinman to issue a writ of *habeas corpus* granting Sheppard's release. The Court also granted the state of Ohio the option of retrying Sheppard within a reasonable time.

The state retried Sheppard in October, 1966, but the defense's case was strengthened by deceased or forgetful witnesses, inadmissible evidence, and Bailey's use of Paul Kirk, a criminal expert who argued that blood splatters on a wristwatch could not have been from flying blood, undermining part of the prosecution's theory. The jury deliberated less than a full day and returned a not-guilty verdict on November 16, 1966.

Impact Bailey's case was aided during the early 1960's by the changing attitude toward judicial fairness and media responsibility and by heightened public interest in the Sheppard murder case. The Supreme Court, under the leadership of newly appointed Chief Justice Earl Warren, had already taken action against overreaching by police and prosecutors, ruling that defendants had a right to an attorney before being questioned and were protected from having evidence found during illegal searches used against them in court. Public interest in Sheppard was first renewed by the 1961 publication of *The Sheppard Murder Case* by Paul Holmes, a Chicago reporter who questioned the conviction. Soon after the book was published, the television show *The Fugitive* aired on American Broadcasting Company, running from September, 1963, to August, 1967. The story was of a doctor, wrongfully convicted of killing his wife, who escapes execution and, while running from the law, searches for the one-armed murderer. The show, which won a best dramatic series award in 1966, was generally assumed to be based on the Sheppard case, although creator Roy Huggins, producer Martin Quinn, and those in-

Sam Sheppard, whose 1954 murder conviction was overturned by the Supreme Court, was retried and acquitted of killing his wife in 1966. (AP/Wide World Photos)

volved with its production denied that they modeled the show after the case. When the show did go off the air after a two-part conclusion, some blamed its falling viewership on the 1966 acquittal of Sheppard. In 1993, the popular television series became the basis of a film, *The Fugitive*, starring Harrison Ford and Tommy Lee Jones.

Subsequent Events After his acquittal, Sheppard had difficulty resuming his life. He returned to practicing medicine but resigned after malpractice suits were filed against him. His marriage to a German woman, entered into during his prison stay, ended in divorce. He became a professional wrestler, married his manager's daughter, and died in 1970.

In 1998, Sheppard's son, Sam Reese Sheppard, released the results of DNA tests (made using blood samples taken at the crime scene in 1954) that he said proved conclusively that a person other than his father was involved in the murder.

Additional Information Sheppard wrote an autobiographical account of the murder, trial, and retrial entitled *Endure and Conquer* (1966); his son, Sam Reese Sheppard, and coauthor Cynthia L. Cooper wrote another detailed account of these events in *Mockery of Justice* (1995).

Rebecca Strand Johnson

See also Crimes and Scandals; Supreme Court Decisions; Television.

■ Silicone Injections

An injection of silicone into the face or breasts for corrective or cosmetic purposes. Though human use was restricted, many illegal injections were performed. Complications including silicone migration and painful cysts surfaced, often years later.

Silicone fluid with additives had been injected for breast augmentations since the 1940's in Japan, Switzerland, and Germany. Additives were thought to lock the inert silicone into the injected area by inducing the formation of fibrous capsules. Most injections were performed by physicians or cosmetologists. Injections gained popularity, particularly among topless waitresses and showgirls, because they did not involve the cutting, hospital stay, and expense of surgical augmentation.

In 1965, Dow-Corning received Food and Drug Administration (FDA) permission to investigate injections of silicone fluid for soft-tissue augmentation. Breast augmentation was forbidden, but the substance was deemed promising for rare, disfiguring conditions that affected the face and body such as hemifacial atrophy and lipodistrophy. Dow's seven investigators followed a closely supervised protocol in working with more than thirteen hundred patients and tracked their progress into the 1970's. They reported few side effects and both cosmetic and psychological benefits.

In the 1960's, women began to report complications from illegal breast injections. The breasts developed solid, painful silicone nodules; occasionally the silicone would migrate along the needle track of the injection. The inflammation and incapacitating pain, called silicone mastitis, could be relieved temporarily by antibiotics and anti-inflammatory agents, but it often returned. For lasting relief, the silicone gel had to be removed using a stab incision. In two reported cases, the patients' swelling and pain were so severe that physicians removed part or all of the breasts. Complications sometimes arose five to nine years after the injections. Patients were told that their reactions were to the silicone; however, the Dow-Corning investigators maintained that the additives were responsible.

Impact In August, 1967, after examining several cases of adverse reactions to silicone injections, the FDA initiated criminal proceedings against Dow-Corning for illegal shipments of silicone fluid. Company officials maintained that medical-grade silicone was shipped only to the seven authorized investigators and to people who signed an affidavit promising it would not be used on humans. They believed the problems probably arose from use of industrial-grade silicone fluid—shipped by Dow and three other companies—which could contain lint, dust, and metal fragments. The FDA suspended its approval for human experimentation by Dow-Corning in November, 1967.

Subsequent Events The FDA began regulating silicone as a device rather than as a drug in 1976. Also that year, Las Vegas physicians published an account of their experiences with local women who had received silicone injections. They estimated that twelve thousand Las Vegas women had been injected, and 1 percent reported problems each year, some traceable to medical-grade silicone. They urged that silicone be avoided except by skilled practitioners in extreme cases such as hemifacial atrophy. In 1992, the FDA obtained consent decrees from three New York physicians stating that they would no longer inject patients with silicone fluid as treatment for acne scars and wrinkles. These injections were causing the same side effects that breast injections had.

Additional Information A detailed discussion of the side effects seen by Las Vegas physicians appears in "Complications of Silicone Injections," by Edward H. Kopf, *Rocky Mountain Medical Journal* 73, no. 2 (March-April, 1976).

Glenn Ellen Starr

See also Medicine; Sex-Change Operations; Women's Identity.

■ Silko, Leslie Marmon

Born March 5, 1948, Albuquerque, New Mexico

A Laguna pueblo writer who gained prominence for her poetry, fiction, and essays. Silko legitimized traditional folk literature of her pueblo in English-language literary genres and helped open the canon of American literature to include literatures of other ethnicities.

Early Life Leslie Marmon Silko was raised in Laguna pueblo reservation in New Mexico by her parents and her father's extended family. Her mother was of European and Cherokee ancestry; her father was of Laguna, Plains Indian, Mexican, and European ancestry. She has written that the search for identity as a half-breed is at the core of her works. Her family included a great-aunt, Aunt Susie, who taught Silko the stories of the Laguna oral tradition. Silko attended day school in Albuquerque from 1958 to 1964 and then the University of New Mexico, where she received a B.A. in English. She married, had two children, and finished three semesters of law school.

The 1960's Silko began writing during the late 1960's, when N. Scott Momaday, a Kiowa, won the Pulitzer Prize for his Southwest novel *House Made of Dawn.* He was the first American Indian to receive a national award for literature. Momaday's example inspired American Indian writers in Albuquerque, including Silko, Joy Harjo, Simon Ortiz, William Oandasan, Geary Hobson, and Luci Tapahonso. Silko published her first story in *New Mexico Quarterly* (1969). Hobson published the first anthology of contemporary Native American writers, *The Remembered Earth,* containing Silko's essay "An Old Fashioned Indian Attack," which made a strong statement against appropriation of Native American cultures by "white Indian" poets.

In the late 1960's, Silko wrote some stories that later became part of the book *Storyteller.* She touched on subjects that she would revisit throughout her career: the oral tradition of Laguna culture, identity, ceremonial healing, and the landscape. She claimed Native American cultural material for writers who were a part of that culture.

Later Life After she received a National Endowment for the Arts grant, Silko quit law school and began writing and teaching. She continued to publish, including a book of poetry, *Laguna Woman* (1974) and seven stories in *The Man to Send Rain Clouds* (1974). In 1977, she published *Ceremony,* a poetry-containing novel that presents a war veteran's healing ceremony. In 1981, she received a MacArthur Foundation grant, which supported her next novel, *Almanac of the Dead* (1991). She continued to express personal and political views in essays, collected in *Yellow Woman and a Beauty of the Spirit* (1996).

Impact At the time of the American Indian movement, Silko articulated the independent identity of American Indian literature. A traditionally raised Laguna, she gave contemporary form to centuries-old, orally transmitted Laguna narratives and helped open the canon of American literature to Native American writers.

Additional Information In 1993, Melody Graulich edited *Yellow Woman,* which contains an interview with Silko, a collection of essays, and a bibliography. Another source is *The Delicacy and Strength of Lace: Letters Between Leslie Marmon Silko and James Wright* (1986), which contains correspondence between Silko and the poet James Wright.

Denise Low

See also American Indian Movement (AIM); *House Made of Dawn.*

■ Simon, Neil

Born July 4, 1927, Bronx, New York

One of the most popular American playwrights of the 1960's. Simon's comedies helped capture, at times even to create, the archetypal images of modern life in the United States.

Early Life Son of a Bronx garment salesman who abandoned the family several times, Marvin Neil Simon learned independence early. After brief duty in the Air Force Reserve, Simon joined his brother Danny writing comedy for radio and the new medium of television. In 1953, he married Joan Baim, with whom he had two daughters. Throughout the fifties, the Simon brothers wrote for increasingly prestigious shows, culminating in the classic *Your Show of Shows,* for which Simon won an Emmy Award in 1957. Simon won a second Emmy in 1959 for his work on the *Sergeant Bilko* show, confirming a reputation as one of the top writers in television.

The 1960's The Broadway production in 1961 of his first full-length play, *Come Blow Your Horn,* was the first in a string of nine hit comedies in as many years in Simon's most prolific decade. Each of Simon's nine plays of the 1960's explores different aspects of life in that decade. The first four all share a common motif of mismatched couples, a theme receiving its

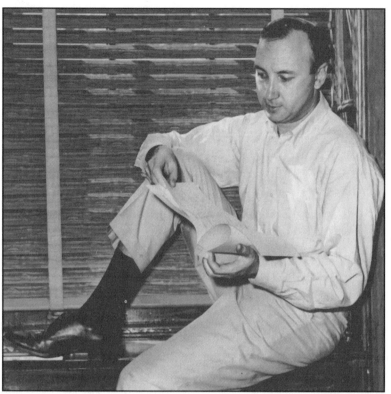

Neil Simon produced a series of very popular comedic Broadway plays during the 1960's, including The Odd Couple *(1965), which was later adapted for the screen.* (Library of Congress)

classical expression in Simon's most famous work, *The Odd Couple* (1965). In *Come Blow Your Horn*, the mismatched pair are brothers, one hedonistic, the other straight-laced. *Little Me* (1962), though Simon's contribution was merely fleshing out an existing plot, concerns the misalliance of a poor girl and a high-society bachelor. *Barefoot in the Park* (1963) contrasts a fun-loving new bride and her staid new husband. The remaining five plays look at different implications of the sexual revolution: *Sweet Charity* (1966) presents the modern myth of the whore with the heart of gold, and *The Star Spangled Girl* (1966) the opposite extreme in the wholesome Midwestern virgin pursued by a libertine. In *Promises, Promises* (1968), an innocent bystander of the sexual revolution offers his bachelor apartment to his libidinous boss; *Plaza Suite* (1968) is a triptych of scenes in the same hotel room, two of them involving adulterous affairs. *The Last of the Red-Hot Lovers* (1969) is also a trio of vignettes, this time of a single male character who attempts to seduce a different woman in each scene.

The tremendous success of these comedies led to lucrative screen versions of *Barefoot in the Park* and *The Odd Couple,* for which Simon wrote the screenplays but had little to no control over the final product. Simon considered his collaboration with Italian screen writer Cesar Zavatini on *After the Fox* (1966) to be marred by Simon's lack of control; Zavatini and the director spoke no English.

Later Life Many reviewers doubted that Simon could keep up the play-a-year pace he established in the 1960's, but through the 1970's, he averaged nearly two a year, eight stage comedies and eleven screenplays. The 1980's saw Simon's plays become increasingly serious, particularly the autobiographical trilogy *Brighton Beach Memoirs* (1982), *Biloxi Blues* (1984), and *Broadway Bound* (1986). Critical acceptance came at last with these plays, as well as *Lost in Yonkers*, which won the 1991 Pulitzer Prize for Drama.

Impact Simon's comedies dominated the stage in the 1960's not only by outlasting the competition but also by begging imitation. The attention Simon received for such centrality was not always positive: many playwrights and critics felt that Simon lowered the quality of Broadway theater by bringing a television style of comedy to the stage. After Simon received his Pulitzer, however, that criticism diminished. Few deny that late twentieth century American comedy was largely shaped by Simon.

Additional Information For critical commentary on all of the early plays, see *Neil Simon* (1983), by Robert K. Johnson. Simon's 1996 autobiography *Rewrites* offers valuable background to the plays.

John R. Holmes

See also Literature; Theater.

■ Simon and Garfunkel

One of the most popular duos of the rock-and-roll era. Their rich harmony, creative forms, and deeply personal lyrics gave their music a powerful aesthetic force that captured the spirit of the folk music tradition and the imaginations of music listeners around the world.

Paul Simon and Art Garfunkel grew up blocks apart in Queens, New York. In 1955, at the age of fourteen, they recorded their first song, "The Girl for Me." They signed their first recording contract a year later as Tom and Jerry. In 1957, their first hit, "Hey Schoolgirl," reached number fifty-four on Billboard's top one hundred and earned them an appearance on *American Bandstand.*

After high school, they followed separate paths: Garfunkel went to college, and Simon pursued a singing/songwriting career. They reunited briefly in 1964 as Simon and Garfunkel, giving concerts and recording *Wednesday Morning, 3 A.M.*, an album of folk songs. The album flopped, but its acoustical version of "Sounds of Silence" became the key to their future success. Parting ways again, Simon moved to London where he recorded a solo album, *The Paul Simon Song Book*, which provided material for later Simon and Garfunkel albums. Their breakthrough came in 1966 when a producer released "Sounds of Silence" overdubbed with "electric" music; it became their first number-one hit. Simon returned to the United States, and they began working together full-time.

In March, 1966, they released an album with the new "Sounds of Silence" as the title track; another album, *Parsley, Sage, Rosemary, and Thyme*, followed in November. The success of both albums thrust them into the national spotlight. In 1967, they were invited to perform at the Monterey Pop Festival, and in 1968, they were asked to record the soundtrack for *The Graduate.* The soundtrack won three Grammy awards, and "Mrs. Robinson" became their second

The singing and songwriting duo Simon and Garfunkel (Paul Simon, right, and Art Garfunkel) enjoyed commercial and critical success in the 1960's, producing memorable songs such as "Sounds of Silence" and "Mrs. Robinson." (AP/Wide World Photos)

number-one hit. They released *Bookends*, another successful album, later that year. They released their final and most popular album, *Bridge over Troubled Water*, in February, 1970, and won six Grammy Awards.

Impact In the late 1960's, Simon and Garfunkel had three number-one hits and won top music honors: two songs of the year, an album of the year, and nine Grammy Awards. Their highly thoughtful and creative music, coupled with their commercial success, placed them among the most compelling apostles of the spirit of the 1960's. Their appearances for political and social causes and their intimate concert tours inspired audiences with a personal manifestation of that spirit.

Subsequent Events After the release of *Bridge over Troubled Water*, Garfunkel left the duo to pursue an acting career and develop other creative interests, and Simon went on to a successful solo career. In 1981, Simon and Garfunkel gave a reunion concert in Central Park to an audience of more than five hundred thousand. In 1990, they were inducted into the Rock and Roll Hall of Fame.

Additional Information See Victoria Kingston's *Simon and Garfunkel: The Definitive Biography* (1996), and *Simon and Garfunkel: Old Friends* (1991), by Joseph Morella and Patricia Barey.

Richard L. Mallery

See also Folk Music; *Graduate, The*; Monterey Pop Festival.

■ Sinatra Kidnapping

Date December 8, 1963

The kidnapping of Frank Sinatra, Jr., the son of the well-known singer. Media coverage of the kidnapping and subsequent trial made front-page news, but rumor and innuendo persisted about the younger Sinatra's possible involvement in the crime.

Origins and History Frank Sinatra, Jr., was the second child born to the famous singer. He entered the University of Southern California as a music major but dropped out in 1962 to pursue a singing career. After performing at Disneyland and making several television appearances, Sinatra was offered a job by the Tommy Dorsey Band. Comparisons to his father's singing style were numerous, but Sinatra received good notices and reviews for shows at the Flamingo in Las Vegas, the Americana Hotel in New York, and the Coconut Grove in Los Angeles.

The Kidnapping Just before a performance at Harrah's Club in Lake Tahoe on December 8, 1963, Sinatra and his trumpet player, John Foss, were having dinner in his motel room when someone knocked on the door. A male voice stated that he had a package to deliver. When Sinatra opened the door, the man pointed a gun at him and pushed his way into the room. The kidnapper ordered Sinatra and Foss to lie face down on the floor, blindfolded them, and taped their hands while another individual stood watch in the hallway. The men then took Sinatra and fled in their car to Los Angeles. At one point, the getaway car met a roadblock near Carson City. The kidnappers took Sinatra out of the trunk, made him crouch in the back seat, covered him with a blanket, and told him to remain quiet. The men passed through the checkpoint without incident after explaining that they had stopped in order to remove snow chains from the tires. In the meantime, Foss managed to free himself and called the authorities. California and Nevada police launched a massive, two-day search.

Sinatra's father was at home in Palm Springs when he received the news. He immediately took a plane to Reno where he and several Federal Bureau of Investigation (FBI) agents awaited the kidnappers' ransom demands. On December 10, he received a telephone call demanding $240,000 in small used bills. The kidnappers wanted him to drop off the money between two parked school buses at a Los Angeles gas station. The famous singer left the ransom money at the designated point and waited to see if the men would release his son unharmed.

The kidnappers held the young Sinatra captive in a small house in Canoga Park, California. On December 11, two of the abductors left to pick up the ransom money while a third accomplice guarded Sinatra. Sinatra seized the opportunity; he persuaded the kidnapper that the others would run off with the money. The ploy worked, and the man decided to release Sinatra on the San Diego freeway near the Mulholland Drive exit. Sinatra flagged down a Bel Air patrol car and identified himself. One of the officers, George C. Jones, tried to take the young man home, but reporters surrounded Sinatra's mother's residence a few miles away. Jones eventually put Sinatra in the trunk of his car and drove him to safety, just one day short of his father's forty-eighth birthday.

The FBI arrested three men, John Irwin, Barry Keenan, and Joseph Amsler, for the crime and recovered $233,855 of the ransom money. The men were charged with conspiracy to kidnap and went to trial in early February, 1964. The trial lasted one month, and the federal grand jury returned guilty verdicts. Amsler and Keenan received life sentences, and Irwin, who provided information to the FBI, got seventy-five years. The sentences for Amsler and Keenan were later reduced to twenty-five years. In 1967, Irwin pleaded guilty to reduced charges in a U.S. Court of Appeals rather than face a new trial, and he was put on five year's probation.

Impact During the trial, defense counsel Gladys Root and George Forde suggested that the young Sinatra had arranged the abduction as a publicity stunt. Members of the media jumped at the suggestion. One British television show, *That Was the Week*

That Was, satirized the kidnapping as a hoax. Sinatra's father vehemently denied the charge and sued Independent TV for damages. He won and donated his share of the money to the Sunshine Home for Blind Babies.

Subsequent Events The kidnapping failed to slow down the young Sinatra's singing career; he made his film debut in *A Man Called Adam* in 1966. However, he refused to answer questions about the incident, stating he wanted to put the past behind him.

Additional Information Information about the kidnapping can be found in Nancy Sinatra's book, *Frank Sinatra: My Father* (1985), and in various issues of *The New York Times* from 1963 through 1964.

Gayla Koerting

See also Crimes and Scandals; Percy Murders.

■ Sit-ins

A method of civil rights protest involving the occupation of a food service counter seat for extended periods of time.

In February, 1960, four African American students protested the whites-only policy at a Greensboro, North Carolina, Woolworth's lunch counter by seating themselves at the counter and refusing to leave until served. (Library of Congress)

Sit-ins were an important part of the fight against racial segregation in the South.

On February 1, 1960, four African American college students entered a Greensboro, North Carolina, Woolworth's and sat at the lunch counter. They were refused service because they were not white, but they remained seated until closing as an act of protest. In the following weeks, others who opposed "whites only" food service policies sat at Greensboro lunch counters for hours at a time. Six months later, the city's lunch counters were open to both African American and white patrons. This form of nonviolent protest came to be known as a "sit-in."

Sit-ins were an important part of the Civil Rights movement. Early in 1960, the technique quickly spread from Greensboro to other areas of the South. Typically, well-dressed African Americans, occasionally accompanied by white people, sat at segregated lunch counters from opening until closing. Despite their own peacefulness, protesters were sometimes physically abused or arrested. Eventually, stores lost money because of the disturbances and were forced to comply with protesters' demands. Sit-ins became the most effective tool for lunch counter desegregation across the South. In a broader sense, sit-in victories brought African Americans one step closer to equality.

Additional Information For more information on the development and impact of sit-ins, consult Miles Wolf's *Lunch at the 5 & 10* (1990) and Martin Oppenheimer's *The Sit-in Movement of 1960* (1989).

Robert D. Lukens

See also Civil Rights Movement.

■ Six-Day War

Date June 5-10, 1967

The third Arab-Israeli war. Israel decisively established its military (air and ground) superiority vis-à-vis its Arab neighbors in the Six-Day War.

Origins and History The Six-Day War was not an isolated event in the post-World War II history of the Middle East but rather the culmination of building tensions between Israel and its Arab neighbors, in this case, Egypt, Syria, and Jordan. Israel's existence since its creation in 1948 had been an uneasy one, engaged as it was in immediate war with neighboring countries in 1948-1949 and in a second war with Syria

in 1956. The Six-Day War constituted the third Arab-Israeli war and was so named because the conflict was won by Israel in only six days.

The Conflict The war of 1967 was preceded for several years by a series of armed skirmishes between Israel and Egypt or Syria. It was not always clear who was at fault in these incidences, and each side blamed the other. On May 22, 1967, Egypt announced that it was blockading the Straits of Tiran (Gulf of Aqaba), an important shipping route that serviced the Israeli port of Eilat. Israel had previously made it clear that it would regard the closure of the shipping route as an intolerable act of aggression on the part of Egypt; therefore, this act made war inevitable. Relations between Egypt and Jordan, strained for many years before the Six-Day War, were dramatically improved, and Jordan joined the military alliance that existed between Egypt and Syria. The three Arab states put forth a united front and were aided in their war effort by Iraq, Kuwait, Sudan, Algeria, and Saudi Arabia. Between the end of the second Arab-Israeli war and the start of the 1967 conflict, the Soviet Union had increased its influence in the affairs of the region and established itself as an Arab ally. However, at the same time, Israel had become more firmly established as an ally of the United States and other Western countries.

The Six-Day War began when Israel struck Egyptian airfields in a surprise, preemptive attack on June 5, 1967. The attack destroyed about 60 percent of the country's fighter planes. Israel simultaneously launched a ground attack on the Gaza Strip and Egypt's Sinai Peninsula. Jordan and Syria were also attacked by Israel, which, under the direction of Minister of Defense Moshe Dayan, achieved air superiority quickly and appeared poised for victory from the very first day. A cease-fire was declared on June 10; Israel had already occupied the West Bank, Gaza Strip, East Jerusalem, Syria's Golan Heights, and the Sinai Peninsula.

Impact Israel had gained an overwhelming victory in the Six-Day War and was reluctant to make concessions. The Arab states were humiliated and therefore loathe to negotiate a settlement, preferring to focus on preparations for the next armed conflict. This would occur in 1973, when Egypt and Syria, seeking to regain territory lost to Israel during the war, launched a surprise attack on Israeli occupation forces in the Golan Heights and the Sinai Peninsula on October 6 (the Jewish holy day of Yom Kippur). As a result of the Six-Day War, Palestinians in the West Bank and Gaza Strip were forced to live under Israeli rule, and the Palestinian struggle against Israel began.

In the United States, the nation's special relationship with Israel ensured that public opinion would favor Israel in the conflict. However, the nation's experience with Vietnam made Americans generally wary of becoming involved in another war. American Jews overwhelmingly expressed their support of Israel and collected generous sums of money for its war effort. Many Jews who had lost touch with their roots renewed their identification with Israel. After the Six-Day War, Israel, which had hitherto been looked upon as the underdog in the eyes of the world, now began to be viewed as a strong player in the Middle East. Palestinian resistance to the Israeli occupation remained a volatile issue for the remainder of the twentieth century.

Additional Information Thorough treatments of the Six-Day War can be found in Walter Laqueur's *The Road to Jerusalem* (1967) and Theodore Draper's *Israel and World Politics* (1967).

Tinaz Pavri

See also American Nazi Party; Cold War; *Liberty Incident*.

■ Skyjackings

An attempt to divert an aircraft from its flight plan through force or the threat of force. Skyjacking is a form of extortion that involves seizing an aircraft and taking its crew and passengers hostage for criminal, political, or transportation purposes.

Skyjackers have been seizing civilian aircraft and their passengers and crews since 1931, when Peruvian revolutionaries hijacked a plane to drop propaganda leaflets. From 1945 to 1952, political dissidents trying to escape to freedom from communist-controlled Eastern European countries committed nearly all the skyjackings. From 1958 through 1969, skyjackings were predominately a Western Hemisphere phenomenon. Of the 177 worldwide skyjacking attempts during this period, 80 percent originated in the Western Hemisphere and 77 percent involved refugees to or from Cuba. The Cuba-related skyjackings began in 1958, after communist Fidel Castro overthrew the government.

Israeli Minister of Defense Moshe Dayan (right) stands in front of the Wailing Wall in Jerusalem, captured in the Six-Day War of 1967. (AP/Wide World Photos)

Only a handful of skyjacking attempts occurred during the early and mid-1960's. The first aircraft hijacking originating in the United States occurred in May, 1961. A man identifying himself as Elpirata Cofrisi, the eighteenth-century Spanish pirate, hijacked a plane over Florida and forced it to fly to Havana, Cuba. Two more U.S. commercial airliners were hijacked during the summer of 1961 by passengers wanting to go to Havana. That same year, fear that the number of airplane hijackings would increase prompted Congress to make skyjacking a federal offense punishable by imprisonment or death under the Federal Aviation Act of 1958. However, the rate of skyjackings skyrocketed in 1968 and remained high through 1972. The year 1969 was the biggest ever for skyjacking, with eighty-five skyjacking attempts worldwide.

The first skyjacking for extortion occurred in 1968. On July 23, the Popular Front for the Liberation of Palestine skyjacked an Israeli airliner to Algiers. The terrorists demanded that Israel free Palestinian guerrillas in return for the passengers' release. The longest hijacking occurred in October, 1969. An absent-without-leave U.S. Marine named Raphael Minichiello hijacked a Los Angeles to San Francisco flight and redirected it to Rome. The first skyjacking for money in the United States occurred in June, 1970, when a man held a plane hostage at Dulles Airport and demanded $100 million.

Impact In the early 1970's, airport security measures were initiated, often with only limited success. Armed guards called "sky marshals" were stationed on aircraft. In 1973, the United States pioneered the search of passengers and their baggage at the boarding gates. X-ray machines and metal detectors have been added to the arsenal of airport security. Despite some spectacular incidents, the rate of skyjackings has been low since the 1960's.

Subsequent Events One of the most notorious of all U.S. skyjackings occurred in November, 1971. D. B. Cooper boarded a flight in Portland, Oregon, demanded $200,000, and parachuted out of the plane with the money. He was never seen again; some believe he perished, others that he successfully escaped.

The skyjacking rate began to decline in late 1972. Increased aviation security such as rigorous passenger and baggage searches, increased worldwide emphasis on antiterrorist measures, and changing political realities (a lessening of Cold War tensions) explain the decline. However, an increase in the sabotage bombing of airborne aircraft has accompanied this decline.

Additional Information For an in-depth study of skyjacking, see *Kidnap, Hijack, and Extortion: The Response* (1987), by Richard Clutterbuck, a counterterrorism expert.

Fred Buchstein

See also Bay of Pigs Invasion; Castro, Fidel; Cuban Missile Crisis; Travel.

■ *Slaughterhouse-Five*

Published 1969
Author Kurt Vonnegut, Jr. (1922-   )

The antiwar novel that became an instant success. It inflamed a generation of anti-Vietnam War protesters across the United States and earned overnight popular acclaim for its author.

The Work *Slaughterhouse-Five: Or, The Children's Crusade, A Duty Dance with Death,* highlights Billy Pilgrim, who, like Vonnegut, survived the firebombing of Dresden, Germany, by finding refuge in a meat locker under the slaughterhouse where he was employed as a prisoner of war. After the war, Pilgrim marries and becomes a successful optometrist in Ilium, New York; however, he cannot escape the horror and atrocity of war. Believing himself to be "unstuck in time," Billy alternates among his memories of World War II, his life as a civilian in a world grown desensitized to violence and brutality, and a rich fantasy life on the planet Tralfamadore. On display in a Tralfamadorian zoo, Billy is mated with an Earthling named Montana Wildhack, a pornographic film star with whom, unlike with his real-life wife, Billy can share his memories of Dresden. While reliving his war experiences, Billy meets Roland Weary, a cruel and sadistic foot soldier who glorifies in the gruesome aspects of war and an ironic perception of himself as heroic, and Edgar Derby, a high school teacher who volunteered his service because he believed in the nobility of the Allied cause. Vonnegut's brilliant characterization further adds to his picture of war as a brutal, dehumanizing force.

Impact When Vonnegut dramatized his World War II experiences, including the February 13, 1945, firebombing of Dresden, then a cultural haven, by the Allied forces, he spoke to a nation torn, outraged, and struggling with its involvement in the Vietnam War. In chapters 1 and 10, Vonnegut directly addresses the reader and echoes the rallying cry of college students across the nation; he reminds us that nothing sensible can be made of war, no revelation, no absolution, nothing to further the evolution of humans. By presenting us with Billy Pilgrim, a man incapable of passion and who can no longer embrace life's trivial joys or sorrows, Vonnegut mourns the annihilation of the human spirit by the brutal mechanisms of war. An instant success, *Slaughterhouse-Five* was praised by *The New York Times* and *Time* and *Life* magazines, forcing literary critics to reevaluate Vonnegut's five earlier novels. While Vonnegut was signing contracts with the film industry, students all across the United States were touting the novel as evidence that U.S. involvement in Vietnam could result in nothing but senseless brutality, slaughter, and the ultimate death of hope or salvation.

Related Work *Slaughterhouse-Five*, the 1972 film written by Stephen Geller, directed by George Roy Hill, and starring Michael Sacks as Billy Pilgrim, provides a Hollywood version of the novel.

Additional Information For a review of *Slaughterhouse-Five* that focuses on Vonnegut's vision of war and the country's reaction to this vision, see *Extra Success* (1969), by Robert Scholes.

Priscilla June Glanville

See also *Cat's Cradle*; Film; Literature.

■ Smith, Margaret Chase

Born December 14, 1897, Skowhegan,
   Maine
Died May 29, 1995, Skowhegan, Maine

The first woman to be elected to both houses of Congress and the first to have her name advanced for the presidency at the national convention of a major party. An independent Republican, she defended the actions of the military during the Vietnam War.

Early Life After graduation from high school, Margaret Madeline Chase worked as a telephone operator, circulation manager for a weekly newspaper, and executive at a woolen mill. In 1930, she married newspaper owner Clyde H. Smith. When her husband was elected to Congress in 1936, Smith accompanied him to Washington, D.C., as his secretary. After her husband's death in 1940, she was elected to represent Maine in his place. Smith was reelected until 1948 when she chose to run for the Senate, defeating three prominent Republicans in the primary and easily sweeping the general election. Her "declaration of conscience," delivered on the Senate floor in 1950, attracted national attention because she was the first Republican senator to publicly denounce the inquisitorial methods of Senator Joseph McCarthy, who was engaged in a communist witch-hunt.

The 1960's An independent Republican, Senator Smith voted against her party one-third of the time. She helped defeat President Richard M. Nixon's nominees to the Supreme Court and irritated her Republican colleagues with her early support of government-financed medical care for the elderly. A consistent supporter of civil rights legislation, she voted in favor of various acts passed in the 1960's. To help defeat the filibuster against the Civil Rights Act of 1960, she slept in her office, appearing in freshly pressed dresses to answer the frequent quorum calls.

Smith was mentioned as a possible vice presidential candidate in 1952 and again in 1968. In 1964, she entered the New Hampshire Republican presidential primary but ran a poor fifth. A second-place finish to Barry Goldwater in Illinois, with 30 percent of the vote, encouraged her to continue her campaign to the party's national convention, where her

Senator Margaret Chase Smith, an anticommunist who would emerge as a strong supporter of the war in Vietnam, visits the U.S. Naval Base at Guantanamo Bay, Cuba, in December, 1962. (Library of Congress)

name was placed in nomination. After the convention, although Smith supported Goldwater's presidential campaign, she was openly critical of his praise of extremism.

Smith had been a proponent of military preparedness as a congresswoman and continued to support the armed forces as a senator. She became the ranking Republican on the Armed Services Committee and also served on the Defense Subcommittee of the Appropriations Committee. She exerted a powerful influence over defense policy and spending, which she used to protect Maine's shipbuilding and defense industries and to advance the role of women in the military.

Always a strong anticommunist, Smith attacked President John F. Kennedy for repudiating the massive retaliation threat made by President Dwight D. Eisenhower. In a Senate speech on September 21, 1961, she argued that only the threat of nuclear warfare restrained the Soviet Union and that Kennedy's reluctance to use such weapons weakened the United States' ability to deal with the communist nation. Soviet premier Nikita Khrushchev denounced her speech, but to Smith, the resolution of the Cuban Missile Crisis the next year proved the accuracy of her belief that only willingness to use nuclear arms would cause the Soviets to back down. Smith strongly supported the Vietnam War, praising the mining of Haiphong harbor, the stepped-up bombing of North Vietnam, the use of defoliant chemicals such as Agent Orange, and the bombing of supply lines in Cambodia. She considered opponents of the war misguided and uninformed.

Later Life By 1970, Smith was increasingly out of touch with both American opinion and the reality of the Vietnam War. Invited to speak at a Colby College (Maine) rally protesting the shootings at Kent State University, she was shocked by the strength of youthful antagonism to the war. Students were amazed when she proved unaware of U.S. military activity in Laos and uninterested in the fact that her mail was running six to one against the U.S. incursion into Cambodia. Although she easily won a contested Republican primary in 1972, she lost to her Democratic challenger in the general election. Smith retired to Skowhegan, where she turned her home into a museum housing the records and memorabilia she had accumulated during her distinguished career.

Impact Although not a feminist and rarely concerned with gender politics, her successful career inspired other women to emulate her example. Her support of the Vietnam War encouraged President Nixon's expansion of the conflict.

Additional Information Smith describes and defends her political career in *Declaration of Conscience* (1972); Patricia Ward Wallace provides a balanced portrait in *Politics of Conscience: A Biography of Margaret Chase Smith* (1995).

Milton Berman

See also Civil Rights Act of 1960; Cuban Missile Crisis; Goldwater, Barry; Kennedy, John F.; Presidential Election of 1964; Vietnam War.

■ Smith, Tommie, and John Carlos Protest

Date October 16, 1968

An electrifying protest during the 1968 Olympic Games in Mexico City. Tommie Smith and John Carlos, African American sprinters who were members of the United States Olympic track team, staged the event.

Origins and History Tommie Smith, born in 1944 and a native of Clarksville, Texas, was a San Jose State College student in California who simultaneously held thirteen world records in track. John Carlos, born in 1945 and from Harlem, was a world record holder for the 220-yard dash who attended East Texas State College but moved to San Jose to join a proposed boycott of the 1968 Summer Olympics.

The Protest Smith and Carlos were members of the Olympic Project for Human Rights, a division of the Olympic Committee for Human Rights. The responsibility of the committee was to draw attention to off-the-playing-field inequities affecting African American athletes. The committee, founded and chaired by Harry Edwards, former track and basketball star and a sociology professor at San Jose, formed the project specifically to boycott the 1968 Olympics. The committee and project were the natural extension of a series of rallies and demonstrations and a number of books by African American athletes. Some of the activities that preceded the organization of the committee were the publication of basketball star Bill Russell's book *Go Up for Glory*, rescheduling of American Football League's East-West game, and boycott of a New York Athletic Club track meet. At San Jose, sixty of the seventy-two African American students (total enrollment at the school was twenty-four thousand) got together to demand social, economic, and political changes.

In addition to domestic issues, the project also protested the Olympic committee's decision to let athletes from South Africa, where apartheid was still practiced, compete in the Olympic Games. Some of the project's more notable supporters were political and civil rights leaders such as Martin Luther King, Jr., Stokely Carmichael (Kwame Toure), H. Rap Brown, and director of the Congress of Racial Equality (CORE) Floyd McKissick; entertainer Dick Gregory; and athletes Lew Alcindor (Kareem Abdul-Jabbar), and Bill Russell. Olympic legends Jesse Owens, Ralph Metcalf, and Rafer Johnson, all of whom were African Americans, opposed the boycott.

The Olympic committee withdrew its invitation to the South African athletes before the 1968 Olympic track and field events began, so the project decided to forgo boycott plans and instead encouraged individual participants to protest. Smith and Carlos, running in the 200-meter sprint, finished first and third, Smith setting a world record time of 19.8 seconds. The pair mounted the victory stand wearing black socks without shoes as a symbol of African American poverty in the United States. Smith wore a black scarf to represent African American pride

At the 1968 Summer Olympics, U.S. sprinters Tommie Smith (gold medalist) and John Carlos (bronze) raised gloved fists to protest discrimination against African Americans. They were stripped of their medals and sent home. (Library of Congress)

and a black glove on his right hand to stand for black power. Carlos wore the mate to Smith's black glove on his left hand to symbolize unity. As they received the gold and bronze medals, they raised black gloved hands to form an arch of unity and power and bowed their heads to honor the civil rights leaders slain in the struggle. Immediately after the ceremonies, Smith and Carlos were suspended from the Olympic team and ordered to leave Mexico within forty-eight hours. In the long jump event, African American Bob Beamon, who set a world record, and Ralph Boston accepted their medals wearing long black stockings without shoes. After the 400-meter race, African Americans Lee Evans, Larry James, and Ron Freeman, who finished first, second, and third, disappointed followers when they did not show some form of protest. Later, Evans made a public apology.

Impact Immediately after the protest by Smith and Carlos, the United States Olympic committee served notice that "severe" penalties would be inflicted on any athlete—regardless of color—who publicly protested during the games. Ultimately, an awareness of racial mistreatment of African American athletes emerged. U.S. colleges and universities began to address charges that African American athletes who were recruited to play on college teams were sometimes denied off-campus housing, that guarantees of employment made to these recruits often failed to materialize, and that the pay for post-graduation jobs was often not as high as the recruiters had promised. Open acts of discrimination at social functions were investigated, and attempts were made to correct the absence and imbalance of African Americans on coaching staffs and in campus administrative positions.

Additional Information An in-depth account of the protest by Tommie Smith and John Carlos can be found in *The Revolt of the Black Athlete* (1969), by Harry Edwards, and a contemporary view can be gained from the July, 1968, issues of *Sports Illustrated.*

Adolph Dupree

See also Alcindor, Lew (Kareem Abdul-Jabbar); Brown, H. Rap; Carmichael, Stokely; Civil Rights Movement; Congress of Racial Equality (CORE); Gregory, Dick; King, Martin Luther, Jr.; Olympic Games of 1968; Powell, Adam Clayton, Jr.; Russell, Bill; Sit-ins; Sports.

■ Smoking and Tobacco

The inhaling and exhaling of the addictive drug nicotine found in tobacco. The relationship between smoking of tobacco, especially cigarettes, and cancer became a major issue in health and politics.

The habitual smoking of cigarettes by large numbers of people in the United States began early in the

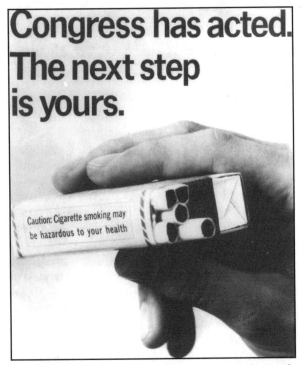

This American Cancer Society poster draws attention to the warning label required on all cigarette packages starting January 1, 1966. (AP/Wide World Photos)

twentieth century. Previously, smoking was limited mostly to pipes and cigars used by the upper class. Following the large increase in smoking, the United States surgeon general, in 1957, publicized his belief, based on scientific studies, that excessive cigarette smoking might be a cause of lung cancer.

By the early 1960's, concern had arisen over the increase in cigarette smoking. The average number of cigarettes consumed per capita annually in the United States had reached 3,888 from 49 in 1900. Habitual adult smokers had reached 42 percent from 15 percent in 1930. The increase had been greater for women than for men as sexist attitudes that stigmatized women smokers disappeared. The United States was a major producer and consumer of tobacco. In 1961, President John F. Kennedy was asked to appoint a special commission to study the effects of smoking on health.

In 1964, the U.S. surgeon general's Advisory Committee on Smoking and Health, after reviewing about one thousand reports and six thousand report summaries, released the most comprehensive report ever compiled on the consequences of cigarette smoking. The committee concluded that "Cigarette smoking is a health hazard of sufficient importance in the United States to warrant appropriate remedial action," that cigarette smoking definitely caused lung cancer, and that other negative effects such as heart attacks also resulted. As a result of the committee's report, in 1965, the U.S. Congress passed legislation requiring a warning label on tobacco products stating "Caution; Cigarette smoking may be hazardous to your health." Denmark and Italy joined England and the United States in the 1960's in passing legislation to discourage cigarette smoking.

Impact Because of the concern over the health consequences of cigarette smoking, the surgeon general continued to release medical reports at the rate of almost one a year after 1964. Numerous other medical and sociological reports were conducted by both antismoking and tobacco interests. The attack on smoking led to major decreases in cigarette usage in the United States. The average number of cigarettes smoked per capita annually peaked in 1963 at 4,345 and then began a major decline.

Subsequent Events Bans on advertising have increased, and stronger warnings have been required on cigarette packages. A great deal of money and effort have been put into antismoking education. In the 1980's attention focused on the health hazard faced by nonsmokers who inhale side-stream, or second hand, cigarette smoke, resulting in the prohibition of smoking in many public buildings. By 1996, the annual per capita use had decreased to 2,482 cigarettes. In 1996, one tobacco company settled class-action lawsuits brought against it by individual states, and in 1997, the tobacco industry began making financial settlements with a number of states amounting to billions of dollars, with the money to be used for research targeting the prevention and curtailment of youth smoking and to recoup costs incurred by states in treating people with smoking-related illnesses.

Additional Information A detailed study of both the economic and medical consequences of cigarette smoking can be found in *The Economic Costs of Smoking and Benefits of Quitting* (1984), by G. Oster, et al.

Abraham D. Lavender

See also Cancer; Medicine.

■ *Smothers Brothers Comedy Hour, The*

Produced February, 1967-June, 1969

A television variety show extremely popular among high school and college-age youth. Tom and Dick Smothers and their guests made satirical comments about sacrosanct topics that provoked censorship.

The Work The Smothers Brothers, Tom and Dick Smothers, who mixed folk songs with comedy, launched a variety show, *The Smothers Brothers Comedy Hour*, on the Columbia Broadcasting System (CBS) on Sunday, February 5, 1967. The show featured social commentary, utilizing innuendo and satirical skits to emphasize message development. It captured a 36 percent share of the viewing audience, outdrawing the well-established show *Bonanza* by a 10 percent share. Tom and Dick Smothers attributed the large audience following to the program's social relevance. Many of the show's skits and acts dealt with political and religious topics with which the CBS executives were uncomfortable. The Smothers Brothers' most notable guest was comedian Pat Paulsen, who launched a satirical run for president to complement the 1968 election in a way that older and conservative viewers found highly offensive. In addition, many of the guests and performers, includ-

The Smothers Brothers, Tom (right) and Dick, used their show to feature socially relevant music and political and religious satire that brought them into conflict with the television network's censors. (AP/Wide World Photos)

ing folksinger Pete Seeger, used the show to make statements against the Vietnam War.

The show started to have major censorship problems with CBS executives shortly after it started its second season; these problems heightened in the third season. CBS canceled the program because the Smothers Brothers had failed to submit a videotape in time for network preview. The comedy duo argued that the program had gotten too controversial and that the network was looking for any excuse to get rid of the show. CBS disagreed with the pair's statements, pointing out that there was a rising cost issue and that the show's ratings had started to slip. Also, the network alleged that there was a contract dispute, and that the social climate of the viewers was changing.

The Smothers Brothers successfully sued CBS for the dismissal but were not able to revive their show on a regular basis until the next decade on the American Broadcasting Company (ABC) network.

Impact Other television shows had been censored during the 1950's and 1960's, including those that featured entertainers such as Groucho Marx and Jack Paar. However, censorship in these cases was usually limited to the excision of language or specific acts. *The Smothers Brothers Comedy Hour* helped to establish that in American television, almost no subject would be too sacred for derisive and satirical treatment.

Additional Information For further information on the Smothers Brothers and their show, see *Broadcasting in America* (1982), by Sydney W. Head with Christopher H. Sterling.

Earl R. Andresen

See also Censorship; Media; Social Satires; Television; *Tonight Show, The.*

■ Social Satires

Comedy that poked fun at contemporary issues such as politics, prominent people, government, family, Cold War, and Vietnam. Satire, with its biting edge, found a receptive audience, particularly among members of the counterculture, in the turbulent 1960's.

Film, television, and live performances welcomed a growing satirical movement that had its origins in late 1950's coffeehouse clubs and later grew to national prominence in all three media. The biting satire in each medium befitted the social, political, and cultural upheaval of the revolutionary 1960's.

Live Performances Original sketch comedy performed by Chicago's Compass Players in the early 1960's demonstrated a sophisticated approach to live theatrical comedy not often encouraged or attempted. This comedic approach was built upon improvisation, which gave actors great freedom to express a sharper political edge in the changing social milieu. The Compass Players later became the renowned Second City comedy troupe. Actors and writers included Mike Nichols and Elaine May (a successful team for many years), Alan Arkin, Bob Newhart, George Kirby, and Avery Schreiber. The Second City (its name a confident counter to New York City's hold on national theater) became a center for young actors to practice improvisational theater.

The themes and style of much of the improvisation and political humor in Second City was influenced by comics of the late 1950's such as Lenny Bruce and Mort Sahl. Both comics developed their acts to suit a new educated class of Americans during the Cold War. Sahl, who always performed with a rolled up newspaper in his hands, was primarily a political comic, satirizing the American political system. He made his reputation at clubs such as The Hungry I in San Francisco, Mr. Kelly's in Chicago, and The Bitter End in New York City. Bruce, who started in vaudeville, built his reputation as an angry gadfly of the state, often shocking audiences with his deconstruction of language (often deemed obscene by judges), his criticisms of the hypocrisy of social classes, and his perceptions of human nature. Bruce became celebrated as much for his legal trouble as for his comic vision, which featured frank discussions of sexuality and an overall brashness. Bruce's brand of comedy opened doors for a new generation of performers in the late 1960's who would use satire as their main comic impulse. Bruce died of a drug overdose on August 3, 1966, in Los Angeles. Comics who followed in the path of Sahl and Bruce included Woody Allen, Shelly Berman, Phyllis Diller, Alan King, Joan Rivers, Bill Cosby, Don Rickles, and Richard Pryor.

Television The culture of live troupe comedy possessed a cachet that television producers wished to capture and turn into profit. Many of the performers from live sketch groups and stand-up comics performed on programs such as *The Tonight Show* (the original host in the 1950's was Steve Allen, followed by Jack Paar, then Johnny Carson in the 1960's), *The Steve Allen Show*, *The Jack Paar Show*, *The Jackie Gleason Show*, and most notably on *The Ed Sullivan Show*, where mainstream Americans were introduced to the burgeoning spirit of the satirical 1960's.

By the middle of the decade, satirical material had become a regular feature on television, leading producers to promote new shows that fostered sketch comedy or variety formats. The National Broadcasting Company (NBC) fall schedule for 1967 slated a new program entitled *Rowan and Martin's Laugh-In*, which featured inventive uses of televisual form (borrowed from television comic pioneer Ernie Kovacs) such as rapid zoom-in style close-ups, previously edited filmed segments, quick and often frenetic editing, and a youthful ensemble cast that relied on topical humor, often of the risqué variety. The popularity of *Rowan and Martin's Laugh-In* was immediate and prompted older established stars to make appearances. Performers such as Bob Hope, Johnny Carson, John Wayne, and frequent guest Sammy Davis, Jr., offered one-liners in brief cameo spots. Even 1968 presidential candidate Richard M. Nixon appeared and delivered the long-running gag line "Sock it to me" with a curious expression on his face. The cast included Lily Tomlin, Goldie Hawn, Arte Johnson, Joanne Worley, Judy Carne, Henry Gibson, Ruth Buzzi, and Alan Sues. The material used in this show was somewhat satirical but was presented so quickly and whimsically that the full punch of social satire was never fully achieved. *Rowan and Martin's Laugh-In* was canceled in the spring of 1972.

Another satirical program of the 1960's was *The Smothers Brothers Comedy Hour* on Columbia Broadcasting System (CBS), introduced in fall, 1967. From the start, the Smothers Brothers, a folk-singing comedic duo of brothers Tom and Dick, featured topical political humor, youthful musical guests and stand-up comics, double-entendre jokes, and an overall antiestablishment comic viewpoint. Part of the appeal of the Smothers Brothers is that they relied on conventional aspects of sketch variety formats: broad gag-line comedy, established stars as guests (including veterans George Burns and Jack Benny), musical guests, and topical humor. The ideological balancing act formed by combining traditional formats with controversial material that consistently ruffled the feathers of the censors led to a ratings success. Although the Smothers Brothers knocked *Bonanza* out of the number-one spot (and all but ended its ten-year run on televison) and remained in the top twenty in the ratings, of all the television programs of the 1960's, *The Smothers Brothers Comedy Hour* had the most problems with censors because of the controversial material produced. Besides satirizing political figures and the government in general, the show was sharply critical of U.S. involvement in the Vietnam War.

Folksinger Pete Seeger, after much debate by the censors, was finally allowed to sing his Vietnam War protest anthem "Waist Deep in the Big Muddy" (which censors hoped would not be taken as the song was meant—as a symbol of the unpopular war), but singer Harry Belafonte was not granted permission to sing "Lord Don't Stop the Carnival," which was to accompany video tapes of the many confrontations between protesters and police at the 1968

Democratic National Convention in Chicago. In April, 1968, guest singer Joan Baez, whose husband David Harris was facing a three-year jail term for resisting the draft, made on-air comments about his struggle that were cut by CBS censors. The Smothers Brother were outraged and called a press conference in New York to announce their displeasure with the network. CBS would have none of it, canceling the program immediately.

The Smothers Brothers Comedy Hour provided a useful example of the difficulty of balancing art and commerce. In the end, the brothers' satirical style was too much for the status quo deemed essential to running a television network. Ironically, a few years later, CBS executives revamped their entire comedy line-up by replacing older shows such as *Gunsmoke, The Beverley Hillbillies,* and *Petticoat Junction* with issue-oriented shows such as *All in the Family, The Mary Tyler Moore Show, Good Times,* and *Maude* in an effort to reach younger demographics and achieve higher revenues from advertisers.

Film Some of the best examples of film satire would come just after the 1960's with films such as *Catch-22* (1970), *Little Big Man* (1971), *Nashville* (1975), and *Shampoo* (1973). However, some of the most striking films of the 1960's belong to the satire genre.

Mike Nichols's *The Graduate* (1967), a coming-of-age film made during the sexual revolution, portrays the overachieving Benjamin Braddock (Dustin Hoffman) as a confused, alienated upper-middle-class college graduate who is manipulated into a love affair with a married woman. In a search for something genuine in his life, Benjamin is met with promises of a future in "plastics." Nichols illustrates the hypocrisy and superficiality of upper-middle-class life in the suburban United States.

Stanley Kubrick directed two satires in the 1960's, *Lolita* (1962) and *Dr. Strangelove: Or, How I Learned to Stop Worrying and Love the Bomb* (1964). Kubrick's adaptation of Vladimir Nabokov's *Lolita*, starring James Mason, Peter Sellers, and Sue Lyon, treated the relationship between the older man and the young girl as a symbol to question middle-class sexual mores and satirize suburban pseudointellectualism.

Dr. Strangelove is the quintessential satire of the military system set during the Cold War. The film demonstrates, with frightening hilarity, what could happen in the event of a nuclear confrontation. The film's theme is predicated on the notion that humankind's sexual consciousness is revealed through military conventions. Each of the characters is given a humorous sexual name and many visual signifiers of sex are presented for comic relief.

Other fine satirical films of the 1960's include *How I Won the War* (1967) and *Petulia* (1968), both directed by Richard Lester; *The Manchurian Candidate* (1962), directed by John Frankenhemier; *Butch Cassidy and the Sundance Kid* (1969), directed by George Roy Hill; *Medium Cool* (1969), directed by Haskell Wexler; and *Wild in the Streets* (1969), directed by Roger Corman. Also, it is arguable that documentaries of the 1960's produced by Fred Wiseman, Alan and David Maylses, Richard Leacock, D. A. Pennebaker, and Ed Pincus are satirical in their approach to analyzing American institutions.

Impact The lasting effect of social satire in the United States in the 1960's was political awareness. The main comedic thrust of all three media—film, television, live performances—centered on reframing the context for political humor during a very turbulent decade of American life. Even if the comedic sequence was not explicitly about politics but drew its laughs from satirizing certain specific aspects of American culture (as was the case in a great deal of the sketch comedy troupes' material), it followed the theme of breaking down social conventions. The effect social satire from the 1960's had on performers is incalculable (many comics of the 1990's such as Dennis Miller, Richard Beazer, and Elayne Boosler consider Bruce to be an influence on their satirical work). The social and political context of the 1960's provided the means for a generation of artists to respond with enriching and often very biting social satire that helped define the era of dissent.

Additional Information More about the Smothers Brothers and their show can be found in Aniko Bodroghkozy's "The Smothers Brothers Comedy and the Youth Rebellion" in *The Revolution Wasn't Televised* (1997). Information on satirical films can be found in David Bordwell and Kristin Thompson's *Film History: An Introduction* (1994) and Ethan Mordden's *Medium Cool: The Movies of the 1960's* (1990). Harry Castleman and Walter J. Podraik's *Watching TV: Four Decades of American Television* (1982) provides a look at satire and television.

John P. Shields

See also Baez, Joan; Bruce, Lenny; *Butch Cassidy and the Sundance Kid*; Censorship; *Dr. Strangelove*; *Ed Sullivan Show, The*; *Graduate, The*; *Medium Cool*; *Smothers Brothers Comedy Hour, The*; Television; *Tonight Show, The*.

■ Sonny and Cher

A husband-and-wife singing duo. Their upbeat and fresh love songs brought them success.

Salvatore "Sonny" Bono started in the music business in the 1950's. He was a songwriter and a producer of various recording artists. In 1962, Sonny and Jack Nitzsche cowrote "Needles and Pins," which became a hit single for the Searchers in 1964. Sonny divorced his wife, Donna Lynn, in 1963 and married Cherilyn Sarkasian LaPier in Tijuana, Mexico, a year later. He had met Cher, who was working as a background singer, at a recording session run by the renowned producer Phil Spector.

After some early missteps, the couple decided to become a singing duo and use their own names, Sonny and Cher, to identify their act. They signed with Atco in 1965. In August of that year, "I Got You Babe" a song written and produced by Sonny—reached number one on the American singles charts. Although a very hard worker, Sonny became adept at projecting a carefree image.

With long hair and hippie clothes, Sonny and Cher caught on with the public. Their first album, *Look at Us* (1965) became a hit. That same year, the pair also released solo material. With their newfound influence, they produced their own clothing line in 1966. Department stores across the country carried Sonny and Cher bell-bottom pants, bobcat vests, and blouse outfits. During the year, they had a private audience with Pope Paul VI in Rome, Italy. Their fresh and innocent image held them in good stead during the late 1960's. In addition to "I Got You Babe," some of their other notable singles include "But You're Mine," "Have I Stayed Too Long," "Baby Don't Go," and "The Beat Goes On." In 1969, Cher gave birth to their daughter Chastity. By 1970, Sonny and Cher had moved on to be a cabaret act appearing in Las Vegas. They began to mix comedy with singing, a mix that would lead to a television show.

Impact As a duo, Sonny and Cher burst onto the scene as fun-loving romantics whose folk-rock style and hippie attire fit the era, while offering a balance to the more politically radical or drug-influenced acts. The pair brought a refreshing enthusiasm to whatever they did.

Subsequent Events In 1971, Sonny and Cher began a highly successful television variety show, *The Sonny and Cher Comedy Hour* (1971-1977). With the success of the show, their music again became popular. Unfortunately, they were divorced in 1975. Cher concentrated on her solo career for the rest of the 1970's. During the 1980's, Cher began an acting career that would culminate in her winning an Academy Award for her performance in the film *Moonstruck* (1987). In 1983, Sonny opened a restaurant in Los Angeles. During the 1980's, he also appeared in some television programs.

Always adept at reinventing himself, Sonny was elected mayor of Palm Springs, California, in 1988. In 1994, Sonny was elected to the House of Representatives from California's forty-fourth congressional district. Tragically, he was killed in a skiing accident at South Lake Tahoe, California, on January 5, 1998.

Additional Information In 1991, Sonny Bono published his autobiography, *And the Beat Goes On.* Lawrence J. Quirk's biography of Cher, *Totally Uninhibited: The Life and Wild Times of Cher*, was also published in 1991.

Jeffry Jensen

See also Music.

■ Sontag, Susan

Born January 16, 1933, New York, New York

An outspoken critic and advocate of contemporary culture. Sontag brought to American criticism a sophisticated sensibility honed in both the United States and Europe.

Early Life Susan Sontag grew up in Arizona and California and attended a semester at the University of California, Berkeley, before departing for the University of Chicago, where she was schooled in a great books view of criticism and philosophy that she applied to the cultural developments of the 1960's. She pursued graduate work at Harvard, earning a master's degree in 1957, and taught briefly at several colleges.

The 1960's Sontag's watershed year was 1964. Her essay, "Notes on Camp," was published in the *Partisan Review* and received national attention in *Time* magazine. With an encyclopedic list of events and attitudes, the essay formulated a thesis that attempted to capture the dynamism of the 1960's and its playful sensibility. At the end of the year, *The Evergreen Review* published her essay, "Against Interpretation," which argued that critics had devalued contemporary art by concentrating on its content—reducing it to a series of statements or messages. Sontag argued that art was not reducible to points in a critical essay and that the efforts of content-driven critics ignored the style and tone of art, depriving readers of the whole experience that only art can provide.

In 1965, *Commentary* published Sontag's "The Imagination of Disaster," a searching investigation of the appeal of science-fiction films, which made this popular genre a noteworthy benchmark for the discussion of postwar culture. After the success of her first book, *Against Interpretation and Other Essays* (1966), Sontag became a full-time writer, lecturing at universities and speaking at public cultural events in Europe and the United States. The publication in 1967 of "The Pornographic Imagination" and "The Aesthetics of Silence" enhanced her reputation not only as a commentator on contemporary culture but as a critic/philosopher who was extending the work of modern European and American masters of literature and criticism. Sontag recounted her controversial trip to Vietnam in *Trip to Hanoi* (1968) and collected her most important essays of the late 1960's in *Styles of Radical Will* (1969). She also wrote and directed two films in Sweden, *Duet for Cannibals* (1969) and *Brother Carl* (1972).

Later Life In 1975, Sontag was hospitalized for breast cancer. Based on her struggle with that disease, she wrote *Illness as Metaphor* (1978), followed by *AIDS and Its Metaphors* (1989). *On Photography* (1977) received the National Book Critics Circle Award for Criticism. Her novel, *The Volcano Lover* (1992) was both a popular and critical success.

Impact Sontag became one of the famous faces and voices of the 1960's. Quoted in intellectual journals as well as in mass circulation magazines, her words were believed to capture the spirit of the age. With her long dark hair and casual clothing—usually slacks—she epitomized a new generation of thinkers and public intellectuals, protesting the Vietnam War, traveling to Hanoi and Cuba, and in general lending her name to leftist causes and battles against censorship and other forms of political repression.

Additional Information Sontag's interviews, including many translated from European languages, appear in *Conversations with Susan Sontag* (1995), edited by Leland Poague. The book also provides the most complete chronology of her life and a comprehensive introduction to her work.

Carl Rollyson

See also Art Movements; Film; Happenings; Literature; Theater.

■ Sound of Music, The

Released 1965
Director Robert Wise (1914-   )

One of the most successful, profitable, and popular motion picture musicals ever produced. The film made $79 million on a budget of $8.2 million and, in 1965, was nominated for ten Academy Awards and won five, including awards for Best Picture and Best Director.

The Work *The Sound of Music* is based loosely on the true story of the Austrian Von Trapp family. In the film, the young novice, Maria (Julie Andrews), is training to become a nun at an Austrian abbey but is obviously unsuited to a life of quiet obedience. She is persuaded by the Mother Abbess (Peggy Wood) to leave the convent and take a job as governess to the children of the widowed Austrian navy captain, Baron Von Trapp (Christopher Plummer). The seven Von Trapp children have managed to drive away several previous governesses, but Maria wins them over with her charm, common sense, and good humor. At first, the authoritarian Von Trapp, who calls his children by blowing a whistle, is skeptical of Maria's methods; but eventually, her charm wins him over, and he realizes that he is in love with her and not with his baroness fiance (Eleanor

Julie Andrews played the governess in the immensely popular and successful 1965 motion picture musical The Sound of Music. *(Museum of Modern Art/Film Stills Archive)*

Parker). The baroness scares Maria at first and sends her running back to the abbey in alarm, but Maria realizes that she is in love with Von Trapp and returns to marry him. Immediately following their wedding, the Nazis invade Austria and annex it, and the baron is under pressure to serve the Third Reich. With the aid of the baron's friend, Max Detweiler (Richard Haydn), who is in charge of the acts at the Salzburg Folk Festival, and the nuns of Maria's former abbey, the Von Trapps escape the Nazis and flee Austria.

Impact *The Sound of Music* was an enormous financial success for Twentieth Century Fox, exceeding all expectations. The film achieved a permanent place in popular culture with such songs as "Do-Re-Mi," "My Favorite Things," and the title song, "The Sound of Music." It is perhaps the best film of a musical by the composer team Richard Rodgers and Oscar Hammerstein II not only because of its remarkable box-office earnings but also because of its success in converting a musical stage production into a film. Two criticisms of the film are that it is historically inaccurate and emotionally manipulative, but its feel-good lyrics and sense of wholesomeness have made it a classic among musical films.

Related Work Director Wise's first successful and critically acclaimed motion picture musical, *West Side Story* (1961), which he codirected with Jerome Robbins and for which they received the Academy Award for Best Director, prepared him for the making of *The Sound of Music*. Like *The Sound of Music*, this film also won the Academy Award for Best Picture.

Additional Information For a detailed description of the history and filming of *The Sound of Music*, see the sections on the film in *Rodgers and Hammerstein* (1992), by Ethan Mordden, and *Oscar A to Z* (1995), by Charles Matthews.

Gregory Weeks

See also Film; Music.

■ Southern Christian Leadership Conference (SCLC)

One of the most effective and controversial of the African American civil rights organizations of the 1960's. It waged a nonviolent campaign that led to the passage of legislation for the abolition of racial segregation in the South.

Origins and History The Southern Christian Leadership Conference (SCLC) was created in 1957 in the wake of the successful Montgomery bus boycott from which the Reverend Martin Luther King, Jr., emerged as a national leader. Organized through a series of conferences in Atlanta, Georgia, and New Orleans, Louisiana, SCLC brought Northern liberals and left-oriented activists such as Bayard Rustin and Stanley Levison together with church-based black civil rights advocates in the Deep South. SCLC remained a church-centered organization made up of local and state groups affiliated by charter, with an all-black board of directors mostly from the Deep South. Sponsorship from within the African American church gave SCLC a distinctive character and helped generate a broad popular following, particularly in those communities where SCLC's successes were of the greatest consequence.

Activities The Civil Rights movement was already well under way in 1960 when student-led sit-ins in Greensboro, North Carolina, led to a mass mobilization of African American youth across the South in protest against segregation. SCLC's King helped create the Student Nonviolent Coordinating Committee (SNCC), and a partnership soon developed between the two organizations. By the 1960's, King had become SCLC's first president and a dominant influence, employing the assistance of a trained and disciplined staff of advisers, field directors, organizers, and fund-raisers. King and SCLC rejected the interracialism of the Congress of Racial Equality (CORE) and the legal strategy of the National Association for the Advancement of Colored People (NAACP), preferring direct-action protest; nevertheless, the SCLC cooperated closely with other civil rights organizations throughout the critical years from 1961 to 1965. Early successes for SCLC were modest, however, with failure at Albany, Georgia, caused by white resistance and black community divisions. SCLC's strategy at this time featured a nonpartisan appeal for the creation of a spiritual, nonviolent army that would promote civil disobedience in order to challenge racial prejudice and discriminatory laws. Operating through a mixture of Christian social gospel, the teachings of India's Mohandas Gandhi, and the pragmatic opportunism of U.S. democracy, King and SCLC proclaimed their mission to redeem the soul of the nation.

In Birmingham, Alabama, through the spring and summer of 1963, SCLC experienced its most dramatic and compelling success by focusing national attention on violent white resistance to desegregation. Its strategy included a calculated effort to engage federal support, leading to the March on Washington in August, which involved SNCC, NAACP, CORE, and a number of other civil rights groups. In the fall, a national consensus in support of civil rights objectives gained strength after the assassination of President John F. Kennedy, whose administration had become cautiously allied with SCLC and its leadership.

With the passage of the Civil Rights Act of 1964, SCLC shifted its focus to voting rights and was joined by SNCC and other civil rights groups in a campaign that targeted the most hostile areas of the Deep South. Unsuccessful efforts at St. Augustine, Florida, coincided with mounting friction between SCLC and other organizations such as SNCC, CORE, and the NAACP over issues of funding, strategy, and leadership. However, during the first three months

One of the leaders of the Southern Christian Leadership Conference, Hosea Williams (right), meets with John Lewis, chairman of the Student Nonviolent Coordinating Committee, in 1965. (Library of Congress)

of 1965, protests in Alabama culminated in a march from Selma to Montgomery that successfully dramatized the plight of African Americans denied the right to vote, resulting in the passage of the Voting Rights Act of 1965.

SCLC had never enjoyed complete stability, but as early as 1964, the organization suffered a financial setback with the expiration of the Gandhi Society, a fund-raising subsidiary. With the loss of top-level staff members, such as executive director Wyatt T. Walker, SCLC spun into confusion spawned by internal schisms and external political pressures. Only King's highly public profile, unique personality, and forceful mediation enabled the top staff members, many of whom possessed large egos and volcanic tempers, to work together successfully through 1965 and 1966. In 1965, SCLC reached a peak staff membership of more than two hundred people, with an income of $1.5 million, supported by contributions drawn from diverse sources throughout the nation, including community church groups, the business world, organized labor, and major foundations. After the summer of 1965, a new strategic shift within SCLC resulted in an emphasis on economic issues such as jobs, housing, and the mounting crisis in the nation's inner cities, and many civil rights advocates became involved in opposition to the Vietnam War. Relations with other organizations, particularly SNCC, continued to deteriorate, and King became the target of special Federal Bureau of Investigation covert intelligence operations designed to discredit him and disrupt the SCLC's activities. The mood among top staff members became increasingly pessimistic as the popular response to urban rioting and antiwar protests provided signs that the United States was becoming more divided and hostile toward civil rights activism.

In the early 1960's, SCLC had derived organizational strength from Deep South civil rights centers that grew out of the African American church. However, by 1966, when SCLC launched its attempt to combat segregation in Chicago, the organization had begun to suffer from weak management, factional rivalries, and a deteriorating financial condition with expenses exceeding revenues. By the end of the year, it was clear that

Chicago remained impervious to SCLC tactics, while black nationalism, with its rhetoric of confrontation, and the Black Power movement emerged as explosive forces among African Americans.

In 1966, SCLC became politically isolated because of an altered atmosphere within national politics, deeper splits among civil rights organizations, and King's criticism of the war in Vietnam. Although SCLC had often worked effectively with SNCC, attempts to dominate the student wing of the movement helped to alienate key leaders, driving them more swiftly in the direction of a militant black nationalism. As overall support for nonviolent spiritualism in response to white resistance began to fade through the mid-1960's, organizational weaknesses within SCLC found preachers pitted against intellectuals for staff leadership, with board members going as far as to oppose King because of his support for antiwar protests. By 1966, all the major civil rights organizations, including SCLC, were enjoying less popular support, and SCLC saw continuing staff departures and top leaders becoming demoralized and cynical. Convinced that the Vietnam War presented the primary stumbling block to successful social action, a deeply distressed and disillusioned King turned to economic radicalism and black power, questioning every aspect of his leadership through the final months leading up to his assassination in the spring of 1968. Already beset with declining contributions and shattered staff morale because of the failed campaign in Chicago, SCLC was nevertheless able to restore staff discipline and financial stability by the time of King's death in Memphis and the early stages of the Poor People's Campaign in Washington.

Impact Probably the most influential of the 1960's civil rights organizations, SCLC was a vital force in the making of national policy from 1961 to 1965, when major civil rights reforms were enacted by Congress with the backing of the president and the courts. Although later civil rights legislation was far less effective, southern states saw the gradual curtailment of racial segregation, the growth of an African American voter constituency, a dramatic increase in African American elected officials, and the overall end of institutionalized white supremacy. King and SCLC, meanwhile, became national symbols of the American aspiration for a society free of racial discrimination.

Subsequent Events After King's assassination, SCLC leadership was in the hands of Ralph Abernathy, Andrew Young, Jesse Jackson, and other nationally recognized figures. Campaigns focusing on public school integration continued to operate into the early 1970's when the organization splintered. Jackson broke from SCLC in late 1971 to create his own organization, People United to Serve Humanity. In 1972, former SCLC executive director Young became the first African American since Reconstruction to win a seat in the U.S. House of Representatives for the state of Georgia. Although SCLC continued under the presidency of Abernathy up to 1977 and Joseph E. Lowery through the 1980's, the organization lacked the resources, the national constituency, and the high public profile to sustain the 1960's style of protest.

Additional Information In-depth studies of SCLC are featured in David J. Garrow's *Bearing the Cross: Martin Luther King, Jr., and the Southern Christian Leadership Conference* (1986) and Adam Fairclough's *To Redeem the Soul of America: The Southern Christian Leadership Conference and Martin Luther King, Jr.* (1987) and Thomas R. Peake's *Keeping the Dream Alive: A History of the Southern Christian Leadership Conference from King to the 1980's* (1987).

John L. Godwin

See also Abernathy, Ralph; Birmingham March; Civil Rights Act of 1964; Civil Rights Movement; Congress of Racial Equality (CORE); Hoover, J. Edgar; Jackson, Jesse; King, Martin Luther, Jr.; March on Selma; March on Washington; National Association for the Advancement of Colored People (NAACP); Poor People's March; Sit-ins; Student Nonviolent Coordinating Committee (SNCC); Voting Rights Legislation; Young, Andrew.

■ Space Race

A race between the United States and the Soviet Union to achieve technological superiority in space. It resulted from the psychological and physical struggles between the forces of democracy and communism locked in a Cold War.

Belligerent defensive postures assumed by the United States and the Soviet Union propelled the emergence of the Cold War in the 1950's. The resulting arms race concentrated on the perfecting of the atomic bomb and the development of hydrogen and nuclear weapons. Although some scientists conducted experiments and tests relevant to space travel, until October 4, 1957, space voyages remained a scientific daydream to be realized only by future generations. The Soviet launch of Sputnik, the first manmade earth satellite, was followed only one month later by a second satellite that carried a dog into orbit. Suddenly, the United States shifted its defense priorities to include space technology, and the race into outer space had begun. Wernher von Braun, supervisor of the U.S. Army's Guided Missile Division at Huntsville, Alabama, took advantage of the situation to suggest publicly that a lack of financial support for programs significant to the development of space travel had placed the United States in a secondary, and quite vulnerable, position. To compensate, President Dwight D. Eisenhower created the National Aeronautics and Space Administration (NASA).

The United States Takes Off   NASA celebrated the launch of its first successful satellite, Explorer 1, in 1958. Other satellite successes followed, but the unreliable Vanguard rockets slowed the program's progress. The apparent success of the Soviet program further aggravated NASA's uneven achievement. Sputnik 3 demonstrated superior thrust control and carried a payload far heavier than that of the U.S. satellites. However, the Soviet program was also clouded by failures.

The Soviets had gained a foothold in space, but the Americans would pose a far greater challenge. At project administrator Braun's insistence, NASA concentrated on manned space flights and established the Moon as its ultimate destination. No longer remote and inaccessible, the mysteries of the Moon included a landscape dotted by more than thirty thousand craters and jagged mountain chains with peaks higher than Mount Everest. The secrets of the far side of the Moon inspired even greater curiosity. In 1958, NASA created Project Mercury to place a man in space within two to three years and requested volunteers for the projected launchings. The Mercury project would be followed by two more stages, Gemini and Apollo.

The Soviets were also interested in the exploration of the Moon. Lunik 1 was designed not only to probe the atmosphere of the Moon but also to take a 450-day journey around the sun. Similar Soviet missions convinced a watchful American public that NASA's efforts had to increase. In March, 1959, the United States placed Pioneer 4, the second manmade satellite, in orbit around the sun. The success of this mission assured Americans that the country was only a matter of months behind in the space race. However, in the fall of 1959, the Soviets launched two important lunar missions: Lunik 2, which delivered an instrument package, and Lunik 3, which photographed the elusive dark side of the Moon. This Soviet triumph loomed even larger when, in November, 1959, a U.S. Atlas-Able rocket aimed at the Moon exploded and fell, burning in the Atlantic Ocean.

Manned Flight   The failure of NASA to keep pace with the Soviet Union caused much concern among the American public. As politicians and other Americans focused on the lack of sufficient booster power, NASA tried to shift the public's attention to newer developments. NASA announced that McDonnell Aircraft Corporation would build the Mercury capsule for manned space flight and showcased seven volunteers who would become astronauts. With considerable fanfare, NASA introduced the nation's new heroes: M. Scott Carpenter, L. Gordon Cooper, John Glenn, Virgil I. "Gus" Grissom, Walter M. Schirra, Alan B. Shepard, Jr., and Donald "Deke" Slayton.

Space travel became a truly human venture on April 12, 1961, when Soviet cosmonaut Yuri Gagarin become the first man to orbit Earth. In August, Gherman Titov blasted off in Vostok 2 for a twenty-five-hour mission that took him on seventeen trips around Earth. The United States edged into manned space flight with two suborbital flights in 1961. Shepard became the first U.S. astronaut in space in a fifteen-minute flight on May 5, 1961. Several weeks later, Grissom completed an eighteen-minute flight.

Armed with these successes, President John F. Kennedy appealed to Congress and the public to embark on an accelerated program that would place an American on the Moon before the end of the decade. However, the successes of Project Mercury continued to lag behind Soviet achievements. As U.S. astronauts struggled to gain experience with weightlessness, the Soviets displayed their domination of the race to the Moon by launching the "space twins," an impressive operation involving two spacecraft. Cosmonaut Andrian Nikolayev piloted Vostok 3 into a synchronous orbit with Pavel Popovich's

Vostok 4. In a splendid demonstration of maneuvering in space, both cosmonauts were able to communicate with each other, and Nikolayev reported that he could see Popovich's craft through his port window.

The Soviet program set several flight duration records and successfully launched one craft with a three-man crew. Project Mercury was followed by the Gemini space program, which officially began in 1964. NASA directed the objectives of this next phase in space exploration toward expanding rendezvous and docking procedures with two vehicles orbiting in space, perfecting reentry methods and landing techniques, and studying the physiological reactions of crew members to weightlessness. As the Gemini program drew to a close, U.S. astronauts had logged nearly two thousand hours in space. As Soviet efforts concentrated on flight longevity, the Americans were gaining experience in steering and maneuvering spacecraft. For the first time in the space race, American technology nearly matched the pace of the Soviet Union.

Lunar Landing Project Apollo, the final drive toward a lunar landing and the United States' final push in the space race, depended on the use of the Saturn launch vehicle, a cluster of rockets that used liquid hydrogen as a propellant. The dangers of a race to the Moon became a stark reality when on January 27, 1967, tragedy struck. Astronauts Grissom, Edward H. White, and Roger B. Chaffee died when a fire erupted inside the Apollo 1 craft during a routine test on the launch pad. NASA suspended the Apollo project to investigate the cause of the fire (an unfortunate spark in the pure oxygen atmosphere of the capsule) and to redesign the spacecraft to eliminate other hazards. In October, 1968, Project Apollo resumed its schedule with the launch of Apollo 7 and Apollo 8, missions that photographed the lunar surface and gathered vital information for future missions.

The space race reached it zenith when Apollo 11 dispatched a lunar module that landed two men on the Moon's surface. On July 20, 1969, astronaut Neil A. Armstrong became the first man to set foot on the Moon, and the space race, essentially, was over, "won" by the United States. "That's one small step for man, one giant leap for mankind," declared Armstrong. Before returning to the spacecraft piloted by astronaut Michael Collins, Armstrong and

his colleague, astronaut Edwin E. "Buzz" Aldrin, collected rock and soil samples, transmitted breathtaking panoramic views of the lunar surface, and raised the U.S. flag. The astronauts left behind a plaque that hinted at the new spirit of cooperation that would dominate future space endeavors. It read: "Here Men from Planet Earth First Set Foot Upon the Moon, July, 1969 A.D. We Come in Peace for All Mankind." Between 1969 and 1973, five more American missions visited the lunar surface. The Soviets landed several probes on the Moon but never sent cosmonauts to explore the surface.

Impact The greatest impact of the space race was the dramatic changes in U.S. education that followed both Sputnik and President Kennedy's challenge to go to the Moon. The technological achievements of the U.S. race to the Moon made Americans' daily lives easier in the form of spinoff technologies such as Velcro fasteners and medical prostheses. However, during the 1960's, U.S. successes in the space race were overshadowed by the nation's involvement in Vietnam, urban violence, and the emergence of the New Left, which challenged a society perceived as being increasingly corrupt.

Subsequent Events In 1973, NASA launched Apollo Skylab, a project designed to test both the astronauts' endurance and the extended use of space vehicles. At the end of the program a year later, forty-seven astronauts had accumulated 22,432 hours in space. NASA organized the first international manned space flight in July, 1975. On July 15, the Soviets launched Soyuz with cosmonauts Alexey Leonov and Valerly Kubasov. Seven hours later, Apollo blasted off from Kennedy Space Center with astronauts Thomas P. Stafford, Vance Brand, and Slayton. The two spacecraft met in space, docked, and for nine days exchanged greetings, shared information, and cooperatively conducted research. By 1975, the space race was completely over, and a new spirit of harmony dominated the efforts of humans to explore their universe.

Additional Information A fact-based history of space flight can be found in T. A. Happenheimer's *Countdown: A History of Space Flight* (1997). The book covers space flight from Nazi rockets to the present-day technology.

Kathleen Carroll

See also Apollo Space Program; Arms Race; Cold War; Gemini Space Program; Mariner Space Program; Mercury Space Program; Moon Landing; Science and Technology.

■ Speck Murders

Date July 14, 1966

One of the most notorious crimes of the 1960's. The savagery manifested in the murders of eight student nurses in Chicago stunned not only the neighbors, police, and coroner but also the nation.

Origins and History Richard Benjamin Speck, age twenty-four, of Monmouth, Illinois, an unemployed laborer and seaman, had served previous prison sentences for forgery, burglary, and assaulting a woman.

The Murders On the night of July 13, 1966, Richard Speck gained access to a far southside townhouse used as a dormitory for eight student nurses from Chicago's Community Hospital. Armed with a gun and a knife, he woke the sleeping residents and herded them into one bedroom; he then surprised three more women returning just before curfew and put them in the same room. Claiming that he wanted only money for a trip to New Orleans, he told them they would not be hurt. After collecting the money, he systematically removed the women one by one to other parts of the house, where he stabbed three and strangled five. The victims were Gloria Jean Davy, Valentina Pasion, Merlita Gargullo, Nina Jo Schmale, Pamela Lee Wilkening, Suzanne Bridget Farris, Mary Ann Jordan, and Patricia Ann Matusek.

An exchange student, Corazon Amurao, escaped death by rolling under a bed and hiding. The next morning, Amurao loosened her bonds and, fearing the killer was still downstairs, forced open a second-floor window screen. Once outside on the window ledge, she called for help. Authorities believe that Speck had watched the townhouse from a nearby park and knew that eight women lived there. Amurao probably escaped detection because Jordan was

Richard Speck (left), convicted of murdering eight nurses in Chicago in 1966, heads for court in June, 1967, where he received a death sentence. (AP/Wide World Photos)

in the house to visit her future sister-in-law, Farris, bringing the total number of women in the house to nine (when the killer had been expecting only eight). The police speculated that none of the other women hid, screamed, or fought back because they believed they would not be hurt or were simply paralyzed with fear.

From evidence, including fingerprints, left at the scene, and from Amurao's description, the police identified Speck as the murderer. He was arrested on July 17 for the murder of Farris; on July 26, he was indicted on eight murder charges.

Impact On June 5, 1967, Speck was sentenced to death by electric chair on all eight counts. However, his execution was stayed repeatedly, and on August 30, 1971, the United States Supreme Court lifted his death sentence, as well as that of thirty-nine others, on the grounds that people opposed to the death penalty had been automatically excluded from the juries. He was resentenced to eight consecutive terms varying from fifty to one hundred and fifty years. Proponents of the death penalty were horrified that it would not be enacted on Speck, the perpetrator of a manifestly evil and morbidly gruesome crime.

Additional Information William J. Martin, the prosecutor in the case, and Dennis L. Breo, a Chicago journalist, published a detailed account of the murders in a book entitled *The Crime of the Century: Richard Speck and the Murder of Eight Nurses* (1991).

Sharon Randolph

See also Boston Strangler; Career Girl Murders; Crimes and Scandals; Texas Tower Murders.

■ Spock, Benjamin

Born May 2, 1903, New Haven, Connecticut
Died March 15, 1998, San Diego, California

The pediatrician whose book on child rearing continues to reassure millions of parents. Spock's prominent antiwar and antidraft activities in the 1960's helped to galvanize older and younger generations in opposition to the U.S. government's Vietnam War policies.

Early Life Benjamin McLane Spock's Dutch parents were very strict and expected him to achieve academic and professional success. In 1921, after two years at Phillips Academy in Andover, Massachusetts, Spock was sent to Yale to study architecture. He soon

switched to a premedical curriculum, and after earning his baccalaureate degree in 1925, he proceeded to Columbia University Medical School where he was awarded a degree in 1929. Following several years of postgraduate study in psychiatry, he began private practice in New York City. Between 1944 and 1946, Spock served as a navy psychiatrist, and it was during this time that he wrote *The Common Sense Book of Baby and Child Care* (later retitled *Baby and Child Care*), which when published in 1946 made him a household name in the United States. The book's staggering success led to academic posts in the University of Minnesota (1947-1951), the University of Pittsburgh (1951-1955), and Case Western Reserve University (1955-1967).

The 1960's By the late 1950's, Spock, who was originally a Republican, began to describe himself as a New Deal Democrat and became a supporter of progressive social legislation. He was especially interested in health care initiatives, including Medicare. In 1962, he became a spokesperson for SANE (National Committee for a Sane Nuclear Policy). Spock strongly backed Lyndon B. Johnson in the 1964 presidential campaign, but he turned against Johnson in 1965 when he realized that the president had no intention of withdrawing from Vietnam. From that moment, Spock put his reputation and fame on the line by becoming one of the most recognizable opponents of the United States' participation in the Vietnam conflict. In 1967, he resigned his university post to devote as much time as possible to his antiwar and antidraft activities. In 1968, the U.S. Justice Department succeeded in gaining an indictment against Spock and four others, including Yale chaplain William Sloane Coffin, for aiding and abetting violation of the Selective Service Act. A sensational trial resulted in convictions for four of the men, including Spock, in July, 1968. Spock was sentenced to two years in jail. However, a year later a U.S. Court of Appeals overturned the verdict, citing erroneous instructions by the trial judge.

Later Life During the early 1970's, Spock persisted in his vocal opposition to the war in Vietnam. He participated in every major antiwar demonstration and continued to urge young American males to avoid conscription by whatever means possible. When the Vietnam War ended, Spock shifted his interest to a variety of other social causes while

Pediatrician Benjamin Spock (center front) leads a peace walk in New York City in 1965. (Library of Congress)

producing frequent new editions of his best-selling book. In the 1980's and 1990's, he gradually receded, although never completely, from the national consciousness and spent more and more time in his Virgin Islands residence. In 1998, the ninety-four-year-old doctor, who had been suffering from heart and kidney ailments, died in San Diego.

Impact Spock's impact in the 1960's directly related to the fame and cachet he had earned as the nation's most prominent "baby doctor." After publication of his book in the late 1940's, millions of American children were raised according to the doctor's advice. It was this generation of young people who seemed most threatened by the country's involvement in Vietnam.

Members of the older generation were shocked by the sight of this conservatively dressed, grandfatherly doctor demonstrating side by side with long-haired, strident young radicals. Many blamed him

and his book for creating a generation of what they regarded as rebellious, sexually permissive, antipatriotic hooligans. However, the long-term effect of his behavior was to awaken parents, particularly mothers, and grandparents to the dangers the Vietnam War, or any war, posed for their children. General outrage erupted over his trial in Boston. That this compassionate and peace-loving doctor could be brought to trial at all, much less be convicted, appeared to millions of Americans to be a misuse of government power.

How much influence Spock or the antiwar campaign as a whole had in forcing changes in U.S. policy is debatable, but his contribution toward making the antiwar demonstrations acceptable to "respectable" Americans can scarcely be overestimated. In a more general sense, he aroused suspicion among middle- and upper-class citizens about whether their government could be trusted to act in the nation's best interests.

Additional Information In 1969, Jessica Mitford published *The Trial of Dr. Spock*, which deals with the sensational trial in 1968.

Ronald K. Huch

See also Boston Five Trial; Draft Resisters; Mitford, Jessica; SANE.

■ Sports

Organized athletic contests cultivated for the enjoyment of both participants and spectators. The 1960's saw great expansion of major sports at both the amateur and professional levels.

The four American sports most often regarded as major ones in the 1960's originated and attained prominence at different times. Baseball is no longer regarded as the 1839 invention of Abner Doubleday. Its origins are difficult to disentangle, but it is known that children of the early New England colonists played stick-and-ball games. The sport now known as baseball took on its present configuration when men began to play the game regularly in the 1840's. The first professional team, the Cincinnati Red Stockings, emerged in 1869, and the present major leagues began operation in 1876 (National) and 1901 (American). College students began playing football, which owed much to the earlier games of soccer and rugby, in the 1880's, and early college teams were known to hire professional players on occasion. The first viable professional league was formed in 1920. Ice hockey developed in Canada in the middle of the nineteenth century and by the end of the century had spread to northeastern and north-central areas of the United States. Professional teams arose in Canada early in the twentieth century, expanding into the United States by 1924. Basketball, the only major sport to be invented in the United States, was devised by James Naismith, a Canadian, in 1891 in Springfield, Massachusetts, as a game that could be played in a gymnasium during cold-weather months. It soon became popular in colleges and schools and developed as a professional sport after the end of World War II.

Perhaps the most striking phenomenon of major professional sports in the 1960's was the expansion of leagues, both in numbers of franchises and movement into new geographical areas. The reasons for the expansions included the proportionally greater population growth in the South and West, generally available long-distance travel by air, frequent telecasts of games that tended to create new fans, and the erection of modern facilities for sports events, including all-weather ones. When the Houston Astrodome opened in 1965, for example, fans could watch baseball and football games for the first time in air-conditioned comfort. Other important developments included a much greater prominence of black performers at both the amateur and professional levels and the first movement toward free agency among professional athletes.

Baseball. The major league baseball map remained unchanged for a half-century before 1954, when the St. Louis Browns franchise of the American League became the Baltimore Orioles. Even then, the National League's St. Louis Cardinals remained both the westernmost and southernmost outpost of major league baseball. The major leagues thus began their true territorial expansion in 1958, when the National League's Brooklyn Dodgers and New York Giants relocated to Los Angeles and San Francisco, respectively. Nevertheless, in 1960 the two leagues still had eight teams each, as they had throughout the century, and thirteen of the sixteen teams still represented the same cities they had since 1903. By 1969, however, each league had swollen to twelve teams, including three more in California, one each in Minnesota, Washington, Texas, and Georgia, and one in Montreal, Canada.

The best teams of the decade were the Los Angeles Dodgers and St. Louis Cardinals in the National League and the New York Yankees in the American. The Dodgers and Cardinals each won three pennants, but at the end of the decade the New York Mets became the first expansion team to finish on top. For the first half of the decade, the Yankees continued their long domination of the American League; during the next five seasons, however, four different teams won pennants. The Yankees, Cardinals, and Dodgers triumphed in two World Series each.

There were a number of spectacular individual feats. In 1961, Roger Maris of the Yankees broke perhaps the most notable record in sports by hitting sixty-one home runs, one more than Babe Ruth hit in 1927; it was a record destined to last even longer than Ruth's. In the National League, the great sluggers tended to be African Americans, including Ernie Banks, Willie Mays, Henry Aaron, and Willie

McCovey. Black players were also largely responsible for the revival of base-stealing as an offensive strategy, especially in the National League. In 1960, the Dodgers Maury Wills stole fifty bases, the highest total in the league since 1923. Two years later, his 104 steals set a major league record that would last until 1974.

The best pitchers in the National League were the Dodgers' lefthander Sandy Koufax, Juan Marichal of the San Francisco Giants, and the Cardinals' Bob Gibson. In 1968, Gibson yielded an average of only 1.12 earned runs per game, the lowest in the major leagues in more than fifty years. The veteran Yankee lefthander Whitey Ford, who had starred throughout the previous decade, remained the American League's top pitcher for the first half of the 1960's; thereafter, Denny McLain of the Detroit Tigers took over. In 1968, McLain won thirty-one games to become the first thirty-game winner in either league since Lefty Grove had won the same number thirty-seven years earlier.

The National League, which had a greater concentration of black stars, finally attained parity with, and perhaps surpassed, the American League, which had long dominated interleague competition. National League representatives won six of ten World Series and eleven of thirteen All-Star games during the 1960's. Nevertheless, at the end of the decade, critics complained that black players still had to be better than average to earn a major league paycheck; it is also worth noting that as yet there existed only one black umpire, no black managers, and no African Americans in significant front-office positions.

As the 1960's went along, baseball's proud status as the "national pastime began to look questionable, as professional football and basketball, both of which had seasons that overlapped baseball's, gained rapidly in popularity. More football than baseball games were being telecast nationally. After 1968, a pitching-dominated year that saw Gibson's and McLain's great seasons and a host of low-scoring games generally, a number of rules changes, including a reduction in the height of the pitcher's mound and the size of the strike zone, were instituted to help hitters; thereafter, the offense that fans presumably favored began to improve.

In 1969 labor relations took an important turn when Marvin Miller, an economist whom the Players' Association had elected as its executive director after the 1965 season, charged that the owners were

not supporting the players' pension fund adequately. When most of the players went on strike during spring training that year, the owners quickly capitulated. One seemingly small incident at the end of the same year pointed the way to a new era in player-owner relationships. On December 24, 1969, an outstanding but recently traded outfielder, Curt Flood, sent a short letter to commissioner Bowie Kuhn announcing his refusal to report to his new team the next year unless he was first allowed to consider offers from other teams. According to the long-standing reserve clause in the standard player contract, this was not permitted, but Flood told Kuhn, "I do not feel that I am a piece of property to be bought and sold irrespective of my wishes." He threatened to go to court if necessary, but he received no encouragement from other players who were as much "property" as he. Flood's own long legal struggle would end in failure, but his letter began to blaze a trail that would lead to sweeping changes in the contractual relationships of players and management.

More future major league baseball players were going to college, but typical academic schedules meant very short seasons except in Southern states; the venerable baseball weekly, *The Sporting News*, devoted more attention to American League baseball than to the college game. The minor leagues remained the proving ground for prospective major leaguers.

Football. At first glance, professional football might seem to have expanded more modestly, from twenty teams in 1960 to twenty-six in 1969. As late as 1959, though, there had been only twelve; the next year a new league, the American Football League (AFL), had risen to challenge the older National Football League (NFL). Whereas baseball, with a schedule that necessitated frequent hops from city to city, could not easily accommodate transcontinental trips in the days of railroad travel, major league football had reached the West Coast as early as 1946. By the end of the 1960's, football too was reaching southward to such bases as Atlanta and New Orleans. In 1966, the AFL and NFL agreed to merge in gradual steps. In 1967, the champions of the two leagues met for the first time in an annual contest that would become known as the Super Bowl, and in 1970 the NFL absorbed the ten AFL franchises.

The team of the decade was the Green Bay Packers. Vince Lombardi coached the Packers to NFL championships in 1961, 1962, 1966, and 1967 and to wins in the first two Super Bowl games over AFL opposition in 1967 and 1968. The Packers' Bart Starr and John Unitas of the Baltimore Colts reigned as the best quarterbacks of the 1960's, while the outstanding running backs were Cleveland's Jim Brown, who rushed for a record 1,863 yards in the fourteen-game 1963 schedule, and Gale Sayers of the Chicago Bears, both African Americans. The one position dominated entirely by white players was quarterback.

Football had long been the most popular college sport, and until the late 1960's, it remained far more popular than professional football. In the 1960's, Paul "Bear" Bryant coached the University of Alabama team to three national collegiate championships. Other powerhouses included Notre Dame under Ara Parseghian, Ohio State under Woody Hayes, and the University of Texas under Darrell Royal. Most professional players came directly from college campuses. It was generally expected, for example, that winners of the Heisman Trophy, voted annually to the outstanding college player, would become professional stars—but although this happened with Heisman winners such as Roger Staubach of Navy and O. J. Simpson of the University of Southern California, there were exceptions. For example, the 1964 winner, quarterback John Huarte of Notre Dame, failed utterly to become the latest Notre Dame great to make his mark in professional football.

Basketball. The National Basketball Association (NBA), a compact eight teams in 1960—also with no team west or south of St. Louis—had grown to fourteen by 1969. Six of the seven teams in its Western Conference were based in previously unrepresented cities: Atlanta, Los Angeles, Phoenix, Seattle, San Francisco, and San Diego. In 1967, the American Basketball Association (ABA) began play with eleven teams, many in previously untapped markets in the West, Midwest, and South. The rivalry between the two leagues lasted until 1976, when four of the ABA's franchises were absorbed by the NBA and the remainder disbanded.

No other team dominated a professional sport as the Boston Celtics did basketball in the 1960's. Led by stars such as center Bill Russell and guard Bob Cousy and coach Red Auerbach, the Celtics won the league's championship nine times during the decade. Only in the 1966-1967 season did another team, the Philadelphia 76ers, win a championship. The 76ers' star, Wilt Chamberlain, was Russell's great rival for the honor of being the league's best center. Chamberlain actually had his most awesome season in 1961-1962, when he led the league in rebounds, won the scoring title with an amazing average of 50.4 points a game, and set an all-time record by scoring 100 points in a March 2, 1962, game against the New York Knicks.

In no sport did black athletes prevail as thoroughly as in basketball. At the start of the decade, black stars were sprinkled throughout the league, but by 1969, African Americans constituted a majority on some teams, including the championship Celtics. In the 1969 All-Star game, the top scorers—the great Oscar Robertson of Cincinnati, who was Cousy's successor as the league's perennial assist leader, the flashy Earl Monroe of Baltimore, and the graceful Elgin Baylor of Los Angeles, the league's most prolific scorer after Chamberlain—were African American, as were fourteen of the game's twenty-four participants.

Other stars of the era included Bob Pettit of St. Louis, Rick Barry of San Francisco, and John Havlicek of Boston—all players who would have been outstanding in any era. For much of his Havlicek's career, Auerbach used him as a "sixth man"; despite his status as one of the league's best players, his coach found that he could use him most effectively coming off the bench at key moments in the game. Indeed, the increasingly fast pace of professional basketball was leading coaches to require more depth in their rosters, making strategic substitutions more important than before.

In the college ranks, coach John Wooden's University of California at Los Angeles (UCLA) teams were nearly as dominant as Auerbach's Celtics were at the professional level, winning five National Collegiate Athletic Association championships. UCLA's greatest player of the 1960's was center Lew Alcindor, later known as Kareem Abdul-Jabbar.

Hockey. In the National Hockey League (NHL), expansion came suddenly, with a doubling of franchises, from six to twelve, for the 1967-1968 season. By adding Philadelphia, Pittsburgh, Minnesota, St. Louis, Los Angeles, and Oakland, major league hockey too moved into southern and western territories. The Montreal Canadiens continued a domination stretching back to the 1950's, winning the Stanley Cup, emblematic of supremacy, five times. When Montreal was not winning, the other Canadian team, the Toronto Maple Leafs, usually was, with four Cup victories. The two greatest offensive stars of the era, however, Bobby Hull and Stan Mikita, who between them won seven of the ten individual scoring races, both played for the Chicago Black Hawks, while the same team's Glenn Hall won the most trophies as best goalie. Curiously, the Black Hawks, who had little team success in the decade, also boasted the defenseman with the most awards in Pierre Pilote, but by the end of the 1960's young Bobby Orr of the Boston Bruins had emerged as the league's premier defenseman. Unlike in other major team sports, black players made no impact on hockey in the 1960's, probably because few African Americans had much opportunity to learn the game.

Another characteristic peculiar to hockey continued to be fights during the games. The league was highly ambivalent about such violence, on the one hand instructing its officials to move slowly to break up the fights, which many fans seemed to enjoy, on the other continuing the long tradition of awarding the Lady Byng trophy to the player who demonstrated outstanding sportsmanship and gentlemanly conduct on the ice. During the 1960's, the two great Black Hawks, Mikita and Hull, proved that achievement in hockey did not necessitate violence. Between them, they won three Lady Byngs.

Impact Increasingly, sports were shaping America's leisure in the 1960's. Better travel facilities not only made it possible for athletes and teams to compete on a truly national scale but also enabled fans to get to the stadiums and arenas more easily. With many more televised games, more people developed interest in sports. In particular, the Super Bowl, which at first appealed principally to diehard fans, evolved into a enormously popular television spectacle and social event.

Sports figures had long been heroes, especially to males young and old, but a greater diversity of athletes now gained that status. Professional football players had been relatively anonymous figures to most Americans, but now the face of Joe Namath, the quarterback who led the New York Jets to the first AFL Super Bowl victory in 1969, became one of the most recognizable faces on television screens every-

where. Even performers in less popular sports, such as Cassius Clay (later known as Muhammad Ali) in boxing, Peggy Fleming in figure skating, and Arnold Palmer and Jack Nicklaus in golf, also became instantly identifiable celebrities.

More fans both at the games and in front of television screens made bigger businesses than ever out of sports. Six-figure salaries became the norm for star players. The Columbia Broadcasting System's purchase of the New York Yankees for $11.2 million in 1964 marked the first time a team had a corporate owner. More money meant higher ticket prices and more commercials in telecasts of sporting events.

Subsequent Events Most of the trends of the 1960's continued into the 1970's and beyond. Professional leagues expanded further, and many elaborate new sports facilities sprang up. Athletes, who now left contractual negotiations to their agents, saw their salaries spiral upward. With the coming of cable television, channels devoted wholly to sports challenged the older television networks. African Americans and other ethnic minorities continued to play increasingly important roles in many sports, and fans generally greeted their achievements enthusiastically. Although football still outdistanced it in popularity, soccer, a sport that even very young children can play, gained status steadily. Sports programs for girls and women, virtually nonexistent in many schools and colleges in the 1960's, were instituted, often in response to legal pressure from women's organizations.

Additional Information Wells Twombly's *200 Years of Sport in America: A Pageant of a Nation at Play* (1976) provides a general historical context. Ronald A. Smith's *Sports and Freedom: The Rise of Big-Time College Athletics* (1988) is well-researched and stimulating. Geoffrey C. Ward's *Baseball: An Illustrated History* (1994) offers a decade-by-decade account of major league baseball. *Seventy-five Seasons: The Complete Story of the National Football League, 1920-1995* (1995) is an overview of the league. A literate insider's view of professional basketball is *Life on the Run* (1976) by Bill Bradley, while Gerald Eskenazi's *Hockey* (1969) surveys its topic efficiently from the perspective of the decade's end.

Robert P. Ellis

See also Baseball; Basketball; Brown, Jim; Chamberlain, Wilt; Football; Koufax, Sandy; Maris, Roger; Mays, Willie, Namath, Joe; Russell, Bill.

■ Steinem, Gloria

Born March 25, 1934, Toledo, Ohio

Charismatic humanist and spokesperson for the women's liberation movement. As an advocacy journalist and political activist, Steinem participated in and wrote about the women's movement, black power, antiwar protests, youth rebellion, and the welfare movement.

Early Life A native of Toledo, Ohio, Gloria Steinem spent much of her youth caring for her mentally ill mother. She graduated magna cum laude from Smith College in 1956, then received a Chester Bowles Asia fellowship to study in India, where she joined a radical humanist group and traveled to poverty-stricken areas in the southern part of the country.

The 1960's Soon after returning to the United States, Steinem moved to New York and worked as a freelance journalist, writing funny photo captions for *Help* and penning more serious articles such as "The Moral Disarmament of Betty Co Ed," which explored the birth control pill and its effect on college women, for *Esquire* in 1962. An exposé on the exploitation and degrading job conditions of women working as Playboy bunnies ran in May and June of 1963 in *Show*.

By 1965, Steinem was earning thirty thousand dollars a year as a freelance writer and lecturer. In the late 1960's, when *New York* magazine was founded, Steinem became a contributing editor and political columnist. In 1968, she wrote a distinctively leftist biweekly column for the magazine focusing on feminist issues, antiwar efforts, black power, poverty, welfare, and student movements. She also was popular on the lecture circuit, speaking on feminist issues. She also negotiated a successful television interview series and wrote film scripts.

Later Life Steinem won the Penny-Missouri Award for the article "After Black Power, Women's Liberation," which was published in the April 7, 1969, issue of *New York*. The article, sympathetic to the women's liberation movement, launched Steinem's career as a spokesperson for the feminist movement. In October, 1969, Steinem was invited by the National Democratic Woman's Club in Washington, D.C., to speak about women's liberation. In 1970, Steinem delivered the commencement speech at Smith College on the current issues in feminism, and in Au-

gust, 1971, *Newsweek* featured Steinem on its cover as the personification of women's liberation. In 1972, Steinem became the editor and founder of the new feminist magazine *Ms*.

Impact Steinem, as founder and editor of *Ms*. magazine, the first feminist mass-circulation magazine in U.S. history, influenced the women's liberation movement by covering topics such as pornography, rape, incest, abortion, poverty, lesbianism, politics, women's health care, and battered women and by authoring essays and books on feminist issues.

Subsequent Events In 1971, Steinem cofounded the National Women's Political Caucus, was a member of the Coalition of Labor Union Women, Voters for Choice, Women Against Pornography, and Women USA and established the Women's Action Alliance. In 1977, President Jimmy Carter appointed Steinem to the National Committee on the Observance of International Woman's Year. Also in 1977, she was awarded the Woodrow Wilson Scholarship to Study Feminist Theory at Woodrow Wilson's International Center for Scholars. In 1983, her book *Outrageous Acts and Everyday Rebellions* became a national best-seller.

Gloria Steinem, journalist and political activist, was a vocal spokesperson for the feminist movement in the 1960's. (AP/Wide World Photos)

Additional Information Steinem—social activist, humanist, and feminist—was the target of much criticism from both within and outside the feminist movement. Nevertheless, she spent a lifetime committed to women's liberation. Her brand of feminism implied that women's liberation was also men's liberation. Steinem advocated that people become secure enough to treat others equally. She stated, "It is time to turn the feminist adage around, that political is personal."

Garlena A. Bauer

See also Feminist Movement; Friedan, Betty; Women's Identity.

■ *Steppenwolf*

Published *Der Steppenwolf*, 1927, (English translation, 1929)
Author Hermann Hesse (1877-1962)

The experimental novel that foreshadowed the counterculture of the 1960's. It deals with the midlife crisis of a bourgeois intellectual and his search for self-realization through sex, drugs, music, and alienation from industrial society—all currents that partially characterized the 1960's.

The Work Hermann Hesse, a German neoromantic novelist, wrote *Der Steppenwolf* in 1927 when he was fifty years old. In the book, Hesse's only novel set in a city during the late 1920's, a young businessman discovers the diaries of a middle-class intellectual named Harry Haller in the apartment of his aunt, Harry's landlady. Harry, who refers to himself as a "Steppenwolf," or a wolf of the steppes, is in effect, a wanderer in search of himself. Harry's surrealistic records reveal a depressed fiftyish man on the verge of suicide. He is rescued by the music of a nearby dance hall where he encounters a peddlar with a placard that advertises the attractions of a "Magic Theater—Not for Everybody." In the first portion of the novel, a "Treatise on the Steppenwolf," Harry reveals himself as half man (his civilized bourgeois qualities) and half wolf (his instinctual urges in search of expression). He is guided in his quest by the classical immortals Johann Sebastian Bach, Johann Wolfgang von Goethe, and Wolfgang Amadeus Mozart and also his new friends—bar girl Hermine, prostitute Maria, and jazz musician Pablo. With Hermine as his alter-ego, Harry learns to enjoy life again, with Maria, he discovers the joys of sex, and with Pablo, he explores jazz and mind-expanding drugs. The second part of the novel deals with Harry's experiences in the "Magic Theater," where he is immersed in dreams and wish fulfillment. He makes war on automobiles, makes love to all the women he ever desired, and commits murder. Finally, he discovers his multiple selves and is tried and condemned to enjoy life and not take himself so seriously by the laughing immortals he had mistaken for pompous intellectuals like his former self. His idol Mozart reveals himself at the end as a lover, a rebel, and a romantic—a precursor of a counterculture Hesse had discovered in the 1920's. Harry had achieved a new, life-giving vision.

Impact To some extent, Harry represented Hesse's struggles. Hermine could stand for (in the framework of Hesse's psychologist Karl Jung) his *anima*, or female counterpart. The novel is set in a European city during the jazz age of the 1920's, a period of "wonderful nonsense," dancing, and sex that foreshadowed the 1960's. Although *Steppenwolf* is about the crisis of a man turning fifty, it celebrates a return to vibrant youth. Harry learns to be young again and discovers spontaneity, romantic love, and his instincts. The story is a reworking of Goethe's *Faust*, also a middle-aged man's quest for happiness. The result is Harry's self-discovery and the unification of his two selves. Other themes are a critique of materialistic industrialism, bourgeois hypocrisy, war, and nationalism—all characteristics of the counterculture of the 1960's. Because of all these currents, *Steppenwolf*, neglected in Germany, was rediscovered in the United States during the 1960's. The novel's mix of the real and the surreal, along with all of its other features, made it appealing to those interested in the counterculture. In 1974, the novel was made into a film starring the distinguished Swedish actor Max von Sydow.

Additional Information *Hesse: A Collection of Critical Essays* (1973), edited by Theodore Ziolkowski, sheds light on Hesse's 1920's novel.

Leon Stein

See also Counterculture; Drug Culture; Literature; Sexual Revolution.

■ **Stonewall Inn Riots**

Date June 28-July 2, 1969

Violent clashes between several thousand angry protesters and the New York City police at the Stonewall Inn bar in Greenwich Village. For many, the riot represents the birth of the gay and lesbian rights movement.

Origins and History Until the homophile movement began in the 1950's, organized support for homosexual rights in the United States was limited at best. In the 1960's, the organizations that made up this movement were few in number, primarily existed in large cities, and were highly secretive because of the severe oppression typically faced by gays and lesbians. Late in the decade, however, gay and lesbian activists followed the lead of civil rights and women's liberation protesters in calling for equal rights.

The Riots At approximately 1:30 A.M. on Saturday, June 28, 1969, a small contingent of police conducted what initially began as a routine raid on the Stonewall Inn, a bar that catered primarily to gay men. The police, following standard procedure, immediately arrested patrons who could not produce proper identification or who had violated a state statute that forbid cross-dressing. This time, however, the police were met by a boisterous crowd of onlookers when they began escorting their prisoners toward the police van.

Rather than dispersing as the officers ordered, the crowd appeared intent on voicing its growing resentment toward police harassment of gays. The crowd began to boo the police and surge around the police van. Shortly thereafter, a full-fledged melee ensued. The crowd screamed obscenities at the police and, as its ranks grew, threw trash, bricks, bottles, garbage cans, coins, and even dog excrement at the officers. One participant shattered Stonewall Inn's front window with a trash can. Overwhelmed by the crowd's fury, the police retreated into the bar. Several people then uprooted a parking meter and, using it as a battering ram, tried to break down the bar's front door. Someone squirted lighter fluid through the bar's broken window and tossed in lit matches.

As a fire erupted inside the Stonewall Inn, two dozen members of New York City's Tactical Police Force arrived to quell the crowd and rescue the trapped officers. However, when the force marched up Christopher Street, several hundred members of the crowd circled around the block and approached the force from the rear. The tactical force lashed out,

and the crowd responded in kind, damaging several patrol cars, assaulting police with wet garbage, and chasing several officers from the scene. The tactical force finally cleared the area at approximately 3:30 A.M., but not before four officers and an undetermined number of rioters were injured, thirteen people were arrested, and the Stonewall Inn was damaged extensively.

During the next several days, large crowds of celebrating rioters, street people, and curiosity seekers gathered outside Stonewall Inn. By the time the sun rose on Saturday, the building's facade had been covered with homemade signs and graffiti, some of which read: "Legalize gay bars," "They invaded our rights," and "Support gay power." The crowd chanted, "gay power," "Christopher Street belongs to queens," and "Liberate Christopher Street." The police and the tactical force again attempted to restore order by wielding their billy clubs. However, the crowd was too large to be controlled easily, and a reprise of the previous night's riot followed. At 4:00 A.M. on Monday, the police finally withdrew.

Although inclement weather prevented additional activity on Monday and Tuesday evenings, rioters reappeared on Christopher Street on Wednesday evening. They set trash cans ablaze, threw beer bottles and cans at police, and shouted, "Gestapo!" and "Fag rapists!" The police again responded with force. Although the riots ended this night, they became a powerful symbol for the gay and lesbian movement.

Impact The Stonewall Inn rebellion was not the first instance of active gay and lesbian resistance. However, the furor unleashed on Christopher Street triggered widespread activism on both national and international fronts. Therefore, the riots represent a significant turning point in the gay and lesbian struggle for equal rights and cultural acceptance. In particular, they gave rise to a new sense of identity and self-acceptance for homosexuals, greatly enhanced participation in the gay and lesbian movement, and informed the spirit and tone of gay and lesbian protests.

Nowhere is Stonewall's importance as a rallying cry more notable than in events that commemorate the riots. Chief among these are annual observances and celebrations, Christopher Street Liberation Day and Gay Pride Day. In 1994, the riots' twenty-fifth anniversary was marked by a nationwide commemoration, the highlights of which were Stonewall Twenty-five and the weeklong Gay Games IV and Cultural Festival, both held in New York.

Additional Information Martin B. Duberman's book entitled *Stonewall* (1993) makes excellent use of eye-witness testimony to provide a thorough and insightful account of the riots and their impact.

Beth A. Messner

See also *Boys in the Band, The*; Gay Liberation Movement; Greenwich Village.

■ Stranger in a Strange Land

Published 1961; restored version 1990
Author Robert A. Heinlein (1907-1988)

The award-winning novel, especially popular among students, that reinforced the sexual rebellion and counterculture lifestyle of mid-1960's youth. It provided an adolescent fantasy of a sexual utopia that would remedy alienation from such bourgeois interests as marriage, career, and property.

The Work In *Stranger in a Strange Land*, Valentine Michael Smith, a human orphan raised by Martians, returns to Earth, where a gestapo oversees a totalitarian federation of nations. Lacking familiarity with human customs, Smith, like fugitive Moses, is "a stranger in a strange land" (Exodus 2:22). Smith is instructed by Jubal Harshaw, an aged, individualistic father figure who represents Heinlein's views. Smith possesses special Martian-tutored mental powers (including telekinesis, levitation, and telepathy), and his educational use of them provides the plot for the novel. He founds a church based on the perception of the individual self as divine, the non-possession of property (including spouses), the freedom of sexual expression, the merging of bodies and souls, and the mysticlike communion ("grokking") that dissolves personal identity through a sympathetic merging with others. Smith demonstrates a Christ-like, infallible judgment and a miraculous capacity to cause the unworthy to die painlessly. Nevertheless, at the close of the novel, he is murdered (martyred) by a mob fearful of his messianic repudiation of the conventional Judeo-Christian moral code.

Impact Although *Stranger in a Strange Land* was awarded a Hugo Prize, it was not immediately popular. The novel, filled with ideas indebted to H. G.

Wells's *In the Days of the Comet* (1906), was an unlikely candidate for wide success. However, by the mid-1960's, it had become a cult book popular among students attracted to its counterculture critique of bourgeois social mores, its argument for free love, and its celebration of an altered state of consciousness. The notion that sexual promiscuity and arrested consciousness could supplant hypocrisy and artificiality, cure routine human dissatisfactions, and provide a basis for utopian social structures appealed to these young readers. The pervasive militaristic threat to Smith's freedom and his promise of human escape from time (history) may also have attracted readers troubled by U. S. involvement in Vietnam. Many readers also found a socialistic message in Smith's communitarian antidote for Cold War alienation from nature, others, and self; however, the political views behind Heinlein's Voltairian satire in this novel are murky, especially considering the pervasive cynicism and social Darwinian opinions of Smith's teacher (Heinlein's spokesperson). Later works by Heinlein clarify his political views and suggest that in this novel he is less sympathetic with socialism than with a libertarian emphasis on absolute individual freedom. *Stranger in a Strange Land*, which sold millions of copies, remains Heinlein's most popular book.

Related Work Heinlein's *The Moon Is a Harsh Mistress* (1966) clarifies many of the ideas represented in *Stranger in a Strange Land.*

Additional Information For a reading of the place of *Stranger in a Strange Land* in the development of the themes and characters of Heinlein's fiction, see *Robert A. Heinlein: America as Science Fiction* (1980), by H. Bruce Franklin.

William J. Scheick

See also Counterculture; Free Love; Sexual Revolution.

■ Strawberry Statement, The

Published 1969
Author James Simon Kunen (1948-   )

One of the best expressions of college student alienation during the late 1960's. This book combines a journal of the 1968 Columbia University student protests with thoughts on such subjects as the emerging youth culture and the problems in American society.

The Work In *The Strawberry Statement: Notes of a College Revolutionary,* James Simon Kunen, a nineteen-year-old Columbia University sophomore, attempts to explain his generation of rebellious college students. The first third of the 156-page book chronicles in journal fashion Kunen's somewhat diffident participation in the protests at Columbia University between April 22 and June 4, 1968. Most of the remainder of the book recounts Kunen's summer—during which he is involved with the court system, works on his book, travels to visit draft resisters in Canada, falls in love, and attends Students for a Democratic Society (SDS) meetings—and presents his thoughts on such subjects as long hair, religion, the Vietnam War, and baseball. Throughout the work, he takes a humorously cynical view of both mainstream and radical society. He believes that society is disintegrating but is not ready to join those calling for armed revolution. He says he will give the republic one more chance but suspects that "democracy cannot be revived through democratic means."

Impact Excepts from *The Strawberry Statement* appeared in *New York* magazine (1968) and *The Atlantic Monthly* (1969) before the entire work was published by Random House in 1969. Reviews of the book were generally favorable: The *Saturday Review* found Kunen "sane, level-headed, perceptive, thoughtful," and the *New Republic* regarded the author as a reliable representative of his generation. Although Kunen's criticisms of American materialism, conformity, and the Vietnam War might have put him at odds with the mainstream press, his wit, general skepticism, and reluctance to become an armed revolutionary gained a sympathetic hearing from what he would have regarded as the establishment. However, these latter qualities prevented his book from being widely accepted by the radical Left, which was becoming increasingly ideological and prone to violence. Within two years of its publication, the book was translated into Japanese, German, Swedish, and French, languages of countries that also had significant leftist student movements. In 1995, it was reprinted in the United States, primarily for use in college classes. Ultimately, *The Strawberry Statement* is more significant as an expression of the youth rebellion of the late 1960's than as a work having significant influence of its own.

Related Work *The Strawberry Statement* (1970), directed by Stuart Hagmann, is a dramatization of the book.

Additional Information Other student perspectives on the Columbia University protests appear in *Up Against the Ivory Wall: A History of the Columbia Crisis* (1968), edited by Jerry L. Avorn.

Gary Land

See also Education; Hairstyles; Student Rights; Students for a Democratic Society (SDS); Youth Culture and the Generation Gap.

■ Streisand, Barbra

Born April 24, 1942, Brooklyn, New York

A multimedia star renowned for her exceptional versatility as a singer and actress. Her stage and screen role as Fanny Brice in Funny Girl *earned her acclaim as one of the most popular and talented performers in the U.S. entertainment industry.*

Early Life After graduating from high school at age sixteen, Barbara Joan Streisand began looking for parts in small theatrical productions and taking acting classes in Manhattan. She appeared in minor

In 1969, singer Barbra Streisand receives an Academy Award for Best Actress for her performance in the 1968 film Funny Girl. *(AP/Wide World Photos)*

roles in repertory and Off-Broadway revues from 1958 through 1960. In 1960, after winning a talent contest for amateur vocalists, she changed the spelling of her first name to Barbra and began singing in nightclubs. Her highly praised performances as a cabaret singer led to her first television appearance on *The Jack Paar Show*, broadcast in April, 1961.

The 1960's During the early 1960's, Streisand appeared on New York television talk shows, sang for brief engagements at fashionable nightclubs, and auditioned for parts in Broadway productions. For her first major acting role in the theater as lovelorn secretary Yetta Marmelstein in *I Can Get It for You Wholesale*, she received the New York Drama Critics Circle Award for Best Supporting Actress in 1962. She also appeared on *The Tonight Show* with Johnny Carson in November, 1962, and signed a recording contract with Columbia Records. Her career gained valuable exposure in 1963 with the release of her first two albums and appearances on *The Ed Sullivan Show* and *The Judy Garland Show*.

Streisand began her legendary rise to fame as Fanny Brice in the Broadway production of *Funny Girl*, which premiered March 26, 1964. Also that year, she received two Grammy Awards, Album of the Year and Best Vocal Performance—Female, for *The Barbra Streisand Album*, released the previous year. In 1965, Streisand accumulated a number of prestigious awards, including two Emmy Awards for her television special *My Name Is Barbra*, a Grammy Award for the song "People," and recognition from the recording industry as the Best Selling Female Vocalist.

During the remainder of the 1960's, Streisand emerged as one of the decade's premier talents, starring in two more television specials and winning another Grammy. She reprised her starring role as Fanny Brice in the film version of *Funny Girl* (1968), and on April 14, 1969, she received an Academy Award for her performance. At the end of the decade, she completed her second starring role in a motion-picture musical as Dolly Levi in *Hello, Dolly!*

Later Life Streisand's popularity fluctuated during the 1970's and 1980's as she experimented with different musical genres. Her film roles also varied from dramatic parts in *A Star Is Born* (1976) and *Yentl* (1983) to humorous characters. By the mid-1980's, she had launched her own film production company and provoked considerable controversy as a political activist. After a twenty-year absence from live performing, she appeared on September 6, 1986, in a special concert called *One Voice* to raise money for Democratic Party candidates.

Impact Streisand's success has lent encouragement to many aspiring artists, particularly women. One of the wealthiest and most creative multimedia stars in the United States, she has been admired and criticized for her public support of social and political causes.

Additional Information A collection of newspaper and magazine articles published during three decades, *Diva: Barbra Streisand and the Making of a Superstar*, edited by Ethlie Ann Vare, was published in 1996.

Nancy D. Kersell

See also Film; Music.

■ Student Nonviolent Coordinating Committee (SNCC)

A national organization of student activists that sought to challenge segregation. As tensions mounted in the mid-1960's, the organization became increasingly aggressive and eventually dropped its nonviolent stance.

Origins and History In early 1960, amid a growing number of student civil rights demonstrations, the Southern Christian Leadership Conference (SCLC), led by Martin Luther King, Jr., encouraged students to convene their own organization. In response to the call, a group of student leaders, under the guidance of Ella Baker, a former administrative head of SCLC, formed the Student Nonviolent Coordinating Committee (SNCC, pronounced "snick"). Committed at the outset to nonviolence, SNCC was designed to be thoroughly democratic and to function independently from mainstream groups, including the SCLC. It also became a biracial organization although initially there was some concern that allowing white students to join SNCC might compromise the organization.

Activities Despite its nonviolent philosophy, SNCC was often very aggressive and confrontational in attacking segregation. The organization took on several of the more dangerous civil rights battles including voter registration campaigns in Alabama and

Mississippi. Numerous times SNCC activists were badly beaten, and in the summer of 1964, three activists who had joined the SNCC campaign (Michael Schwerner, Andrew Goodman, and James Chaney) were brutally murdered by southern segregationists including members of the Ku Klux Klan. Nevertheless, SNCC continued its confrontational strategy.

By 1964, frustrated by the slow pace of change and apparent lack of support from the federal government, SNCC members began to splinter into two factions. One group sought to maintain the organization's original principles, and the other chose to reconsider the group's nonviolent approach. Racial tensions within the organization further divided SNCC. African American volunteers were concerned that their white counterparts were taking control of the organization, and white members were growing more critical of SNCC leadership. Amid the internal tensions, many SNCC members became increasingly radical.

During the mid-1960's, SNCC members, under the charismatic leadership of Stokely Carmichael, embraced a new creed of black power. The slogan became a call for economic self-determination and political activism as well as a symbol of black militancy. Carmichael believed that change would come only through dramatic, confrontational appeals. The evolving SNCC philosophy advocated responding to violence with violence. The increasingly strident rhetoric led some members to abandon the organization, but at the same time, it attracted new membership, particularly radical, northern, urban African Americans. Further demonstrating its new direction, SNCC shifted its activities from voting rights and educational issues in the rural South to conditions in urban ghettos.

SNCC, plagued by ineffective leadership and constant internal divisions, saw its membership dwindle to a handful of activists by 1968. The organization was further undermined by its entering into a formal alliance with the Black Panthers and by concern that the organization associated with other paramilitary groups. The last two SNCC chapters, Atlanta and New York, ceased operation in early 1970.

Impact SNCC activists helped to focus the nation on the problem of institutionalized racism by taking a leading role in several major civil rights demonstrations during the 1960's. In 1961, SNCC members

A Detroit newspaper reported that the Student Nonviolent Coordinating Committee, a civil rights organization led by Stokely Carmichael, circulated this black power pamphlet in 1967. (AP/Wide World Photos)

helped the Congress for Racial Equality (CORE) operate Freedom Rides that challenged the constitutionality of segregated interstate busing laws in the South. The rides attracted much media coverage, which brought the Civil Rights movement into middle-class white suburban homes for the first time and helped pressure President John F. Kennedy into paying more attention to civil rights issues. The rides were immediately followed by the Albany, Georgia, demonstrations, in which SNCC members sat in whites-only sections of local bus stations to test interstate transportation laws that made segregated facilities illegal.

In 1964, SNCC organized a voter registration and educational campaign in Mississippi. A biracial effort carried out by college student volunteers, the second phase of the campaign, in which young workers were to educate voters, became known as Freedom Summer. This campaign further enlightened Americans about the plight of African Americans in the South. The student volunteers who participated in the campaign were able to register more than seventeen thousand African American voters and provided more than three thousand children with educational instruction. The efforts, however, came at a price. During the summer, at least sixty-seven bombings and arson fires were directed at the volunteers. In one incident, three activists, Schwerner, Goodman, and Chaney, were killed. That same summer, SNCC helped organize the forming of the Mississippi Freedom Democratic Party, which challenged the credentials of the Mississippi delegation to the 1964 Democratic National Convention when it met to nominate Lyndon B. Johnson. SNCC members were also among the organizers and participants in most of the civil rights marches during the mid-1960's, including the March on Washington in 1963 and the march from Selma to Montgomery in 1965.

Subsequent Events Though SNCC disbanded early in the 1970's, several of the organization's leaders and former members remained activists on both the local and national levels well into the 1970's. Among the more notable former SNCC members are James Forman, who became involved in African American economic development; John Lewis, who in 1988 won election to the House of Representatives; Charles Sherrod, who was elected mayor of Albany, Georgia; and Robert Moses, who became director of a nationwide literacy program. Other former members became involved in protesting the Vietnam War and in the women's rights movement.

Additional Information Clayborne Carson's *In Struggle: SNCC and the Black Awakening in the 1960's* (1981) discusses SNCC's role in the context of the Civil Rights movement in the South. A personal memoir is available in *The River of No Return: The Autobiography of a Black Militant and Death of SNCC* (1990), by Cleveland Sellers and Robert Terrell. In 1998, Cheryl Lynn Greensberg edited a collection entitled *A Circle of Trust: Remembering SNCC.*

Paul E. Doutrich

See also Black Panthers; Black Power; Carmichael, Stokely; Congress of Racial Equality (CORE); Freedom Rides; Freedom Summer; March on Selma; Mississippi Freedom Democratic Party; Schwerner, Goodman, and Chaney Deaths.

■ Student Rights Movement

A social movement occurring on college campuses during the 1960's. Student activists focused their efforts on securing freedom of speech, reforms in curriculum and programs, and a more liberated campus lifestyle.

The student rights movement refers to the political protests by U.S. college and university students in the 1960's to secure the interests of these students. The goals of this general social movement were to improve the circumstances in terms of rights and privileges of these students, especially regarding freedom of speech, educational reform, and campus lifestyle. This focus on students as a group whose rights needed defending began with the Free Speech movement at the University of California, Berkeley, in October, 1964, to secure First Amendment freedom of speech rights for students on that campus and to press for educational reform and student independence from *in loco parentis* administrative control over student lifestyles.

The Free Speech movement was the first 1960's student movement to emphasize students' rights apart from concerns of the Civil Rights movement. Before this movement, politically active 1960's college students protested and sought change for the difficult circumstances of other groups such as African Americans via participation in the Civil Rights movement and the poor via participation in programs such as those that were part of the War on Poverty. However, from 1964 on, college students saw themselves as a group whose political, cultural, and personal needs should be furthered.

On October 1, 1964, mathematics student Jack Weinberg, who was collecting funds for the Congress of Racial Equality (CORE), a civil rights organization, was told he could no longer do this on the Berkeley campus. Because the U.S. Supreme Court had long before decided activities such as collecting donations for political causes was an aspect of free speech, Weinberg's inability to collect funds represented a loss of free speech rights. Students from all political sectors—conservative to liberal to radical—formed the Free Speech movement to regain their rights, which were restored by December, 1964, after a dramatic faculty vote with 88 percent of the Berkeley faculty favoring students' rights to free speech.

Lifestyles In addition to free speech, students pressed for freedom to experiment with different cultural lifestyles. Authors and researchers Richard Flacks, Kenneth Keniston, and Theodore Roszak found that, especially among politically active students, countercultural values were supplanting more traditional Protestant ethics. Therefore, instead of adhering to traditional values such as individualism, emotional inhibition, materialism, and upward mobility, students in the 1960's were embracing values such as humanitarianism, intellectualism, romanticism, communitarianism, and emotional expressiveness, including the increasing acceptability among college students of living together without benefit of matrimony.

An examination of the research reveals that by themselves, the countercultural values influenced students to withdraw from the existing social system and join in such countercultural institutions as rural communes. However, when 1960's students embraced both countercultural values and radical political values, they were especially likely to participate in political protests.

Educational Reform Another focus of the student rights movement was educational reform. Students argued that education in the modern "multiversities"—that is, large-scale, multifunctional, research-oriented, and often impersonal universities—did not meet many legitimate student needs. Therefore, they called for changes in the educational system, demanding smaller classes instead of large lectures, teaching-oriented rather than research-oriented professors, less reliance on impersonal bureaucracy, and greater attendance to students' intellectual and personal needs.

One significant reconnection of the student rights movement to movements concerned with rights of African Americans and other ethnic minorities was the late-1960's student participation in the American version of the Third World movement. Although this Third World movement involved primarily African American, Chicano, Asian American, and Native American students, some white students participated as well. The Third World movement was

One student plays guitar and others sleep after about nine hundred students were locked in Sproul Hall by University of California, Berkeley, police after staging a sit-in to protest restrictions on free speech. (Library of Congress)

not a duplication of the Civil Rights movement. It was led by students, not prominent adults such as Martin Luther King, Jr. It was more politically radical because it aimed to eliminate racism by reforming entire social institutions instead of gradually changing racial attitudes and practices and more campus- and student-based because it focused on forming ethnic studies departments in colleges and universities such as San Francisco State and the University of California, Berkeley. The resulting significant, widely publicized conflicts on those two campuses appeared to lead administrators at other schools to institute ethnic studies programs with less acrimony.

Impact Several authors, including Todd Gitlin, Nigel Young, and Flacks, have described the impact of the Free Speech movement—which received worldwide publicity—as crystallizing, for many American college students, the idea that students could be an independent political force and influence the issues affecting their own lives. This self-image of students as a political force presented a marked contrast to the self-image held by apolitical or conservative American college students in the 1950's, as documented by Rose Goldsen in *What College Students Think* (1960), a national survey of college students in the 1950's. In an intriguing footnote, she noted that a 1960 anti-ROTC (Reserve Officers Training Corps) petition at the Berkeley campus—successfully focusing on students' rights to attend the university without having to take ROTC—might signify a coming political activism. Goldsen correctly anticipated that many 1960's students would perceive themselves as viable political actors able to influence policies affecting college students, an idea given great impetus by the success of the Free Speech movement.

Students were successful in bringing about some educational reforms. Campus administrators throughout the country listened to the criticisms aimed at "multiversity" education and began to institute educational changes that continued into the 1990's. From 1965 to the late 1990's, American universities have instituted programs emphasizing smaller classes for college students, increased student-professor interaction, and student involvement in professors' research. Schools have also attempted to reduce bureaucratic red tape for students and increase the involvement of administrators in students' instruction. Students have begun to serve on faculty and

university committees, including recruitment committees, grievance committees, and academic senates. Colleges have also expanded student services for career, educational, medical, and personal counseling.

So many educational reforms were made that sometimes it seemed as if university administrators were listening to Free Speech movement leader Mario Savio's speeches on the subject and taking notes to create improved programs for students. The changes were not, however, purely altruistic moves on the part of administrators. As one university analyst noted, the Free Speech movement was not just another "California curiosity." It pointed to serious problems in the multiversity that could lead to further disruptions. To lessen the likelihood of further campus disruptions or to prevent them from occurring on more peaceful campuses, many administrators decided to take the advice to voluntarily institute educational reforms.

Whether educational reforms actually reduced conflicts is difficult to determine because of the escalation of U.S. involvement in the Vietnam War after 1965, which generated increasingly large protests among college and university students. No amount of educational reform could prevent the conflicts between the students and university administrations and between the students and police or national guard forces over U.S. policies in Vietnam. As the 1960's wore on, educational reform became less and less of a motivation for student protests, replaced by antiwar issues.

Many 1960's countercultural values, such as concern for humanitarian issues, emotional expressiveness instead of inhibition, and concern with meaningful community, have been incorporated into the larger society, as have programs of educational reform and accompanying students' rights of free speech and assembly. The student rights movement of the 1960's came full-circle in terms of the rights of ethnic minority students and minority groups generally. The early 1960's movement had this focus as did the later 1960's movement. Finally, the student rights movement abated only after students' rights regarding issues such as free speech, educational reform, alternative lifestyles, Vietnam War protests, and Third World programs came to be realized by events such as the free speech and educational reform victory for students at the University of California, Berkeley, more relaxed policies regarding campus living quarters, the widespread institutionalization of ethnic studies programs, and the ending of the Vietnam War.

Additional Information For a study of the legal aspects of student rights from a historical perspective, see Frank R. Kemerer's *Constitutional Rights and Student Life: Value Conflict in Law and Education, Cases, and Materials* (1979). For more detailed information about the movement in Berkeley, see the classic book, *The Berkeley Student Revolt* (1965), edited by Seymor Martin Lipset and Sheldon S. Wolin, which contains texts of speeches made by Free Speech movement leader Savio.

James L. Wood

See also Black United Students; Chicano Movement; Counterculture; Free Speech Movement; United Mexican American Students (UMAS).

■ Students for a Democratic Society (SDS)

The dominant student organization of the New Left. SDS was a loose federation with chapters on more than three hundred college campuses. Most members were students who believed they must take radical action against racial discrimination, poverty, militarism, and especially the war in Vietnam.

Origins and History The American Left had all but vanished during the 1950's, largely because of an anticommunist environment embodied in Senator Joseph McCarthy of Wisconsin, who launched assaults on suspected communists in various organizations. The Student League for Industrial Democracy (SLID), which traced its origins to the labor struggles of the 1930's, tried to disassociate itself from the communists, whom they perceived as authoritarian, manipulative, secretive, and undemocratic. To emphasize its differences, the group called itself part of the New Left. Inspired by the Civil Rights movement emerging in the South, white SLID members attending the University of Michigan at Ann Arbor helped organize boycotts against chain stores that practiced racial segregation in the South and, in June, 1962, under a new name, Students for a Democratic Society (SDS), the group hosted a conference at a United Automobile Workers camp in Port Huron, Michigan.

The 1962 SDS convention issued a manifesto, the Port Huron Statement, proclaiming the group's commitment to a form of democracy in which each citizen would directly participate in public affairs as much as possible. To prevent a core group of leaders from dictating policy, SDS was to have a loose structure. Each campus chapter would be relatively independent, most decisions would be made by group consensus, and leadership positions would rotate annually.

Activities Perhaps the most important early activity of SDS was the Economic Research and Action Project (ERAP) in which SDS members lived in poor urban communities to assess the needs of the residents in those neighborhoods and help empower them to address those issues. ERAP organized rent strikes and won concessions from local welfare officers.

Initially identifying themselves as liberals who were carriers of core American values, SDS members were inspired by President John F. Kennedy's call to action and then by President Lyndon B. Johnson's support for civil rights and initiation of the War on Poverty. However, many became suspicious of Johnson's pledge not to expand the Vietnam War during the 1964 presidential campaign. As the Vietnam War escalated, it increasingly became the focus of SDS activity and analysis. A consensus emerged that the war was not a mere mistake stemming from a fundamentally sound policy carried out too zealously but rather a manifestation of a society controlled by a small corporate elite who orchestrated foreign and domestic policy to ensure their continued wealth and power. Poverty, racial discrimination, militarism, and an aggressive foreign policy that SDS termed imperialism for its apparent aim of dominating other countries were all seen as symptoms of the same core cause.

By the mid-1960's, most SDS members viewed themselves as radicals and saw liberals as members, or at least allies, of the corporate elite because of liberals' attempts to contain protest so that it did not threaten the rich and powerful. In particular, they felt that liberals bore most of the responsibility for the Vietnam War. To rally opposition to the war and galvanize that opposition into a mass movement that would bring about a radical transformation of American society, SDS organized teach-ins on college campuses around the country, supported draft resistance, and sponsored nationwide gatherings that converged on Washington, D.C., and antiwar marches that attracted tens of thousands of participants in cities such as New York, Chicago, Boston, San Francisco, and Los Angeles.

A consensus emerged within SDS that universities did not produce objective, value-neutral knowledge but that they trained professionals and conducted research in service to the powerful corporate elite. Students demonstrated against the university itself, opposing the Reserve Officers' Training Corps (ROTC), war-related research, and on-campus recruitment for the military and for weapon-producing corporations such as Dow Chemical. In April, 1968, the Columbia University chapter of SDS took over several buildings, effectively shutting the university down. When the university administration called the police, activity did not return to normal; instead, the protest erupted into a campus-wide student strike. The Columbia demonstration was followed by similar strikes and building takeovers on hundreds of campuses over the next several years.

By 1968, SDS had at least 350 chapters totaling at least forty thousand members, and the number of people who identified themselves as part of the New Left was much larger. Despite its success, SDS was becoming an organization plagued with internal problems. Its commitment to openness and tolerance and loose organizational structure made it possible for a small minority to speak indefinitely at meetings and seize control of the agenda. Supporters of progressive labor, whom most SDS members regarded as authoritarian, dogmatic, manipulative, and antidemocratic, took advantage of this opportunity and became so persistent, and some would say disruptive, that by 1969, it became almost impossible for SDS to function as a viable coalition. Soon SDS dissolved into small factions, including the Weathermen, and ceased to lead the New Left as a unified organization.

Mark Rudd, Columbia University president of Students for a Democratic Society, takes center stage at a campus protest in 1968. (Archive Photos)

Impact Whether or not they formally joined SDS, hundreds of thousands of young people—students and nonstudents—began to identify themselves with the radical New Left. Both students and nonstudents began to question the fundamental values of the society they were about to inherit. The antiwar movement eventually won sympathy even among soldiers and high-ranking representatives of the government, the corporations, the universities, and the media and may have influenced President Johnson not to seek a second term.

Subsequent Events Although SDS essentially dissolved in 1969, the New Left continued to grow for several years. In 1970, a national student strike simultaneously shut down hundreds of campuses. Largely to appease student discontent, the voting age was lowered to eighteen, and many universities granted students more voice in governing campus affairs. Fear of provoking a radical movement may have motivated presidents Johnson and Richard M. Nixon to gradually withdraw from Vietnam.

Additional Information Kirkpatrick Sale's *SDS* (1973) is a comprehensive history of the organization. In 1989, R. David Myers edited *Toward a History of the New Left*, a collection of memoirs and reflections of former students who had been active in SDS. Steven Kelman's *Push Comes to Shove* (1970) presents the reaction of one of the opponents of SDS.

Yale Magrass

See also Chicago Seven Trial; Days of Rage; Moratorium Day; National Mobilization Committee to End the War in Vietnam (MOBE); Pentagon, Levitating of; Students Rights Movement; Vietnam War; Weathermen; Yippies; Youth Culture and the Generation Gap.

■ Summer of Love

Date Summer, 1967

The experiment in antiestablishment, alternative living, centered in the Haight-Ashbury district of San Francisco. Thousands of hippies and visitors abandoned conven-

On June 21, 1967, hippies from San Francisco's Haight-Ashbury district gather in Golden Gate Park to celebrate the solstice during the Summer of Love. (AP/Wide World Photos)

tional, materialistic society for a lifestyle of simplicity, sharing, drugs, and rock music.

Origins and History The characteristic features of the Summer of Love emerged from an unlikely combination of college students, antiwar activists, hippies, and antiestablishment radicals, many of whom formed organizations in and around San Francisco during 1966. Shops selling drug paraphernalia, Indian-print clothing, beads, and other accoutrements of the alternative culture occupied the run-down community of Haight-Ashbury. By July and August, thousands of "psychedelic residents" were flocking to the Bay Area, where marijuana and hallucinogenic drugs were cheap and residents usually were allowed to practice alternative lifestyles.

The Event Setting the stage for the Summer of Love was a mass meeting on January 14, 1967, known as a Gathering of the Tribes for Human Be-in or simply a Human Be-in. For the first time, most of the diverse antiestablishment groups supported a single event. Hippies, Diggers (members of a communal group), musicians, artists, and leftist political activists joined to hail "a new concert of human relations" led by the young, which recognized "the unity of all mankind." Tens of thousands of people flocked to the Polo Field in Golden Gate Park to hear counterculture gurus such as Jerry Rubin, Allen Ginsberg, and Timothy Leary decry American materialism and extol the virtues of drugs, which were freely distributed. Local bands such as Quicksilver Messenger Service, Big Brother and the Holding Company, Country Joe and the Fish, and the Jefferson Airplane provided additional incentive for the gathering.

By the spring of 1967, the hippie movement was becoming institutionalized. On April 5, representatives of counterculture groups joined in forming the Council for a Summer of Love, for the purpose of organizing celebratory events for the hundreds of thousands of seekers and tourists expected to inundate San Francisco. In May, the Council announced a series of festivals. The most important was the Monterey International Pop Festival, June 16-18, which attracted more than a hundred thousand people. Among the groups performing at this historic concert were the Animals, Simon and Garfunkel, Big Brother and the Holding Company, the Grateful Dead, Jefferson Airplane, Steve Miller, the Who, and the Jimi Hendrix Experience. The music most closely identified with the Summer of Love,

however, was the Beatle's *Sgt. Pepper's Lonely Hearts Club Band*. Released in June, the album remained at number one on the charts for fifteen weeks.

Impact By September, most of the visitors to San Francisco had departed. The Summer of Love suggested both the possibilities and the limitations of the counterculture. Though the festivals and "happenings" had been largely peaceful, hospitals were increasingly flooded with victims of drug overdoses. A series of drug-related murders tarnished promises of a drug-enhanced utopia. In addition, the example of the alternative communities of the Bay Area had not been able to lessen the urban violence that had broken out in July in many cities across the nation nor to alter the continued escalation of U.S. involvement in Vietnam. However, national publicity generated by the events in San Francisco that summer spread many of the values and sentiments held by the Summer of Love participants to young people across the United States.

Additional Information Charles Perry provides a well-documented chronicle of the Summer of Love in *The Haight-Ashbury: A History* (1984).

John Powell

See also Be-ins and Love-ins; Communes; Counterculture; Death of Hippie; Drug Culture; Flower Children; Ginsberg, Allen; Grateful Dead; Haight-Ashbury; Hendrix, Jimi; Hippies; Jefferson Airplane; Joplin, Janis; Leary, Timothy; LSD; Marijuana; Monterey Pop Festival; *Sgt. Pepper's Lonely Hearts Club Band*; Sexual Revolution; Simon and Garfunkel; Yippies; Youth Culture and the Generation Gap.

■ Super Bowl

The annual football game pitting the National Football League champion against the American Football League champion, first played January 15, 1967. As television propelled football into the spotlight, the Super Bowl became the game's showcase attraction.

The National Football League (NFL), which was formed in 1922, held off four rival leagues before the American Football League (AFL) began play in 1960. On June 8, 1966, the leagues agreed to merge in 1970, a deal that included an annual World Championship Game. However, NFL teams viewed the AFL teams as upstarts and did not want to lose to teams from a league still considered a rival.

On January 15, 1967, legendary coach Vince Lombardi led his NFL champion Green Bay Packers into Los Angeles Memorial Coliseum to take on the AFL's Kansas City Chiefs. Though officially the World Championship Game, the contest was dubbed the Super Bowl, a name created by Chiefs owner Lamar Hunt, after his daughter's high-bouncing "Super Ball" toy. Lombardi's Packers were heavy favorites and did not disappoint, winning 35-10.

The Packers returned to the title contest January 14, 1968, facing the Oakland Raiders in Miami's Orange Bowl stadium. Again the Packers were favored, and again they triumphed, 33-14.

Just when things looked bleak for the AFL, along came quarterback Joe Namath and his New York Jets in 1969. Namath's AFL champions were heavy underdogs against the Baltimore Colts in the first game officially named a "Super Bowl." Before the January 12 game in Miami, the flamboyant Namath guaranteed a Jets win and backed up his vow, leading New York to a 16-7 victory. Namath became an instant celebrity and the AFL had its first world championship, though many in the NFL felt the victory was a fluke, a case of fortune smiling on an inferior team.

The 1969 season champion was determined January 11, 1970, in New Orleans' Tulane Stadium—the final game before the merger. Hunt's Chiefs triumphed in the AFL's swan song, defeating the Minnesota Vikings 23-7 and ending NFL notions of superiority.

Impact With the televising of the 1958 NFL championship game, football began to shift from a regional game, in which fans in a few cities cheered for "their" teams, into a national one. That process continued through the 1960's, and as football became a prominent part of American life, it found the perfect centerpiece for its new television success. The Super Bowl, with its pageantry and heroes, lived up to its name and became an event everyone had to watch.

Subsequent Events After the leagues merged in 1970, the annual confrontation featured the winners of the two NFL conferences. By 1997, when the Packers won Super Bowl XXXI, various Super Bowls made up seven of the ten most-watched television

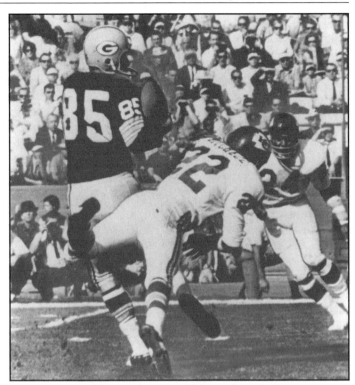

The Green Bay Packers defeat the Kansas City Chiefs on January 15, 1967, in the first Super Bowl. (Library of Congress)

programs ever, and the game annually was viewed by more than 120 million people. The game also was a financial success—by the 1990's, tickets that cost $12 in 1967 cost more than $100, and commercial airtime that once sold for $85,000 per minute rose to $850,000 per half-minute.

Additional Information *The Super Bowl* (1990), a National Football League-produced book, offers detailed descriptions of the first twenty-five Super Bowls. *The Official National Football League Record and Fact Book* (published annually) includes Super Bowl statistics and records.

Eric Strauss

See also Football; Lombardi, Vince; Namath, Joe; Sports.

■ Supersonic Jets

Airplanes capable of sustained level flight faster than the speed of sound. Until 1969, when the prototypes of two supersonic airliners, the Tu-144 and the Concorde, first exceeded the speed of sound, the only airplanes that reached such speeds were experimental and military aircraft.

The first airplane to fly at supersonic speed in level flight (on October 14, 1947) was the rocket-powered Bell X-1, an experimental aircraft designed in the United States to test the practicability of supersonic flight, which some theorists had thought impossible. During the 1950's, a growing number of jet-powered aircraft, built in the United States and elsewhere, were capable of still higher speeds. The United States Air Force received its first supersonic interceptor, the North American F-100 Super Sabre, in 1954.

During the 1960's, the air forces of the United States and several other major nations put into service many supersonic aircraft that had been developed or designed in the 1950's. Outstanding examples in the U.S. Air Force were the Republic F-105 Thunderchief, a fighter-bomber (brought into service in 1960); the Convair B-58 Hustler, a four-engine nuclear bomber capable of twice the speed of sound (1960); the Northrop T-38 Talon, a trainer (1961); the MacDonnell F-4C Phantom, a two-seat tactical fighter (1963); and the Lockheed SR-71A, a reconnaissance plane capable of twenty-one hundred miles per hour (1966). In 1967, the U.S. Air Force received its first "swing-wing" airplane, the General Dynamics F-111, a supersonic fighter-bomber that had first flown in 1964. With the incorporation of these and other types of aircraft during the 1960's, the U.S. Air Force became largely supersonic in its fighter and bomber divisions. The United States Navy flew aircraft of similar performance.

Jet airplanes were not the fastest winged flying machines in the 1960's. The rocket-powered North American X-15A-2 reached 4,534 miles per hour in October, 1967. However, it flew at such great altitude, once reaching sixty-seven miles, that it was less an airplane than a spacecraft.

In the 1960's, design of supersonic airliners advanced quickly, with the United States, the Soviet Union, Britain, and France competing to supply what promised to be an enormously profitable future market. The first supersonic transports to fly were the Soviet Tupolev Tu-144 (December, 1968) and the British-French BAe/Aérospatiale Concorde (March, 1969). Prototypes of both flew faster than sound in 1969.

In the United States, the Boeing 2707 seemed superior in design to both the Concorde and the Tu-144. However, just as construction of the prototype was starting, Congress canceled government funding of the project in March, 1971. Without that help, Boeing could not proceed with the 2707.

Impact The importance of supersonic jets for the United States in the 1960's was largely military and strategic. The high speed (both horizontal and in rate of climb) of these powerful airplanes helped maintain the United States' superiority over potential foes (although speed in itself provided little advantage in the peculiar conditions of the Vietnam War). The Soviet Union tried to match U.S. advances in airplane performance. The high cost of doing so contributed to the later collapse of the Soviet system.

Additional Information The best single source of information on supersonic jets is Roger E. Bilstein's *Flight in America: From the Wrights to the Astronauts* (1994). Another good source of information is *Jane's Encyclopedia of Aviation* (1993).

Peter Bakewell

See also Concorde; Travel.

■ Supreme Court Decisions

Overwhelmingly liberal and progressive decisions reflecting the larger social revolution. The Supreme Court of the 1960's helped establish social policies that continued to set the tone in the United States for the next two decades.

A real watershed occurred in the Supreme Court in 1937, when President Franklin D. Roosevelt, frustrated by the Court's refusal to uphold New Deal legislation, proposed a plan to "pack" the Court with justices of his own choosing. His plan failed in Congress, but Roosevelt still succeeded in reorienting the Court so that it upheld his progressive economic and social agenda.

One of the most important of Roosevelt's Supreme Court appointments was Justice Hugo Black, a First Amendment fundamentalist whose emphasis on a literal reading of the Bill of Rights helped fuel the so-called "due process revolution." This profound change in constitutional interpretation ultimately revolutionized state law enforcement and criminal court procedures by "incorporating" the guarantees of the first eight amendments into the due process clause of the Fourteenth Amendment and making them applicable to the states as well as to the federal government.

During the next thirty-five years, the Court gradually found that most of the individual protections of the Bill of Rights applied to the states. The primary opponent of this sea of change in the Court was Justice Felix Frankfurter, who urged judicial restraint, arguing that the elected branches of governments were the proper catalysts for social change. Although Frankfurter's attitude held sway during the early years of the Cold War, when the Court frequently upheld the convictions of purported subversives in the face of free speech defense arguments, Black's view finally triumphed. By the time Chief Justice Earl Warren assumed the helm of the Supreme Court in 1953, the Court had entered a new era, one that stressed individual liberties and downplayed economic regulation, which had been the Court's earlier focus.

The first major opinion that Warren wrote for the Court was one of the most significant opinions in the history of the nation. *Brown v. Board of Education of Topeka, Kansas* (1954) did away with the doctrine of "separate but equal," which had made racial segregation the law of the land since 1896, placed the emphasis squarely on a new rights consciousness, and set the tone for the Warren Court.

Defendants' Rights During the Warren era, this new awareness of the rights of minorities and of people in general, along with the burgeoning due process revolution, produced a series of highly controversial decisions affecting criminal defendants, who were most often tried in state courts. Clarence Earl Gideon, who had been convicted of a felony in Florida without benefit of legal counsel, was moved to appeal his conviction directly to the U.S. Supreme Court by means of a handwritten application. In *Gideon v. Wainwright* (1963), the Court declared that states were obliged to supply legal representation for all indigent defendants charged with serious crimes. In *Mapp v. Ohio* (1961), the Warren Court had extended the exclusionary rule preventing the admission in court of improperly obtained evidence to state criminal proceedings, and in *Miranda v. Arizona* (1966), the Court expanded and combined the exclusionary rule with the right to counsel to disallow involuntary confessions.

Privacy and Speech In *Griswold v. Connecticut* (1965), the Court went so far as to recognize a new constitutional right, the right to privacy, which protected an individual's prerogative to control his or her own body through use of previously banned contraceptives. The right to privacy was closely

aligned with the right to free speech, another important aspect of society's—and the Court's—new rights consciousness. On the one hand, in *New York Times Company v. Sullivan* (1964), the Warren Court upheld the right of the press to publish truthful attacks on individuals deemed to be public figures. On the other hand, however, in *Katz v. United States* (1967), the Court outlawed the use by law enforcement of unwarranted wiretaps because even a suspected lawbreaker had an "expectation" of privacy when holding telephone conversations.

First Amendment Rights The Warren Court was also obliged to hear First Amendment challenges to the suppression of pornography. In the first of these, *Roth v. United States* (1957), Justice William Brennan, the architect of obscenity law, declared that obscenity was not protected by the First Amendment because it is "utterly without redeeming social importance." However, a few years later, when a state supreme court declared that John Cleland's 1749 novel, *Memoirs of a Woman of Pleasure* (*Fanny Hill*), could be suppressed even though it was not unqualifiedly worthless, the U.S. Supreme Court reversed this judgment. In *Memoirs v. Massachusetts* (1966), Justice Brennan enunciated a new test for obscenity, one that provided First Amendment protection for all but the most explicitly prurient material. Pornography flourished, fueling yet another backlash against the liberalism of the Warren Court.

Another First Amendment guarantee, the right of free association, was often combined in the Warren Court with the right of free speech to overturn earlier Cold War convictions of alleged subversives such as labor leaders and Communist Party members. Although sometimes decided on different legal grounds, decisions such as *United States v. Robel* (1967) reversed the criminal status of persons charged mainly with guilt by association. Free speech and free association were also used to advance the civil rights struggle in cases such as *National Association for the Advancement of Colored People v. Button* (1963), which upheld the prerogative of groups such as the National Association for the Advancement of Colored People (NAACP) to take collective action seeking political redress through the courts.

The ruling in the NAACP case helped prompt passage of the Civil Rights Act of 1964, which was immediately challenged in court. In *Heart of Atlanta*

Motel v. United States and *Katzenbach v. McClung*, which the Warren Court decided on the same day in 1964, the public accommodations provision of the act was upheld, in effect guaranteeing African Americans the right to travel by ensuring that they could stay at any lodging and eat in any restaurant open to the public. In cases such as *Jones v. Alfred B. Mayer* (1968), the Court employed Reconstruction-era civil rights statutes to outlaw racial discrimination by private persons.

One Person, One Vote Like the due process revolution, the reapportionment revolution, which guaranteed political equality by establishing the principle of one person, one vote, was grounded in the Fourteenth Amendment. In what Chief Justice Warren called the "most vital decision" made during his tenure, *Baker v. Carr* (1962), the Court cited the equal protection clause of the Fourteenth Amendment as justification for opening the federal courts to those seeking equal representation. In *Wesberry v. Sanders* (1964), the Court interpreted the equal representation requirement to mean that the populations of electoral districts for the House of Representatives must be nearly equal in size. And in *Reynolds v. Sims* (1964), the Court extended the principle of one person, one vote to state legislatures, most of which were thereby rendered unconstitutional. Within two years, nearly every state was obliged to redraw its legislative districts. With the reapportionment revolution, members of minority groups, who had been largely concentrated in urban areas, were for the first time given an opportunity to elect their own representatives to national and state legislatures. Votes that previously had counted little were given proper weight when the size of election districts was equalized.

Impact The judicial activism that characterized the Warren Court reflected—and added to—the larger social revolution going on in the United States in the 1960's. President Lyndon B. Johnson, who had been a power in the Democratic Party since the days of Franklin D. Roosevelt, sought to replicate the social reforms of the New Deal with a program he called the Great Society, which included the War on Poverty intended to eliminate such problems as illiteracy, pollution, and urban blight. Johnson's predecessor, President John F. Kennedy, had introduced civil rights legislation in response to the concerns expressed during the early, nonviolent stages of the

Civil Rights movement. After Kennedy was assassinated in 1963, the Johnson administration shepherded the Civil Rights Act of 1964 through Congress. Before the 1960's were over, Congress would pass two more important pieces of legislation aimed at combating racial discrimination: the 1965 Voting Rights Act and the 1968 Fair Housing Act.

Through rulings such as *Brown v. Board of Education of Topeka, Kansas*, the Warren Court had helped to create a climate that was hospitable to such legislation, which the Court upheld when it was challenged. The American people, for their part, soundly rejected efforts to jettison the Great Society initiatives and roll back New Deal reforms when they rejected Barry Goldwater, Johnson's Republican opponent in the 1964 presidential election.

Meanwhile, however, certain segments of society felt the Warren Court had gone too far. Many people believed that the Court's emphasis on "criminals' rights" and freedom of expression had led to a general lawlessness. As reasons for their unease, they pointed to the assassinations of civil rights activist Martin Luther King, Jr., and Robert F. Kennedy in 1968 and to the violence and mayhem that sometimes attended late 1960's public protests against racial inequality and U.S. involvement in Vietnam. An informal movement to impeach Warren gained popularity.

Warren officially stepped down on June 23, 1969. During the preceding sixteen years, he had headed a Court that clearly saw itself as an active participant in the process of governing and shaping the nation and its priorities. Clearly, the Warren Court had radically altered the American social landscape—perhaps forever.

Subsequent Events In 1968, the "silent majority" that had not wholeheartedly supported the reforms of the previous decade elected Republican candidate Richard M. Nixon as president. Shortly after he assumed office, Nixon appointed Warren Burger as Warren's replacement. Burger had been an outspoken opponent of what he saw as the Warren Court's leniency toward criminals, and Nixon looked to him to move the Supreme Court back toward a conservative agenda. Instead, Burger concentrated his efforts on reforming the court system, while holdovers from the Warren era—particularly Justices William O. Douglas and Brennan—continued to advance liberal causes. In the landmark case of *Roe v. Wade*

(1973), the right of privacy was used to justify a woman's right to abortion, and the Court endorsed other newly asserted rights such as gender equality and affirmative action. Burger himself wrote the majority opinion in *United States v. Nixon* (1973), the decision that led directly to Nixon's resignation under threat of impeachment.

One member of the Burger Court, however, was clearly dedicated to reinjecting the nation's highest tribunal with conservative values. Profound public reaction to the social and economic ills of the 1970's swept Republican Ronald Reagan into office in 1980. In 1986, when Burger resigned his post, Reagan elevated Associate Justice William H. Rehnquist to head the Court. Over the next decade, Rehnquist's efforts to move the Supreme Court back toward the political Right would prove to be largely successful.

Additional Information For an overview of the causes and effects of the Supreme Court's jurisprudence in the 1960's, see Richard L. Pacelle's *The Transformation of the Supreme Court's Agenda: From the New Deal to the Reagan Administration* (1991). *The Warren Court in Historical and Political Perspective* (1993), edited by Mark Tushnet, provides an array of opinions on the Warren Court's significance, and *Inside the Warren Court* (1983), written by Bernard Schwartz with Stephen Lesher, affords a more intimate view of the workings of the Court during the 1960's. Richard C. Cortner's *The Supreme Court and the Second Bill of Rights: The Fourteenth Amendment and the Nationalization of Civil Liberties* (1988) is a useful analysis of the incorporation doctrine and the due process revolution.

Lisa Paddock

See also Abortion; Burger, Warren; Civil Rights Act of 1964; Civil Rights Movement; *Engel v. Vitale*; *Flast v. Cohen*; *Gideon v. Wainwright*; Great Society Programs; *Griswold v. Connecticut*; *Heart of Atlanta Motel v. United States*; *Jacobellis v. Ohio*; Johnson, Lyndon B.; *Katzenbach v. McClung*; Liberalism in Politics; *Memoirs v. Massachusetts*; *Miranda v. Arizona*; *New York Times Company v. Sullivan*; Reapportionment Revolution; War on Poverty; Warren, Earl.

The Supremes were an extremely successful Motown singing group. In 1969, the group's members were (clockwise from left) Diana Ross, Cindy Birdsong, and Mary Wilson. (National Archives)

■ Supremes

A female soul trio. Under the direction of Berry Gordy, Jr., the Supremes became Motown's flagship act and achieved crossover success and worldwide recognition.

The original members of the Supremes, Diana Ross, Florence Ballard, and Mary Wilson, met as teenagers in Detroit, Michigan, and began performing as the Primettes. Motown's Berry Gordy, Jr., signed them in 1961 and suggested that they change their name; Ballard suggested "the Supremes." After a slow start, the Supremes had their first number-one hit in 1964 with "Where Did Our Love Go?" During the next few years, twelve Supremes singles climbed to number one on the *Billboard* charts. In 1967, the name of the group was changed to Diana Ross and the Supremes, and Ballard left the group. She was replaced by Cindy Birdsong. Ross left the group in 1969 to pursue a solo career and was replaced by Jean Terrell.

Impact The Supremes more than realized Gordy's dream of crossover success. Their appeal transcended racial and generational lines, paving the way for other African American artists. In an era of racial upheaval, they became important symbols of African American success.

Subsequent Events Ballard died in 1976, and Ross achieved lasting success as a solo artist. The Supremes went through several changes in personnel before disbanding in 1977. In 1988, the group was inducted into the Rock and Roll Hall of Fame.

Additional Information Alan Betrock's *Girl Groups: The Story of a Sound* (1982) contains more information on the Supremes and other female groups.

Christl Reges

See also Motown; Music.

■ Surfing

Surfing, the art and sport of riding a surfboard across the face of a breaking wave. Surfing spread throughout the world during the 1960's and had a profound impact on the music, films, and youth culture of the decade.

The sport of surfing originated between 1500 B.C. and A.D. 400 among the oceanic cultures of Polynesia. The sport nearly became extinct when nineteenth century missionaries prohibited its practice by Hawaiians and other Pacific Islanders. A revival began in Hawaii about 1900 when young Euro-Hawaiians "rediscovered" surfing. Hawaiian surfers Duke Kahanamoku (the father of surfing) and George Freeth played an instrumental role in introducing surfing to the world through their exhibitions and demonstrations in California and Australia. Technological innovations during the 1950's made lightweight and maneuverable boards available to the general public, and surfing subcultures appeared in California, Hawaii, and Australia.

In California, surfing produced a unique and unconventional lifestyle exported to the world through films, popular music, and magazines. Surfers created their own style of dress, language, and attitude. The standard dress included a white T-shirt, striped Pendleton shirt, white Levi jeans, and Ray-Ban sunglasses. Surfers also popularized phrases such as "like wow," "daddy-o," "stoked," "kook," and "wipeout." The introduction of specialized magazines such as *Surfer* and *Surfing* further advertised the

surfer image and helped to popularize the sport. By 1970, *Surfer* had a monthly circulation of one hundred thousand, and it remains the principle publication of the surfing world.

The first surfing or beach film, *Gidget*, the story of a teenage girl who spends much of her time on the beach with her boyfriend and other surfers, appeared in 1959, and since then, more than two hundred beach films have dealt with the surf culture. Popular 1960's beach films include the two *Gidget* sequels, *Gidget Goes Hawaiian* (1961) and *Gidget Goes to Rome* (1963), *Ride the Wild Surf* (1964), and *Beach Blanket Bingo* (1965). Bruce Brown's *Endless Summer* (1964) was one of the first pure or authentic surf films. This film was not the typical boy-meets-girl beach film of the Gidget genre. Considered by many as "the" surf film, *Endless Summer* follows two surfers around the world as they search for the perfect wave. This film influenced surfers to leave their local beaches on "searches" or "surfaris." California surfers trekked up and down the Pacific coast, ventured into Mexico, surfed Hawaii's North Shore, and explored Australia's coastline. The growing popularity of surfing during the 1960's is evident by the fact that Brown debuted his film in Wichita, Kansas, where it was the most popular film for two weeks during mid-winter.

The 1960's also saw the emergence of surf music—a California-based pop music style. Surf music is characterized by a raw and energetic guitar-based sound. Bands such as Dick Dale and the Del-Tones, the Ventures, and the Surfaris played primarily instrumental songs, and bands such as the Beach Boys added vocals with surf themes and terminology. More than eight hundred surf bands recorded songs during the early 1960's, and songs such as "Surfin' Surfari" (1962), "Wipeout" (1963), and "Surfer Girl" (1963) became big hits.

Surfing in the 1960's was characterized by a massive increase in the surfing population, the formation of surf clubs, and the promotion of professional contests. California's surfing population, for example, grew from 5,000 surfers in 1956 to 150,000 in 1963. By 1963, there were sixty-five surf clubs in California. Because the general population viewed surfers as deviant and subversive, local surf clubs sought to improve the behavior of their members and enhance the image of the sport by promoting organized surf contests. Contestants earned points for the number of waves caught, length of ride, style, and sportsmanship. National organizations such as the United States Surfing Association also appeared during the 1960's in an effort to organize the sport of surfing. Competitions eventually evolved into a professional surfing circuit, dominated by a distinct class of elite professional surfers. The professionalization of surfing, however, led to conflict among the surfing population. "Soul surfers," who surfed for the love of surfing, believed that clubs and contests restricted creativity and self-expression.

Impact Surfing had a tremendous impact on 1960's era culture. Thousands of American and international youths took up the sport and created and perpetuated a lifestyle based on the beach and surfing. The mass media exported beach and surf themes to the world through films, music, and popular literature. The surf culture was one of the earliest counterculture movements of the 1960's, and it influenced other movements such as the hippies. The popularity of surfing and its ensuing organization during this decade led to its recognition as a legitimate professional sport and an accepted leisure activity.

Additional Information An overview of the history of surfing can be found in *The History of Surfing* (1983), by Nat Young, a former professional surfer.

Mark R. Ellis

See also Beach Films; Beach Boys; Counterculture; Gidget Films.

■ Susann, Jacqueline

Born August 20, 1918, Philadelphia, Pennsylvania
Died September 21, 1974, New York, New York

A best-selling author of the 1960's. Susann's popular novels of sex and drug use among the rich and famous garnered an unprecedented three consecutive number-one spots on The New York Times best-seller list.

Early Life The daughter of Rose and Robert Susan, Jacqueline Susann (her mother added an "n" to encourage proper pronunciation) received early encouragement for her writing but was determined to enter show business as a performer. She debuted in *The Women* in 1937; small parts in minor plays followed. In 1939, she married Irving Mansfield. Failing to get a "big break," she turned to writing; her first play opened in 1946 to disastrous reviews. Her son Guy, born December, 1946, was diagnosed as

Jacqueline Susann penned best-selling fiction such as Valley of the Dolls *(1966), a sex and drug-filled story of young women in the entertainment world.* (AP/Wide World Photos)

autistic and institutionalized in 1949. Still seeking acting success, Susann appeared in commercials and minor television roles throughout the 1950's.

The 1960's In 1963, Susann wrote *Every Night, Josephine!* about her pet poodle; it reached number ten on *The New York Times* best-seller list. Determined to reach number one, she brought a tougher kind of plot and franker treatment of sexuality to the standard romance novel format. The result was *Valley of the Dolls* (1966), the story of three young women in the entertainment world. Though judged "literary trash" by most critics, the book was number one on *The New York Times* best-seller list for a record-breaking twenty-eight weeks. The 1967 film adaptation set box-office records. (Interest in the film was renewed in 1969 after costar Sharon Tate was murdered by followers of Charles Manson.) Susann's 1969 novel, *The Love Machine* (a dual reference to television—the "love machine"—and the novel's womanizing protagonist), reached number one on *The New York Times* list within six weeks of publication.

Susann knew people wanted to read a story that enabled them to escape the tedium and trouble in their own lives. For plots, she turned to what she knew: the worlds of Hollywood and Broadway (which *Valley of the Dolls* brought together for the first time), infidelity (her father was notorious for his many affairs), chronic illness (her breast cancer and 1962 mastectomy remained a lifelong secret), and drug use (she had smoked and taken pills since she was fourteen).

Later Life In 1973, Susann wrote *Once Is Not Enough,* another number-one best-seller. Her final project, the novella *Dolores,* loosely based on the life of Jacqueline Kennedy Onassis, appeared in the February, 1974, issue of *The Ladies Home Journal;* Susann died of cancer seven months later. In 1976, Mansfield published *Dolores* in book form; it also became a best-seller. A final posthumous novel, the science-fiction fantasy *Yargo,* was published in 1979.

Impact Understanding that books were a product like anything else, Susann quickly became an expert on the intricacies of book selling, blending promotion, personal appearances, and celebrity tie-ins. Her forthright personality made her a media natural, and she made the most of all airtime. She robbed the critics of their power through the sheer number of readers and fans she brought into the bookstores, and her grassroots approach to marketing changed the face of publishing. Her success is undisputed; *Valley of the Dolls* was credited by the *Guinness Book of World Records* as the best-selling novel of all time, a record that held for almost three decades.

Additional Information Barbara Seaman's 1987 biography, *Lovely Me: The Life of Jacqueline Susann,* provides a comprehensive account of Susann's life.

Jennifer Davis-Kay

See also Literature.

■ *Switched-on Bach*

Released 1968
Performer Walter Carlos (1939-   )

The first electronically produced album to scale the pop charts. It modernized baroque music and popularized electronic music.

The Work Walter Carlos, who had degrees in both physics and music, was one of a number of musicians experimenting with electronic music in the 1960's. He was a client and collaborator of Robert Moog, the inventor of the modular synthesizer. Although most electronic compositions were modernistic and atonal, Carlos produced electronic renditions of classical pieces. Using bulky and primitive equipment in his Manhattan apartment, Carlos laboriously programmed music by the baroque master Johann Sebastian Bach, including selections from *The Well-Tempered Clavier,* the Brandenburg concertos, "Jesu, Joy of Man's Desiring," and "Wachet Auf." Columbia Records released the recordings as *Switched-on Bach* in 1968.

Impact *Switched-on Bach* won three Grammy Awards, and was the first classical music album to reach platinum. Moog called the album "the most stunning breakthrough in electronic music to date." Its frenetic tempo and eerily hollow sound, combined with the stately associations of Bach's music, produced a result that many listeners found exciting and modern. A pioneer in electronic music, Carlos later became a pioneer in another field of technology: sex-change surgery. Walter Carlos became Wendy Carlos, and later editions of *Switched-on Bach* identify Wendy Carlos as the artist.

Related Work Carlos's soundtrack for Stanley Kubrick's film *A Clockwork Orange* (1971), with music by Beethoven and others, was also a commercial success.

Additional Information Herbert Russcol, in *The Liberation of Sound: An Introduction to Electronic Music* (1972), assesses the creation and reception of *Switched-on Bach.* Joel Chadabe's *Electronic Sound* (1997) provides a broader historical context for Carlos's work.

Jeremy Mumford

See also Music.

T

■ Taylor, Elizabeth

Born February 27, 1932, London, England

An international film star. She dominated headlines in the early 1960's with her film successes and the scandals of her private life.

Early Life Elizabeth Rosemond Taylor is the daughter of an art dealer and an actress. The family moved from London, England, to Los Angeles, California, where Elizabeth signed with MGM in 1943. She achieved fame after appearing as Velvet Brown in

National Velvet (1944). A lovely child, Taylor developed first into a beautiful teenager, then a woman with compelling violet eyes and extraordinarily beautiful features. Every film magazine documented her life, describing, in turn, her engagement to football star Glen Davis, her first marriage to hotelier Nicky Hilton in 1950, and her marriage to actor Michael Wilding in 1952. Her fairy-tale marriage in 1957 to film producer Michael Todd ended with his death in a airplane crash in 1958. After Todd's death, Taylor sought consolation from singer Eddie Fisher, a close friend of Todd. Taylor and Fisher, who was

Motion picture star Elizabeth Taylor arrives at Princess Grace's birthday party in Monaco in 1969 wearing the Cartier diamond, worth more than a million dollars, given to her by husband Richard Burton, who accompanied her. (AP/Wide World Photos)

married to film star Debbie Reynolds, became romantically linked, creating a scandal that diminished public sympathy toward the newly widowed Taylor. The pair were married in 1959.

The 1960's Taylor regained the public's sympathy after a very serious bout with pneumonia in the early 1960's, then went on to win an Academy Award for her performance in *Butterfield Eight* (1960). Taylor was given the starring role in *Cleopatra* (1963), for which she received an unprecedented payment of one million dollars. While making the film, she fell in love with costar Richard Burton, a well-known British actor who played Mark Antony. The scandal and media coverage produced by the Taylor-Burton romance surpassed that created by the earlier Taylor-Fisher affair. Taylor and Burton separated from their respective partners and were married in 1964. Their turbulent marriage lasted almost a decade. Burton and Taylor made a number of pictures together, most notably *Who's Afraid of Virginia Woolf?* (1966). Taylor received her second Academy Award for her performance in this film. Taylor and Burton were known for their extravagant lifestyle and the diamonds purchased with their enormous wealth.

Later Life Although Taylor described Burton as the great love of her life, their marriage ran into trouble in the 1970's. The couple separated and reconciled several times, divorced, remarried, and divorced again in 1976. In 1978, Taylor married John Warner and assisted in his campaign to become a senator from Virginia. They divorced in 1982. The often-photographed Taylor experienced problems with her weight and alcohol, and her film career waned, although she appeared in television and feature films. In the 1980's and 1990's, she developed her own successful line of perfumes and did extensive charitable work, especially on behalf of AIDS. In 1991, she married construction worker Larry Fortensky, whom she had met at a treatment center for drug and alcohol abuse. They were divorced in 1997. Though Taylor was semiretired, her celebrity status ensured that each illness, surgery, and romance—rumored or true—would continue to receive extensive media coverage.

Impact Taylor, a glamorous movie star, dominated celebrity headlines in the early 1960's. A strongly independent woman, she launched the trend of skyrocketing fees for actors and lived her life according to her own standards. Although she won two Academy Awards, Taylor's acting career has been overshadowed by her own personality and celebrity.

Additional Information Among the many works on Taylor, *Who's Afraid of Elizabeth Taylor?* (1978), by Brenda Maddox, provides an interesting look at both the child and the woman. Dick Sheppard's *Elizabeth: The Life and Career of Elizabeth Taylor* (1975) chronicles her life in the 1960's.

Norma Corigliano Noonan

See also Film; Marriage; *Who's Afraid of Virginia Woolf?*.

■ Teachers Strikes

Illegal strikes by thousands of teachers who ignored the laws and withheld their services. Teachers were growing increasingly militant in an attempt to empower themselves in educational decision-making processes.

Teachers organizations have been a part of U.S. history since shortly after the Revolutionary War. The National Education Association (NEA) was created in 1858 and had its roots in the New York Society of Associated Teachers of the 1790's, the Connecticut teachers discussion clubs of 1799, and the National Teachers Association (1857). The American Federation of Teachers (AFT) was formed in 1916 when several individual teacher organizations from northern Illinois and Indiana joined together. The first teachers organization to have withheld services was the Chicago Federation of Teachers in 1915.

According to the NEA, teachers strikes are defined as instances in which teachers called for work stoppages, took professional days away from the classroom, or in general, withheld their services from a school. Although it was illegal for public servants to strike, from July, 1960, through June, 1970, there were 500 teachers strikes, 331 by NEA affiliates, 135 by AFT affiliates, and the rest by independent unions or nonunion groups. During this period, 500,000 school personnel withheld their services for more than 5.2 million man-days of classroom instruction. The majority of the teachers strikes occurred in the states with economies based on industry rather than agriculture. Although fewer strikes occurred in the southern states, no geographic area was spared from strikes. Thirty-three states and the District of Columbia experienced at least one teacher strike. Of these, only seven states

Teacher Strikes by State, July, 1960 - June, 1970

State	Teacher Strikes	Personnel Involved	Man-days Lost	State	Teacher Strikes	Personnel Involved	Man-days Lost
Alaska	1	500	250	Missouri	11	3,834	6,057
California	27	34,545	299,474	Montana	2	818	1,636
Colorado	4	3,721	26,398	Nevada	2	3,200	5,600
Connecticut	15	6,791	19,574	New Hampshire	3	1,345	3,460
District of				New Jersey	34	17,261	121,634
Columbia	5	3,446	3,446	New Mexico	3	3,058	15,218
Florida	4	32,000	423,800	New York	23	128,998	3,250,717
Georgia	2	98	346	North Dakota	1	200	4,400
Idaho	1	300	300	Ohio	65	16,500	40,926
Illinois	53	29,258	95,219	Oklahoma	5	24,822	26,932
Indiana	14	28,666	75,671	Pennsylvania	42	29,763	75,503
Iowa	2	209	592	Rhode Island	7	2,675	24,285
Kentucky	7	55,060	191,810	South Dakota	1	441	3,969
Louisiana	4	2,607	16,271	Tennessee	4	851	5,808
Maryland	8	10,855	37,705	Utah	3	10,325	20,950
Massachusetts	10	9,226	48,216	West Virginia	3	114	272
Michigan	125	45,240	350,774	Wisconsin	8	1,844	11,106
Minnesota	1	2,000	30,000	**Totals**	**500**	**510,571**	**5,238,319**

Source: National Education Association Research Bulletin 48, 1970

were responsible for 74 percent of the strikes (Michigan experienced 125 strikes, Ohio 65, Illinois 53, Pennsylvania 42, New Jersey 34, California 27, and New York 23) and accounted for more than 80 percent of the lost man-days of classroom instruction.

During the 1960's, six states (Florida, Indiana, Kentucky, Oklahoma, Pennsylvania, and Utah) experienced statewide strikes lasting from one to fifteen days. Although some of the strikes lasted no more than one day, the longest strike occurred in 1968-1969 when New York City teachers walked out for fifty days. That single incident, involving more than 50,000 teachers, accounted for more than 90 percent of the total lost man-days for all teacher strikes in 1968-1969.

As the 1960's progressed, the number of strikes along with the number of school personnel involved and man-days lost continued to increase. In the 1961-1962 school year, only one teachers strike occurred nationwide. However, in 1969-1970, the number of strikes was 180. The number of school personnel involved grew from just over 5,000 in 1960-1961 to more than 118,000 in 1969-1970. Likewise, the number of man-days lost increased from 5,000 in 1960-1961 to more than 2.7 million man-days during the 1968-1969 school year.

Impact To understand why teachers of the 1960's were willing to withhold services at the risk of losing their jobs, it is important to remember the development of collective bargaining between organized labor and management. Collective bargaining gave labor a platform on which to exercise operational concerns about day-to-day business functions of companies. Teachers had no voice in the management of classroom education (items such as curriculum, class size, book selection, and building maintenance). Although local issues varied from state to state, collective bargaining remained the key to solving the empowerment problem. According to George D. Fischer, NEA president in 1969, the teachers of the day were determined to get involved with decision making in education, and the strike was becoming an acceptable tool to try to improve the quality of education for students and staff. Teachers were no longer willing to remain powerless when it came to educational reform and the operation of their schools.

The striking teachers sought gains not only in the area of pay scales but also in working conditions and participation in policy making. As a result, the strikes brought about decreased class size, duty-free lunch periods, more teacher involvement in the textbook selection process, more time to prepare lessons, and improvements in the physical school environment.

Some of the accomplishments of teachers strikes should be attributed to the early successes of the AFT-sanctioned strikes that encouraged the NEA to accept the concept that labor unions could work for professional educators. The AFT more than doubled its membership during the 1960's, and the NEA also expanded significantly. Because the era of professionally prudent persuasion had failed to improve the situation for teachers, the NEA gradually evolved from promoting sacrifice in the name of professionalism (it was considered unprofessional to talk about money) to an association that supported affiliates who went on strike and represented their members in crisis bargaining. White-collar workers saw that unionism had gained a degree of respectability in the educational community, which made it acceptable for other public service occupations.

Subsequent Events Strikes by teachers continued past the 1960's, and other civil servants, including police officers and firefighters, followed suit with work stoppages and sickouts. Debate continued over the right of such public employees to strike.

Additional Information For a history of the AFT, see *Teachers and Power* (1972), by Robert J. Braun. For data on the teachers strikes of the 1960's, see the *NEA Research Bulletin* 48, October, 1970.

Richard D. Cronk

See also Education; Unions and Collective Bargaining.

■ Teachings of Don Juan, The

Published 1968
Author Carlos Castaneda (1925?-1998)

An account of studying with a Yaqui sorcerer named Don Juan. The sorcerer's teachings featured the use of peyote as part of an ongoing and sincere spiritual quest.

The Work *The Teachings of Don Juan: A Yaqui Way of Knowledge* was Castaneda's doctoral thesis in anthropology submitted to the University of California, Santa Cruz. It details Castaneda's visits with don Juan, a seventy-year-old Yaqui sorcerer whose religious practices feature the use of peyote to provoke mystical visions. With don Juan's guidance and through the liberal ingestion of peyote, Castaneda is taught to become a "man of knowledge," entering an alternately marvelous and frightening supernatural dimension in which the ordinary laws of time and space are suspended.

Impact *The Teachings of Don Juan* was widely regarded as giving a powerful legitimacy to the use of psychedelic drugs. In endorsing the mind-altering peyote and in treating a nonwestern culture as a spiritual resource, Castaneda created one of the seminal works of the "consciousness revolution" of the 1960's.

Related Works *The Teachings of Don Juan* was the first of a tetralogy that continued in *A Separate Reality: Further Conversations with Don Juan* (1971), *Journey to Ixtlan* (1972), and *Tales of Power* (1974). Together these books have sold millions of copies around the world.

Additional Information Richard de Mille has collected articles discussing the paranormal and peyote among other topics in a 1980 book called *The Don Juan Papers: Further Castaneda Controversies.*

Margaret Boe Birns

See also Drug Culture; *House Made of Dawn*; Religion and Spirituality.

■ Teatro Campesino, El

A bilingual Chicano theater group. The company began as a propaganda tool for the California farmworkers' strike and remained dedicated to Chicano political and social issues.

Origins and History El Teatro Campesino ("the farmworkers' theater") was founded by Luis Valdez in Delano, California, in 1965 to help César Chávez and the United Farmworkers' Organizing Committee with activities in support of the grape boycott and farmworkers' strike. The group's purpose was to inform workers of developments in the strike and maintain strikers' morale during difficult times. They were at first unabashedly propagandistic and focused on the single purpose of helping win the strike. By 1967, however, the group had officially separated from the organizing committee, and its focus had begun expanding to include other issues

El Teatro Campesino, a bilingual theater group that began as a propaganda tool for the striking grapeworkers, performs in Modesto, California, in 1975. (Lou Dematteis)

of importance to California's Chicano, or Mexican American, population, including educational inequality and racial stereotyping. However, the group remained committed to its ideal of creating bilingual theater for a working-class Chicano audience. In 1968, the company won a prestigious Obie (Off-Broadway) Award in recognition of "creating a workers' theater to demonstrate the politics of survival." By 1969, the group had achieved international recognition, appearing at venues that included the World Theater Festival in France.

Activities The earliest works of El Teatro Campesino were semi-improvised ten- to fifteen-minute playlets, called *actos*, performed by and for striking workers. These were based on real people and events of the evolving strike and, because they followed no set script, were adaptable to various audiences and circumstances. The style of the company was influenced by the work of playwright Bertolt Brecht, who had used untrained actors and non-naturalistic staging in his political dramas. The *actos* often involved

audience participation and incorporated humor, music, and elements of Mexican folklore, while relying on minimal sets, props, and costumes. As the company evolved, the original *actos* were supplemented with longer, usually scripted, works that moved beyond the farmworkers' concerns to present an inclusive celebration and affirmation of all Chicano culture.

Impact With its ever-growing audience, El Teatro Campesino was clearly filling a need for entertainment and education among working-class Chicanos. Local, community-based theater groups began to spring up wherever there was a Chicano community to be served. Many of these groups reflected the concerns of their specific local populations, urban or rural. The success of the company helped to legitimize Chicano and other types of bilingual theater in California and throughout the United States.

Subsequent Events By the early 1970's, El Teatro Campesino was well-established enough to purchase land in San Juan Bautista, California, and open its own playhouse. Valdez achieved commercial success in the Los Angeles theater with his 1978 play *Zoot Suit* and went on to write for film and television. The company has continued to grow and win major awards, but it has never lost touch with its roots as a political and social organization.

Additional Information In 1985, the company published *El Teatro Campesino: The First Twenty Years*, documenting its evolution, and ten of the early *actos* by Valdez are collected in his 1971 book *Early Works*.

Janet E. Gardner

See also Chicano Movement; Grape Workers' Strike; Theater Arts.

■ Telecommunications Satellites

The technological development that made possible instantaneous, global communication. Telecommunications satellites have resulted in vast changes for civilians, governments, and the military.

Beginning in the late 1920's, scientists described the parts of a satellite communications system that would function by relaying electromagnetic signals from transmitters and to receivers. They theorized about and described the necessary components for geostationary satellites in orbits that would make possible instantaneous, global communication. Research continued toward these ends, and by December 19, 1958, an Atlas launch vehicle boosted the first satellite into Earth orbit and transmitted President Dwight D. Eisenhower's Christmas address to the nation. This development made the world aware of the possibilities of satellite communication.

Telstar was launched into low orbit on July 10, 1962. Although in 1960 the United States Army had launched its own communication satellite, Courier 1B, and the National Aeronautics and Space Administration (NASA) and Bell Laboratories had collaborated on Echo 1, both satellites were passive, merely relaying electromagnetic signals from transmitters to receivers. Telstar was the first active communication satellite—that is, amplifying and repeating signals—as well as the first communication satellite to be privately owned (by Bell Telephone and American Telephone and Telegraph). On July 11, 1962, Telstar relayed the first live television images across the Atlantic Ocean.

Telstar was followed in late 1962 by Relay 1, which RCA provided for NASA. By 1964, after two failures,

Hughes Aircraft's Syncom 3 achieved geosynchronous orbit, which allowed the satellite to remain fixed over the same spot on Earth's surface and also provided American audiences with television transmissions from the Tokyo Olympic Games. Intelsat 1, the "Early Bird," was launched on April 6, 1965, by Hughes for Comsat, a corporation created by Congress in 1962 as a joint venture between the U.S. government and private businesses and which became an important member of the multinational International Telecommunications Satellite Consortium (Intelsat), also formed in 1962. Intelsat 1, an important step in the commercialization of satellite communications, relayed such diverse images as those of Houston heart surgeons, French nuclear scientists, and U.S. troops patrolling in the Dominican Republic. NASA's Applications Technology Satellite (ATS1) made history on December 16, 1966, when it photographed the full disk of Earth.

Impact Telstar inaugurated what became an orbital and frequency traffic jam. Along with weather and military usages, satellites provided the benefits of Search and Rescue operations (SARSAT) and Global Positioning (GPS), among a plethora of other applications. By the end of the twentieth century, satellite communications had become ubiquitous. For many, the greatest impact has been on television transmission, which allows viewers immediate access to events and information previously available only on film or in printed media. Instantaneous coverage showing the horrors of the Vietnam War, for example, may have speeded the end of that conflict or at least increased opposition to the war.

Additional Information *ACTS: System Overview*, published by NASA in 1994, contains detailed information about developments in telecommunications technology and application.

Sharon Randolph

See also Communications; Science and Technology.

■ Television

A dominating cultural presence. During the 1960's, television played extensive and varied roles depending on the age and ethnic experience of the viewer.

By 1960, almost 90 percent of U.S. homes had at least one television set. Official viewing statistics suggested that, on average, people were watching tele-

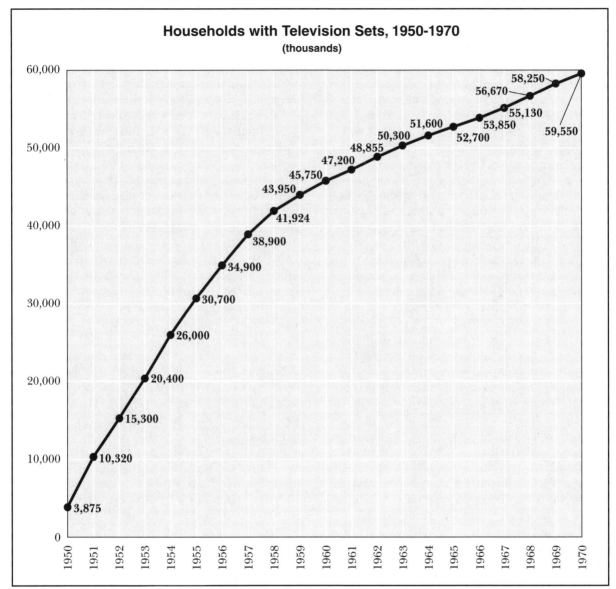

Households with Television Sets, 1950-1970
(thousands)

Source: Kurian, George, *Datapedia of the United States, 1790-2000, America Year by Year.* Lanham, Maryland: Bernam Press, 1994.

vision about five hours per day. Although these figures measured the amount of time the set was on and not whether anyone in the house was actually watching television or even in the room, they are nonetheless a convincing index that television had seized an easy lead over all other forms of mass information and entertainment. The switch to primarily color programming in the mid-1960's only served to increase the lure of this medium.

The paradox was that although more people than ever before were simultaneously exposed to similar or even identical audiovisual messages, they received them within their own individual dwellings and as part of their family lives. The videocassette recorder (VCR) was not yet a household item, so that at least in single-set households (the great majority), viewers were compelled to watch only one program and together. Paternal authority and sibling rivalry appeared to be equally manifest in deciding which program a family watched. What viewers made of programs was yet another story; research shows conclusively that many viewers are not just passive.

The screen was dominated by the "big three" networks—the Columbia Broadcasting System (CBS), National Broadcasting Company (NBC), and the American Broadcasting Company (ABC)—although the decade also saw the founding of very small-scale national public television in the form of the Public Broadcasting Service (PBS) in 1969. The move from live television produced in New York to recorded programs produced in Hollywood had been accomplished by the end of the 1950's, but the actual production of programs was farmed out to independent companies and to established motion-picture firms such as Warner Brothers. Increasingly, the networks concentrated on selling programs, leaving to other companies the financial risk of making them. However, this enabled some of the independent companies to create more innovative entertainment, judged by the standards of the time, than would be seen in later decades.

The high cost of financing this gigantic enterprise also led to a decline in direct advertiser involvement in programs, with multiple sponsorship replacing the single-sponsor model of earlier broadcasting. At the same time, with the economy initially booming through industrial growth related to the Vietnam War, plenty of advertising dollars were available to fuel expensive television productions. The networks were kings; cable television was not yet a powerful influence.

The event that put television on the political map was the surprising impact of the first-ever televised debate between presidential candidates in 1960. Commentators then and since have suggested that John F. Kennedy's telegenic appearance helped nudge the number of votes he won, just past the total received by his opponent, Vice President Richard M. Nixon, who was judged to have done better in the debate than Kennedy by those who listened on the radio. The Kennedy-Nixon debates created a discourse about the supposed political power of television that would become quickly entrenched as popular wisdom.

Civil Rights and Black Power During the decade, the publicly visible emphasis of African Americans' political activism shifted increasingly from civil rights demonstrations, mostly in the states where segregation was legally enforced, to urban protest outside the South. The changing images on the television screen had a number of consequences.

Television news footage in the early 1960's again and again showed African Americans, unarmed and offering no resistance, stoically withstanding police dogs, billy clubs, water cannons, and jail sentences, not to mention bystanders who screamed abuse and threatened violence against them. Without the pictures, the violence meted out against African Americans would likely have gone unremarked, and the enduring viciousness of their persecutors unnoticed.

Additionally, and crucially, these images were picked up by television news services around the world, meaning that the United States' self-defined mission as leader of the democracies against Soviet repression was very badly dented—not least in many Third World nations newly represented in the United Nations, for whose allegiance the United States had to constantly compete with the Soviet Union. In turn, this secondary television impact forced U.S. administrations to turn their attention to the civil rights issue.

The portrayal of African American activists and individuals influenced the feelings of many television viewers toward this minority group. After Martin Luther King, Jr., delivered his "I Have a Dream" speech at the 1963 March on Washington, the civil rights leader, portrayed in the 1950's as a disruptive militant, became defined as a peace statesman and was contrasted favorably with Malcolm X and the Black Panther Party, who held more radical views and were sometimes labeled merchants of hate. Television also broadcast footage of the frightening violence in many cities' African American areas, most notably the Watts section of Los Angeles in 1965; Detroit, Michigan, and Newark, New Jersey, in 1967; and Washington, D.C., in 1968—yet by and large the networks glossed over the fact that those dead and injured in these "riots" were nearly always African Americans who had been shot or beaten by the police or the National Guard. Given this presentation, what seemed paramount was the riots' "danger" to white Americans.

The atmosphere of violence was fed by the assassinations of President Kennedy, Malcolm X, King, and Senator Robert Kennedy. It seemed as though individuals who frequently appeared on television and had a commitment of one kind or another to solving racial issues were destined for the morgue. Television coverage rapidly built an image of a problem incapable of solution. This image was furthered by the absence of African Americans in any professional capacity in television news, which meant that the networks lacked any African American input from within their ranks on how to help the general public, of whatever background, understand the present or the past of U.S. race relations. Typically, newscasters dealing with racial issues spoke as one white American to another. African American voices took the shape of insurrectionary sound bites that seemed simply to confirm fears rather than address solutions.

The 1968 Kerner Commission Report (a report on the cause and prevention of urban violence prepared by President Lyndon B. Johnson's National Advisory Commission on Civil Disorders) included a notable chapter critiquing the news media, including television, for their failures in race relations coverage. It strongly underlined the role of predominantly white staffing on poor and negative coverage of African American issues. The report was not endorsed, however, by the president.

The War in Southeast Asia When the networks first began to expand their nightly newscast from fifteen minutes to thirty in 1963, one of the first topics was the conflict in Vietnam. From then until 1972, when U.S. military casualties began to drop relative to those of the South Vietnamese, but three years before the U.S. pullout, the Vietnam War and the subsequent expansion of the war into Cambodia and Laos were very regularly in the news.

A strong wing of opinion, not least in the Pentagon, has regarded a prime cause for the U.S. defeat in Vietnam to be television coverage. This hypothesis holds that by bringing into the living room grisly pictures of war carnage and of body bags filled with young Americans and by covering domestic antiwar activity, the public's morale was increasingly sapped. Over time, the public simply became unable to pay the necessary price of winning. Explanations vary as to why television journalism might have covered the war and protests in this way. Some researchers hold that because television is a visual medium, this type of impact was unavoidable. Others theorize that journalists routinely seek out conflict and the negative. A third group believes that top journalists mostly belong to a select coterie of left-leaning social critics educated in northeastern Ivy League schools.

The problems with the hypothesis, however, are severe. One is that much of the evidence indicates that television coverage of the war was not hostile, indeed that the networks supported U.S. troops and the government's stance and avoided questioning the war until domestic protest against it was already widespread and a story in its own right. In a famous incident in 1967, distinguished veteran journalist Fred Friendly publicly resigned his CBS position when the company chose to screen a fourth rerun of *I Love Lucy* rather than cover the first Senate hearings on the war. Other problems with the hypothesis include the assertion about the personal political leanings of top journalists. Even if these political leanings are accurately described, journalists are not free agents who can write anything they choose. The hypothesis also supposes that all other aspects of the U.S. involvement in the war were in order, which is the subject of debate rather than an established fact.

Youth and Student Rebellion The virtual absence of the sixteen-to-twenty-four age group from television viewing during the 1960's was a major headache for the networks. Effectively, at least on campus, and often on the streets, this cohort felt the action was elsewhere. First the Beatles, then the Rolling Stones, the Grateful Dead, and the Doors—not to mention the earlier Bob Dylan and Joan Baez—opened up a cultural space foreign to the older generation and to most television executives. Young people's attention was captivated by the new musical scene, experimentation with hallucinogenic drugs and sexual license, and student political protest regarding civil rights and the Vietnam War.

Television coverage of student protest and youth rebellion was initially minimal, but when it became full, it was often unsympathetic to hostile. A classic instance was CBS's decision in 1969 not to cover live the huge Moratorium Day march in Washington, D.C. against the war. Instead of following the main group of a half-million participants, it focused on a very small number of demonstrators who broke away and threw rocks at the Pentagon. Often news of demonstrations would focus on the presence of Vietnamese flags among the demonstrators rather than the objectives of the march as a whole. In 1968, leading television anchor Walter Cronkite initially described the Chicago police at the Democratic National Convention clashes as "thugs," but a week later, he publicly withdrew the statement.

A television show that to some degree echoed

many of the struggles taking place and whose history encapsulates the conflicts of the war was *The Smothers Brothers Comedy Hour.* Targeted precisely at television's absent sixteen-to-twenty-four age group, it began by featuring an airhead character, Goldie O'Keefe, whose conversation was littered with in-jokes and in-the-know allusions to drug taking. The network executives probably had little or no idea of what the terms meant. Then in the second and third season, the jokes became more heavily politicized. CBS pulled the plug on the show in 1969. Mainstream commentators complained of censorship, and the alternative youth press tried to organize a movement to get the program reinstated.

Impact It is perhaps the case, therefore, that the degree of alienation felt in the 1960's by many young people and by many people of color concerning the Vietnam War, civil rights, and some of the traditions held dear by their parents, was very likely intensified by the distance the three television networks evinced from their concerns. Cinema bridged the gap a little, but television hardly at all. At the same time, however, the steady projection of cultural norms in most programming and all television advertising meant that for older Americans, the shocks and dramas in the news could appear threatening but not challenging. Arguably for most, therefore, television strengthened a traditional cultural and political consensus, as evinced by the size of the votes for presidential candidates Nixon and George Wallace in 1968 and in 1972.

Additional Information *Tube of Plenty: The Evolution of American Television* (1975), by Erik Barnouw, provides an overall look at television in the 1960's. For further information on television's interactions with the decade's social and political movements, read *The Whole World Is Watching: Mass Media in the Making and Unmaking of the New Left* (1980), by Todd Gitlin; *The Revolution Wasn't Televised: Sixties Television and Social Conflict* (1997), edited by Lynn Spigel and Michael Curtin; *The "Uncensored War": The Media and Vietnam* (1986), by Daniel C. Hallin; and *Blacks and White TV: Afro Americans in Television Since 1948* (1991), by J. Fred MacDonald. A closer look at the Smothers Brothers show can be found in "On the Edge of Tastelessness: CBS, the Smothers Brothers, and the Struggle for Control," by Steven Allen Carr in the summer, 1992, issue of *Cinema Journal.*

John D. H. Downing

See also Advertising; Assassinations of John and Robert Kennedy and Martin Luther King, Jr.; Civil Rights Movement; Communications; "I Have a Dream" Speech; Kennedy-Nixon Debates; Kerner Commission Report; Media; Moratorium Day; *Smothers Brothers Comedy Hour, The*; VCRs; Vietnam War; Youth Culture and the Generation Gap.

■ Tennis

One of the most important periods in the development of modern tennis. The domination of the sport by Australian men, the emergence of women's tennis, and the introduction of open tennis helped the game become a major participation and spectator sport.

Tennis in the 1960's was still a game controlled by the private clubs and the conservative establishment of tennis. Three of the major tournaments in the Grand Slam were played on grass, and the other was played on red clay in Paris. Hard courts were gaining in popularity in public clubs but still had not been accepted for top play. Players in all tournaments were still required to dress completely in white, all players in the major tournaments played only for expense money and trophies, and tiebreakers were not yet introduced.

Men's Tennis. Australia stamped its image on the male tennis world during the 1960's by winning seven Davis Cups and finishing as runner-up in two others. Led by Rod Laver, Ken Rosewall, and Roy Emerson, Australian players won the singles championship at Wimbledon eight times and the U.S. Championship six times during the period. The top American player during the early 1960's was Chuck McKinley, who won Wimbledon in 1963 and teamed with Dennis Ralston to win the Davis Cup from the Australians the same year. During the final years of the decade, Arthur Ashe emerged as the top American player. In 1968 and 1969, the U.S. Championship was divided into a tournament for amateurs and an open tournament for professionals and amateurs. Ashe won both tournaments as an amateur in 1968 and became the first male African American to win a Grand Slam title. In that same year, Ashe teamed with Stan Smith to wrest the Davis Cup from Australia. The United States was able to defend the title for the next three years.

Women's Tennis. Unlike in the men's game, the top female players were from a variety of countries. Six women from four countries won Wimbledon during the decade. The best American player from 1960 to 1963 was Darlene Hard, who retired in 1964 after winning twenty-one grand slam singles and doubles titles. She won the U.S. Championship twice and the French title once. In 1961, a seventeen-year-old American named Billie Jean Moffitt won the doubles championship at Wimbledon and returned in 1965 as Billie Jean King to advance to the singles finals before losing to Margaret Court. King would go on to win the singles title at Wimbledon in 1966, 1967, and 1968 and would eventually win six singles titles at Wimbledon and a record twenty titles in singles, doubles, and mixed doubles in the tournament. She was runner-up in the first U.S. Open in 1968 and eventually won that title four times. King also led the battle for equal pay for female players and the establishment of a women's tour. In 1969, one year after the establishment of open tennis, Gladys Heldman, the founder of the magazine *World Tennis*, established three tournaments for female professionals, marking the beginning of the women's tour.

The most important event in tennis in the 1960's was the decision to include top professionals in the major tournaments. Prior to 1968, all major tournaments were open only to amateurs. The top players seldom remained amateur after winning a number of major tournaments, and critics complained that major tournaments were offering second-class tennis. In addition, the amateurs still competing in tournaments found tournament directors willing to pay them considerable expense money to ensure their participation. There was pressure on the tennis establishment to allow professionals to compete in the major tournaments so that top players could continue to perform in these showcase events. In 1967, the All-England Club announced that professionals would be allowed to participate at Wimbledon beginning the following year, and Rod Laver returned to win his third and fourth championships. Laver received $3,800 for his singles victory, and the ladies champion, Billie Jean King, received $1,300. All other major tournaments quickly followed suit.

Impact The decade was a period of change, as metal racquets were introduced by top players, women's tennis established the Federation Cup, giving the women an international competition similar to the men's Davis Cup, new and colorful champions emerged, and the public demanded and finally received open tennis.

Additional Information Herbert Warren's *Game, Set, Match: The Tennis Boom of the 1960's and 70's* provides information about changes in the sport during the 1960's and about major players.

Joe Blankenbaker

See also Ashe, Arthur; Hard, Darlene; King, Billie Jean.

■ Terry, Megan

Born July 22, 1932, Seattle, Washington

Experimental playwright who first came to prominence in the 1960's with the New York Open Theater. A pioneer in feminist drama and in the development of transformational drama.

Early Life Megan Terry (born Megan Duffy) has been involved with theater since she attended a Seattle Repertory Playhouse production when she was seven. During her teens, she spent considerable time at the Playhouse learning the craft of theater from Florence and Burton James. After high school, Terry studied at Banff School of Fine Arts, the University of Washington, and the University of Alberta in Edmonton. While teaching at the Cornish School of Allied Arts, she developed her philosophy of playwriting as improvisation. In the late 1950's, Terry moved to New York where her career as a playwright developed and flourished.

The 1960's During the 1960's, Terry was both active and highly visible in New York theater. She was a founding member of the New York Open Theater, where she was playwright-in-residence from 1963-1968. At the Open Theater for which she wrote eight major works, one of her most significant contributions was *Viet Rock: A Folk War Movie* (1966), her first collaborative workshop play and the first American play about the Vietnam War. At the Open Theater, Terry's experimentation with Viola Spolin's transformation technique resulted in a new theatrical form, the transformation play, which requires actors to improvise constantly in response to changes in setting or action or even character that occur several times during the course of a play. Among Terry's best transformation plays from the 1960's are *Calm Down Mother*, *Keep Tightly Closed in a Cool Dry Place*, and *The*

Gloaming all written and premiered in 1965—and *Comings and Goings* (1966), which Terry has said is the most frequently produced of her plays. In 1970, she wrote *Approaching Simone*, dramatizing the life of philosopher Simone Weil. That play won the 1969-1970 Obie Award for Best New Play.

Later Life Terry moved to Omaha, Nebraska, in 1974 to join JoAnn Schmidman, an Open Theater actress who in 1968 had founded the Omaha Magic Theater, a feminist theater troupe. As playwright-in-residence at the Magic Theater, Terry continued to write for the stage and also for television. She has written in excess of fifty plays, a number of which have been translated and produced outside the United States. These plays include *Babes in the Bighouse* (1974), *Kegger* (1982), *American King's English for Queens* (1978), and *100,001 Horror Stories of the Plains* (1976).

Impact Terry is generally credited by theater historians and critics as the chief architect of the transformation play, a type of drama that fit in well with the 1960's disregard for tradition and its forms and conventions. Her plays touch on the Vietnam War, feminism, and social problems such as substance abuse and combine visual arts, dance, music, and sculpture.

Additional Information Elizabeth Natalle's *Feminist Theatre: A Study in Persuasion* (1985) provides a short biography of Terry along with critical analysis of her works.

E. D. Huntley

See also Rock Operas; Theater Arts; Theater of the Absurd.

■ Tet Offensive

Date January 30-March 31, 1968

A surprise attack by Viet Cong and North Vietnamese forces on provincial capitals, district towns, villages, and U.S. bases. It proved to be a turning point in the Vietnam War when it increased opposition to continued involvement in the conflict.

Origins and History By 1968, U.S. military forces in Vietnam had increased to more than half a million. The role of the U.S. soldier had progressed from adviser to principal combatant, and strategies such as continuous bombing of North Vietnam and search-and-destroy operations had failed to bring the war to a conclusion. The death toll continued to rise, reaching fifteen thousand Americans dead by the end of 1967, and opposition to the war effort grew at home.

The Offensive Planning for the Tet Offensive began in the middle of 1967 in Hanoi, the capital of North Vietnam. Although the precise goals of the offensive remain uncertain, North Vietnamese military leaders apparently believed that the time had arrived for a large-scale effort that would encourage massive popular uprisings in favor of the North and lead to a final victory over the Americans and South Vietnamese.

The three-day Tet holiday, a celebration of the lunar new year, began on the night of January 30. Despite the announcement of a cease-fire by the Viet Cong, U.S. officials had received intelligence indicating that an enemy initiative was likely. Nonetheless, they were unprepared for what was to come.

Among the Vietnamese entering Saigon, the South Vietnamese capital, in the days before Tet were hundreds of Viet Cong. After midnight, early in the morning of January 31, they retrieved previously hidden weapons and moved toward their targets, which included the United States Embassy. At 3:00 A.M., an antitank rocket opened a hole in the outer wall of the embassy compound, initiating an attack that would not end until shortly before noon. Heavy fighting occurred throughout Saigon, including in Cholon, the Chinese section of the city. The Viet Cong methodically executed individuals believed to be loyal to the South Vietnamese government, and hundreds of residents died in the crossfire between American and South Vietnamese forces and the Viet Cong.

Throughout South Vietnam, eighty-four thousand North Vietnamese and Viet Cong troops attacked thirty-six of the forty-four provincial capitals and scores of towns and villages as well as American installations. Next to Saigon, the most significant target was Hue in northeastern South Vietnam, an ancient capital city of great beauty and historical significance. Six thousand North Vietnamese regulars marched into the city on January 30, accompanied by commissars carrying dossiers of people marked for execution. As U.S. Marines approached Hue to liberate the city, North Vietnamese rounded up and killed—sometimes burying alive—govern-

A Viet Cong attack forces U.S. soldiers to take cover behind a wall of the single officers quarters in Saigon on January 31, 1968, during the Tet Offensive. (National Archives)

ment officials, teachers, military officers, priests, and men of military age.

Fighting between Marines, aided by South Vietnamese, and the North Vietnamese raged for twenty-four days. The effort to recapture Hue finally proved successful but at a huge cost. The death count reached 142 U.S. Marines and 384 South Vietnamese soldiers, and 2,800 South Vietnamese citizens had been executed by the invading forces. Between 5,000 and 8,000 North Vietnamese were killed. At the conclusion of the battle, whole sections of Hue lay in ruins. More than half of the homes had been leveled, and large numbers of historical treasures were destroyed.

In the final analysis, the North Vietnamese and Viet Cong were unable to hold any areas that they attacked. They suffered huge losses, and much of the Viet Cong infrastructure was destroyed. The popular uprising that planners had expected never occurred, and soldiers, demoralized by the heavy losses, defected from the north in greater numbers.

Impact Although the Viet Cong and North Vietnamese suffered a major military defeat, they ultimately won a psychological victory in the Tet Offensive. Previously, a large majority of Americans had supported the Vietnam War, believing, as their political and military leaders stated, that they could see the "light at the end of the tunnel." The impact of the Tet Offensive, however, demonstrated that the war was far from over and the enemy was capable of penetrating even the most supposedly secure of positions, including the U.S. Embassy in Saigon. Clearly, a much greater commitment would be required to bring the communists to their knees.

The American public appeared disinclined to make that commitment, and President Lyndon B. Johnson was unwilling to ask it of them. General Earle Wheeler, chairman of the Joint Chiefs of Staff, returned from a visit to Vietnam in late February, 1968, to announce that General William Westmoreland, commander of the U.S. forces in Vietnam, needed more than 200,000 additional troops to fight the war successfully, a figure that would increase the troop level in Vietnam to more than 730,000. To meet this request, Johnson would have been forced to order a general call-up of reserves.

Meanwhile, antiwar sentiment continued to rise within the United States. A Harris poll in late March reported that U.S. support for the Vietnam War had dropped from 74 percent to 54 percent, and that 60 percent of respondents considered the Tet Offensive a defeat for U.S. objectives. In the presidential campaign, Johnson faced strong challenges to his renomination from Senators Eugene McCarthy and Robert F. Kennedy.

In a televised speech on March 31, Johnson announced to the nation that he had decided to halt unilaterally the bombing of North Vietnam except just above the demilitarized zone, while sending an additional 13,500 troops to Vietnam. He added, "I shall not seek, and I will not accept, the nomination of my party for another term as your president." Johnson had decided against the extensive buildup requested by his generals and necessary for a military solution to the war. In coming to this decision, he had set the United States on a new path, one that would lead to peace talks in May, a gradual reduction in the U.S. war effort, a passing of the military torch to the South Vietnamese, and, ultimately, victory for North Vietnam.

Additional Information Don Oberdorfer offers a landmark account of the Tet Offensive in *Tet! The Turning Point of the Vietnam War* (1984). George Donelson Moss's *Vietnam: An American Ordeal* (1990) also describes the offensive, and Peter Braestrup's *Big Story* (1977) looks at reporting the event. Westmoreland's *A Soldier Reports* (1976) tells the story from the viewpoint of the general in charge of U.S. forces in Vietnam.

Edward J. Rielly

See also Gulf of Tonkin Incident; Johnson, Lyndon B.; My Lai Incident; Paris Peace Talks; Vietnam War.

■ Texas Tower Murders

Date August 1, 1966

One of the most infamous events of the 1960's. A sniper ascended the clock tower on the campus of the University of Texas, Austin, and randomly shot dozens of people below. In the end, more than forty people were either dead or wounded as a result of the killing spree.

Origins and History Twenty-five-year-old Charles Joseph Whitman was an Eagle Scout, a former U.S. Marine, and a student at the University of Texas when he assumed the unlikely role of mass murderer. The recent separation of his parents and his mother's subsequent move to Austin had been tremendous sources of stress for the troubled Whitman. The clock tower's one-hundred-meter-high observation deck had long been a popular tourist attraction when Whitman, who exemplified the all-American youth, turned the tower into a landmark of terror.

The Murders Late on the night of July 31, 1966, Whitman went to the apartment of his mother, Margaret Whitman, stabbed her several times with a bayonet, and shot her once in the back of the head. He left a note by his mother's bedside stating that he was upset about having killed her but felt that doing so was the only way to relieve her suffering. The suffering Whitman referred to was the physical and emotional abuse that, for years, his father had inflicted upon his mother. After murdering his mother, Whitman returned home and stabbed his wife, Kathy, killing her as she slept. He also left another note, this one explaining his feelings of desperation, his struggle to maintain rational thought, and his wish that, after his death, his brain would be examined for physical abnormalities.

Early the next day, Whitman called his wife's place of employment, claiming that she was ill and, as a result, would be taking the day off. He made a similar call to explain his mother's absence later that morning. Whitman then loaded a Marine-issue footlocker with various weapons and supplies. His arsenal included numerous rifles, handguns, a shotgun, and seven hundred rounds of ammunition. Whitman then drove to a campus parking lot, placed the trunk on a dolly, and wheeled his arsenal to the clock tower's elevator, which he rode up as far as he could. He lugged the trunk up some stairs and soon reached the tower's observation deck. A University of Texas employee, paid to greet visitors as they entered the area, met Whitman as he emerged from the stairs. He immediately split her skull with the stock of his shotgun and then shot her. He then barricaded the door to the stairwell and fired on a family of tourists who were about to enter the observation deck, killing two and wounding two. Whitman then positioned himself behind the face of the clock and with a rifle began indiscriminately shooting at people below. The time was approximately 11:48 A.M. when the shooting began. Had the sniper arrived a bit earlier, there would have been thousands of students walking through campus, leaving classes that ended at 11:30 A.M. Nevertheless, Whitman continued shooting for more than ninety minutes. Whitman, himself, was under heavy gunfire not only from the 130 or so local, state, and federal law enforcement officers who had converged on the scene but also from an undeterminable number of local citizens. Police eventually broke into the barricaded observation deck and fatally shot Whitman. In all, including his wife and his mother, Whitman killed fifteen people and wounded thirty-one.

Impact The day after the tower murders, a psychiatrist who had seen Whitman on a single prior occasion told a mystified national television audience that the killer had come in seeking help, had been experiencing hostile urges, and had admitted to having thought about shooting people from the campus clock tower. Whitman's brain was later examined, as he had hoped, and a small tumor was found. The tumor may have been the cause of the severe headaches that Whitman complained of at the time; and a panel of experts agreed that the tumor may possibly have had an indirect effect on his actions. The tower murders occurred in the wake of the much-publicized Richard Speck murders. Only weeks before Whitman's rampage, Speck had murdered eight female nursing students in Chicago. The combination of events stunned the nation, and apparently caused another Texan, a fifteen-year-old boy, to kill a local law enforcement officer. The boy said that after hearing reports of the two events, he had fostered an uncontrollable urge to kill that he could not explain.

Additional Information A detailed account of the sequence of events surrounding the Texas tower murders and an in-depth look at Whitman can be found in *Mass Murderers* (1992), by the editors of Time-Life Books.

Trent Marshall

See also Boston Strangler; Career Girl Murders; Crimes and Scandals; Genovese Murder; Percy Murder; Speck Murders.

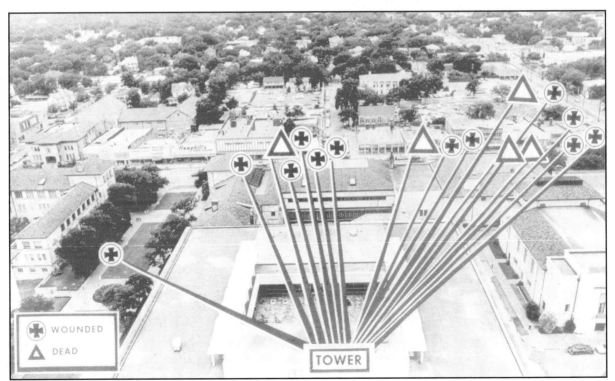

This photograph, taken facing west in the tower at the University of Texas, Austin, shows where some of sniper Charles Whitman's victims fell. More than forty people were killed or wounded during his shooting spree. (AP/Wide World Photos)

■ Thalidomide

A drug primarily known for causing devastating birth defects. Thalidomide became the watchword for the dramatic and appalling outcome of profit-motivated science.

In the late 1950's and early 1960's, thalidomide was prescribed to pregnant women to relieve morning sickness. Because the drug was an effective hypnotic, with low toxicity and an incredibly high fatal dose, use of the drug had spread quickly after 1958 in Europe, Australia, Canada, and Japan. In those countries, thalidomide would eventually be found responsible for the births of thousands of children with malformed or nonexistent limbs.

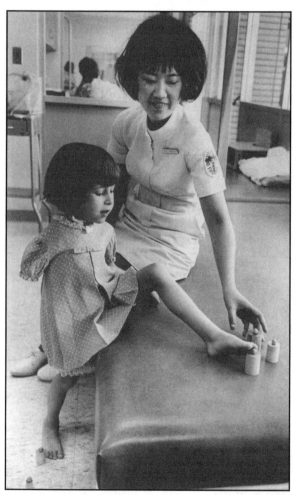

An occupational therapist works with six-year-old Barbie Hanavan, a thalidomide child, who was to have surgery at Rancho Los Amigos Hospital in Downey, California, in 1969. (AP/Wide World Photos)

In September, 1960, Frances Oldham Kelsey, a pharmacologist new at the Food and Drug Administration (FDA, the watchdog agency that approves new drugs for market), suspected that the results of safety trials on thalidomide were spurious and requested further proof of the drug's safety from the William S. Merrell Company, purchaser of the American license for thalidomide. Kelsey's insistence on proof of safety saved the United States from similar disasters, although support for her position was not immediate. Merrell applied political pressure and the FDA was preparing to dismiss Kelsey when the February, 1961, issue of the *British Medical Journal* reported nerve damage in long-term users of thalidomide.

On November 29, 1961, West Germany banned all use of thalidomide after pediatrician Widukind Lenz made public his findings that the drug unequivocally caused congenital abnormalities when pregnant women took it. Although in November, 1961, Merrell withdrew its FDA application for the general use of thalidomide, the company had dispensed free samples (under the name Kevadon) to U.S. doctors. At least three children with birth defects from mothers who were prescribed thalidomide for morning sickness were discovered. Merrell did not withdraw the drug from experimentation until March, 1962. Because of her tenacity and credentials, Kelsey was named to head the new FDA department to regulate drug testing and was praised from the Senate floor for her professional acumen and persistence. On July 7, 1962, Kelsey was presented the Presidential Award for Distinguished Service.

Impact Though thalidomide was never widely used in the United States, controversy surrounding the drug eventually produced several changes in pharmaceutical testing and dispensing. In October, 1962, President John F. Kennedy signed legislation to enforce strict regulations for new drug testing. Additionally, the FDA created a new department to oversee drug testing. Most physicians became more cautious when prescribing drugs for pregnant women, and drug companies were more accountable for their testing and dispensing procedures, as well as their advertising.

Subsequent Events Thalidomide, and later drugs such as DES (diethylstilbestrol), prompted careful study of the side and long-term effects of drugs given to pregnant women. However, thalidomide has become recognized as one of the dangerous but useful drugs. In 1998, the FDA cautiously approved the use of Thalidomide to treat certain symptoms of Hansen's disease (leprosy). In some countries it has been used in combination with the drug cyclosporine to treat immune system reactions in many bone marrow transplant patients.

Additional Information An exhaustive study of thalidomide can be found in *Suffer the Children: The Story of Thalidomide* (1979), an anthology of articles about thalidomide originally published in *The Times* of London.

Sharon Randolph

See also Medicine.

■ Theater

Ignoring artistic and political boundaries, theater in the 1960's explored new relationships with the audience while challenging that audience to find different meaning in the world.

Before World War II throughout Europe and the United States, poets, philosophers, and artists questioned reality, the purpose of life, and the meaning of art. In New York, theater groups explored the same socialism that later netted participants accusations of being communist. Antonin Artaud, writing in the 1930's in France, claimed that theater would allow humans to create the new impulses that were to arise out of the chaos of social repression. His Theater of Cruelty would force audiences to confront that which lay repressed in them. He taught that Western theater, which was language based, needed to look outside its traditions to Asian theater for its style. Germany's theater thrived with innovations of dramatists such as Bertholt Brecht. After World War II, Eastern Europe, owing to the terms of the Warsaw Pact, labored under totalitarian communist governments in thrall to the Soviet Union. Britain was hearing from a new group of playwrights termed "Angry Young Men," typified by John Osborne and Harold Pinter, who displayed the emptiness of British middle-class life. Although there had been Depression-era rebellion on the American stage, theater in the United States became cheerful and upbeat in response to World War II and after the war largely followed the model of Broadway blockbusters that gave rise to road companies performing popular shows in various cities across the nation.

European Influences As the 1960's dawned, theater companies in Eastern Europe used their stages to comment on political repression. From Czechoslovakia and Poland came the voices of Josef Svoboda, Václav Havel, and Jerzy Grotowski, using theater to question the harsh realities of life and forge new relationships between actor and audience. By ignoring large theaters, these writers and producers were able to create an intimacy that forced the audience to confront the playwright's challenges.

German theater, largely state subsidized, flourished with documentary dramas highlighting political or social atrocities, either past or present. Soul searching about the recent war produced plays questioning Germany's inhumane role as well as criticizing policies in other countries. Playwrights such as Rolf Hochhuth (*The Deputy*, 1963) charged that Pope Pius XII had not taken a decisive enough stand against the Nazis, and Heinar Kipphardt (*The Case of J. Robert Oppenheimer*, 1964) joined Peter Weiss, whose *The Persecution and Assassination of Jean-Paul Marat by the Inmates of the Asylum of Charenton Under the Direction of the Marquis de Sade* (1964, commonly known as *Marat/Sade*) suggested that the world was, in fact, an asylum.

The British theater, unlike that of Eastern Europe, changed from inside its venerable institutions. The Royal Shakespeare Company, filled with young talent (actors Paul Scofield, David Warner, and Judy Dench), expanded into a year-round venue, producing a season of Artaud, among other things. Peter Brook, perhaps the best known of the company's directors, sought new drama from Europe and, by 1962, had the company performing a translation of German playwright Weiss's *Marat/Sade*. Even when directing Shakespeare, Brook looked for new ways of translating the text into performance. His *A Midsummer Night's Dream* (1970) included trapezes and dance to envelope the audience in his magical world. He searched for ways to make the play relevant to modern audiences. Both of these plays were imported to the New York stage.

Experiments As the cost of producing plays on Broadway increased, producers sought relatively inexpensive sites for their offerings. They imported successful plays from London or searched for alternate venues in New York. Off-Broadway allowed traditional as well as riskier pieces to gain audiences with less financial outlay on the part of producers, and Joseph Papp's Public Theater took a leading role. Papp had gained a following for his Shakespeare in the Park series of free summer Shakespeare performances. It was the Public Theater that initially produced *Hair*, which later was transferred (with some changes) to Broadway. At the same time, the Ford Foundation began funding theaters in U.S. cities outside New York, and local professional theaters proliferated. These theaters produced both proven drama and works by new playwrights.

Early favorites in the local theaters were Neil Simon and Edward Albee, who led the country in writing new plays, some of which were first produced Off-Broadway, and many of which had absurdist themes. However, those who wanted an alternative to tradition began creating theaters in smaller sites around New York—Off-Off-Broadway.

The La Mama Experimental Theater Club began life in a basement but had its own building by the end of the decade. Café La Mama tried to make the play an integral part of both audience and actor and encouraged new writers and new directors. Tom O'Horgan, one of the leading La Mama directors, featured physical activity along with technical effects in plays he mounted.

The La Mama opened the gates for a flood of experimental theaters that, by the end of the decade, peppered cities across the continent. Chicago hosted several flourishing companies, as did Toronto, Los Angeles, and San Francisco. Although some of these theaters produced plays written by known playwrights, many wrote their own plays or performed improvisational theater.

As the decade spun increasingly out of control politically and socially, these experimental theaters tried to capture their audiences in the message of their productions. The empty rooms that served as theaters provided the open space for physical innovation. In some cases, this meant eliminating the traditional barrier that had existed between actor and audience, and members of the audience interacted with the actors, helping to create the drama. In some plays, the audience sat all over the room, and the performance areas also were scattered. Actors frequently went among the audience, talking to the patrons and encouraging their participation. In the spirit of the times, many of these small groups charged no standard admission price; rather, they would pass the hat at the end of the perform-ance, asking the audience members to give what they could.

Politics on Stage Also reflecting the tenor of the times, African American theater developed a separate voice in the theater. Lorraine Hansberry led the way, gaining mainstream critical acclaim for *A Raisin in the Sun* (1959), her tragedy involving an African American family. LeRoi Jones (later Amiri Baraka), tried to create a movement separate from white theater. By trying to instill racial pride in their audiences, Jones and the other African American playwrights frequently alienated white audiences.

Equally political were the Bread and Puppet Theater and the San Francisco Mime Troupe, which used performance as the vehicle to depict political positions. The Vietnam War provided much fodder for the theatrical groups, and they performed outside or anywhere there was space.

By 1970, theater seemed to be without boundaries: It eliminated political boundaries when Eastern European works surfaced in London and New York; it transcended social boundaries as nudity appeared on the Broadway stage and the counterculture invaded; and it eliminated physical boundaries as theater no longer needed a stage. The new technology enabled mixed-media productions, and the theatrical world seemed united by the influx of Asian and Eastern European writers, actors, and directors to the Western European countries.

Impact Although theater has, by and large, returned to its more traditional roots, the experiments of the 1960's still affect it. Many of the local theater groups thrive, using both traditional proscenium and thrust stages as well as the experimental open performance space, which can be adapted as necessary. Directors and actors use physical activity on stage where before the 1960's, the acting would have been more sedate. Audiences, too, are not surprised if expected to take an active role in the performance.

Additional Information A closer look at theater in the 1960's is provided in Edwin Wilson and Alvin Goldfarb's *Living Theater: A History* (1994), Oscar G. Brockett and Robert R. Findlay's *Century of Innovation* (1991), and Oscar G. Brockett's *History of the Theater* (1995).

Tracy E. Miller

See also Albee, Edward; Counterculture; *Hair*; Hansberry, Lorraine; Simon, Neil.

■ Theater of the Absurd

Antirealistic drama that evinced a sense of human futility. It treated human misery and suffering as grim farce and asked such troubling questions as whether language is a viable tool for authentic human intercourse.

Absurdist drama arose from the spiritual and physical devastation of World War II, prompted by the existentialism of Jean-Paul Sartre and Albert Camus. In Europe, such early proponents as Eugène Ionesco, Samuel Beckett, Jean Genet, and Harold Pinter sought to unshackle themselves from the realistic thesis play that had dominated serious theater from Henrik Ibsen's day forward by creating a new form of drama more suited to a world viewed as being devoid of purpose, legitimate moral authority, or even simple human dignity. By the late 1950's, the movement had begun influencing American experimental drama in Off-Broadway and Off-Off-Broadway theaters.

The effect of the European absurdists on America's avant-garde playwrights of the 1960's is more evident in method than in substance. The charnel house nihilism that beset postwar Europe never really fully undermined or overwhelmed American optimism. As a result, many experimental playwrights of the decade, though flirting with absurdist elements and techniques, never succumbed to the devastating ennui and despair that lay beneath them.

Edward Albee probably came closest to the soul of absurdism in his early plays, starting with *The Zoo Story* (1959), which was first staged with Beckett's *Krapp's Last Tape* at the Provincetown Playhouse in New York. Albee's early targets were American middle-class complacency and materialism, which he attacked in short works such as *The Sandbox* (1960), *The Death of Bessie Smith* (1960), and *The American Dream* (1961). These were followed with some of Albee's major contributions to American theater, including *Who's Afraid of Virginia Woolf?* (1962), *Tiny Alice* (1964), and *A Delicate Balance* (1966), plays that tear at the secrets of dysfunctional families with grim humor and, at times, infantile dialogue.

The techniques and darkly comic focus of the absurdists are also evident in the works of important 1960's playwrights such as Arthur Kopit, Jack Richardson, and Jack Gelber. Although Kopit's *Oh Dad, Poor Dad, Mamma's Hung You in the Closet and I'm Feeling So Sad* (1961) is actually a burlesque of the technique, in it the playwright used grotesque comedy for serious material, which he continued to do throughout the 1960's. Richardson, with a focus on the individual as hapless victim, mined the idea that illusion offered a respite from an obscene reality in plays such as *Gallows Humor* (1961), *Lorenzo* (1963), and *Xmas in Las Vegas* (1965). Gelber employed an improvisational technique, first exploited in *The Connection* (1959) then in such plays as *The Apple* (1961) and *Square in the Eye* (1965).

Throughout the 1960's, thanks to the small Off-Off-Broadway theaters such as Caffe Cino, American Place Theater, Judson Poets' Theater, Theater Genesis, and Café La Mama, dozens of other playwrights found hospitable Greenwich Village venues for experimental pieces, many of which reflected at least an indirect absurdist influence. The Village was the proving ground for a broad spectrum of playwrights, including such diverse figures as Megan Terry, LeRoi Jones (Amiri Baraka), Terrence McNally, Jean-Claude Van Itallie, and Sam Shepard.

Impact By the end of the 1960's, the Cold War and the Vietnam War were having a strong erosive force on American optimism. Many playwrights, novelists, and filmmakers incorporated absurdist elements and techniques in works expressing their deep disillusionment with war and their feelings about the generation gap, sexual problems, and the conservative opposition to the drug culture and rock music. As illustrated in works such as Kurt Vonnegut, Jr.'s novel *Slaughterhouse-Five* (1969), the rock musical *Hair* (1967), and Mike Nichols's film *The Graduate* (1967), in the second half of the decade, absurdist works had found their way from Off-Off-Broadway, underground presses, and art-film coffeehouses into "legitimate" Broadway houses, best-seller lists, and commercial motion picture theaters.

Subsequent Events By the late 1970's and early 1980's, popular culture had co-opted many absurdist techniques, particularly in the situation comedies of Norman Lear, including *Mary Hartman, Mary Hartman* (1976-1978), and the spoofs created by film directors such as Mel Brooks.

Additional Information Martin Esslin's classic study, *The Theatre of the Absurd* (third edition, 1980) remains the most helpful source of information on the absurdist movement and its principal playwrights.

John W. Fiero

See also Albee, Edward; *Hair*; *Indians*; *Slaughterhouse-Five*; Terry, Megan; Theater; *Who's Afraid of Virginia Woolf?*

■ Thompson, Hunter S.

Born July 18, 1937, Louisville, Kentucky

One of the first practitioners of "gonzo journalism." Thompson pioneered a style of reporting in which political and social occurrences are presented in the format of realistic fiction.

A journalist almost from birth, Hunter Stockton Thompson began writing for his neighborhood newspaper at age ten. In 1956, Thompson joined the United States Air Force and penned a weekly sports column for the Elgin base's newspaper, *The Common Courier*. Between 1959 and 1965, he served as a correspondent for *Time*, the *New York Herald Tribune* and the *National Observer*. In 1963, in Greenwich Village, he married Sandra Dawn, with whom he had a son, Juan.

In the 1960's, the radical youth of the United States demanded a mode of journalism that would divorce itself from a media they viewed as pandering to the political hierarchy. They found it in Thompson's work. In 1964, Thompson wrote an article for the *Nation*, "Motorcycle Gangs: Losers and Outsiders," and began to challenge the media's representation of the Hell's Angels motorcycle gang. He rode and lived with the motorcycle gang until 1966 when he completed *Hell's Angels: A Strange and Terrible Saga*, one of the best examples of New Journalism participant-observer reporting.

Impact Thompson became known as a champion of the New Journalism, a form noted for its participant-observer approach and that would later become known as "gonzo journalism."

Subsequent Events In 1972, Thompson published *Fear and Loathing in Las Vegas: A Savage Journey to the Heart of the American Dream*, his best-known work, which was widely read by 1970's remnants of the counterculture.

Additional Information In 1993, Jean Carroll published Hunter's biography, *Hunter: The Strange and Savage Life of Hunter S. Thompson*.

Priscilla June Glanville

See also Capote, Truman; *Electric Kool-Aid Acid Test, The*; Hell's Angels; Literature; Metafiction.

■ Thomson, Virgil

Born November 25, 1896, Kansas City, Missouri
Died September 30, 1989, New York, New York

A noteworthy twentieth century American composer. Thomson's music was simple in structure, harmonically diatonic, and melodically traditional in its evocation of American life.

Early Life Virgil Garnett Thomson, who played the piano at age five, enrolled in Harvard in 1919. From 1925 to 1940, he lived in Paris, where he studied composition with Nadia Boulanger and collaborated with Gertrude Stein to write the opera *Four Saints in Three Acts* (1927). In 1936-1937, he composed the music for two documentaries, *The Plow that Broke the Plains* and *The River* and later won a Pulitzer Prize for the score to *Louisiana Story* (1948). From 1940 to 1954, he was music critic for the *New York Herald Tribune*.

The 1960's Thomson lectured at many American universities, was appointed to the French Legion d'honneur, and published *Music Reviewed* (1967). While taking seven years to compose his third opera, *Lord Byron* (1961-1968), he scored John Houseman's film *Journey to America* in 1964. He also wrote for solo voice (*The Feast of Love*, 1964) and chorus (*The Nativity*, 1966-1967).

Later Life Thomson published *American Music Since 1910* (1971) and continued composing and writing music criticism until his death in 1989.

Impact Although strongly influenced by the French composer Erik Satie, Thomson's compositions are notable for their American flavor, particularly their appropriation of hymn tunes and folk melodies coupled to sturdy, simple harmonies.

Additional Information In 1959, Kathleen Hoover and John Cage wrote Thomson's biography and a critique of his work, *Virgil Thomson: His Life and Music*. Thomson published his memoirs, *Virgil Thomson*, in 1966.

David Allen Duncan

See also Bernstein, Leonard; Music.

■ *Thresher* Disaster

Date April 10, 1963

The worst submarine disaster in the history of the U.S. Navy. The loss of the nation's most modern and powerful nuclear submarine heralded reform in the service.

Origins and History The *Thresher* was the first of a new class of nuclear submarines known as "hunter-killers." The construction of nuclear ballistic missile submarines, particularly by the Soviet Union, required a warship to hunt and destroy these vessels in the event of a threat of an undersea nuclear weapons launch. The *Thresher* was laid down at Portsmouth Naval Shipyard in New Hampshire on May 28, 1958, and launched on July 9, 1960. At a cost of forty-five million dollars, with a length of 278 feet, a beam of 31 feet, and a displacement of 3,732 tons while surfaced, this ship amply fulfilled the requirements. Equipped with a nuclear reactor and the most advanced sonar system available, this ship was capable of diving to a depth of 1,000 feet and was the most powerful submarine in the service.

The Loss of the *Thresher* As the prototype of the hunter-killer submarines, the *Thresher* was subjected to numerous sea trials. The U.S. Navy ordered the *Thresher*, under the command of Lieutenant Commander John W. Harvey, to cruise 220 miles east of Cape Cod, Massachusetts, beyond the continental shelf, where the water was 8,400 feet deep. The *Thresher* was to submerge to 1,000 feet to test its performance at maximum depth. The submarine rescue ship *Skylark*, skippered by Commander Stanley W. Hecker, monitored the submarine's progress and stood ready in case of emergency. The *Thresher* began the dive at 7:49 A.M. on April 10. All seemed well until 9:13 A.M. when the *Skylark* received a message from Harvey that the ship was experiencing a "minor problem" and was attempting to surface. Hecker lost communication for the next four minutes. Finally at 9:17 A.M., the *Skylark* received the *Thresher*'s last message, unintelligible except for the phrase "test depth." The crew of the *Skylark* assumed that the full message was "exceeding test depth." Hecker then heard a dull, muffled thud, a sound that the ship might make if it were breaking up. He reported the *Thresher* missing following an exhaustive search. The Navy confirmed the loss of the submarine at dusk after a rescue vessel spotted an oil slick and debris on the surface. The entire crew of 126 died.

Impact The disaster resulted in a court of inquiry into the loss of the submarine. It concluded that the probable cause was a cracked fitting or a faulty seal in a cooling pipe. The court concluded that flooding disabled the ship's electrical system, which shut down the nuclear reactor. The *Thresher* consequently lost propulsion and sank beneath its test depth. The inquiry also uncovered poor shipbuilding practices in the construction of the *Thresher* that may have contributed to its loss. The result was an improved quality-control system in naval shipyards and the development of new, deep-sea rescue submersibles to respond to future disasters at sea. Many Americans were worried that the nuclear reactor on the submarine might leak and contaminate the ocean, but U.S. Navy officials assured the public that there was no danger of leakage.

Additional Information John Bentley wrote a detailed work on the disaster and the events following it entitled *The "Thresher" Disaster: The Most Tragic Dive in Submarine History* (1965).

Eric W. Osborne

See also *Scorpion* Disappearance; *Trieste* Dive; *Triton* Submarine.

■ Tiny Tim

Born April 12, 1922?, New York, New York
Died November 30, 1996, Minneapolis, Minnesota

A performer most famous for singing "Tiptoe Through the Tulips" in a falsetto voice while playing the ukulele. His novelty act provided moments of comic relief in the 1960's.

Early Life Tiny Tim, born Herbert Khaury, grew up in New York City's Washington Heights. His ambition was to become a singer just like his idols on old 78 recordings. He was influenced by 1930's singer Cliff "Ukele Ike" Edwards and by Nick Lucas, who first sang "Tiptoe Through the Tulips" on the radio in the Depression. Tiny Tim, as Larry Love in the early 1950's, sang old songs and wore his hair long and stringy and his clothes mismatched and clashing. His act attracted a small group of loyal fans in Greenwich Village's lesbian night clubs and small coffeehouses. The name he gained fame with was Tiny Tim, taken from Charles Dickens's *A Christmas Carol*.

Thirty-seven-year old singer Tiny Tim and seventeen-year-old Victoria May Budinger (her mother, Emma Budinger, stands behind them) sign their wedding license in New York. Their wedding was held on The Tonight Show *on December 17, 1969.* (AP/Wide World Photos)

The 1960's By 1968, Tiny Tim was an international sensation. His debut record, *God Bless Tiny Tim* (1968), sold more than two hundred thousand copies, and "Tiptoe Through the Tulips" was a hit around the world. He was a regular on American television. Some thirty-five million viewers saw his wedding to his first wife, Miss Vicky (Victoria May Budinger), on Johnny Carson's *The Tonight Show.* For two golden years, Tiny Tim commanded big money. He was a regular on *Martin and Rowan's Laugh-In* and *The Ed Sullivan Show.* The music industry underwent a transition in the late 1960's. As heavy protest and the art rock movements gained popularity, ukuleles and falsettos lost appeal. Because his records no

longer sold, Tiny Tim was abandoned by the music industry at the close of the decade.

Later Life By mid-1970, his career had begun a relentless skid. Although he never regained his huge popularity, Tiny Tim continued performing. He made a few recordings and took whatever gigs he was offered, from circuses to benefits. He sang in his natural baritone as well as his better-known falsetto voice. By 1992, Tiny Tim was destitute. He bounded back by accepting one-night stands and personal appearances.

In the 1990's, he released a few compact discs and appeared on television with Howard Stern, Conan

O'Brien, and Roseanne, telling stories about old-time singers and songwriters. Tiny Tim said that the key to his success was his originality.

Impact Even in an age of countercultural excesses, Tiny Tim stood out. His nostalgic tiptoe through the past represented love and peace, not war and politics. For a nation caught up in social revolution, political protest, and the Vietnam War, Tiny Tim provided comic relief.

Additional Information In 1976, Harry Stein published a biography of Khaury entitled *Tiny Tim*.

Marian Wynne Haber

See also *Ed Sullivan Show, The*; Music; *Tonight Show, The*.

■ *To Kill a Mockingbird*

Published 1960
Author Harper Lee (1926-   )

A novel that provides one of the most compelling indictments of racial prejudice in the South. Although set in the 1930's, the book reflects the time period in which it was written with its exposure and condemnation of a social code that perpetuates unequal justice.

The Work Narrated by precocious Jean Louise "Scout" Finch, who ages from six to eight in the novel, *To Kill a Mockingbird* depicts the initiation of Scout, her older brother Jem, and their friend Dill into the adult world of prejudice and injustice. Growing up in Maycomb, Alabama, in the 1930's, the three children are fascinated by the story of Arthur "Boo" Radley, who, following some youthful misdeed, has been forced into seclusion by his fanatically religious family and subsequently victimized by the community's prejudice and fear. Although the children view him as a monster to be feared, they simultaneously desire to know and understand him. Meanwhile, their lives are disrupted by the appoint-

Lawyer Atticus Finch (Gregory Peck) defends Tom Robinson (Brock Peters) in the 1962 film adaptation of To Kill a Mockingbird *(1960), a novel about racial injustice in the South.* (Museum of Modern Art/Film Stills Archive)

ment of Scout's father, Atticus Finch, as defense attorney for an African American man, Tom Robinson, accused of raping a white woman, Mayella Ewell. The children's introduction to racial prejudice and injustice is swift and severe. Although Finch clearly proves that Robinson is innocent, the all-white jury finds him guilty, and Robinson is subsequently killed in an escape attempt. Mayella's father, Bob Ewell, revealed in the trial to be a liar, seeks revenge on Atticus Finch and, in a drunken rage, tries to murder Scout and Jem. Boo Radley, who had befriended the children in secret, rescues them. The novel ends with Atticus's fear that society will pay for its injustice but also with the belief that in spite of his losing the case, a small step has been made toward racial justice.

Impact Although frequently referred to as a regional novel, *To Kill a Mockingbird* quickly proved to have universal appeal. A best-seller, it received mixed critical reviews but was awarded the Pulitzer Prize and soon became one of the most widely read contemporary novels in U.S. high schools. Objections to its mild profanity, inclusion of racial epithets, depiction of hypocrisy in religion, and reference to rape led to occasional short-term censorship in public schools and libraries but ultimately only increased the popularity of the novel. Written during one of the most turbulent periods of race relations in the United States, *To Kill a Mockingbird* effectively reflects and indicts the social code of the South, which conflicted with established law in failing to provide justice for all, regardless of race. As race relations were being tested in both the courts and the streets, readers responded emotionally and intellectually to a literary work that advocated equal justice for all humanity.

Related Work A 1962 Academy Award-winning film version of *To Kill a Mockingbird* (screenplay by Horton Foote, directed by Robert Mulligan) capitalized on and expanded the popularity of the novel.

Additional Information For extended interpretation and criticism of the novel, see *"To Kill a Mockingbird": Threatening Boundaries* (1994), by Claudia Johnson, and *Harper Lee's "To Kill a Mockingbird"* (1995), edited by Harold Bloom.

Verbie Lovorn Prevost

See also Film; *Guess Who's Coming to Dinner*; *In the Heat of the Night*; Literature.

◼ **Tommy**

Released 1969
Composer The Who

A rock opera involving psychedelic images, messianism, and media culture. This seminal work remains one of the best examples of its genre.

The Work The rock opera *Tommy* was the creation of a British rock band, the Who, formed by Pete Townshend, Roger Daltrey, John Entwistle, and Keith Moon. The rock opera tells the story of a boy, Tommy, who becomes deaf, dumb, and blind after witnessing the killing of his father. At first, neglected by his family and abused by his wicked uncle and cousin, he is lost in his own trauma. However, through a stroke of fate, he becomes a pinball champion, has his senses restored, and becomes a quasi-messianic cult leader. He comes to understand that he is trapped in a media circus run by his mother and stepfather and, inciting his followers to abandon him, attempts to tread a purer, more inward spiritual path. Famous songs from the work include "Pinball Wizard," "I'm Free," and "We're Not Gonna Take It."

Impact *Tommy* demonstrated that rock music was capable of accommodating the passion and pageantry traditionally associated with opera. One of the most ambitious works of rock music ever, it showed that popular music could address issues of fundamental concern to young people in the 1960's and early 1970's.

Related Works *Jesus Christ Superstar* (1971) was a rock opera with many thematic and musical similarities to *Tommy*. The melody, anger, and passion of the Who's earlier albums, *My Generation* (1965) and *On Tour: Magic Bus* (1968), are crucial background for understanding the rock opera. The Who wrote a second rock opera, *Quadrophenia*, in 1971, and a film version of *Tommy* was released in 1975.

Additional Information In 1996, Richard Barnes—a friend of Townshend for more than twenty years—published *The Who: Maximum R&B*, a book that details his experiences with the Who.

Nicholas Birns

See also Music; Rock Operas.

■ *Tonight Show, The*

Produced 1954-

The longest running and most successful talk show in television. It was hosted in the 1960's by Jack Paar and Johnny Carson.

The Work *The Tonight Show* has been seen nationally since 1954. The program originated in New York and was hosted live by Steve Allen (1954-1957), followed by Jack Paar (1957-1962), who began producing the show on a tape-delayed basis, then Johnny Carson (1962-1992), and Jay Leno beginning in 1992. In 1972, the show moved to California.

Paar was an outspoken, witty, and emotionally explosive host whose guests included John F. Kennedy, Richard M. Nixon, and Robert F. Kennedy. He is remembered for telling a bathroom joke that he considered appropriate but was edited from the program by the National Broadcasting Company (NBC) censors. An enraged Paar walked off the set the following night but returned to the show a month later.

A more casual and spontaneous Johnny Carson took over what became *The Tonight Show Starring Johnny Carson* in 1962. Viewers soon became accustomed to his nightly monologue, comedy skits, studio audience games, informal celebrity interviews, and humorous manner that became characteristic of the show. One of Carson's most memorable shows was the wedding of entertainer Tiny Tim and "Miss Vicki" in 1969. Although numerous rivals such as Joey Bishop, Merv Griffin, and Joan Rivers challenged Carson for late-night programming dominance, he maintained rating superiority for thirty seasons.

Impact *The Tonight Show* has entertained tens of millions of late-night viewers for more than four decades and accounted for approximately one-fifth of NBC network profits through the years.

Subsequent Events Carson's last appearance, May 22, 1992, culminated more than forty-five hundred shows hosted by the comedian. His final show attracted approximately fifty-five million viewers.

Additional Information A book tracing the early history of *The Tonight Show* is Terry Galanoy's *Tonight!* (1972).

Dennis A. Harp

See also Television; Tiny Tim.

■ Travel

One of the fast-changing aspects of life in the United States in the 1960's. On the ground, Americans were traveling more in private automobiles, less in public conveyances, and increasingly taking to the air for longer trips.

Only after the Civil War did more than a tiny proportion of the population travel far from home, but by 1870, even small communities in the East were likely to boast a railroad station, and well-to-do Americans crossed the Atlantic Ocean in steamboats to visit Europe. At the turn of the century, with the automobile just beginning to compete with horses and wagons on local roads, a network of rails crisscrossed the continental United States. By the 1920's, the mass production of inexpensive automobiles offered a serious alternative to travel by railroad. Although brothers Wilbur and Orville Wright demonstrated their first airplane as early as 1903, commercial aviation was not implemented for decades. From 1930 to 1945, the Great Depression and World War II slowed the expansion of travel but increased ridership on public transportation in urban areas. Thereafter, automobile and air travel increased significantly.

Cars Win, Trains Lose An increasing percentage of the eighty million automobiles registered in the United States in 1960 were the recently developed compact models whose production jumped by one million vehicles that year. Most standard-size cars came equipped with automatic transmissions. In the early 1960's, sales of foreign cars (except for Volkswagens) declined, but later in the decade, Japanese-made models became popular. From 1960 to 1969, both U.S. drivers and automobile registrations increased by more than twenty million; the number of drivers passed one hundred million in 1966. One measure of Americans' mobility was the creation of the new cabinet post of the Department of Transportation in 1966.

People continued to ride buses, although patrons in smaller cities and towns faced rising fares and decreasing service. The real losers were the nation's railroads. Although the number of passengers carried declined only slightly during the 1960's, miles traveled by passenger trains and by passengers themselves both dipped sharply, the former figure from just over 200 million miles to half that figure, the latter from 21 million to 12 million miles. Travelers

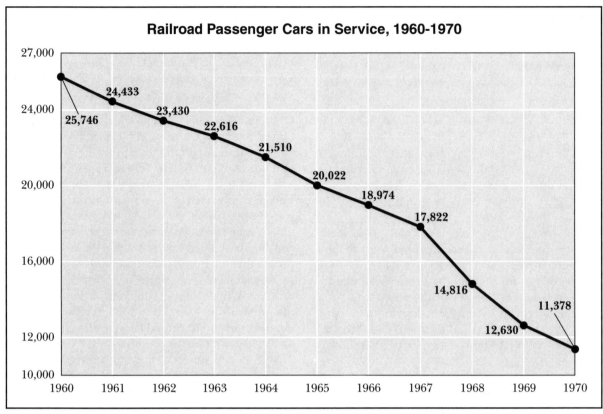

Railroad Passenger Cars in Service, 1960-1970

Source: Kurian, George, *Datapedia of the United States, 1790-2000, America Year by Year.* Lanham, Maryland: Bernam Press, 1994.

were commuting to work in urban centers by train, but the industry increasingly abandoned routes and stations in less populated areas.

Americans Take to the Air The spectacular rise in air travel cut deeply into train ridership. About forty-five million civilian Americans boarded planes in 1960, most of these powered by piston engines, the transition to jet planes having begun only the previous year. By 1969, the annual count of passengers had nearly quadrupled, and jet-propelled aircraft carried virtually all long-distance travelers. The nation's busiest airport, O'Hare in Chicago, in August, 1967, accumulated more than sixty thousand landings and takeoffs—one every forty-four seconds. Business travel by air, while increasing briskly, did not keep pace with the mounting number of passengers bent on visits and vacations. The percentage of business travelers decreased from around 80 percent early in the decade to levels in the 60 percent and even 50 percent range by 1969. As the 1960's proceeded, Americans almost completely abandoned ocean lin-

ers in favor of jet planes that reduced travel time from days to hours.

The facilities of airports in large population centers were strained as never before, and by 1967, the Federal Aviation Agency was proposing limits on operations at five major airports. To expand airports or build new ones adequate to handle the larger jets (a Boeing 747 with a capacity of 490 passengers was projected for 1970) was becoming extremely difficult. In addition, the prospect of even larger supersonic jet planes loomed on the horizon.

Impact Americans now traveled more frequently and for longer distances, but the volume of automobile traffic created many problems. In response to one of them, the interstate highway system, triggered by an act of Congress in 1956, matured during this decade. By 1965 nearly half of the system's planned forty-one thousand miles had been completed. In one sign of things to come, California in 1960 passed the first state legislation to combat exhaust pollution. In 1965, Ralph Nader's best-seller *Unsafe at Any*

Speed provoked the adoption of many new safety standards in the second half of the decade.

People could now ride comfortably in the stable, large jet aircraft and were regularly offered meals, films, and other enticements aloft. However, an unfamiliar danger—skyjacking—arose. In 1968, the number of successful hijackings of U.S. planes reached eighteen, more than in any previous year, and that number rose to a shocking thirty in 1969.

The landscape changed. Highways cut wide swaths, and abandoned railroad stations became a familiar sight. The high seas still saw large ocean liners, but for the most part they no longer served as transportation to desired destinations but as cruise ships on which people enjoyed the boat ride and stops at resorts.

Subsequent Events Most of the transportation trends of the 1960's continued, including the virtual completion and even expansion of the original interstate highway system. Foreign automobiles, especially compacts, continued to command a large share of the market, but smaller subcompacts fell out of favor with motorists, who viewed them as offering too little protection on highways that increasingly were shared with gigantic commercial vehicles. By the 1980's, air-conditioning and many other amenities became standard features of automobiles, and tens of thousands of campers and other types of recreational vehicles appeared on the highways. Passenger travel by railroad staged a limited comeback after 1970 with the consolidation late that year of existing rail lines into the government-subsidized Amtrak.

In the air, two trends did subside. The supersonic Concorde, jointly developed by France and Great Britain, was more costly and had a greater environmental impact than first imagined, so airlines in the United States did not adopt the aircraft. After skyjackings peaked in 1969, new security procedures and devices greatly reduced their incidence.

Additional Information Harry Bolles Lent's *The Automobile, U.S.A.: Its Impact on People's Lives and the Na-*

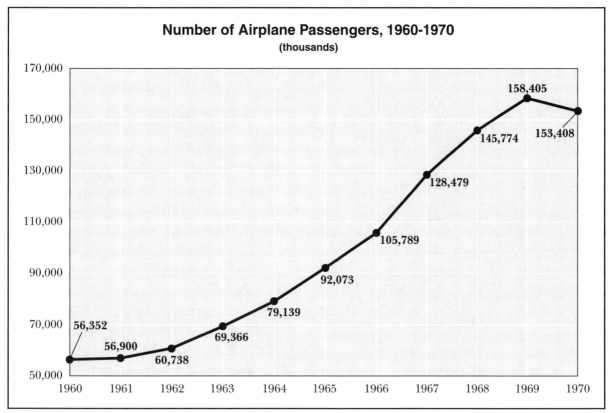

Number of Airplane Passengers, 1960-1970
(thousands)

Source: Kurian, George, *Datapedia of the United States, 1790-2000, America Year by Year.* Lanham, Maryland: Bernam Press, 1994.

tional Economy (1968) is a valuable source of information on travel. A later if somewhat more specialized source is Paul J. Ingrassia's *Comeback: The Fall and Rise of the American Automobile* (1994). For information on other modes of travel see Maury Klein's *Unfinished Business: The Railroad in American Life* (1994) and Joe Christy's *American Aviation: An Illustrated History* (1994).

Robert P. Ellis

See also Automobiles and Auto Manufacturing; Concorde; Interstate Highway System; Japanese Imports; Motor Vehicle Air Pollution Act of 1965; Nader, Ralph; Skyjackings; Supersonic Jets.

■ *Trieste* Dive

Date January 23, 1960

Submersible deep ocean dive. The bathyscaphe Trieste *dove to the deepest point on the ocean floor.*

Origins and History The two-thirds of Earth's surface that is water has remained largely a mystery because of the human inabilities to withstand submarine pressure and to breath underwater. Bathyscaphe research is an attempt to create a vehicle for manned exploration of the ocean depths. In 1931, Auguste Piccard, a Swiss professor, made his first balloon ascension into the stratosphere. He determined that the same physical principles could be used to develop a balloon that would descend to the bottom of the ocean. He developed and tested the FNRS-2 in 1948, successfully diving to forty-six hundred feet. For ten years, he refined and tested his bathyscaphe with the assistance of the Belgian, Swiss, French, and Italian governments. In 1958, the *Trieste* was purchased by the United States and put under the Office of Naval Research. Piccard's son, Jacques Piccard, was retained as the pilot. Increased funding resulted in Project Nekton, a plan to descend in a manned bathyscaphe to the deepest point on earth, the Challenger Deep in the Mariana Trench off the coast of Guam.

Project Nekton For the descent, it was necessary to build a sphere strong enough to withstand sixteen thousand pounds of pressure per square inch and heavy enough to sink. The sphere of the *Trieste* was seven feet, two inches in diameter. It was supported by a float of thin sheetmetal that held thirty-four thousand gallons of gasoline. Gasoline was chosen to fill the float instead of air because it is lighter than water, does not mix with water, and is not highly compressible. The float had slits along the bottom that allowed seawater in as the gasoline compressed or was ejected. A porthole of six-inch-thick plexiglass provided a view of the ocean floor. On Saturday, January 23, 1960, at 8:23 A.M., the *Trieste*, manned by Piccard and Lieutenant Don Walsh of the U.S. Navy, began its descent seven miles down to the floor of the Challenger Deep. For the first 26,000 feet, they traveled at 200 feet per minute through the twilight zone, into the black stillness of the abyssal zone, and finally past the normal sea floor into the trenches of the hadal zone. Iron ballast was released to slow the descent as they approached the bottom. At 1:06 P.M., they landed on the trench floor at 35,800 feet. As the *Trieste* settled, Piccard saw a foot-long flatfish scurry across the ocean floor, answering the question of whether life exists at that level. The water temperature was 36.5 degrees Fahrenheit. At 1:26 P.M., eight hundred pounds of ballast was released, and the bathyscaphe began its three-and-a-half-hour elevator-like ride from night to predawn to daylight.

Impact Submersible research has steadily increased, with vehicles being built worldwide. In addition to their many military applications, submersibles are used for oceanographic exploration, marine archeology, tourist adventures, oil and mineral exploration, sonar and volcanic research, and marine ecology studies.

Additional Information Auguste Piccard's 1956 book *Earth, Sky, and Sea* discusses the construction of the *Trieste*. *Seven Miles Down* (1961), by Jacques Piccard and Robert Dietz, covers Project Nekton.

Myrna Hillburn-Clifford

See also Science and Technology; *Scorpion* Disappearance; *Thresher* Disaster.

■ Trips Festival

Date January 21-23, 1966

The first concert and multimedia celebration open to the public. This music festival became closely identified with the hippie scene in 1960's San Francisco.

Origins and History In the mid-1960's, a group of isolated activities coalesced to produce new entertainment activities for an alternative youth culture. Ken Kesey's acid trips (events at which participants experimented with LSD, or lysergic acid diethylamide) had been attracting attention; Chet Helms had been overseeing jam sessions of Big Brother and the Holding Company in the basement of a Victorian house on Page Street in San Francisco; and Bill Graham was coordinating a series of three concerts to raise money for the Mime Troupe, a group of street actors that he was managing. These elements all came together when, in January, 1966, Stewart Brand, a photographer and friend of some of Kesey's associates, decided to celebrate the changing culture of San Francisco with a large event that would inaugurate a loose, free-form entertainment involving music, light shows, acrobatics, and the active participation of the audience. Graham organized the proceedings and secured the newly constructed Longshoremen's Hall near Fisherman's Wharf, which would accommodate three thousand people.

The Festival For three nights, audiences danced to the Grateful Dead and Big Brother and the Holding Company and witnessed an array of spectacles. Gymnasts bounced about on a "stroboscopic trampoline"; Hell's Angels oversaw a pinball machine; there were readings from the Beatles' works and presentations by poets Allen Ginsberg and Marshall MacLuhan; and members of Kesey's Merry Pranksters, dressed in outlandish costumes, ran about the hall and performed as the Psychedelic Symphony. The activities were chaotic and largely impromptu, but the spirit was jovial, even ecstatic. Tom Wolfe described it as "an LSD experience without LSD."

Impact The event popularized LSD and the idea of taking hallucinogenic "trips" brought on by ingesting LSD and similar drugs. More important, the nature of popular music in San Francisco began to change. Rock bands up to this point did not join the local musicians union because their jam sessions and concerts did not generate much money, and the musicians did not take their commercial potential seriously but instead were motivated by the sheer pleasure of performing. When the musicians union discovered how successful the event had been, rock music became a significant business. Graham's reputation as a rock promoter grew, and his fund-raising concerts at Fillmore auditorium quickly burgeoned into weekly concerts. When *San Francisco Chronicle* columnist Herb Caen mentioned the Trips Festival favorably, rock music suddenly gained a margin of respectability in the established press. Also, the fes-

tival was a precursor of larger rock festivals that would be held in the next few years.

Additional Information Gene Anthony offers a detailed account of the festival and its origins in *The Summer of Love: Haight-Ashbury at Its Highest*; Wolfe places the incident in the context of Kesey's adventures in *The Electric Kool-Aid Acid Test*.

David W. Madden

See also Altamont Music Festival; Ginsberg, Allen; Grateful Dead; LSD; Monterey Pop Festival; Newport Folk Festivals; San Francisco as Cultural Mecca; Summer of Love; Woodstock Festival.

■ *Triton* Submarine

The first U.S. submarine to have two nuclear reactors and a three-level hull. Its underwater around-the-world voyage boosted the nation's prestige during the Cold War.

During World War II, the Soviet Union developed the largest submarine force in the world and sustained this numerical superiority during the early years of the Cold War. The U.S. Navy needed a long-range submarine able to stay submerged for long periods and sustain high speeds underwater. None of the existing methods of propulsion produced adequate speeds until the nuclear-powered USS *Triton* was launched in 1958. The *Triton* was the only submarine ever built with two nuclear reactors. It had a surface displacement of 5,940 tons and submerged displacement of 7,780 tons. The 447-foot long ship cost $100 million. Initially, its primary mission was to explore the feasibility of using nuclear submarines to deploy cruise missiles, to operate as a radar picket for aircraft carrier groups, and to serve as an integral member of the early defense warning system against Soviet interballistic missiles.

In 1959, the USS *Triton* was commissioned with one of the best-known submariners, Captain Edward L. Beach. In 1960, the *Triton* became the first submarine to circumnavigate the globe while submerged. It traveled 30,708 miles in sixty days and twenty-one hours.

Impact This history-making voyage served to enhance the nation's prestige during the Cold War. It also demonstrated the submerged endurance and sustained high-speed capabilities of nuclear submarines. In recognition, the *Triton* was awarded the Presidential Unit Citation, and Captain Beach received the Legion of Merit from President Dwight D. Eisenhower.

Subsequent Events In 1967, the *Triton*, along with fifty other boats, was designated for deactivation because of defense cutbacks. It was decommissioned in 1969 and scrapped in the 1980's.

Additional Information Norman Friedman's *U.S. Submarines Since 1945* is a major reference on nuclear submarines.

John Alan Ross

See also Cold War; *Scorpion* Disappearance; *Thresher* Disaster.

■ Twiggy

Born September 19, 1949, London, England

Twiggy, the seventeen-year-old British model known for her slender, boyish figure, steps off the plane in New York in 1967. Behind her is her partner and manager, Justin de Villeneuve. (AP/Wide World Photos)

A Cockney teenager who became the world's top model. Twiggy's waiflike appearance helped popularize the Mod look in fashion.

Born in a working-class section of London, Leslie "Twiggy" Hornby was the youngest of three daughters born to William and Helen Hornby. As a child, she was often teased about the slender figure that would later become her trademark.

After dropping out of school at the age of fifteen, Twiggy began modeling under the guidance of her boyfriend/manager, Justin de Villeneuve, who nicknamed her Twiggy. Within months, she had been declared "the face of 1966" by a London newspaper and was one of England's most sought-after models. In 1967, she made a much-publicized visit to the United States, where she was photographed by Richard Avedon and profiled by several magazines. Under de Villeneuve's management, she brought out a line of clothing bearing her name and agreed to endorse a wide range of products. By the close of the decade, however, she had given up modeling to pursue an acting career.

In the years following her modeling career, Twiggy worked as an actress, a singer, and a dancer. She appeared in Ken Russell's film *The Boyfriend* in 1971 and on Broadway in 1983 in *My One and Only*.

Impact With her boyish figure and cropped hair, Twiggy personified the youthful, miniskirted look of the 1960's. Her working-class background and Cockney accent also represented the ongoing breakdown of class barriers in England. Her slender figure also ushered in a new level of desirable thinness for models and women.

Additional Information Michael Gross's 1995 book, *Model*, examines the careers of leading fashion models, including Twiggy.

Janet E. Lorenz

See also British Invasion; Fashion and Clothing; Hairstyles; Miniskirts; Mod.

■ Twist

One of the most influential dance fads in popular music history. Ignited by recording artist Chubby Checker, the twist touched off a revolution in dance styles across the world.

Widely regarded as a 1960's innovation, the twist has its roots in a twisting, gyrating dance performed in African American communities in the 1800's. Its modern genealogy can be traced to the 1930's when a gospel recording group, the Sensational Nightingales, created a song inviting dancers to "do the twist." In 1957, they passed the song on to rhythm-and-blues artist Hank Ballard, who modified it to create "The Twist." African American teenagers promptly fashioned a provocative new dance to accompany Ballard's up-and-coming hit record.

By July, 1960, "The Twist" had made its way to *Billboard*'s Hot One Hundred list. Dick Clark, host of the popular television show *American Bandstand*, was certain that this new dance would become a sensation. Concerned that Ballard's risqué reputation would tarnish *American Bandstand*'s wholesome image, Clark asked aspiring young singer Chubby Checker to produce a cover of the song aimed at a more pop-oriented audience. Debuting on Bandstand's sister program, *The Dick Clark Show*, in August, 1960, the amiable and telegenic Checker sang "The Twist" and demonstrated the dance to mainstream America. The song subsequently leapt into the Top Forty and, by September, had soared to number-one status. The dance quickly became a craze, the first since the Charleston of the 1940's, capturing the fancy of white as well as black teenagers. Requiring no basic steps and allowing liberal improvisation, the simple "no touch" dance was likened to extinguishing a cigarette with one's feet while drying one's back with a towel. In 1962, "The Twist" made history when it reached *Billboard*'s number-one spot an unprecedented second time.

The simplicity of the twist soon lured adults into the rage. At a trendy Manhattan nightclub, the Peppermint Lounge, Joey Dee and the Starliters played twist music all night long as the jet set rubbed shoulders with the working class. The twist became the darling of high society, gaining fans among celebrities such as Marilyn Monroe, Elizabeth Taylor, Marlon Brando, and Tennessee Williams as well as high-ranking politicians and European royalty.

In the early 1960's, twenty twist-inspired songs made the Top Forty, including Grammy Award-winning "Let's Twist Again," "Peppermint Twist," and "Twist and Shout." The twist mania spread abroad before the dance became passé in the mid-1960's.

Chubby Checker demonstrates the twist, one of the most popular modern dances, to the press in London in December, 1961. (AP/Wide World Photos)

Impact The twist ushered in an era in which dance partners did not touch each other. It spawned an array of dance crazes including the pony, mashed potato, jerk, watusi, and hully gully and eventually led to the birth of the discotheque (a nightclub featuring dance records instead of live music performances) in the United States. Flaunting the era's rigid moral codes, the uninhibited dance allowed people to ignore social convention and freely express themselves with their bodies. Within a few short years, the twist not only crossed over racial lines but also cut across class and generational lines, making an indelible imprint on the nation.

Additional Information For a comprehensive history of the song and dance, see *The Twist* (1995), by Jim Dawson.

Karen L. Gennari

See also *American Bandstand*; Dances, Popular; Music.

■ *2001: A Space Odyssey*

Released 1968
Director Stanley Kubrick (1928-1999)

A stunning cinematic marvel. This science-fiction film revolutionized special effects in terms of scale and realism and proved highly provocative in its suggestion of extraterrestrial intervention in human evolution.

The Work Originally titled *Journey Beyond the Stars*, *2001: A Space Odyssey* evolved over several years of close collaboration between director Stanley Kubrick and the English science-fiction writer Arthur C. Clarke. The screenplay was based on Clarke's story "The Sentinel," in which astronauts on a roving mission to extract mineral samples from the mountains of the moon discover a pyramidal structure left by space travelers eons before, presumably as a kind of cosmic signpost for those terrestrial creatures who might evolve sufficiently to be able to journey to the moon and find it.

In *2001: A Space Odyssey*, the first such signpost is a black monolith, a slender slab of smooth marble, which proto-human apes discover in their desert habitat. Touching the slab creates the spark of realization that leads to the use of tools and—in an unsettling preview of human history—weapons. The man-ape who touches the slab understands that the bone in his hand is useful not only for obtaining food but also for dominating other apes. In a famous scene, a triumphant man-ape tosses his bone-weapon into the air, and the bone's trajectory dissolves into the orbit of a twenty-first century man-made spacecraft high above the earth, transporting the audience instantaneously and dramatically to the age of human space travel.

The rest of the film follows the astronauts on their quest for the meaning of the mysterious second signpost—an identical black monolith discovered on the moon in the year 2001. The astronauts' attempt to retrace the monolith's signal (the sudden and brief emission of a beam of energy aimed at one of the moons of Jupiter) is endangered by the on-board computer HAL, who runs chillingly amok. The one surviving astronaut, Dave Bowman (Keir Dullea), manages to disconnect HAL and pilots a single pod of the spacecraft toward the presumed destination, a black monolith aligned mysteriously with Jupiter and its moons. What follows is a tour of

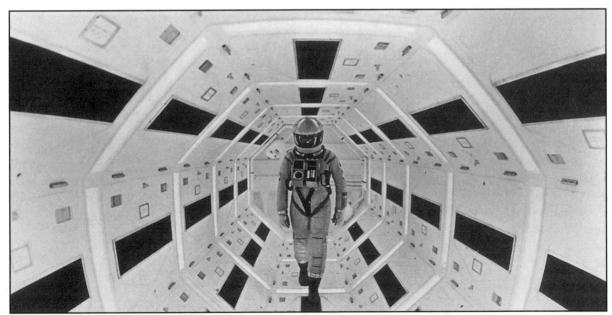

An astronaut walks down a futuristic passageway in the 1968 film 2001: A Space Odyssey. *(Museum of Modern Art/Film Stills Archive)*

the universe—a dynamic visual roller coaster that careens past awesome galactic and planetary systems. At the end of the journey, the astronaut faces not the extraterrestrials who left the signposts that guided him there but himself in the imploded present, past, and future. He is simultaneously young, old, dying, and—in the dramatic final scene—cosmically reborn as a star-child.

Impact With *2001: A Space Odyssey,* the genre of science-fiction films came of age. The film achieved a level of unity of theme and visual effect that had never before been reached. The videotape, or "flat," version of the film is a pale derivative of the visual and aural experience created by Super Panavision projection and its accompanying stereo technology. *2001: A Space Odyssey* is strikingly original for a science-fiction film of the 1960's in that, among other things, it does not feature monstrous aliens or the effects of radiation and lacks romance or sex. Implicit in the film's execution—minimal dialog and strong visuals—is the idea that ultimate reality would be experienced nonverbally, that is, primarily through the sense of sight. The enigmatic ending, the result of many revisions and rather too patly explained in the novel published after release of the film, is perhaps the most superb example of the film's evocative power.

Related Work A film based on Arthur C. Clarke's sequel, *2010,* was released in 1984, with Roy Scheider in the starring role. Critics praised the film's ambition, but as Robert Corliss of *Time* magazine quipped, the film was an "amiable footnote" to Kubrick's classic.

Additional Information The fascinating story of the making of the four-year, $11 million film and its critical and popular reception is told in Jerome Agel's *The Making of Kubrick's 2001,* published in 1970.

Mark R. McCulloh

See also Apollo Space Program; Computers; *Dr. Strangelove*; Film.

■ Tyler, Anne

Born October 25, 1941, Minneapolis, Minnesota

A writer known for her gentle humor and eccentric characters. Tyler holds a distinctive place among contemporary American authors.

Early Life From the age of six, Anne Tyler experienced a southern childhood: first at Celo, a wilderness community in the mountains of North Carolina, where her mother and father, Phyllis and Lloyd Tyler, joined a Quaker community; then in Raleigh, North Carolina, where she attended high school and discovered in the works of Eudora Welty that a writer may create literature from the ordinary things in life. At Duke University, she majored in Russian and studied creative writing with author Reynolds Price. She published short stories in the *Archive,* Duke's literary magazine, and twice received the Anne Flexner Award for creative writing. After earning her bachelor's degree, Tyler pursued graduate studies at Columbia University.

The 1960's Tyler returned to Duke in the early 1960's to work as a Russian bibliographer in the university library. She published short fiction in popular magazines such as *Seventeen, Mademoiselle,* and *McCall's* and in more sophisticated periodicals, including *The New Yorker, Harper's,* and *Southern Review.* She won a *Mademoiselle* magazine award for writing in 1966, and in 1969, one of her stories appeared in *Prize Stories 1969: The O. Henry Awards.*

After marrying Thigh Mohammed Madeiras, an Iranian psychiatrist and writer she met at Duke, in May, 1963, Tyler moved to Montreal, Canada, and spent six months working on her first novel, *If Morning Ever Comes* (1964). In 1965, she gave birth to her first daughter, Tech, and published her second novel, *The Tin Can Tree.* In 1967, a second daughter, Metra, was born, and the family settled in Baltimore, Maryland, which became the setting for most of her subsequent fiction.

By the end of the 1960's, Tyler had attracted both readers and critical attention. The two novels she published during the decade depict confining family situations, characters desiring their separate identities yet needing to be connected, and the circling journey narrative she continued to use in her later works. Calling herself a "southern writer," Tyler skillfully selects details and conveys small town speech to evoke setting and character in these novels. Her mature works continue to be marked by major themes such as movement without change or change without movement and the sense of remoteness from present life that afflicts many of her characters.

Later Life Between 1970 and 1977, Tyler published five novels. In 1977, she received the American Academy and Institute of Arts and Letters Award for Literature. Her 1980 novel, *Morgan's Passing*, brought wide recognition and the Janet Heidinger Kafka Prize. For *Dinner at the Homesick Restaurant* (1982), she won the PEN/Faulkner Award for Fiction. *The Accidental Tourist* (1985) received the National Book Critics Circle Award and *Breathing Lessons* (1988) the Pulitzer Prize. Her 1990's novels, including the best-selling *Ladder of Years* (1996), feature familiar themes.

Impact Tyler, who ignores the latest trends in writing, holds a unique place in contemporary American literature. She concentrates on the values of perception and memory in characters who are seldom evil or good, although occasionally mistaken. She continues to attract readers who enjoy her wit, handling of detail, and compassionate humor.

Additional Information Overviews of Tyler's career and novels appear in *Southern Women Writers: The New Generation* (1990), edited by Tonette Bond Inge, and *Fifty Southern Writers After 1900* (1987), edited by Joseph M. Flora and Robert Bain.

Bes Stark Spangler

See also Literature.

U

■ U-2 Spy Plane Incident

Date May 1, 1960

The downing of a U.S. reconnaissance plane deep inside Soviet territory scuttled a Soviet-U.S. summit and reminded Americans that the smoldering Cold War was a threat to the nation's security.

Origins and History In 1953, the administration of President Dwight D. Eisenhower authorized thirty-five million dollars to build thirteen U-2 high-altitude spy planes. These aircraft were designed to photograph Soviet military installations and other strategic sites. Bases in Pakistan, Norway, Germany, England, and Japan gave the planes an opportunity to penetrate deep into Soviet territory.

President Eisenhower was initially skeptical that any gains from U-2 flights would outweigh the risks; therefore, he required each flight be subject to his personal review and authorization. The first flight in 1956 provoked only private protests from the Soviets, and Eisenhower continued to authorize flights through spring, 1960.

The official cover for the program stated that the U-2s were weather research planes operated and flown by U.S. civilians. By 1960, it was an open secret among many U.S. journalists and Washington, D.C., officials that the U-2s were spy planes. A report to that effect appeared in *Model Airplane News* magazine. Several U-2s crashed outside the United States, including one that crash-landed at a Japanese civilian glider facility. However, to most Americans in 1960, the idea that the United States would violate Soviet air space to conduct espionage seemed far-fetched.

The Incident The stimulus for the May 1, 1960, flight may have been a visit to the Soviet Union by Vice President Richard M. Nixon in the fall of 1959. On a tour of Sverdlosk, Nixon spotted a new type of radar dome that aroused the curiosity of U.S. military experts. Soviet winter weather delayed a U-2 flight over the city until April, 1960. Eisenhower authorized a flight for April 25, then reluctantly approved an extension to May 1 because of weather conditions.

U.S. officials knew a U-2 could be lost over Soviet territory, so the U-2 was equipped with a mechanism to destroy its camera equipment, and the pilots were given a suicide device and exhorted (not ordered) to avoid capture. The Eisenhower administration also had a prepared response if the Soviets announced that a U-2 had crash-landed. When the U-2 spy plane crashed on May 1, Soviet premier Nikita Khrushchev announced the event but withheld the information that the pilot and cameras survived the crash. After the United States released its prepared

In May, 1960, a U-2 spy plane flown by Francis Gary Powers, shown wearing a U.S. Air Force uniform, crash-landed during a reconnaissance mission over the Soviet Union. (Archive Photos)

statement, Khrushchev shocked the United States and the world by announcing that the camera and Francis Gary Powers, pilot of the plane, were being held under guard.

Eisenhower faced a classic Cold War no-win situation. If he denied knowledge of the flights, it would fuel criticism of his hands-off leadership style. If he took responsibility, he would go down in history as the first president to admit publicly that he had authorized a campaign of espionage. Possibly because of his military background, Eisenhower decided to take responsibility for the failed mission.

The response from Khrushchev was a mixture of outrage, ridicule, and threats that culminated in his withdrawal from the Paris summit. Powers went on trial in Moscow in August, 1960, with the Soviets taking great advantage of the propaganda potential as U.S. officials appeared unable to help Powers, although the Central Intelligence Agency secretly paid for two lawyers to travel to Moscow to aid the pilot. Before the end of the month, Powers received a ten-year prison sentence. In February, 1962, Powers was released in an exchange for Soviet agent Rudolf Abel. The U-2 pilot returned to the United States, where he died in a helicopter crash in 1977.

Impact After the crash, many people have speculated about the impact of the U-2 incident on Soviet-American relations. Because of the brief thaw in the Cold War before May, 1960, the incident is often portrayed as a disastrous setback to the reduction of international tension. However, the Soviet record before May, 1960, had been one of volatile zigzags under the erratic leadership of Khrushchev. As for the May, 1960, summit, it is doubtful the Soviets expected much from a meeting with a lame duck president. However, the U-2 incident was rich in public symbolism, reminding the world of the precarious balance of terror in 1960. In the United States, many people realized that President Eisenhower had been caught publicly making a false statement. This fact itself proved scandalous and blemished the president's character and reputation.

Additional Information A very detailed account of the U-2 incident researched using documents released through the Freedom of Information Act is *Mayday: Eisenhower, Khrushchev, and the U-2 Affairs* (1986), by Michael R. Beschloss.

Michael Polley

See also Cold War; Khrushchev's UN Visit.

■ Underground Newspapers

News publications during the 1960's that addressed the concerns of a new youth culture. Readers of these papers were often weary of the Cold War, fed up with conformity and hypocrisy, and disturbed by U.S. involvement in Vietnam.

The *Village Voice* originated in 1955 as a Greenwich Village community newspaper that paid particular attention to the arts and was dedicated to preserving Village amenities. In 1958, Paul Krassner founded *The Realist*, a magazine that mixed fact and opinion with satire and surrealism. These publications were models for the underground newspapers that followed.

The Birth of the Underground Press In 1964, Art Kunkin, an intellectual tool-and-die maker with some experience in radical publishing, began publishing the *Los Angeles Free Press* (the *Freep*). In 1965, the *Berkeley Barb* (in Berkeley, California) was started in conjunction with a mass demonstration that attempted to stop a train carrying troops. The *East Village Other* (*EVO*) also was founded in 1965 in New York as competition to the *Village Voice*, but it soon became more radical. The *San Francisco Oracle* was founded in 1966; its graphics-oriented pages reflected the psychedelic and hippie lifestyle of Haight-Ashbury. Intended as "a graphic expression of man's highest ideals: music, art, ideas, prophesy, poetry, and the expansion of consciousness through drugs," it represented the short-lived flower child era and folded in 1967.

In June, 1966, the Underground Press Syndicate (UPS) was formed, consisting of *EVO*, the *Barb*, the *Freep*, the *Oracle*, *The Paper* (Lansing, Michigan), and *Fifth Estate* (Detroit, Michigan). UPS membership grew first to twenty-five and then to more than a hundred as new papers arose all over: *Kudzu* (Jackson, Mississippi) and *The Great Speckled Bird* (Atlanta, Georgia) in 1968; *Space City!* (Houston, Texas) and *Street Journal* (San Diego, California) in 1969. *Rat*, founded as an alternative to *EVO* in 1968, regarded the flower children as a mostly media-inspired phenomenon. The *Berkeley Tribe* was founded in 1969 by disaffected *Barb* staff members.

By 1970, underground newspapers were established in more than two hundred U.S. cities and towns. In 1970, journalist Robert J. Glessing made a list of more than four hundred and fifty underground newspapers. In addition, anywhere from five hundred to three thousand high school underground papers existed. The number of papers, mostly weeklies, continued to grow until 1971, when there may have been as many as eight hundred.

The Readers and Topics These newpapers were avidly read by students, intellectuals, radicals, hippies, street people, drug users, pacifists, mystics, poets, dropouts, draft resisters, homosexuals, black militants, musicians, and all those who identified with the new youth movement. It was a rich and exciting time: The 1964 Free Speech movement began as a struggle for the right to promote and raise funds for causes, primarily civil rights, and to organize politically on campus but became a broader anticensorship movement. The human potential movement attempted to train people to be sensitive and open, Eastern spiritual philosophies became popular, sexual freedom came to include gay liberation, radicalized women realized the necessity for women's liberation, and the ecology movement emerged. However, increasingly the focus of the underground press was the steadily growing antiwar movement. The underground papers covered these countercultural issues in a personal, poetic, frank, free-form, passionate, and creative style that acknowledged, as *EVO* put it, a world of physical, mental, and spiritual facts. Drugs were considered a catalyst of self-awareness. Rock music was considered revolutionary and self-actualizing.

Although Kunkin intended the *Freep* to be both political and cultural, some tension always existed in the underground papers between the sociocultural and spiritual aspects of the counterculture and politics. Coverage from 1967 to 1969 became more political, but as many editors and writers became disillusioned with political factionalism, turmoil, doctrinaire approaches, and the seeming futility of their efforts, coverage tended to shift back to alternative lifestyles, communal living, ecology, mysticism, rock music, arts, the legalization of marijuana, and just survival.

Sex Sells There was an attempt to create an alternative economy, and rock music, records, concerts, dance clubs, coffeehouses, head shops (shops selling drug paraphernalia), clothing stores, yoga studios, and bookstores advertised in the underground papers, but the most important advertisers in the beginning were record studios and concerts. How-

ever, the record ads began to fall off after 1969. With the fall of obscenity statutes, sex-related advertisements, both display and classified, became increasingly important. They helped to make *EVO* 50 percent advertising in 1969 and to increase circulation. In 1972, a *Los Angeles Free Press* staffer estimated that one-third of the readership came from the sex advertisements. The publisher of a New York paper called *Other Scenes* found that a nude girl on the cover doubled circulation. This created a contradiction in that the counterculture advocated sexual freedom but opposed commercialization of sex, exploitation of women, and anything dehumanizing.

The underground press was subjected to serious repression. Publishers, staff members, and vendors were subject to arrest for vagrancy, obstructing traffic, drug possession, and obscenity, and offices suffered vandalism, arson, and even bombing. The papers were kept under surveillance by the local police, the Federal Bureau of Investigation, and even U.S. Army intelligence.

Impact The underground press became, as journalist Laurence Leamer wrote, "the one broad, unifying institution" of the counterculture. It helped forge a mass radical youth culture and had a lasting impact in promoting feminism, environmentalism, natural foods, alternative health, and what came to be called New Age spirituality.

Subsequent Events In 1972, Kunkin bought his own offset press because of pressure on his printer to stop printing his paper. It proved to be a financial drain, and legal expenses forced him to sell the *Los Angeles Free Press* in 1973. Some staff members had already formed a competing paper called the *LA Staff*, and Kunkin started a new paper called the *LA Weekly News* (*LAWN*), which merged with the *LA Staff*, but by then interest in underground newspapers had passed.

Free lifestyle and entertainment weeklies eventually appeared, maintaining some of the philosophical and political values of the underground papers but targeting the sophisticated consumerism of affluent yuppies.

Additional Information For detailed studies of the underground press, see Robert J. Glessing's *The Underground Press in America* (1970); Abe Peck's *Uncovering the Sixties: The Life and Times of the Underground Press* (1985); Laurence Learner's *The Paper Revolu-*

tionaries: The Rise of the Underground Press (1972); Ken Wachsberger, Abe Peck, and William M. Kunstler's *Voices from the Vietnam Era Underground Press* (1993); and *The Underground Reader* (1971), edited by Mel Howard and Tom Forcade.

William L. Reinshagen

See also Censorship; Communications; Counterculture; Drug Culture; Free Love; Free Speech Movement; Hippies; *MAD* Magazine; Media; Youth Culture and the Generation Gap.

■ Unemployment

An important social and economic problem during the 1960's. Although the overall unemployment rate was low (particularly after 1965), certain population subgroups, including Native Americans living on reservations, residents of urban ghettos, and workers age sixteen to twenty-four, suffered from high rates of joblessness.

Historically, high rates of unemployment have been associated with significant declines or depressions in economic activity. Especially severe depressions occurred in 1837-1843, 1873-1879, and 1929-1933, resulting in widespread destitution of workers and their families.

During the mass unemployment in the 1930's, widely differing estimates of the level of joblessness indicated the need for reliable information on the number of employed and unemployed persons. A small group of economists and other social scientists in the Works Progress Administration developed an objective national survey measure of labor-force behavior based on actual activity during a survey week. Responsibility for the national sample survey (begun in 1940) was ultimately given to the Bureau of the Census, and the survey remains the basis of the national statistics on employment and unemployment.

During the early post-World War II period (1945-1959), unemployment was generally not a serious economic problem. However, the jobless rate for 1958 did reach a postwar high of 6.8 percent, reflecting the impact of the 1957-1958 recession.

The Statistics Unemployment in the 1960's was relatively high at the beginning of the decade but fell steadily from 6.7 percent of the labor force in 1961 to 3.5 percent in 1969. The major factor causing a relatively high jobless rate in 1961 was the 1960-1961 recession. As a result of declining production levels, unemployment rose from 5.5 percent of the work force in 1960 to 6.7 percent in 1961.

The period of prosperity that followed the mild recession of 1960-1961 was the longest in the nation's history, lasting until 1969. Economic activity took a very strong upswing in 1965 and 1966, reflecting the positive impact of a tax cut in 1964 and the nation's growing involvement in the Vietnam War. The rate of economic growth remained very high from 1967 until late 1969 because of increases in both military and civilian expenditures.

Rapid economic expansion was associated with concomitant declines in the rate of unemployment. The rate fell to 5.2 percent in 1964, 3.8 percent in 1966, and 3.5 percent in 1969. From 1966 through 1969, the unemployment rate was below 4 percent (the full employment rate). This was a period of genuine labor shortage.

Unemployment of Women During the 1960's, the relative unemployment rates of women as compared with men steadily increased. In the early part of the decade, the unemployment rate for women was 11 percent greater than the unemployment rate for men; by the end of the decade, that gap had increased to nearly 60 percent.

There are two major explanations for this phenomena. First, the greatest expansion in production and employment occurred in industries such as construction and heavy manufacturing, which employed mostly men. In addition, the rapid expansion of the military draft and in the overall size of the armed forces reduced the unemployment rate among men, especially younger workers, after 1965.

Unemployment of Minorities Although the unemployment rates of both blacks and whites fell during the 1960's, the relative rate of black unemployment remained more than double that of whites during the entire decade. The passage of antidiscrimination legislation as part of the Civil Rights Act of 1964 did not affect the relative black unemployment rate during the remainder of the decade.

Migration is a partial explanation for the unfavorable employment status of the African American worker. During the 1960's, 1.5 million African Americans migrated from the South to the cities of the North and West. The majority of these migrants moved from rural, agricultural occupations to urban, nonagricultural pursuits. Because the unemployment rates in nonagricultural occupations tend

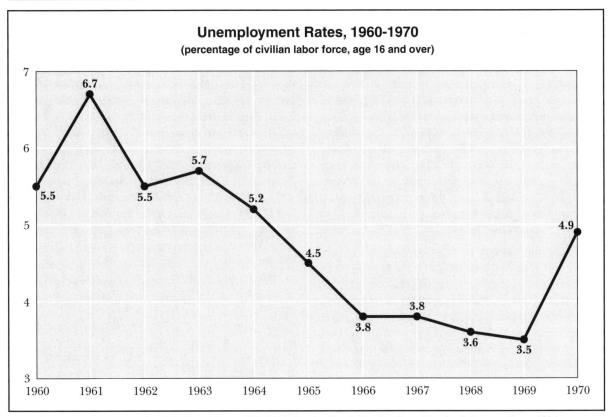

Unemployment Rates, 1960-1970
(percentage of civilian labor force, age 16 and over)

Source: Kurian, George, *Datapedia of the United States, 1790-2000, America Year by Year.* Lanham, Maryland: Bernam Press, 1994.

to be higher than those in agricultural jobs, movement from rural to urban jobs probably caused an increase in the total level of African American unemployment.

Moreover, entry into some occupations in the North usually required union membership. Some of those unions (especially in the construction trades) discriminated against African Americans and effectively froze them out of a number of craft occupations. Conversely, in the South, these craft jobs were filled mostly by nonunion workers, giving African Americans a somewhat better opportunity for employment.

Long-Term Unemployment During a recession, the proportion of unemployed who are jobless fifteen weeks or more (the long-term unemployed) increases. Many of those who lose their jobs during a recession work in industries that are sensitive to business downturns. These industries do not rehire workers until business conditions show a definite improvement. Therefore, many of these people re-

main unemployed for several months, joining the ranks of the long-term unemployed. In addition, it is much more difficult for a laid-off worker to find another job when the total unemployment rate is rising than when the level of unemployment is steady or declining.

Long-term unemployment rose from 24.8 percent of total unemployment in 1960 to 32.5 percent in 1961, reflecting the impact of the 1960-1961 recession. The remainder of the decade was characterized by falling jobless rates caused by the uninterrupted 1961-1969 economic expansion. Long-term unemployment fell to 25.6 percent of total unemployment by 1964 and was only 16.9 percent of the total from 1965-1969.

Impact In response to the relatively high unemployment rates in the early 1960's, federal jobs programs were initiated and expanded. These programs (such as the Manpower Development and Training Act of 1962) provided training for those who became unemployed because of technological change; public employment for youths, the aged, and those on welfare; subsidies to private employers to hire, train, and employ disadvantaged workers; and basic education for adults.

The Economic Opportunity Act of 1964, the core of the War on Poverty, established two major work programs for unemployed youth from low-income families: the Job Corps, which provided vocational education for teenagers, and the Neighborhood Youth Corps, which focused on preventing students from dropping out of high school. Evaluative research indicated that both these programs had a positive effect on the employment status of these disadvantaged young people.

Additional Information Further information on unemployment during the 1960's can be found in *Human Resources and Labor Markets: Labor and Manpower in the American Economy* (1972), by Sar A. Levitan, Garth Mangum, and Ray Marshall; *Education, Unemployment, and Economic Growth* (1974), by Alan Sorkin; and Lowell Galloway's *Manpower Economics* (1971).

Alan L. Sorkin

See also Business and the Economy; Economic Opportunity Act of 1964; Prosperity and Poverty.

■ Unidentified Flying Objects (UFOs)

One of the great mysteries of the space age. More popularly referred to as "flying saucers," unidentified flying objects (UFOs) excited the public imagination with visions of extraterrestrial visitors.

The appearance of "foo fighters" in the skies of Europe during World War II proved to be a precursor of Kenneth Arnold's famous sighting of a formation of "flying saucers" near Mount Rainier in 1947. Thousands of additional sightings of unidentified flying objects (UFOs) were reported over the years to the U.S. Air Force's investigating project, which was called, in turn, "Sign," "Grudge," and, in the 1950's and 1960's, "Blue Book." From the outset, attention focused on the merits of the extraterrestrial explanation, which was attacked by scientists but vocally supported in the 1950's by so-called "contactees" who claimed to have met the occupants of the flying saucers and found them to be quite human and benevolent ambassadors to earth from distant planetary systems. Civilian groups such as the Aerial Phenomena Research Organization (APRO) and the National Investigations Committee on Aerial Phenomenon (NICAP) sprang up to support the extraterrestrial theory and, especially in the case of NICAP, to charge that the Air Force was involved in a cover-up of the truth.

The UFO phenomenon reached a new height in the 1960's with a series of dramatic incidents, one of the most famous of which took place on the night of September 19-20, 1961, when Betty and Barney Hill saw a strange object approach their car while driving on U.S. Route 3 in New Hampshire. Unable to account for two and a half hours of their time and experiencing repeated nightmares, the couple sought the help of a Boston psychiatrist and, while under hypnosis, appeared to relive the trauma of being abducted and examined by space aliens. Although the psychiatrist concluded that their story was a fantasy, it made them nationally famous and lent a threatening air to the UFO phenomenon. Whereas the popular view of UFO occupants in the 1950's had been one of benevolent humans, the Hills were among the first of many "abductees" who would depict UFO occupants as menacing and decidedly nonhuman. The second most famous UFO sighting of the decade, which also involved a close encounter with occupants, took place at Socorro, New Mexico, on April 24, 1964, when police officer Lonnie Zamora reported seeing a car-sized elliptical object on legs sitting in a remote patch of desert with two figures in overalls standing nearby. As Zamora drove closer, the figures got in the object, and it took off, leaving imprints and scorched foliage behind. Zamora's standing as a police officer lent credibility to his story, and the Air Force concluded that his sighting was unexplained. Later, two corroborating witnesses were found who lent additional weight to Zamora's report.

The Scientific Reaction Although most scientists chose to ignore UFOs in the 1960's, a few took them seriously. James McDonald, a physicist at the University of Arizona, became prominent in the mid-1960's as the leading scientific advocate of the extraterrestrial theory of UFO's, a view he held until his tragic death by suicide in 1971. In 1965, Jacques Vallee, a French-born computer scientist, published the first of his many books on UFOs, in which he developed the theory that UFOs are electromagnetic manifestations with the ability to control human perceptions. On the other side of the fence, the principal scientific "debunkers" of UFOs in the 1960's were Donald Menzel, a Harvard University astronomer who attributed UFO sightings to hoaxes and miragelike atmospheric conditions, and Philip Klass, a science reporter whose favorite explanation was a plasmalike electrical phenomena. Other common "scientific" explanations for UFOs were misidentified balloons, birds, aircraft, and celestial bodies.

The UFO phenomenon reached its peak in 1966, when the number of sightings reported to the Air Force exceeded a thousand for the first time since the "flap" years of 1952 and 1957. Of these sightings, however, only thirty-two were officially classified as unexplained. One set of sightings that yielded a controversial explanation took place at Dexter and Hillsdale, Michigan, on March 20-21, 1966. Police officers, a civil defense director, a college dean, and dozens of college students were among the witnesses to UFOs that hovered and maneuvered on two successive nights, attracting such attention that the Air Force sent its scientific consultant, J. Allen Hynek, to

the scene. Hynek gave a famous press conference in which he suggested that the Hillsdale sighting was caused by "swamp gas," an explanation that was widely scoffed at by UFO advocates and that inspired jokes and cartoons in the media.

UFOs Go Hollywood A public opinion survey conducted in 1966 showed that 5 percent of the American public had seen a UFO, a percentage that equated to five million adults. Quick to take advantage of the public fascination with the subject, the American Broadcasting Company (ABC) television network put its series *The Invaders* on the air in the fall of 1966, featuring Roy Thinnes as an architect who discovers the presence of aliens disguised as earthlings. The Air Force, tired of being burdened for more than twenty years with the thankless task of investigating UFO reports, contracted in October, 1966, with the University of Colorado for an eighteen-month scientific study of UFOs. Dubbed the Condon committee after its scientific director, Edward U. Condon, the project spent more than a half-million

This unidentified flying object (UFO) appeared in the sky near Tallahassee, Florida, at sundown on two consecutive days in November, 1965. Sightings such as this made many people believe in extraterrestial visitors. (AP/Wide World Photos)

dollars and investigated dozens of prominent UFO cases before finally concluding, in December, 1968, that there was no evidence for the extraterrestrial origin of UFOs and "no scientific or military justification for further study of UFOs." However, a 1966 memo from the project's coordinator, Robert Low, was leaked to the press and seized upon by UFO advocates as evidence of bad faith on the part of researchers because Low had stated that "The trick would be, I think, to describe the project so that, to the public, it would appear a totally objective study but, to the scientific community, would present the image of a group of nonbelievers trying their best to be objective but having an almost zero expectation of finding a saucer." UFO believers also pointed out that despite the project's conclusions, its final report failed to conclusively explain a fourth of the sightings studied. The Air Force was quick to accept the Condon committee's finding that further scientific study of UFOs was not justified, and Project Blue Book was terminated on December 17, 1969.

Impact From the Bay of the Pigs to Vietnam, the 1960's witnessed a growing credibility gap between Americans and their government. To suspect the government of a cover-up of UFOs was not a stretch to many Americans, and the UFO phenomenon probably incrementally increased the credibility gap, especially when explanations such as swamp gas were offered. Perhaps it was also natural that in a decade of great social upheaval and political strife, many Americans would find either solace or uneasiness in the thought that UFOs represented an alien presence in the skies. Also, even if the vast majority of UFO reports could be explained away, a residual core of unexplained sightings remained, and as one Air Force officer told the press in 1968, "Some reports you can't exactly ignore." This unexplained core was sufficient to give the entire UFO phenomenon a lasting air of mystery and fascination and to make it a permanent fixture in American popular culture.

Subsequent Events UFO sightings continued for decades, and with the Air Force out of the picture, the job of investigating them fell entirely to private groups. Hynek, the erstwhile Air Force consultant, emerged in the 1970's as the leading scientific proponent of the view that UFOs should receive serious study, and he authored a series of books on the subject and founded the influential Center for UFO

Studies. The phenomenon of animal mutilations began to attract widespread attention in the 1970's and was quickly linked to UFOs, just as it had been in 1967 when the death of "Snippy," a horse in Colorado, inspired similar speculation. Abduction cases became a more established part of UFO lore, and by the 1990's, the ultimate UFO case emerged in the form of stories about a supposed UFO crash at Roswell, New Mexico, in 1947, thus bringing things full circle.

Additional Information The final report of the Condon committee was published as *Scientific Study of Unidentified Flying Objects* (1969). The most vigorous critique of the committee's work was *UFOs? Yes! Where the Condon Committee Went Wrong* (1968), by David Saunders and R. Roger Harkins. Vallee's first book on UFOs was *Anatomy of a Phenomenon* (1965), and "debunker" Klass's first book was *UFOs—Identified* (1968). A skeptical overview of the UFO phenomenon may be found in *Watch the Skies! A Chronicle of the Flying Saucer Myth* (1994), by Curtis Peebles.

Larry Haapanen

See also Condon Report.

■ Unions and Collective Bargaining

Organizations and tools working for the labor movement. In the 1960's, union membership remained high, and wages and other benefits improved appreciably; however divisive issues such as the Vietnam War and the Civil Rights movement tore apart the liberal coalition and weakened organized labor.

After struggling for years to attain legitimacy within the United States, organized labor flourished in the mid-twentieth century. In spite of the Taft-Hartley Act, enacted in 1947 over President Harry S Truman's veto, which weakened some of the legal protections afforded labor by the National Labor Relations Act of 1935, trade unions represented a larger percentage of the workforce than at any other time in the past. In 1950, fourteen million Americans belonged to trade unions, representing 31.5 percent of the total nonagricultural workforce. As of 1960, the numbers stood at seventeen million and 31.4 percent respectively. Studies showed that trade union membership paid dividends, as unions negotiated collective bargaining agreements that included

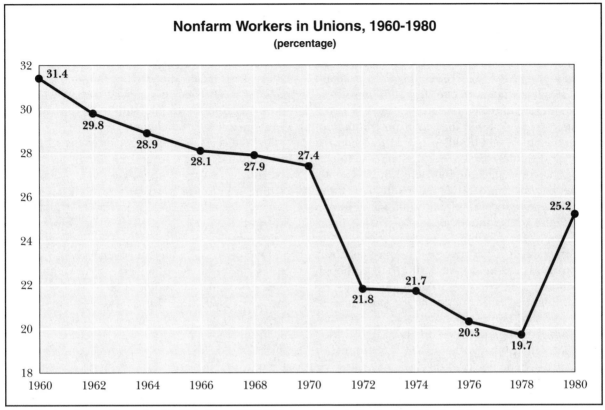

Nonfarm Workers in Unions, 1960-1980
(percentage)

Source: Kurian, George, *Datapedia of the United States, 1790-2000, America Year by Year.* Lanham, Maryland: Bernam Press, 1994.

COLA's—guaranteed cost of living allowance increases—and unprecedented health and retirement benefits. The 1955 merger of the American Federation of Labor (AFL) and the Congress of Industrial Equality (CIO) suggested that even brighter days lay ahead. Only ongoing investigations into union corruption and possible ties to organized crime conducted by the McClellan Committee, whose chief counsel was Robert F. Kennedy, seemed to portend trouble.

Power in Unity The elections of 1960 and 1964 illustrated organized labor's newfound might. The AFL-CIO supported both John F. Kennedy and Lyndon B. Johnson as well as many other liberal Democrats who won House and Senate seats. The fact that the votes of union members served as the key to the liberal coalition's successes guaranteed labor a receptive ear in the White House and the back halls of Congress. George Meany, the AFL-CIO's indefatigable president, enjoyed regular meetings with Presidents Kennedy and Johnson. He and his top aides

appeared as frequent witnesses before House and Senate committees. Other top labor leaders, from Walter Reuther, the United Automobile Workers' (UAW) president, to I. W. Abel, the head of the United Steelworkers of America (USWA), exercised similar influence. Further evidence of labor's political might came with the enactment of a slew of liberal legislation, from the Area Redevelopment Act, which provided federal funds for rebuilding impoverished regions such as the Appalachians, and Medicare, long a priority for organized labor, to the Civil Rights Act of 1964 and federal aid to education, both of which labor supported. By pursuing progrowth policies, the federal government benefited labor by keeping unemployment down and wages up. By ensuring the payment of "prevailing wages" and accepting the emergence of large public employee unions, officials on the national, state, and local level augmented labor's prowess. Only in the South did trade unions fail to win political support.

Prominent labor leaders, hefty wage increases, and occasional big strikes contributed to labor's image as a powerful force in the 1960's. In addition to Meany and Reuther, Teamster boss Jimmy Hoffa was a household name in the United States. Even though Meany gained a reputation as a labor bureaucrat and Hoffa as a crook, they were probably the last labor leaders of the twentieth century to enjoy widespread public recognition and attention. Hoffa, in particular, won the admiration of millions of workers in spite of his alleged links to organized crime and feuds with Robert F. Kennedy. (Hoffa disappeared, presumably murdered, in 1975.) Of course, the influence of Meany, Hoffa, and other labor leaders rested on the ability of trade unions to continue to win improved benefits for their members. Wages for production workers increased 44 percent in the 1960's. Those for unionized construction workers grew at an even faster pace. Although the number of large strikes paled in comparison to the number that occurred during the labor strife of the 1930's and immediate post-World War II years, more workers took part in work stoppages during the 1960's than in any other era in U.S. history. In 1969, nearly six million workers participated in some form of walkout, the peak for the decade and about three million more than had gone on strike fifty years earlier, often considered the most turbulent time in labor history. However, the work stoppages of the 1960's rarely involved troops, nor did they revolve around the basic demand for recognition. On the contrary, with liberal politicians ascendent and corporate profits soaring, both of labor's traditional foes, government and big business, accepted big labor as an established part of the American scene.

Labor and the Left Ironically, labor was criticized for its success. Whereas progressives historically had aligned themselves with the cause of labor, many new leftists of the 1960's lambasted the labor movement for becoming too conservative, too mainstream, and too much a part of the establishment. New leftists were particularly critical of organized labor's support for Johnson's policies in Vietnam and the Cold War in general. Meany and other leaders of the old AFL unions clashed with the New Left over Vietnam, both verbally and at times in the streets. Even though the AFL-CIO lobbied for the passage of civil rights reforms, in the latter half of the decade, civil rights activists increasingly censured the labor movement for protecting the privileges of skilled, predomi-

nantly white workers at the expense of less skilled and more poorly paid minority workers. Black power advocates also clashed with labor over the paucity of African American labor leaders. The cultural views of labor—leaders and the rank and file—exacerbated antagonisms between it and the New Left, which was made up largely of youths, many if not most of whom were sympathetic to the counterculture.

A 1970 anti-antiwar rampage of construction workers in New York City, in which "hard hats" screamed, "Get the hippies, get the traitors," while beating up antiwar protesters, symbolized the rift that developed between the New Left and labor during the latter part of the 1960's. However, this action exaggerated or hid important countervailing developments. Although many workers found the antics of the antiwar movement appalling, polls showed that like the public at large, they sought an end to the war. By 1970, a number of prominent labor leaders, most notably Reuther, had split with Meany over his hawkish views. New leftists and trade unionists also found common ground around the struggle of migratory farmworkers, led by César Chávez, to establish a union. Together they helped stage one of the most successful consumer boycotts in U.S. history. At the same time, the restlessness of many young workers, manifested by a number of wildcat strikes and perhaps by household feuds over popular culture and standard mores, compelled some within the labor movement to reach out to segments of the New Left. In Oakland, California, for example, Ronald Dellums won a seat to the U.S. Congress and was repeatedly reelected by forging a coalition of student leftists, African American radicals, and trade unionists.

Impact Many argue that trade unions missed a golden opportunity in the 1960's. Rather than pursuing an aggressive agenda of organizing the unorganized and promoting workplace democracy, labor rested on its laurels and focused too much attention and energy on winning the war in Vietnam. Rather than embracing the women's liberation movement, organized labor initially supported the status quo. As a result, it lost an opportunity to channel the energy of young feminists into the work of organizing millions of unorganized female workers, which in turn would have greatly enhanced labor's power. Similarly, by so strongly supporting the war, labor alienated many new leftists who might have played a crucial role in building support for trade unions among skilled white-collar workers, another highly unorganized sector of the economy. By the early 1980's, so the argument goes, it was too late to mobilize or tap these forces. Instead, beset by a stagnating and changing economy and conservative backlash, labor went into decline. The number and percent of workers who belonged to trade unions decreased precipitously, dipping to pre-New Deal levels by the mid-1990's. Ironically, conservatives scapegoated organized labor for the nation's troubles, accusing it of being a special-interest group and favoring unproductive workplace rules. Prior claims, made by the New Left, that labor was part of the establishment, lent an air of familiarity and legitimacy to these conservative accusations.

Additional Information　Two good overviews of labor during the twentieth century are Robert H. Zeiger's *American Workers, American Unions, 1920-1985* (1986) and James Green's *The World of the Worker: Labor in Twentieth Century America* (1980). For works that focus more on the 1960's, see Peter B. Levy's *The New Left and Labor in the 1960's* (1994) and Kim Moody's *An Injury to All: The Decline of American Unionism* (1988). An excellent contemporary study is Andrew Levision's *The Working-Class Majority* (1974).

Peter B. Levy

See also　Business and the Economy; Chávez, César; Liberalism in Politics; Prosperity and Poverty; Teachers Strikes.

■ United Mexican American Students (UMAS)

A late 1960's organization of Chicano students located primarily in California and Texas. It brought together activist Chicano students who aimed to strengthen the cultural identity of students to combat discrimination.

Several student groups formed during the mid-1960's in support of such major Chicano organizations as La Raza Unida and the United Farm Workers. These groups began to coalesce into a formal organization in 1966 and met in 1967 at Loyola Marymount University in Los Angeles to launch the United Mexican American Students (UMAS).

The group worked to improve the status and rights of Chicano students at the high school and university level. UMAS organized several school walkouts and protests in the late 1960's and early 1970's to attack racism and second-class citizenship, including a 1968 East Los Angeles school strike in which high school students boycotted school to demand better education and more cultural sensitivity on the part of their teachers. UMAS also worked with schools in the Mexican American community, tutoring students and teaching them cultural pride.

Following a 1969 conference in Denver, UMAS joined with other student organizations to develop El Plan de Santa Barbara, which focused on redirecting university attention to the needs of Chicano students and to organizing the community politically. The new organization became El Movimiento Estudiantil Chicano de Aztla (MEChA). It marked a major development in the political consciousness of student activists in that it emphasized militancy. The student movement began to view colleges as strategic agencies for political change. Critical to this strategy was the development of Chicano studies programs and the recruitment of Chicano faculty and administrators. Additionally, student activists also began to participate much more widely in a variety of leftist activities such as those of La Raza Unida. Despite some early successes, UMAS and its successors declined precipitously by 1971. Internal squabbles, the graduation of early activists, and the creation of a number of similar organizations undercut UMAS support.

Impact　UMAS was successful in developing a student voice within the Chicano movement. It effectively called attention to the plight of Chicano students and played a key role in the development of Chicano studies departments within colleges and universities. It served as a catalyst in developing intellectual leadership within the movement and helped to radicalize a generation of students. UMAS also provided important support to the United Farm Workers and La Raza Unida.

Subsequent Events　By 1973, internal struggles and other factors effectively dissipated UMAS. The student movement revitalized somewhat in 1975 to protest continuing educational problems and to provide wider support to César Chávez and the farmworkers. By 1977, the student movement was no longer viable.

Additional Information　Two works provide the complete history and analyze the impact of UMAS: *Mexi-*

can Students por La Raza (1977), by Juan Gómez-Quiñones, and Carlos Muñoz, Jr.'s *Youth, Identity, Power: The Chicano Movement* (1989).

R. David Myers

See also Brown Berets; Chávez, César; Chicano Movement; Grape Workers' Strike; Young Lords.

■ Updike, John

Born March 18, 1932, Shillington, Pennsylvania

An author who captured the American middle class in its private moments. His tales of the changing sexual mores of suburbia and the emptiness of American society resonated with many readers.

Early Life During his college years, John Updike expected to pursue an art career. A graphic artist, he was especially adept at cartoons. After earning a bachelor's degree at Harvard University in 1952, Updike studied on a Knox Fellowship at the Ruskin Center of Drawing and Fine Arts in Oxford, England, 1954-1955. He and his wife, Mary Entwistle Pennington, whom he married on June 26, 1953, had four children before their divorce. The young Updike began earning his reputation with short stories in the *New Yorker*, and in 1959, he published his first novel, *The Poorhouse Fair*.

The 1960's A groundbreaking and especially productive period for an already prolific writer, the 1960's saw Updike publish ten volumes of fiction as well as numerous stories in magazines, one of which won him the O. Henry Prize in short fiction for 1967-1968. Of particular interest is his 1960 novel *Rabbit, Run,* the first of a four-volume series (*Rabbit Redux*, 1971; *Rabbit Is Rich*, 1981; and *Rabbit at Rest*, 1990) that would span some forty years of Updike's career and become a landmark of contemporary American fiction. The story of Harry "Rabbit" Angstrom, a faded small-town basketball star who feels out of place in domestic life and the workaday world, *Rabbit, Run* embraces the main themes that would occupy the author's attention in his 1968 *Couples* and for decades to come: the complex relationships between lovers, the spiritual shabbiness of modern life, and our attempts to create religious meaning out of secular events.

Updike's 1963 novel, *The Centaur*, earned the National Book Award and the writer's election to the National Institute of Arts and Letters.

Later Life In 1974, Updike's first marriage ended, and in 1977, he married Martha Bernhard. He continued to write novels and short fiction into the 1990's. Some of his memorable works with themes similar to those in the Rabbit series include *Marry Me: A Romance* (1976), *Museums and Women and Other Stories* (1972), *Problems and Other Stories* (1979), and *Trust Me* (1987).

Additional Information Biographical and critical information on Updike are provided by Updike's *Self-Consciousness: Memoirs* (1989), Julie Newman's *John Updike* (1988), and Robert Detweiler's *John Updike* (1984).

Carroll Dale Short

See also Cheever, John; Literature; Tyler, Anne.

■ Urban Renewal

Projects designed to eliminate blighted urban areas. These programs had the goal of providing decent, affordable housing for every family in the United States.

The United States government first initiated urban renewal programs during the 1930's. In these early programs, the government attempted to eliminate slums by purchasing buildings in blighted areas, razing them, and replacing the structures, often with towering concrete housing projects such as those in Chicago and New York. A legal challenge to this practice in 1935 resulted in the federal government's granting funds to local authorities for urban renewal projects. The next major effort at urban renewal came with the passage of the Housing Act of 1949. The act dealt with the elimination of substandard and otherwise inadequate housing through the clearance of slums and blighted areas and set forth the goal of a decent home and a suitable living environment for every family in the United States. Local governments could acquire properties in deteriorated residential areas, clear them, and redevelop the area with the help of federal funds. The act required that any development be in line with a community plan.

The Housing Act of 1954 changed the focus of the governmental programs. In addition to slum clearance, it emphasized conserving housing that was still serviceable and preventing the development of new slums. Each project that was funded under the 1954 act had to be part of a plan to improve the community. As a prerequisite to receiving government funds for projects, a city had to have a workable program to combat slums and blight. This program consisted of a detailed analysis of the housing and other characteristics of each neighborhood and an action plan to prevent or eliminate blight within each community. The analysis examined housing conditions with emphasis on the location and extent of blight and the adequacy of public and private community facilities and services. The plan to eliminate or prevent blight involved comprehensive community land-use and development plans, financing, citizen participation, and a relocation program for displaced families. The workable program requirement was based on the principle that certain forms of federal assistance could bring permanent benefit only to those communities that were making a real effort to help themselves.

By 1960, the number of roads and highways had greatly increased, and many higher-income, white families had moved to the suburbs. In addition, in the construction of many of the highways and interstates, some urban neighborhoods had been divided or destroyed. The changing nature of the inner city and the problems that it brought lent urgency to the need for urban renewal. By 1960, more than eight hundred urban renewal projects had been started in about four hundred U.S. communities. The projects ranged from small efforts involving less than a hundred families to very large programs affecting more than ten thousand families. The late 1950's and early 1960's was the first time in U.S. history that planned urban renewal had gained such prominence.

Although the concept of urban renewal first concentrated on the physical aspects, it gradually came to be viewed as a means of achieving a better life within a community. However, in a survey conducted during the decade, Americans still cited primarily physical improvements as goals of urban renewal. Ranked in terms of priority, the goals they mentioned were clearing slums, renewing blighted areas, upgrading substandard houses, remodeling downtown areas, building new public structures, and solving traffic problems. In 1965, President Lyndon B. Johnson signed legislation that created the Department of Housing and Urban Development (HUD) to coordinate the many urban renewal and housing plans that were being developed.

In 1966, Congress passed the Demonstration Cities and Metropolitan Development Act, known as the Model Cities Act. This act supplied up to 80 percent of the costs of redevelopment projects related to housing, welfare, or transport. It was specifically designed to address the social and economic aspects of urban renewal in addition to the physical concerns. The Model Cities program required the participation of the city's residents and comprehensive planning that examined the program's effect on the entire city. To receive support, a program had to demonstrate how it would improve the social and physical problems of the city.

Impact The stated purpose of urban renewal is to improve housing by the elimination of substandard and other inadequate housing. This objective has been pursued using a wide variety of means. Early programs concentrated on the elimination of blighted areas and the construction of public housing. These programs, however, were often criticized because they displaced the often low- or lower-income people who lived in the blighted areas that were razed. Critics also said the programs tended to favor the creation of housing for the middle class rather than housing that would serve the inner-city residents' needs. Later programs tried to address the inner-city residents' social needs in addition to the physical redevelopment of urban areas; however, these projects still tended to result in displacement and gentrification. The Model Cities Act, although generally regarded as not having any major lasting effect on urban renewal problems, did make participation by residents and concerned citizens a part of many future government projects.

Subsequent Events In 1974, the Housing and Community Development Act combined a number of community development and housing programs. One of the act's provisions, the Community Development Block Grant program, funded by the federal government, delegated responsibility to the state and local governments for creating and administrating programs involving housing and redevelopment. Although President Jimmy Carter revived urban recovery projects in the late 1970's, the federal government largely withdrew from funding urban renewal projects during the 1980's, leaving the task of funding as well as planning to state and city governments.

Additional Information Jane Jacobs's *The Death and Life of Great American Cities* (1961) provides a discussion of the causes of urban decline as well as information on what makes a city livable. John B. Will-mann's *The Department of Housing and Urban Development* (1967) presents a history of this department and its early activities.

See also Great Society Programs; Housing Laws, Federal; Johnson, Lyndon B.; Prosperity and Poverty.

V

■ Vatican II

Date October 11, 1962-December 8, 1965

The twenty-first ecumenical council of the Roman Catholic Church. Seeking to bring the Church up to date, it modernized worship, opened dialogue with other religions, and engaged the church in society.

Origins and History The newly elected Pope John XXIII called for an ecumenical council to spiritually renew the church and open the way for its unification with all Christians. He said that developments in science and technology, the effects of economic prosperity, and the growing secularization of society had created a spiritual crisis. The solution lay not in renewed condemnation of errors but in applying "the medicine of mercy." His conciliatory attitude set the tone for the conference.

The Council More than twenty-five hundred people attended the opening session of the Second Vatican Council on October 11, 1962. By the council's end, twenty-eight non-Roman Catholic churches had participated, though without speaking or voting rights. The council adopted sixteen documents during its annual autumn sessions, finishing on December 8, 1965, under the leadership of Pope Paul VI.

The council acknowledged the first Vatican council's affirmation of papal infallibility but added that infallibility also resides in the body of bishops when

Mass is celebrated at the opening ceremonies of the Second Vatican Council on October 11, 1962. (Library of Congress)

they exercise doctrinal authority along with the pope. It thus affirmed collegiality, the principle that the bishops as a group continue the authority of the apostles. In addition, although the traditional emphasis had been on the role of the clergy, the council stated that laypeople are called to holiness and missionary service through their various vocations. For the first time, laypeople were allowed to participate in the Mass and encouraged to read the Bible—functions traditionally reserved for clergy. The council, instead of viewing the church as a hierarchy, saw it as a community of the people of God, with each person having an appropriate, not subordinate, role.

Perhaps the most visible change was the introduction of parish worship in local languages instead of Latin. New levels of participation and respect were granted to non-Western cultures. Church unity was seen as sustainable through a degree of diversity not only by centrally imposed uniformity.

Before the Second Vatican Council, the principle influence on the church was the Council of Trent (1545-1563), held in an era of reaction to the Protestant Reformation. Vatican II abandoned the earlier defensive posture and adopted a conciliatory attitude that sought to reunite the Church with what it had come to consider separated brethren rather than heretics and schismatics. As part of this process, the long-standing opposition to interfaith dialog was reversed, and other Christian groups were seen as possessing elements of the one true church. Religious liberty was also affirmed. However, although the council acknowledged some truth and goodness in other religions, it called upon Catholics to proclaim Christ as the lord and savior of all humanity.

As it had since the late nineteenth century, the Church joined its proclamation to global social concerns by addressing, among other things, governmental roles, economics, and labor issues. The Second Vatican Council emphasized the dignity of humans as bearers of the image of God, proclaiming the need for freedom, affirming equality as the foundation for social justice, and avowing that people and societies are interdependent.

Impact The council widened a rift in the church between traditionalists, who wanted it to merely clarify traditional teaching, and progressives, who wanted nothing less than a complete restructuring of the Church. Critics of the council saw in its docu-

ments inconsistencies resulting from the clash between the opposing sides. In the years following the conference, traditionalists feared the Church was drifting from its cherished heritage, and progressives called on the Church to remain true to the reforms it began. Supporters of the council hailed it as opening a new era of a truly global church.

Additional Information R. F. Trisco's article, "Vatican Council II," in *New Catholic Encyclopedia* (1967) gives an overview, and *Documents of Vatican II* (1975), edited by Austin P. Flannery, provides the council's texts.

Brian Morley

See also Religion and Spirituality.

■ VCRs

A machine that records images and sound on magnetic tape for later playback. Videocassette recorders (VCRs) eventually became popular devices for home entertainment and led to the development of videodiscs and camcorders.

The first videotape recorder was demonstrated in 1951. In 1956, the Ampex Corporation of California sold the first successful video recorder, a reel-to-reel machine, and by 1959, the company was manufacturing color video recorders.

During the 1960's, many companies engaged in research to produce smaller, cheaper VCRs. This research assisted the development of optical recording on videodiscs, first demonstrated by the Telefunken Corporation in 1966. In 1969, the Sony Corporation of Japan marketed an open-reel VCR device, featuring a one-half-inch tape in a cassette, which led to the universal-automatic (U-matic) format, three-quarter-inch tape. Although intended for home use, the price of this VCR essentially limited it to commercial purposes such as training tapes for businesses.

Impact VCRs have had a profound effect on the way people seek entertainment and enhance their education. As VCR technology advanced and prices fell in the 1970's and 1980's, use of the machines rapidly spread. VCRs ultimately came to be used for playing back prerecorded motion pictures and educational and self-help videos as well as for recording television broadcasts to be viewed at a more convenient time. They allow people to watch one program while taping another on a different channel, to watch favorite programs or films over and over, and to fast forward through commercials or segments they dislike or replay scenes numerous times. VCRs enable people to enjoy films or study education videos at their convenience.

Subsequent Events In the 1970's, VCRs became essential equipment in the television industry, and the first commercially successful home VCR appeared in 1975. Portable VCRs that operated on batteries were combined with color video cameras in the late 1970's to produce camera-recorders (camcorders) for making home videos that could be played back instantly. Telecasts, educational materials, and self-help videos were recorded on videotape.

Additional Information The history, technology, and applications of VCRs can be found in *Multimedia: Technology and Applications* (1991), edited by John A. Waterworth.

Alvin K. Benson

See also Communications; Lasers; Media; Science and Technology.

■ Vietnam War

Date October, 1957-April 30, 1975

The United States' greatest overseas conflict of the 1960's and 1970's. The Vietnam War is the longest war in which the nation has been involved and one of the most domestically wrenching, costly, and widely reported and analyzed events in U.S. history.

Origins and History After the French were defeated in 1954 in their attempt to retain imperial control of Vietnam, the country was divided into the independent nations of North (communist) and South (anticommunist) Vietnam. Based on President Harry S Truman's Cold War policy (the United States must help any nation threatened by communists) and out of a fear of the validity of the domino theory (if one Southeast Asian nation fell to the communists, the others would also fall, one after the other), the next three U.S. presidents—Dwight D. Eisenhower, John F. Kennedy, and Lyndon B. Johnson sent increasing amounts of money, men, and

Helicopters like these were used to rescue downed fliers and pick up injured men, among other tasks. (London Daily Express/Archive Photos)

Wounded paratroopers in the heavy jungle twenty-five miles northeast of Saigon lie on litters as they wait for helicopters to lift them to treatment centers in October, 1965. (AP/Wide World Photos)

materials to South Vietnam, resulting in a concomitant escalation of the war.

Early Chronology Vietnam seems always to have been the object of attempted domination by foreigners—first the Chinese, then the French, followed by the Japanese, and again the French, who were finally thwarted in their bid to reassert imperial authority by Ho Chi Minh, a Vietnamese patriot, communist, and leader of the National Liberation. In May, 1954, the Vietminh (members of Ho's Revolutionary League for Vietnamese Independence) annihilated French forces at Dien Bien Phu, and in July, the two sides signed peace agreements, known as the Geneva Accords, at Geneva, Switzerland. Vietnam was temporarily divided into North Vietnam and South Vietnam at the Seventeenth Parallel, with national elections set for 1956 to reunify the country. Ho Chi Minh established a communist government in the North and Ngo Dinh Diem became president of South Vietnam in 1955. Diem, who had done little to relieve the hardships of peasant life in rural South Vietnam and therefore had become unpopular, feared a communist sweep of the planned nationwide elections and therefore refused to allow them to take place. However, he was able to persuade President Eisenhower to continue to funnel aid directly to Saigon (capital of South Vietnam) and to train the South Vietnamese army. As early as 1954, General J. Lawton Collins, Eisenhower's special envoy, had arrived in Saigon with the promise of one hundred million dollars in aid to affirm U.S. support for Diem.

In October, 1957, members of the Vietminh who had stayed in South Vietnam rebelled against Diem's rule in accord with the decision reached in Hanoi (capital of North Vietnam) that thirty-seven armed companies be organized in the Mekong Delta region in the South. In 1959, North Vietnam began infiltrating regular troops and sending weapons into the South along a supply route known as the Ho Chi Minh Trail. The communist insurgents began shifting from hit-and-run, small-scale operations to full-scale military action against government-controlled villages in the South. Two U.S. military advisers, Major Dale Buis and Sergeant Chester Ovnand, became the first Americans killed in what would be called the Vietnam era.

In 1960, communist leaders in Hanoi formed the National Liberation Front for South Vietnam. Diem dubbed them Viet Cong, meaning communist Vietnamese. By 1961, with discontent over the Diem regime mounting and more than ten thousand Viet Cong soldiers attacking South Vietnamese army bases, President Kennedy began to expand military aid to South Vietnam. Between 1961 and 1963, he increased the number of U.S. military advisers and troops from nine hundred to more than sixteen thousand. The American Military Assistance Command, the so-called "MAC-V," was created in South Vietnam in 1962.

Against a backdrop of mounting turmoil and intensifying protests against Diem in 1963, Kennedy supported a group of South Vietnamese generals who opposed Diem's policies. On November 1, 1963, the generals staged a coup, but against Kennedy's wishes, they also assassinated Diem and his brother, Ngo Dinh Nhu, the next day. Tragically, Kennedy survived the brothers by only twenty days, being assassinated on November 22 in Dallas.

Policy Changes: Tonkin to Tet Escalation of the war effort characterized the years from 1964 through 1968, with U.S. troop strength reaching its apex of 543,000 in early 1969. On August 4, 1964, President Johnson announced that the U.S. destroyer *Maddox* had been attacked by North Vietnamese patrol boats in the Gulf of Tonkin on August 2 and that a second incident had followed. The president ordered immediate air strikes against the North. Although some people doubted the veracity of at least the second reported attack, the U.S. Congress responded by passing the Tonkin Gulf Resolution on August 7, giving the president extraordinary powers to act in Southeast Asia. Though war was not officially declared, Johnson used the resolution as the legal basis for escalating the conflict.

The Viet Cong began staging attacks against U.S. military installations at Pleiku on February 7, 1965. Within seventeen days, Operation Rolling Thunder—sustained U.S. bombing of North Vietnam—was initiated. In March, 1965, in order to defend Danang airfield, Johnson sent the U.S. Marines to Vietnam, making them the first official ground combat forces to enter the war.

Johnson also approved the request of General William Westmoreland (field commander of U.S. forces in Vietnam) for forty-four additional combat battalions. By December, 1965, U.S. troop strength reached nearly 200,000. The following two years witnessed additional troop build-ups. Between 1965 and 1967, the United States relied mainly on saturation bombing of North Vietnam and search-and-destroy ground missions in the South to achieve its objectives. However, due to the iron will and troop strength of the North Vietnamese communists, the opposing sides fought to a destructive draw.

The year 1968 was a turning point in the Vietnam War. On January 31, the start of Tet (Vietnamese New Year celebration), a massive new coordinated offensive was unleashed by North Vietnamese and

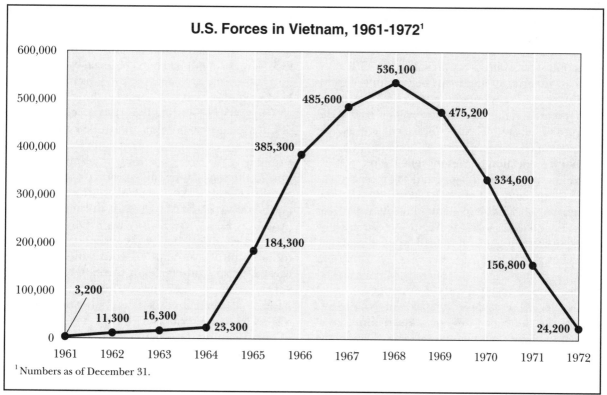

U.S. Forces in Vietnam, 1961-1972[1]

[1] Numbers as of December 31.

Source: U.S. Department of Defense

South Vietnamese police chief Nguyen Ngoc Loan executes a Viet Cong officer February 1, 1968. For many Americans, this photograph symbolized the brutality of war. (AP/Wide World Photos)

Viet Cong soldiers. They attacked South Vietnamese cities and towns with great fury. The Tet Offensive stunned Americans, and many began doubting the validity of the cause in light of the cost, in terms of both money and men. Domestic protests against the war rose significantly. Tet also forced changes in U.S. military policy—a decrease in the bombing of North Vietnam, a rejection of Westmoreland's request for an additional 206,000 troops, and the replacement of Westmoreland as field commander by General Creighton Abrams. President Johnson called for peace negotiations with the North Vietnamese government and publicly announced he would not seek reelection.

Protest and Tragedy The 1969 inauguration of newly elected President Richard M. Nixon was greeted by the Viet Cong with a series of brutal attacks on South Vietnamese villages. Seeing the need to reduce U.S. participation in the war, Nixon announced on June 8, 1969, the new policy of Vietnamization, the gradual takeover of the war effort by the South Vietnamese army and a concomitant with-

drawal of U.S. troops from Vietnam. At year's end, U.S. troop strength had been reduced by 60,000, but not before massive antiwar demonstrations were held in Washington, D.C., in the fall.

The years 1970 through 1972 saw a continuation of intense antiwar protests across the United States in addition to ongoing reductions in U.S. troop strength in Vietnam. Increasing widespread opposition to the war can be linked directly to television. Some of the most shocking and tragic images of this period occurred on May 4, 1970, during an antiwar protest at Kent State University in Ohio. National Guardsmen fired their weapons into a crowd of demonstrators and killed four students while wounding nine others. Soon thereafter, the Senate voted to repeal the Tonkin Gulf Resolution. The nation was again shocked when, on November 12, 1970, Lieutenant William L. Calley, Jr., went on trial at Fort Benning, Georgia, for his role in the 1968 civilian massacres at My Lai, a small hamlet in South Vietnam. In March, 1971, Calley was convicted of war crimes and sentenced to a ten-year prison term, prosecutors having proven his army unit guilty of murdering between one hundred and two hundred noncombatants in a premeditated fashion.

Public abhorrence of the war and distrust of U.S. officials deepened in 1971 when *The New York Times* published a series of documents called the Pentagon Papers, which described secret decisions and actions of U.S. leaders regarding the conduct of the war. Unfortunately, North Vietnam initiated a major invasion of the South in March, 1972, and President Nixon responded by ordering the mining of Haiphong harbor and the intensified bombing of all North Vietnam. These actions halted the invasion and led to peace talks, conducted primarily by Henry Kissinger, Nixon's chief foreign policy adviser, and Le Du Tho of North Vietnam. On January 27, 1973, a cease-fire agreement was signed in Paris by the United States, North Vietnam, South Vietnam, and the Viet Cong. Secretary of Defense Melvin Laird soon announced the end of the military draft in the United States, and the last U.S. ground forces left Vietnam on March 29, 1973. By mid-year, Congress began sharply reducing aid to South Vietnam. This encouraged the Viet Cong to renew the fighting, and by March, 1975, South Vietnamese troops were forced to retreat from strategic areas of their country. Still, President Gerald R. Ford—Nixon's successor—would declare in a speech delivered on April 23 that the war was finished. That month Congress approved three hundred million dollars in emergency aid for Vietnam, which proved to be mainly for the evacuation of Americans from Saigon. The war effectively ended when North Vietnam captured Saigon and the South surrendered to the communist North.

Impact Certain aspects of the Vietnam War can be quantified. About 58,000 Americans were killed between 1961 and 1975, and approximately 365,000 were wounded. Total loss of human life in both North and South Vietnam ran to some 2.1 million persons. The United States Air Force dropped 6.7 million tons of bombs on Southeast Asia, which was two and one-half times the amount dropped on Germany during World War II. Almost 5.2 million acres of forest and crop land were sprayed with nineteen million gallons of defoliant to aid U.S. forces in their prosecution of the war. The landscapes of North and South Vietnam were literally changed, and crop lands as well as plant and animal life were permanently damaged. U.S. air strikes de-

stroyed much of North Vietnam's industrial and transportation systems. But the South, where most of the fighting occurred, ended up with approximately ten million homeless inhabitants—half the population. In addition, the United States spent between $150 billion and $170 billion on the war.

Other aspects of the Vietnam War and its effects on the American people cannot be so easily measured. The psychological costs of the war were tremendous. It was the first foreign conflict in which the U.S. military failed to achieve its objectives. It damaged the pride, confidence, and spirit of hope of many Americans. It was the nation's first televised war, and uncensored scenes of horror were brought directly into the homes of ordinary people on a daily basis. These horrific scenes left viewers with bitter and painful memories. Most affected were the 2.7 million men and women who fought in the war and their families. Some veterans were irreparably scarred, physically and psychologically. They suffered from high rates of divorce, drug and alcohol abuse, and homelessness. Returning veterans of previous wars had been welcomed home as heros; however, Vietnam veterans were criticized, mocked, abused, or ignored. In an attempt to heal some of the social wounds and rifts persisting in the United States as a result of the sharp divisions over the Vietnam War, President Jimmy Carter, a one-time professional military officer, officially pardoned most of the ten thousand wartime draft evaders on January 21, 1977 (the day after his inauguration).

As a result of the Vietnam War, Congress and the public became more vocal in openly challenging the president on U.S. military and foreign policy issues. Though Americans disagree on the lessons of the Vietnam War, careful review of possible U.S. involvement in overseas conflicts seems to have been one of its legacies. Many Americans questioned the validity of a U.S. obligation to police the globe.

Additional Information The classic complete history of the Vietnam War, which has also been made into a documentary television series, is Stanley Karnow's *Vietnam—A History* (1983). More specific treatments of the United States' role in Vietnam are found in George C. Herring's *America's Longest War: The United States and Vietnam, 1950-1975* (1979), Guenter Lewy's *America in Vietnam* (1978), and George Donelson Moss's *Vietnam, an American Ordeal* (1990).

Andrew C. Skinner

See also Agent Orange Controversy; Draft Resisters; Gulf of Tonkin Incident; Johnson, Lyndon B.; Kissinger, Henry; March Against Death; Moratorium Day; My Lai Incident; Nixon, Richard M.; Paris Peace Talks; Tet Offensive.

■ Voting Rights Legislation

The Voting Rights Act of 1965, the preeminent voting rights legislation of the decade. It affirms the principles regarding the elimination and prohibition of open practices of racial discrimination in voting in the Civil Rights Acts of 1957, 1960, and 1964 and the Twenty-third and Twenty-fourth Amendments to the Constitution of the United States.

The Twenty-fourth Amendment to the United States Constitution was enacted in July, 1964. This amendment sought to protect the right of U.S. citizens to vote by banning any poll or other voting tax. It also provided Congress with the power to enforce the amendment using appropriate legislation. Although this and other laws had been passed to protect the rights of African American and other minority voters, these groups remained disenfranchised and continued to have difficulty registering to vote in many sections of the country. The Voting Rights Act of 1965 was designed to address the denial of minority citizens of the most basic right of U.S. citizenship—the right to vote.

The right to vote is central to the full political participation of all citizens because it gives them the power to elect officials who make decisions affecting their rights. However, many minority citizens had not been able to exercise their right to vote freely because state and local officials and private citizens had made efforts to prevent them from casting their ballots.

Dallas County Sheriff Jim Clark grabs the collar of Amelia Boynton of Selma, Alabama, and forces her to move along after an argument that ensued as Boynton and other African Americans lined up to register to vote at the courthouse in January, 1965. (AP/Wide World Photos)

Major Expansions of Voting Rights

Date	Action	Significance or Intent
1870	Fifteenth Amendment	Guaranteed the vote to African Americans.
1920	Nineteenth Amendment	Guaranteed the vote to women.
1961	Twenty-third Amendment	Gave District of Columbia residents right to vote in presidential elections.
1964	Twenty-fourth Amendment	Prohibited use of poll taxes or other taxes to restrict voting rights.
1965	Voting Rights Act	Banned voting tests in the South and some other areas.
1970	Voting Rights Act	Suspended literacy tests for voting.
1971	Twenty-sixth Amendment	Extended vote to eighteen-year-olds.
1972	*Dunn v. Blumstein*	Supreme Court held that long residency requirements for voting were unconstitutional.
1975	Voting Rights Act	Required that voting information be bilingual in parts of twenty-four states.
1982	Voting Rights Act	Extended 1965 act for twenty-five years.

African Americans, Mexican Americans, Asian Americans, some Caucasian Americans, and various ethnic and racial minority groups backed the Voting Rights Act of 1965. Major civil rights organizations lending support included the National Association for the Advancement of Colored People (NAACP) and the Student Nonviolent Coordinating Committee (SNCC). Politicians and leaders such as Martin Luther King, Jr., Ralph Abernathy, Hubert Humphrey, and President Lyndon B. Johnson also championed the act. These organizations and individuals were deeply involved in trying to get legislation enacted that would prohibit the numerous practices used to deny minority citizens the right to vote. These tactics included physical intimidation and harassment, the use of literacy tests, a poll tax, English-only elections, and racial gerrymandering. The results of these practices were low voter registration and turnout among minorities and the election of only a few officials who were members of racial or ethnic minorities. In many areas, minorities were almost totally excluded from the political process.

Opponents of the act were mainly southern politicians such as Governor George Wallace, Senator Allen Ellender, Senator Sam Ervin, and Governor J. P. Coleman and private citizens' groups such as the White Citizens Council, the Ku Klux Klan, and the Council of Federated Organizations (COFO).

Provisions of the Act The U.S. Congress responded to the demands of civil rights activists who were demonstrating during the 1960's by passing the Voting Rights Act of 1965. President Johnson signed it into law in August, 1965. The act overcame some of the weaknesses in the Civil Rights Act of 1964. It authorized federal voting examiners to register voters for federal and state elections, suspended literacy tests, banned the use of poll taxes, and provided limited federal approval of new state registration laws and voting statutes. Penalties were also established for those who sought to deny any person the right to vote.

The general provisions of the act protect the voting right of American citizens in several important ways. These provisions prohibit voting qualifications or procedures that would deny or abridge a person's right to vote because of race, color, or inclusion in a minority language group. The general provisions make it a crime for a public official to refuse to allow a qualified person to vote or for any person to use threats or intimidation to prevent someone from voting or helping another to vote. The act also contained special provisions that provided additional voting protections to citizens in certain jurisdictions. Unlike the general provisions, which are permanent and apply nationwide, the special provisions were temporary and applied only to those jurisdictions that met certain criteria.

Section II of the Voting Rights Act of 1965 prohibits the use of voting laws, practices, or procedures that discriminate in either purpose or effect on the basis of race, color, or membership in a minority language group. This section covers all types of voting practices and procedures, including those relating to registration, voting, candidacy qualifications, and type of election systems.

Section V was designed to prevent states and other governmental entities with a history of voting discrimination from continuing to devise new ways to discriminate and prevent citizens from voting. These jurisdictions are required to submit any proposed voting changes in their election practices prior to implementation for federal approval by either the attorney general or the federal district court for the district of Columbia. They must demonstrate that the proposed voting changes do not have the purpose or effect of discrimination against protected racial or language minorities. This process is referred to as the preclearance process. Minority language groups protected by the act are Native Americans, Asian Americans, Alaskan natives, and persons of Spanish heritage.

Jurisdictions covered include the states of Alabama, Alaska, Arizona, Georgia, Louisiana, Mississippi, South Carolina, Texas, and Virginia and counties and towns in California, Colorado, Connecticut, Florida, Hawaii, Idaho, Maine, Massachusetts, Michigan, New Hampshire, New York, North Carolina, South Carolina, South Dakota, and Wyoming.

Impact The law had an immediate impact. By the end of 1965, a quarter of a million new African American voters had been registered, one-third by federal examiners. Although passage of the Voting Rights Act of 1965 resulted in an increase in minority voter registration from approximately 29 percent to 52 percent of the minority population by the end of the decade, some persistent and serious obstacles remained. For example, some jurisdictions resisted provisions requiring the printing of materials related to registration and voting in the applicable minority language and the providing of oral assistance.

Subsequent Events The Voting Rights Act of 1965 was subsequently readopted and strengthened in 1970, 1975, and 1982.

Additional Information A comprehensive study of the impact of the Voting Rights Act of 1965 and other civil rights legislation can be found in *Freedoms, Courts, Politics: Studies in Civil Liberties* (1972), by Lucius J. Barker and Twiley W. Barker, Jr. A complete analysis of the act can be found in *The Voting Rights Act: Unfulfilled Goals* (1981), written by the U.S. Commission on Civil Rights.

Cherri N. Allison

See also Abernathy, Ralph; Civil Rights Act of 1960; Civil Rights Act of 1964; Civil Rights Act of 1968; Johnson, Lyndon B.; King, Martin Luther, Jr.; Ku Klux Klan (KKK); March on Selma; Mississippi Freedom Democratic Party (MFDP); National Association for the Advancement of Colored People (NAACP); Student Nonviolent Coordinating Committee (SNCC); Wallace, George.

W

■ Wallace, George

Born August 25, 1919, Clio, Alabama
Died September 13, 1998, Montgomery, Alabama

The most prominent political leader of white resistance to the blacks' struggle for civil rights in the 1960's. Wallace articulated white lower- and middle-class resentment of the decade's social trends not only in his native Alabama but also in other parts of the nation.

Early Life Born to poor southeast Alabama farmers, the feisty young George Corley Wallace excelled in boxing and politics, earning Golden Glove titles and a state senate page appointment. He participated in student government as he worked his way to a University of Alabama law degree. After service as a bomber crew member in World War II, he was an Alabama state legislator and later a district judge. As a protégé of populist Governor Jim Folsom, he was a moderate on race issues and a liberal regarding social services. However, in his 1958 gubernatorial bid, he underestimated growing white anger over blacks' efforts to gain their civil rights and lost to a candidate who emphasized a policy of resisting integration. Afterward, Wallace vowed to outdo political opponents in fighting African American advances.

The 1960's Wallace won the 1962 governor's race by attacking both civil rights activists and federal efforts made on their behalf. He proclaimed "segregation forever" in his inaugural address and gained a national reputation for white political resistance to integration when he stood in the doorway of the admissions office of the University of Alabama to symbolize his opposition to black enrollment. He maintained discreet ties with white supremacist groups while publicly disparaging the violence that they and white law officers exhibited against black protesters in Birmingham, Alabama.

Eager to prove his appeal elsewhere, he appeared on national television news shows and spoke at Harvard University. He also entered three 1964 northern Democratic presidential primaries. Although he failed to win, he still garnered impressive support.

In 1965, he further established his position by publicly opposing the March on Selma. Alabama law prevented successive terms as governor, so Wallace helped his wife, Lurleen, become governor in 1966. This guaranteed the public exposure needed for his 1968 presidential campaign.

Wallace ran as an Independent Party candidate. He hoped to win enough electoral votes either to create an electoral deadlock so that he could set terms for its resolution or at least to lay the foundation for a later successful run. Wallace won five Deep South states, nearly won two other southern states, and drew noteworthy northern support. He failed, however, to gain sufficient electoral votes to reach his goal because his workers misdirected funds and his rhetoric and past actions scared away many potential voters. His running mate, former Air Force general Curtis LeMay, also hurt Wallace's chances when he publicly stated that he would consider using atomic weapons against North Vietnam.

Later Life Wallace's wife died of cancer in 1968, and he married Cornelia Snively in 1971. A lone gunman shot and permanently crippled him during the May, 1972, Maryland Democratic presidential primary, effectively ending his 1972 campaign and contributing to his 1978 divorce. He made a half-hearted run at the presidency in 1976 and served three more governor's terms. The passing years and constant bullet-wound pain mellowed him. He publicly asked African Americans to forgive his past actions and eventually gained substantial support from black Alabamans because he appointed more African Americans to government office than any other Alabama governor.

Impact Wallace's views changed over his career, indicating his political shrewdness and the impact of events. Although his many highly publicized stands against racial integration were ineffectual, he tapped a vein of white working- and middle-class anger in the United States.

White racism and fear of increasing black unrest were partial reasons for his popularity in the South

Alabama governor and staunch segregationist George Wallace, shown here speaking to a crowd at a National Guard armory near Baltimore in 1964, unsuccessfully ran for president as an independent in 1968. (AP/Wide World Photos)

and other parts of the nation. He criticized the federal government and Supreme Court, institutions that many southerners and a growing number of other Americans considered out of touch or too imperious. He called for "law and order," words that many perceived as code for an anti-African American stance but that also appealed to nationwide alarm over rising crime rates. He also attacked intellectuals, members of the counterculture, and student protesters, whom many Americans blamed for the bewildering social and political changes of the 1960's.

Wallace thus presaged a rightward turn in U.S. politics in the ensuing decades. In the 1972 presidential race, President Richard M. Nixon tacitly supported Wallace's decision to run as a Democrat. Wallace won a couple of primaries by exploiting

white resistance to court-ordered busing to achieve integration before he was shot in Maryland. Nixon's "southern strategy," featuring a conservative social message and resistance to busing, was an attempt to attract Wallace's supporters.

Additional Information One sweeping assessment of Wallace's life and political impact is *The Politics of Rage* (1995), by Dan Carter.

Douglas Campbell

See also Birmingham March; Busing; Church Bombings; Civil Rights Movement; Conservatism in Politics; Counterculture; John Birch Society; Kennedy, Robert F.; King, Martin Luther, Jr.; Ku Klux Klan (KKK); March on Selma; Nixon, Richard M.; School Desegregation; Supreme Court Decisions.

■ War on Poverty

A set of social and urban programs initiated during Lyndon B. Johnson's presidency. Although these program never received more than a small percentage of the Johnson administration's social welfare budget, they attracted a great deal of public attention and helped to transform the racial politics of a number of American cities.

Defined largely by the Economic Opportunity Act of 1964, the War on Poverty was intended to promote opportunity, stimulate community action, introduce new social services, and expand transfer payments. The idea had both intellectual and political origins. In 1960, socialist Michael Harrington published *The Other America*, demonstrating the persistence of poverty in the supposedly affluent society. Social scientists such as Richard Cloward and Lloyd Ohlin began to reevaluate social policy, arguing that poverty and social disorder stemmed from blocked social and economic opportunities in poor communities, created in part by overly bureaucratic service institutions such as schools, welfare agencies, and the police. Local institutions and the poor needed to be brought together in order to better coordinate antipoverty efforts.

Attracted by this theory of blocked opportunity, Attorney General Robert F. Kennedy enlisted Ohlin's help in running the President's Commission on Juvenile Delinquency in 1961. This commission generated the basic concepts behind the War on Poverty—in particular, the idea that the poor would participate in the formulation and administration of local programs (community action). Along with the promotion of opportunity through education and job training, this idea—community action—became the heart of the War on Poverty.

The Civil Rights movement also helped put the issues of poverty and community action on the national agenda. Martin Luther King, Jr., and other civil rights leaders began to argue that economic opportunity and political equality were of a piece. Throughout the urban North, meanwhile, local African American activists led protests against job and housing discrimination, urban renewal, police brutality, and inadequate and paternalistic local public service bureaucracies. Community action seemed to have a local constituency ready to reform the social welfare establishment. An antipoverty proposal submitted to the Johnson administration in late 1963 called for a series of local federally funded demonstration projects that would accumulate knowledge about how to coordinate and implement local poverty wars. This proposal became the

basis for the Economic Opportunity Act of 1964, which created the Office of Economic Opportunity (OEO) to administer community action. The phrase "maximum feasible participation" of the poor, contained within Title II of the legislation, caused little debate; Johnson and Congress assumed that despite the language of community action, local officials and politicians would run the new programs. OEO officials and local community activists had other ideas.

The Economic Opportunity Act faced little opposition in Congress or elsewhere initially. The legislation was strongly pushed by the Johnson administration and was supported by liberals, labor unions, civil rights organizations, and by Democratic city mayors who hoped to use the new money and programs for political gain. Johnson, a great admirer of president Franklin D. Roosevelt and his New Deal social programs, hoped to use the War on Poverty and his later Great Society legislation to step out from the politi-

President Lyndon B. Johnson and his wife, Lady Bird, leave the home of an Appalachian man, father of eight, who has been out of work for two years. As part of his War on Poverty, the president traveled to the region to see conditions firsthand. (AP/Wide World Photos)

cal shadow of his martyred predecessor and extend Roosevelt's legacy.

Criticism of and opposition to the War on Poverty—and in particular the Community Action Programs—developed quickly. OEO administrators took "maximum feasible participation" seriously and held local Community Action Programs to strict representational guidelines in late 1964 and early 1965. Although the overwhelming majority of local programs remained in the hands of of city hall and established agencies, in a number of cities, both the OEO and local activists combined to challenge social and political power. Led by Chicago's Richard Daley, urban mayors—mostly Democrats—began to put pressure on the Johnson administration in the spring of 1965 to roll back what they saw as overzealous OEO bureaucrats. Conservative Republicans and southerners in Congress began to criticize the OEO and held hearings to publicize abuses of power and wastes of federal money at the local level. The War on Poverty also received criticism from black and white leftists, who argued that the OEO and its programs ignored the structural issues of low wages, deindustrialization, and racial discrimination in unions and employment, in favor of a focus on participation, culture, and human capital.

Increasingly concerned about the Vietnam War and a potential voter backlash against social programs and urban riots in the 1966 congressional elections, which did in fact occur, Johnson reigned in the OEO. In late 1967, Congress passed the so-called Green Amendment to the Economic Opportunity Act, giving local mayors the option of taking over local community action agencies. "Maximum feasible participation" of the poor was all but dead by the end of 1967. Although social spending increased significantly during the Johnson years, the War on Poverty was never more than 1 percent to 2 percent of the federal budget. The financial and political costs of the escalating war in Vietnam ensured that the War on Poverty was never more than a mere skirmish.

Impact Although community action garnered most of the headlines, the various social programs of the Johnson administration had a significant impact on the lives of many Americans, poor and not poor. Community action helped give rise to a new cadre of African American political leadership in the urban North and to a variety of locally based efforts to affect social service delivery and economic development. The expansion of public assistance and the creation of new "in-kind" social services (food stamps, legal assistance, health care, Head Start) greatly reduced malnutrition and infant mortality among the poor. However, most of the Johnson administration's social spending (Medicare and the expansion of Social Security and unemployment compensation) primarily benefitted those who were not poor, the elderly in particular. As critics at the time noted, the War on Poverty and Johnson's social legislation generally did little to address issues of employment and income redistribution, preferring to take the politically expedient route of relying upon equal opportunity and economic growth to alleviate poverty. In the end, Johnson and the Democrats paid a high political price for a poverty war that was oversold, underfunded, and ultimately inadequate; the election of 1968 marked the beginning of a conservative Republican ascendancy in national politics, caused in part by a backlash against the perceived liberality of federal programs and the "ungratefulness" of rioting blacks.

Additional Information For an overview of the origins, successes, and failures of the War on Poverty, see Michael Katz's *In the Shadow of the Poorhouse: A Social History of Welfare in America* (1986). Two classic studies of the Community Action Programs are Daniel P. Moynihan's *Maximum Feasible Misunderstanding: Community Action in the War on Poverty* (1969) and David Greenstone and Paul E. Peterson's *Race and Authority in Urban Politics: Community Participation and the War on Poverty* (1976).

Mark E. Santow

See also Civil Rights Movement; Equal Opportunity Act of 1964; Great Society Programs; Head Start; Job Corps; Kennedy, John F.; Kennedy, Robert F.; Liberalism in Politics; Prosperity and Poverty.

■ War Resisters League

One of many organizations that came to prominence in the 1960's by opposing United States involvement in the Vietnam War.

The War Resisters League dates back to 1923 when it was organized as the American arm of the War Resisters International, with the purpose of building public opposition to war. In World War II, the league provided support for conscientious objectors and found new life in the 1960's by agitating against the conflict in Vietnam.

The War Resisters League, in many ways, resembled other pacifist groups in that it organized and supported demonstrations and marches and carried out efforts to educate the public on the war effort. The league also actively supported conscientious objectors who were seeking to avoid the military draft during the 1960's. Like many of the older peace organizations, the league was not marked with excessive militancy.

Impact Although the role of the antiwar movement in actually bringing about an end to the conflict in Vietnam is the subject of debate among historians, little doubt exists that the actions of organizations such as the War Resisters League, taken as a whole, helped foster the largest popular resistance to any war in U.S. history.

Additional Information Charles DeBenedetti provides the most comprehensive treatment of the antiwar movement in his 1990 book, *An American Ordeal: The Antiwar Movement of the Vietnam Era.*

Phillip A. Cantrell II

See also Draft Resisters; National Mobilization Committee to End the War in Vietnam (MOBE); SANE (National Committee for a Sane Nuclear Policy); Vietnam War.

One of the most famous images produced by American pop artist Andy Warhol, pictured in his factory in 1968, was the soup can. (Santi Visalli Inc./Archive Photos)

■ Warhol, Andy

Born August 6, 1928, Pittsburgh, Pennsylvania
Died February 22, 1987, New York, New York

A prolific and innovative artist. Warhol is identified with popular, or pop, art, one of the major art movements of the mid-twentieth century, which for Warhol included cinematography and music.

Early Life Andy Warhol (born Andrew Warhola) was born in Pittsburgh of working-class immigrant parents. His life and career were shaped by the polluted environment of his childhood and the deprivations his family suffered during the Great Depression. He was sickly as a child but showed remarkable artistic talents. His father, who died when Warhol was fourteen, had the foresight to put aside enough money so that his son could begin his studies at the Carnegie Institute of Technology where he majored in commercial art. Soon after finishing his studies

on scholarships, Warhol left for New York City where he became a highly successful commercial artist. In late 1959, Warhol decided he wanted to be an artist—a fine artist rather than a commercial artist.

The 1960's Between the autumn of 1959 and the spring of 1961, Warhol's art underwent a remarkable transformation. He changed from a stylish commercial illustrator to a serious artist realistically painting familiar objects in bold outlines and brilliant colors. Probably his best-known object was the soup can, remembered from his Depression-era childhood. Other objects included soft-drink bottles and scouring-pad cartons often painted in multiple—common in advertising art. Warhol's work was in contrast to the then-prevailing art movement of nonrepresentational abstract expressionism. He became one of the founders of the pop art movement that sought to place artistic value on commonplace items.

Although Warhol's work was dismissed by some art critics, it became popular with the public, and major galleries began to display his work. Seeking to expand artistically, Warhol helped perfect the silk-screen method of reproduction that could produce multiple copies of hand-colored photographic images. His subjects were well-known figures. The process was a commercial success, so much so that in 1965, Warhol announced his "retirement" as a painter in favor of a career in cinematography.

Over the next three years, Warhol produced a series of films with controversial themes but of increasing sophistication. Among the more memorable was *Chelsea Girls* (1966), a seven-hour, largely unedited semidocumentary. He also sponsored a hard-core rock group called the Velvet Underground. His career changed abruptly on June 3, 1968, when an unstable film scriptwriter shot him, nearly ending his life.

Later Life In 1967, Frederick W. Hughes had become Warhol's business associate. Academically trained in art and with connections to museums and wealthy collectors, Hughes persuaded Warhol to abandon filmmaking and return to fine art, especially to the lucrative field of portraiture. He also persuaded Warhol to enter publishing with the launching in 1969 of the film magazine *Interview*. With its striking covers and its off-beat articles about current celebrities, the magazine became both a commercial and artistic success. Other publications included *The Philosophy of Andy Warhol From A to B and Back Again* (1975) and *America* (1985). Warhol was on his way to becoming one of the world's best-known, most prolific, and wealthiest artists when he unexpectedly died the morning of February 22, 1987, after a routine operation for the removal of an infected gallbladder.

Impact The turbulent 1960's, with its race riots, protests against an unpopular war, and the assassination of a president, fostered permanent social changes, including the way Americans viewed art. The division between the acceptable and unacceptable became increasingly blurred. In opposition to the opinions of the purists and self-appointed experts, a realization developed that there is such a thing as popular culture and popular art against which each generation tends to define itself. One of pop art's most notable accomplishments was to de-

mystify fine art and to separate American art from its European antecedents.

Subsequent Events By the terms of his will, the bulk of Warhol's estate was to be used to establish the Andy Warhol Foundation for the Visual Arts. The possibility of a museum was also raised, but disagreement among the executors and the officers of the foundation resulted in prolonged and bitter legal battles. The Andy Warhol Museum, the largest single-artist museum in the United States, finally opened in Warhol's hometown of Pittsburgh in 1994.

Additional Information For a description of Warhol's work in the 1960's, see David Bourdon's *Warhol* (1989); for an account of the legal wrangling that diminished the assets of the foundation see Paul Alexander's *Death and Disaster* (1994).

Nis Petersen

See also: Art Movements; Film; Pop Art; *SCUM Manifesto*.

■ Warren, Earl

Born March 19, 1891, Los Angeles, California
Died July 9, 1974, Washington, D.C.

One of the greatest and most influential chief justices in the nation's history. Under the leadership of Earl Warren, the Supreme Court assumed an activist role in transforming society in the United States.

Early Life Born in California and reared in the progressive politics of California's Republican governor Hiram Johnson, Earl Warren moved up from Alameda County district attorney to state attorney general in 1938. A strong record as an anticrime prosecutor propelled him into the governorship in 1942. Running as a Republican but cross-filing as a Democrat, he won three terms—one time with both party nominations—while becoming more progressive. He was Thomas Dewey's vice presidential running mate in 1948 and an unsuccessful candidate for the Republican presidential nomination in 1952. He strategically aided Dwight D. Eisenhower's 1952 Republican presidential convention victory and was rewarded with the appointment to chief justice in 1953. After his appointment, he is credited with bringing the fractious justices behind the unanimous landmark 1954 school desegregation decision in *Brown v. Board of Education of Topeka, Kansas*.

The 1960's With Justice Felix Frankfurter's retirement and Arthur Goldberg's elevation to the Court in 1962, Warren, previously in the liberal minority with Hugo Black, William Brennan, and William Douglas, found himself in command of solid five-vote majorities on virtually every issue. Goldberg was replaced by another liberal, Abe Fortas, in 1965, and the liberals gained strength with Thurgood Marshall's appointment in 1967. Warren was a strong supporter of the more liberal justices Black and Douglas on free expression and civil liberties but did not take some of their more absolute stands.

The Warren Court transformed U.S. constitutional law in ways that outstripped every other Court, and it provided the greatest single decade of change of any in U.S. history. Although single cases such as *Marbury* (1803) or *Dred Scott* (1857) were often individually significant, no court ever overturned so many federal statutes or transformed so many areas of the law. Only in the 1960's were so many highly controversial decisions handed down. To cite only some of the issues involved—desegregation, civil rights, civil liberties, obscenity, school prayer, legislative reapportionment, incorporation of the Bill of Rights to the states by way of the Fourteenth Amendment, protection of those accused of crimes, and issues surrounding the Vietnam War—is to recognize how significant this decade was for the Court and U.S. society. After retiring from the Court, Warren spent his retirement speaking and writing.

Impact Not generally credited as a great legal scholar, Warren is considered the driving force behind the Court era carrying his name. In the following decades, the legacy of the Court's decisions has transformed U.S. constitutional law and society. Although some of the decisions have been modified, the vast bulk of the rulings remain intact.

Additional Information The standard biography, *Earl Warren: A Public Life* (1982), by Warren's former law clerk, G. Edward White, has been supplemented by an excellent, highly readable biography, *Chief Justice: A Biography of Earl Warren* (1997), by Jack Cray.

Richard L. Wilson

See also Civil Rights Movement; *Engel v. Vitale*; *Flast v. Cohen*; Fortas, Abe; *Gideon v. Wainwright*; *Griswold v. Connecticut*; *Heart of Atlanta Motel v. United States*; *Jacobellis v. Ohio*; *Katzenbach v. McClung*; *Memoirs v. Massachusetts*; *Miranda v. Arizona*; *New York Times*

The Supreme Court under Chief Justice Earl Warren handed down many controversial decisions in areas such as desegregation, civil rights, civil liberties, obscenity, school prayer, and defendant's rights. (George Tames/New York Times Co./ Archive Photos)

Company v. Sullivan; Reapportionment Revolution; Supreme Court Decisions; Warren Report.

■ Warren Report

Published September 27, 1964
Author President's Commission on the Assassination of President John F. Kennedy

The Report of the President's Commission on the Assassination of President John F. Kennedy. It became one of the most controversial government documents in U.S. history.

The Work After President John F. Kennedy was assassinated in Dallas, Texas, on November 22, 1963, his successor, Lyndon B. Johnson, made the Federal Bureau of Investigation (FBI) responsible for investigating the crime and issuing a report. However, he was soon persuaded that a presidential panel would be needed to put the matter to rest and, on November 29, 1963, appointed a commission consisting of Chief Justice Earl Warren, former Central Intelligence Agency (CIA) director Allen Dulles, U.S. Senators Richard Russell and Sherman Cooper, U.S. Representatives Gerald Ford and Hale Boggs, and banker John McCloy. This group became known as the Warren Commission.

The main task faced by the Warren Commission was to identify the assassin of President Kennedy and to consider the existence of a possible conspiracy. Texas Governor John Connally, riding in the same car as the president, had also been wounded, and Dallas police officer J. D. Tippit had been murdered soon afterward in another part of the city. Two days later, the accused assassin of the president, Lee Harvey Oswald, was shot to death in the basement of a Dallas police station. Between the end of November, 1963, and September 27, 1964, when the Warren Commission released its report, the commission and its staff heard testimony from more than a hundred witnesses and entered into evidence thousands of reports from the FBI, CIA, Secret Service, State Department, and other government agencies as well as information from foreign sources. The final report stated that Oswald, acting alone, fired all of the shots that struck President Kennedy and Governor Connally and that he also murdered Officer Tippit. The commission also declared that Dallas nightclub owner Jack Ruby acted alone in shooting Oswald and that it had "found no evidence that either Lee Harvey Oswald or Jack Ruby was part of any conspiracy, domestic or foreign, to assassinate President Kennedy."

Perhaps the most controversial element of the Warren Report was its conclusion that Governor Connally was wounded by a bullet that had first struck President Kennedy.

This so-called single bullet theory was embraced despite the absence of serious damage to the bullet purported to have wounded both men and the fact that Connally can be seen in bystander Abraham Zapruder's famous home movie of the assassination reacting to his wounds after Kennedy reacts to a hit from supposedly the same bullet. Also controversial was the commission's conclusion that all shots were fired by Oswald from the rear of the presidential limousine when the Zapruder film appears to show the fatal shot to Kennedy's head throwing him back-

ward rather than forward in his seat. The report also found no conspiratorial significance in Oswald's 1959 to 1962 stay in the Soviet Union, his pro-Castro activities, or his trip to Mexico City just before the assassination and dismissed as rumor and speculation the attempts by some to find sinister overtones in these aspects of Oswald's background.

Impact The Warren Report had its intended effect: to assure the American public that President Kennedy's assassin had been identified and that there had been no conspiracy. However, its persuasive effect proved temporary as critics of the report revived old questions about the assassination and posed new ones. Following the release of the report, public opinion polls showed that more than half of Americans accepted the conclusion that Oswald acted alone, but by late 1967, only one-fourth of the public believed there had been no conspiracy. Stimulating the public's doubts were articles in such major magazines as *Life* and *Look*, best-selling books such as Mark Lane's *Rush to Judgment* (1966), and New Orleans district attorney Jim Garrison's widely publicized investigation of the assassination (1967-1969). However, the 1969 acquittal of Garrison's main suspect, New Orleans businessman Clay Shaw, was a major setback to those who favored a conspiracy theory.

After the Watergate affair and government spying scandals of the 1970's, doubts about the Warren Report were revived. The U.S. House of Representatives conducted an inquiry from 1976 to 1979 that concluded a conspiracy had probably been involved in the assassination. In 1991, Hollywood director Oliver Stone's film *JFK* cast Garrison's ill-fated investigation in a heroic light and generated sufficient controversy to persuade Congress to open the government's still-secret files on the assassination.

Additional Information A proconspiracy alternative to the Warren Report can be found in Peter Dale Scott's *Deep Politics and the Death of JFK* (1993), and the report's most adamant defense is Gerald Posner's *Case Closed* (1993).

Larry Haapanen

See also Assassinations of John and Robert Kennedy and Martin Luther King, Jr.; Kennedy, John F.; Oswald, Lee Harvey.

■ Washington, D.C., Riots

Date November 22, 1962; August 1-3, 1967

Racial unrest that erupted in the nation's capital. The events were short-lived but had a profound impact on the country as a whole during the Civil Rights movement.

Origins and History Although much of the attention during the Civil Rights movement in the 1960's focused on the South, racial tension also existed in the North, especially in urban areas such as Washington, D.C. The 1962 riot broke out at a football game between two longtime rival high schools, one white and the other African American, and spilled over into the streets. In 1967, other seemingly minor incidents set off a riot.

The Riots On November 22, 1962, two high school football rivals met for a fifth consecutive annual Washington, D.C., championship game. These schools were St. John's, a mostly white Catholic high school, and Eastern, a mainly African American public school. During the game, a player ejected for roughness returned to the field and began fighting. His own teammates subdued him, but his actions began a chain reaction. The fighting spread quickly from the field into the crowd, the parking lots, and surrounding streets. A total of thirty-four people were injured before the police brought it under control.

In 1967, a citywide riot occurred. Earlier that summer, many civil rights leaders, including Martin Luther King, Jr., had warned of possible disorders in several cities including Washington, D.C., but their warnings were largely ignored. Although some accused these leaders of giving people reasons to riot, Federal Bureau of Investigation Director J. Edgar Hoover acknowledged there was no direct evidence supporting this belief. The violence broke out on August 1. The riot started with sporadic fires set mainly in African American neighborhoods. This was followed by rioters throwing rocks and bottles at police officers and firefighters responding to the blaze. In one area, two roaming gangs shot at police. The turmoil subsided on August 3.

Impact After the 1967 racial unrest in Washington and other cities, President Lyndon B. Johnson appointed Illinois Governor Otto Kerner head of the National Advisory Commission on Civil Disorders, known as the Kerner Commission, to study the reasons for the riots and growing racial tension in the nation. The commission eventually concluded that the United States was being divided into two societies, one white and the other black. The commission concluded that the urban areas of the nation faced a downward trend unless action was taken to relieve discriminatory conditions. This gave rise to a new attitude that brought about new government legislation.

Additional Information See Richard and Beatrice K. Hofstadter's *Great Issues in American History* (1982) for extensive materials on racial problems of the 1960's and the attempted solutions. The Kerner Commission Report published in 1968 also contains important information.

Robert Sullivan

See also Chicago Riots; Detroit Riot; Kerner Commission Report; King, Martin Luther, Jr.; New York Riots; Newark Riot; Watts Riot.

■ Water Pollution

Dirty, chemical-laden water became a political issue as more people began to demand clean water for an increasing variety of uses. The problem was first seriously addressed by the Water Quality Act of 1965.

During the nineteenth century, agricultural advances and technological innovations led people to migrate to the cities, where inadequate waste disposal became a direct cause of polluted drinking water, a problem that continued into the twentieth century. Water pollution has three main sources: municipal sewage, industry, and agriculture. In 1900, 2 million Americans obtained drinking water from streams and 24 million dumped sewage into the same streams. By 1960, streams provided 100 million Americans with drinking water and 120 million used the same streams as raw sewage dumps. As late as 1970, the sewage of 10 million people in fourteen hundred communities was still being discharged raw and untreated into U.S. waters and the sewage of an additional 85 million was discharged into rivers and lakes after receiving only primary treatment (removal of settled solids).

Initially, waste treatment was concerned primarily with sewage, but by the 1950's, industry, utilizing increasingly complex processes, had become the greatest user of water and the largest source of pollution. Some industrial wastes could be successfully treated as sewage, but many chemical compounds were not amenable to such treatment, and even nontoxic industrial wastes can disrupt the ecological balance of a river.

The second largest use of water is for agricultural irrigation. When this water eventually returns to a stream, it is often polluted with dissolved solids and salts, chemicals from pesticides and fertilizer, and fecal matter. In sufficient concentrations, these pollutants can render any body of water unsuitable for other uses.

Chemically pure water does not occur naturally; water that is "pure" by public health standards, although containing chemical additives, must merely be free of infectious bacteria, toxic chemicals, and radioactive wastes. Often water that is quite safe to drink contains barely measurable amounts of pollutants that can cause the water to appear cloudy, have an unpleasant odor, or acquire a disagreeable taste.

Because the United States has been extravagant in using and negligent in maintaining unpolluted water, the impetus for change was slow in coming. At the beginning of the 1960's, the pollution of the New York harbor was considered a national disgrace and the Mississippi and Missouri Rivers were still being contaminated by raw sewage, untreated industrial waste, and slaughterhouse by-products. Even a scenic tributary of the Colorado River was defiled by radioactive wastes from uranium mines. Although the nation's water supply was unlikely to be exhausted soon, the supply of clean water was rapidly disappearing. Matters came to a head during the 1960's because of the post-World War II population explosion, an increased demand for electric power, the expansion of new industrial technologies, and a vast increase in manufactured goods.

Industry's opposition to pollution controls and general public apathy had kept state and federal governments from enacting effective water pollution control legislation. Compounding the problem was the important economic role played by industry in many communities. Because local industry provided tax dollars as well as jobs, community leaders were reluctant to press for corrective measures. Without strong legislation, industry generally had no compelling interest in seeking means of alleviating or reducing the noxious chemicals being dumped into local waters. On the other hand, communities that failed to approve the bonds necessary to treat their own sewage could hardly criticize industries for failing to detoxify their effluents.

The U.S. Congress first responded to the growing menace of water pollution by enacting the Water Pollution Control Act of 1948. Because this legislation limited federal enforcement authority and provided little financial assistance to states, it had scant effect. The principal legislative foundation for controlling water pollution began with the Federal Water Pollution Control Act of 1956. This act established procedures for regional conferences to recommend controls and appropriate treatment in local regions with water pollution problems. The authority to act against polluters was left with the states; federal authority was severely limited. This legislation was amended by the Water Quality Act of 1965, which authorized the establishment and enforcement of water quality standards for interstate and coastal waters in order to protect the various uses of water. Although federal authority was broadened, the law was still ineffectual because it attempted to regulate the overall quality of water. Individual states were directed to develop and enforce water quality standards for interstate waters. The federal government was given no power to regulate intrastate water pollution unless temporarily granted this authority by a state's governor.

The Water Quality Improvement Act of 1970, an direct outgrowth of the earlier legislation, extended federal control by allowing federal enforcement of standards for both intrastate and interstate waters if the public health or welfare was at risk. Water quality standards were also extended to include the discharge of toxic wastes or other potentially dangerous pollutants. Federal programs providing grants for state and local governments to construct waste treatment facilities supplemented the regulatory legislation.

Impact As a direct consequence of the water pollution legislation enacted during the 1960's, water pollution has come to be recognized as an expedient component of water resource management, and the provision of adequate and safe water has become the one of the nation's most critical natural resource problems.

The United States has come to realize that dumping sewage and industrial waste into local waters is no longer a viable option. Sewage plants with at least two, but preferably three, stages of treatment are becoming the standard for most municipalities. State and federal laws now require that pollution be abated at the source, whatever the cost to industry. Americans are demanding clean and healthy water for household use and recreational purposes. They have come to realize that the larger the population and the higher the standard of living, the greater the pollution and the greater the competition for clean water. Traditional processes for determining water-use priorities have become obsolete as public values have evolved to national goals demanding the best quality water for the maximum number of applications benefiting the most people. Society has learned that clean water is not free and has become more willing to underwrite the high costs of pollution prevention or abatement.

Subsequent Events Attempting to police polluters and enforce legislation based on water quality standards has proven to be problematic. Therefore, as part of the Federal Water Pollution Control Act Amendments of 1972, Congress established the National Pollutant Discharge Elimination System (NPDES). This legislation shifts the emphasis from the regulation of general water quality to the setting of rigorous and easily monitored standards for wastewater. The Environmental Protection Agency (EPA, established in 1970) was empowered to establish strict effluent limitations for each industry before a discharge permit would be granted. The amendments also extended water quality standards to intrastate waters and mandated that NPDES permits be consistent with the previously adopted water quality standards. During the 1970's, the EPA, in conjunction with the states, focused attention on developing and enforcing the NPDES permit program.

The Clean Water Act of 1977 relaxed somewhat the deadlines of the 1972 water pollution control legislation although it also attempted to abolish all emissions of certain particularly toxic water pollutants. By the 1980's, it became apparent that greater attention to the water quality-based approach to pollution control was needed to protect effectively the nation's waters. Impatience with the states' sluggish progress in adopting new water quality standards for toxic chemicals goaded Congress into enacting the Water Quality Act of 1987. This set of amendments addressed the problem of toxic water pollutants by requiring that the states adopt limiting numerical criteria rather than vague unenforceable statements for bodies of water where toxic pollutants were likely to cause problems.

Additional Information Various factors that led to the water pollution problems of the 1960's are discussed in *Death of the Sweet Waters* (1966) by Donald Carr. A complete report on the progress made during the 1960's in controlling water pollution and regulating water quality can be found in "River of Life, Water: Environmental Challenge" in *Conservation Yearbook No. 6* (1970). *Balancing the Needs of Water* (1989), by James Moore, reviews various uses of water and their often conflicting interactions, the environmental impact of these uses, and water quality standards that attempt to reconcile the requirements of diverse users.

G. R. Plitnik

See also Air Pollution; Carson, Rachel; Environmental Movement; Motor Vehicle Air Pollution Act of 1965.

■ Watts Riot

Date August 11-16, 1965

One of the best known urban uprisings in U.S. history. The Watts riot highlighted the problem of race in the urban West and helped change public attitudes and federal welfare policies.

Origins and History During the 1940's, thousands of African Americans living in the South migrated to Los Angeles, California, in search of better jobs and lives, but they found that conditions in segregated communities such as Watts were only marginally better than those they had left behind. African Americans faced high unemployment, police brutality, segregated schools, inferior housing, and political and social isolation. By 1965, many African Americans were ready for a revolution.

The Riot On Wednesday, August 11, 1965, a routine traffic stop sparked one of the worst urban disturbances in U.S. history. California Highway Patrol Officer Lee Minikus detained a young African American man, Marquette Frye, and his brother Ronald under the suspicion that Marquette was driving while intoxicated. A crowd soon gathered to observe the police, and when the young men's mother, Rena, arrived at the scene, a fracas broke out, and all three Fryes were arrested. Witnesses later testified that the officers, including some members of the Los Angeles Police Department who arrived on the scene shortly after Minikus stopped

National Guardsmen patrol a street in the Watts area of Los Angeles after several days of rioting in August, 1965. (AP/Wide World Photos)

Frye, savagely beat the Fryes as they were being taken into custody. The crowd taunted the officers as the Fryes were being placed into squad cars, and later that night, a large mob of African Americans overturned cars and attacked whites passing through the Watts area.

The violence escalated the next day, and African Americans took to the streets, shouting "Burn, baby, burn" and looting white-owned businesses. Rioters armed themselves with guns and Molotov cocktails, and police in Watts exchanged gunfire with them. The National Guard arrived on Friday to help the officers contain the violence, but the rioting spilled over into the weekend. By Saturday, more than fifteen thousand National Guard troops and Los Angeles police officers were in the streets trying to restore order. However, snipers and rioters harassed the National Guard and the police, and the death toll rose steadily. Violence continued through Mon-

day morning, when law enforcement officials finally restored order and the rioters left the streets.

Thirty-four people died during the rioting, one thousand were injured, and nearly four thousand were arrested. Property damage exceeded two hundred million dollars. Officials estimated that more than thirty-five thousand adults had actively participated in the riots. Although at first the looting and property damage appeared random, a pattern soon became evident: The rioters had not looted most businesses owned by African Americans and generally had not attacked African American homes, schools, churches, or libraries. Most of the rioters' rage centered on white-owned businesses and other symbols of what rioters perceived as white exploitation of the ghetto.

Impact Americans were stunned by the violence of the Watts riot. President Lyndon B. Johnson and his staffers scrambled to use the resources of the War on Poverty to prevent further rioting, and federal planners increasingly allocated antipoverty funds for summer job programs for inner-city youths. Their efforts, however, did not stop similar riots in Chicago, Detroit, New York, and Washington, D.C., during the next several years. Many African Americans saw the Watts riot as symbolizing a new era in the Civil Rights movement, one in which attention would shift to discriminatory practices in the large cities of the North and West and away from segregation in the rural South. African American militancy increased after the summer of 1965, and radical African American leaders moved further away from the doctrine of nonviolence espoused by the Reverend Martin Luther King, Jr. After the Watts riot, many whites criticized the rioters for setting back the progress that had been made in the Civil Rights movement and began to withdraw their support for the movement. The riot and increased militancy of African Americans sparked a conservative reaction around the nation, and when Richard M. Nixon ran on a law-and-order campaign in 1968, this so-called silent majority of conservatives put him in the White House.

Additional Information A contemporary account of the unrest, *Rivers of Blood, Years of Darkness*, by Robert E. Conot, was published in 1967. In 1995, Gerald Horne published an in-depth study of the riots entitled *Fire This Time: The Watts Uprising and the 1960's*.
Daniel E. Crowe

See also Chicago Riots; Detroit Riot; Kerner Commission Report; New York Riots; Newark Riot; War on Poverty; Washington, D.C., Riots.

■ Wauneka, Annie Dodge

Born April 10, 1910, Navajo Nation, near Sawmill, Arizona
Died November 10, 1997, Flagstaff, Arizona

Navajo social reformer and public health activist. Wauneka crusaded for the improvement of the health and welfare of the Navajo people and was a major contributor to eliminating tuberculosis from the Navajo reservation.

Early Life Annie Dodge Wauneka was born to Henry Chee Dodge, the first elected chair of the Navajo tribal council, and his Navajo wife, K'eehabah. Wauneka attended a government boarding school in Fort Defiance, Arizona, and the Albuquer-

Navajo public health worker Annie Dodge Wauneka received the Presidential Medal of Freedom Award in 1963. (AP/Wide World Photos)

que Indian School in New Mexico. She traveled the reservation with her father in his role as chair, observing the poverty-stricken Navajos, attending tribal meetings, and learning to be an interpreter between the Navajos and Anglos. In the early 1950's, she became the first woman ever elected to the Navajo tribal council and also was elected head of the council's health and welfare committee. In the mid-1950's, Wauneka earned a bachelor's degree in public health from the University of Arizona. In the late 1950's, she received the Josephine B. Hughes Memorial Award; the Woman of the Year Achievement Award from the Arizona Women's Press Association; the Outstanding Worker in Public Health Award from the Arizona State Public Health Association; and the Indian Achievement Award of the Indian Council Fire of Chicago.

The 1960's In the early 1960's, Wauneka helped produce two films on health and cleanliness habits; spent two years broadcasting information on health issues in the Navajo language on KGAK radio in Gallup, New Mexico; and served on the U.S. Surgeon General's and the U.S. Public Health Service's advisory boards. Her proudest moment was receiving the Presidential Medal of Freedom Award, presented to her by President Lyndon B. Johnson at a White House ceremony on December 6, 1963, sixteen days after the assassination of President John F. Kennedy. This award is given to those who have made outstanding contributions to the national interest, the country's security, or world peace or who have participated in cultural or other significant public or private endeavors.

Later Life In 1976, Wauneka received an honorary doctorate in public health from the University of Arizona and was chosen as one of ten Women of the Year. In her eighties, she continued to advise the Navajo tribal council and remained involved with Navajo health issues.

Impact Wauneka obtained a deep knowledge of the political and financial realities of tribal life, an unusual asset for a Navajo woman because they were not usually involved in tribal government decisions. Her major accomplishments included the eradication of tuberculosis and other diseases from the reservation. She was instrumental in having the dirt-covered floors of the hogans replaced with wooden floors and having windows installed to help create healthy living conditions. She became an interpreter between Western doctors and the Navajo medicine men, generating cooperation between the two medical systems to rid the reservation of the diseases that most affected the Navajos. She also created a dictionary by translating English words for modern medical techniques into Navajo words, which assisted the relationships between government doctors and Navajo patients.

Additional Information Mary Carroll Nelson's *Annie Wauneka* (1972) offers an in-depth portrayal of this Navajo public health activist. *Indian Women* (1964), by Lela Waltrip and Rufus Waltrip, has an excellent chapter on Wauneka.

Darlene Mary Suarez

See also American Indian Civil Rights Act of 1968; American Indian Movement (AIM); *House Made of Dawn*; *Way to Rainy Mountain, The*; Women's Identity.

■ *Way to Rainy Mountain, The*

Published 1969
Author N. Scott Momaday (1934-   )

Multigenre work by Oklahoma-born Kiowa poet, essayist, novelist, and painter. In this work, Momaday arranged Kiowa traditional stories, autobiographical data, and drawings by his father in a mosaical text representing the author's tribal history and identity from several perspectives.

The Work Occasioned by the death of Momaday's grandmother, Aho, who witnessed the last Kiowa Sun Dance in 1887, *The Way to Rainy Mountain* traces the history of the Kiowas from their emergence through a hollow log onto the arid North American plains. Momaday poetically recounts Kiowa devotion to the sacred Sun Dance doll, Tai-me. His apparent motive for writing was to draw the reader into his "journey" of recovery of the past as he partially creates his own "Indian" identity from the "fragmentary . . . mythology, legend, lore, and hearsay" found in books and family and tribal sources. The graphic arrangement of the work lets the reader piece together compelling fragments, much as Momaday did. Most left-hand pages contain short, traditional Kiowa tales, including stories of how the Kiowas acquired dogs, of Grandmother Spider and Arrowmaker, and of human-animal transformations. Right-hand pages feature brief selections from mainstream history texts and anthropological sources, presenting non-Indian views of the Kiowa; at the bottom of these pages, in italics, are personal, usually autobiographical statements that reveal the author's perspective. These personal passages frequently pay tribute to Momaday's grandmother, whose death and burial, for the author, mark a profound intersection of the unchangeable past, stretching from time immemorial, with the present, replete with creative possibilities. The bold, pen-and-ink drawings of Al Momaday, the author's father, share pages filled with his son's words and serve as a reminder of how Kiowa traditional art thrives. *The Way to Rainy Mountain* explores the mutually interdependent roles of memory, spirituality, and aesthetic imagination in a people's invention of themselves in dialogue with their sunscorched homeland and in the author's own self-creation "as a man" and "as an Indian" in dialogue with the past.

Impact Although *The Way to Rainy Mountain* was not published until 1969, its introduction had appeared in the January 26, 1967, issue of *The Reporter*, where it apparently enjoyed an enthusiastic reception. The excerpt was almost immediately reprinted in numerous college rhetoric texts and literature anthologies as a model for writers. Many of the personal opinions Momaday expressed in *The Way to Rainy Mountain* were originally transformed into the dialogue of the Priest-of-the-Sun character, Tosamah, in the author's Pulitzer Prize-winning first novel, *House Made of Dawn* (1968). Momaday's early works undoubtedly influenced the development of post-1960's Native American literature, including major works by Leslie Marmon Silko and others.

Additional Information For additional commentary on *The Way to Rainy Mountain* and its significant relationship to *House Made of Dawn*, see *Other Destinies: Understanding the American Indian Novel* (1992), by Louis Owens.

Catherine Rainwater

See also *House Made of Dawn*; Silko, Leslie Marmon.

■ Weather Satellites

Spacecraft that orbit Earth and provide meteorological data. Weather satellites supply information that allows more accurate forecasting and better preparation for dangerous storms.

The first photograph of clouds from space was obtained by a U.S. rocket launched on March 7, 1947, and a rocket launched on October 5, 1954, captured the first photograph of a storm from space. Experimental meteorological equipment was included in the U.S. satellites Vanguard 2 (launched February 17, 1959), Explorer 6 (launched August 7, 1959), and Explorer 7 (launched October 13, 1959).

The first series of satellites intended strictly for meteorological use was the Television and Infrared Observation Satellite (TIROS) series. TIROS 1 was launched by the National Aeronautics and Space Administration (NASA) on April 1, 1960. Seven more TIROS satellites were launched from November 23, 1960, to December 21, 1963. These satellites had orbits that prevented them from photographing Earth's polar regions. Unlike previous satellites in the series, TIROS 8 had an automatic picture transmission system that allowed images to be transmitted to Earth as soon as they were produced. TIROS 9

(launched January 22, 1965) and TIROS 10 (launched July 1, 1965) had orbits that allowed them to photograph all parts of Earth's surface. The Environmental Science Services Administration (ESSA) was formed on July 31, 1965, and the TIROS series evolved into the ESSA series. ESSA 1 was launched on February 2, 1966, and was considered to be the first fully operational weather satellite. Eight more ESSA satellites were launched from February 28, 1966, to February 26, 1969.

Meanwhile, NASA began launching the Nimbus series of weather satellites. Nimbus 1, launched on August 28, 1964, had sensitive infrared equipment that allowed it to photograph the nightside of Earth for the first time. Six more Nimbus satellites were launched from May 15, 1966, to October 24, 1978.

Impact Weather satellites became an important part of meteorological forecasting soon after they were developed. They also led to an increase in the ability of meteorologists to determine the position, speed, direction of movement, and power of dangerous storms. TIROS 3 was nicknamed the "Hurricane Spy" when it detected Hurricane Esther (1961) two days before conventional methods. Weather satellites were critical to minimizing the loss of life caused by Hurricane Betsy (1965) and Hurricane Camille (1969).

Subsequent Events The National Oceanic and Atmospheric Administration (NOAA) replaced ESSA in 1970 and began launching a new series of weather satellites. NASA began launching the Synchronous Meteorological Satellite (SMS) series in 1974. The SMS series evolved into the Geostationary Operational Environmental Satellite (GOES) series in 1975. NOAA and GOES satellites continued to be launched into the 1990's and were expected to remain an important part of the U.S. space program well into the twenty-first century.

Additional Information A detailed account of U.S. weather satellites can be found in *Weather from Above: America's Meteorological Satellites* (1991), by Janice Hill.

Rose Secrest

See also Hurricane Betsy; Hurricane Camille; Telecommunications Satellites.

■ Weathermen

Perhaps the most radical and violent group to arise in opposition to the Vietnam War. A splinter group of the Students for a Democratic Society, the Weathermen called for violent revolution in the United States and attempted to achieve their goal through terrorism, especially bombings.

Origins and History Beginning in 1965, the focus of the Students for a Democratic Society (SDS) moved away from social justice and toward protesting the Vietnam War. Consequently, SDS's membership began to grow dramatically and to include more diverse viewpoints. The relatively moderate Progressive Labor (PL) coalition began to gain considerable influence and was opposed by the far more extreme Radical Youth Movement (RYM). The internal dispute came to a head at the 1969 SDS national conference. There, RYM introduced a rambling political document with a title borrowed from a line in a Bob Dylan song: "You Don't Need a Weatherman to Know Which Way the Wind Blows." The paper advocated revolutionary violence to overthrow what its authors regarded as a corrupt and repressive "Amerika." Bernadine Dohrn, one of the document's authors, gave a blistering speech, blasting the other, less revolutionary factions and expelling them from the organization. Those who remained, a relatively small group of the most radicalized members of SDS, took a new name from the Dylan lyric: the Weather Underground, or Weathermen.

Activities The Weathermen recruited working-class white teenagers, reasoning that they were more likely to be alienated from the "system" than college students were. Recruitment methods focused on raids (called "jailbreaks") staged at high schools in the hope of fomenting uprisings among the students. These attempts failed, so the Weathermen escalated their efforts with the Days of Rage in Chicago, October 8-11, 1969—a series of demonstrations designed to provoke the authorities. The Weathermen predicted that tens of thousands of protesters would take part, but only seven hundred actually showed up. For four days, the Weathermen and their supporters listened to speeches, trashed downtown property, and fought the police. The results were injuries on both sides, and the arrest of many of the demonstrators. Contrary to the expectations of the Weathermen, there was no uprising among the youth of Chicago or elsewhere in response to the Days of Rage, but one clear result was that the rest of the antiwar Left in the United States completely disavowed the Weathermen.

Disappointed with the response to the Days of Rage, the Weathermen changed tactics, pared down their membership, and went underground. The new strategy emphasized bombings of "political" targets, chosen in response to events occurring both at home and abroad. A bomb went off at the home of a New York City judge who was presiding over the trial of some Black Panthers, another bomb was exploded at the office of the New York State Department of Corrections following the Attica prison riot, and still another destroyed a Pentagon lavatory after the bombing of North Vietnam was escalated. Each explosion was preceded by a telephoned warning (so that the building could be evacuated) and followed by a communique from the Weathermen, often through the underground press, to justify the selection of their target.

Contrary to widespread belief, the Weathermen's bombs never killed any member of the "establishment" they opposed; the only fatalities involved the Weathermen themselves. On March 6, 1970, a townhouse in New York's Greenwich Village blew up, killing Weathermen Diana Oughton, Ted Gold, and Terry Robbins. The building was being used as a bomb factory, without the knowledge of its absent owner, James Wilkerson, whose daughter Cathy had joined the Weathermen. This incident marked the end of the bombing campaign.

Impact The Weathermen never came close to achieving their revolutionary goals. They did succeed in destroying SDS, the largest organization opposing the Vietnam War. Further, they provided ample material for the Nixon administration's effort to diminish the credibility of the antiwar movement. Nixon pointed to the Weathermen to convince many Americans that all those who protested the war held the extreme views and violent tendencies exhibited by this small group of revolutionaries. This allowed Nixon to maintain substantial middle-class support for his policy of gradual disengagement, called "Vietnamization."

Subsequent Events Most Weathermen drifted away from the group as the Vietnam War wound down, and political infighting broke out among the rest. The organization effectively ceased to exist by 1977. The Weathermen leaders, having spent years on the run, individually surrendered to the authorities over the next decade. A few served brief prison sentences, but much of the evidence against them was old, inconclusive, or tainted by the illegal means employed in gathering it.

Additional Information The 1970 volume *Weatherman*, edited by Harold Jacobs, contains many of the group's speeches, position papers, and communiques. A useful book-length study is Ron Jacobs's *The Way the Wind Blew: A History of the Weathermen* (1997).

J. Justin Gustainis

See also Days of Rage; National Mobilization Committee to End the War in Vietnam (MOBE); Students for a Democratic Society (SDS); War Resisters League.

■ Weight Watchers

Both cause and effect of growing social pressure to stay slim in the 1960's. Weight Watchers brought calorie-control dieting to the masses, at a profit.

Origins and History From the 1880's through the 1950's, science and society combined to promote weight control. As malnutrition and wasting diseases such as tuberculosis waned, obesity became a major health concern. Moreover, from the 1920's through the 1950's, weight increasingly determined attractiveness and social acceptability. The Metropolitan Life Insurance weight tables (developed in 1942-1943) provided the goals, and the counting of calories—discovered in the 1880's and featured in cookbooks by the 1920's—became the method.

Weight-loss groups spread in the 1950's, based on a combination of group therapy (popular after World War II) and Alcoholics Anonymous-style support. TOPS (Take Off Pounds Sensibly), founded in 1948-1952, had thirty thousand members by 1958; that decade also produced various "anonymous" groups, such as Eaters Anonymous and Fatties Anonymous. In the 1960's, weight-loss organizations flourished. Two major groups were founded by married women in their thirties: Overeaters Anonymous, developed by three homemakers in 1960, and Weight Watchers, created by Jean Nidetch, a "formerly fat housewife," in 1961.

Activities Originally, Weight Watchers, like TOPS, closely resembled Alcoholics Anonymous in that it took a generally religious approach that included prayers for deliverance from overeating. More important, it featured group support or even control. Each meeting required members to weigh in before the assembly, and shame or praise was used as a motivator. Nidetch emphasized her own status as one who was beating a weight problem. She stressed that the individual must never feel the battle is over, even when the goal weight is reached. Remembering the days when the individual was overweight was key in Weight Watchers' approach: Participants stood in front of their "before" pictures as they spoke before the assembly, and Nidetch's book equates forgetting the past with sliding back into failure.

However, the real significance of Weight Watchers is that, in 1963, it became the first commercial, nonmedical weight-loss organization. Its first-year revenues were $160,000, and in 1970, it earned $8 million. The concept of combining weight loss with social support was new, although weight-loss products had been around for some time, and this concept became the foundation for much of the diet industry in the late 1960's and subsequent decades. Competing weight-loss companies soon started up, beginning with Diet Workshop, Inc., in 1965.

The concept of a weight-loss group especially appealed to women, many of whom were isolated both by their positions as homemakers and by the stigma of being overweight. The groups also provided a way for active nonworking women, like Nidetch herself, who headed many volunteer organizations before founding Weight Watchers, to influence others and gain recognition. The weight-loss groups provided women employment as counselors, as long as they did not regain the weight. As Weight Watchers became more established, it began to target men as well and rapidly gained male members and leaders. By 1969, Weight Watchers was directing advertisements at male executives.

The Weight Watchers approach was moderate for the time, providing highly structured eating guidelines based on a maximum daily calorie count. Because of Nidetch's emphasis on weight control as a never-ending struggle, the group also offered post-weight-loss support and lifelong maintenance diets, unusual then but consistent with later theories about weight and eating.

Impact Weight Watchers was part of a medical and social trend that favored slenderness and disapproved of heaviness and obesity, a trend driven largely by the baby boomer's desire to look good in clothes and to maintain a youthful appearance. New, revealing fashions such as bikinis and miniskirts meant that more flesh would be exposed and girdles could not be worn, so the flesh itself had to be shaped and firmed. In addition, the Metropolitan Life weight tables were revised during the 1960's so that much of the allowance for the previously accepted midlife weight gain was eliminated, and standards of beauty became more youthful in general. The waiflike, young English model Twiggy promoted the youthful, ultrathin look in the fashion world, and Weight Watchers and similar groups spread the goal of youthful thinness to the masses.

Subsequent Events Weight Watchers continues to succeed financially, with its own magazine, line of prepared foods, and international membership, despite growing competition as the dieting market continues to expand. Weight Watchers has proved flexible over the years, introducing behavior modification techniques and exercises and adapting somewhat to new nutritional research.

The 1990's saw growing public suspicion, based on long-term failure rates of all commercial dieting programs and some feeling that weight need not be so strictly controlled, leading to calls for government regulation of the diet industry. However, the desire to be thin remains potent—and lucrative.

Additional Information Consult Jean Nidetch's own *The Story of Weight Watchers* (1972) and, for a critical view, portions of Hillel Schwartz's history of dieting, *Never Satisfied* (1986).

Bernadette Lynn Bosky

See also Miniskirts; Twiggy; Women's Identity.

■ Welfare State

Expanding national-level social protection. Throughout the 1960's, Congress produced legislation extending the 1930's New Deal concept of an expansive, activist federal government committed to economic and social betterment.

The U.S. welfare state began with the Social Security Act of 1935. The stock market crash of 1929 and the Great Depression of the 1930's created widespread unemployment, about 25 percent of the workforce, and cast doubt on the ability of private-enterprise market principles to maintain U.S. living standards. Between 1934 and 1939, the United States adopted an approach to social protection that ultimately involved the direct provision of welfare and job-related services by the federal government. The New Deal legislation covered loss of income due to temporary loss of job, inability to participate in the labor force due to age or disability, the promotion of the welfare of mothers and children, and the encouragement of adequate state and local public health services. It established a dual system for federally supported income maintenance.

The 1935 act provided for preferred federally administered insurance programs (Federal Old Age Insurance) and less favorable federally aided, state-administered assistance programs for selected groups of "worthy poor" (Old Age Assistance, Aid to the Blind, Aid to Dependent Children). Left to the states was the third group of "unworthy poor," for whom states and localities were to develop programs without federal aid. In 1939, the act was amended to provide survivors' insurance and benefits for dependents. New Deal legislation also separated poor people into two categories, the able-bodied unemployed, for whom jobs were the solution, and those unable to work, for whom financial assistance was to be provided. This dichotomy led to the acceptance of two national objectives: full employment for all who were able and willing to seek work, with minimum wage legislation to help assure that those who worked escaped poverty, and a minimum decent standard of living, through social security, for those in need and not able to work.

The Legislation In 1961, to achieve full employment, President John F. Kennedy sponsored tax reduction legislation, with promises of expenditure control, to stimulate the economy and, by extension, lower the unemployment rate. Other job-related legislation included the Area Redevelopment Act of 1961, intended to bring private industry into such areas as Appalachia, and the Manpower Development and Training Act of 1962, designed to train or retrain workers displaced by economic or technological change. The Kennedy administration rejected the New Deal strategy of government as employer of last resort as exemplified by the Works Progress Administration.

Much of the legislation in the 1960's addressed the issue of poverty. In 1961, Congress approved legislation to make families with an able-bodied unemployed father eligible for Aid to Dependent Chil-

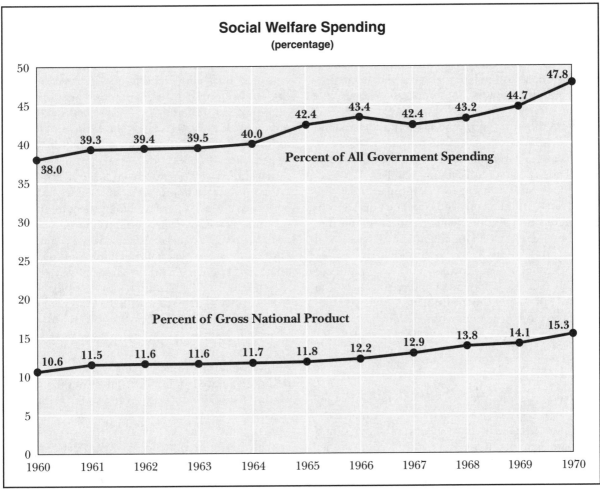

Social Welfare Spending
(percentage)

Source: Kurian, George, *Datapedia of the United States, 1790-2000, America Year by Year.* Lanham, Maryland: Bernam Press, 1994.

dren (ADC) benefits on a temporary basis, thereby acknowledging society's continued obligation to assist those who cannot find work despite market incentives to do so. The Public Welfare Amendments of 1962 encouraged states to provide social services leading to self-care and self-support.

On January 8, 1964, President Lyndon B. Johnson launched a War on Poverty in his state of the union message. The resultant legislation, the Economic Opportunity Act of 1964, authorized a Job Corps to provide work experience and training to youths through conservation camps and urban and rural residential centers, a work-training program to employ local youths, a Community Action Program to assist a variety of local efforts to alleviate poverty, a Head Start program to prepare economically disadvantaged children for elementary school education,

and a series of programs including Volunteers in Service to America (VISTA, a domestic Peace Corps) to assist the poor in rural areas. Funds were available for a range of community-service jobs through both public and private nonprofit sectors of the economy, in effect making the government the employer of first resort for many indigent people. Although the Republican Party claimed that the programs violated principles of federalism, Congress extended the programs in 1965, 1966, and 1967 and appropriated more money each year.

In 1967, Congress enacted a bill raising Social Security benefits and adding restrictions to the welfare program. The public welfare amendments established a mandatory work-training program for all recipients of Aid to Families with Dependent Children (AFDC, or welfare). Mothers of preschool children put them in federally subsidized day-care centers to attend job training. These amendments signified the beginning of a shift in the public philosophy of welfare away from the provision of social services and public cash assistance to impoverished mothers toward job preparation to achieve self-sufficiency.

The War on Poverty program was the cornerstone of Johnson's Great Society, which expanded the role of the federal government beyond that of the 1930's New Deal. Related legislation included the Food Stamp Act passed in 1964 to help meet the nutritional needs of the poor, the Elementary and Secondary Education Act of 1965 that marked the first extension of federal aid for general purposes to local schools, the Model Cities Act of 1966 to demonstrate, through a concentration and coordination of housing, health, education, employment, and social services, the ability to transform decaying urban areas into more hospitable settings, and the Housing and Urban Development Act of 1968 to provide for low- and moderate-income groups over a ten-year period.

Expansion Despite the War on Poverty and other job-related legislation in the 1960's, the major expansion of the U.S. welfare state was the extending of health benefits to the aged and the poor. Chief among the major events was passage in 1965 of Medicare, a program of hospital insurance for those age sixty-five and over, financed through the Social Security system. Medicare contained not only a basic compulsory hospital plan sought by many liberal Democrats in the post-World War II era but also a voluntary supplementary plan covering doctor bills and related services.

The second major expansion of the welfare state in the 1960's was enactment of Medicaid in 1965. Medicaid gave states the option of extending the 1961 program of assistance to the "medically needy" aged (persons who were poor but not poor enough to qualify for welfare) to other needy persons who were not elderly. It substantially increased the number of people who were eligible for federal aid to pay medical bills. In 1965, before enactment of Medicaid, a total of $1.35 billion was spent for medical assistance payments by the states and the federal government, with $600 million of the total in federal funds. In 1966, after the first calendar year of Medicaid, the federal government's share was $975 mil-

lion of $2 billion spent to pay for medical bills for welfare recipients and other needy people. To help contain federal costs of Medicaid, in 1967, Congress set income levels for eligibility of the medically needy.

Social protection legislation in the 1960's addressed not only the elderly's health needs but also their general welfare. The Social Security Amendments of 1961 raised Old Age, Survivors, and Disability Insurance (OASDI) payments, extended coverage to state and local government employees, and raised the payroll tax rate from 3.125 percent each on employers and employees in 1962 to 4.625 percent each from 1969. In addition, the amendments permitted men to receive reduced monthly benefits at age sixty-two instead of sixty-five. In 1965, The Older Americans Act established the Administration on Aging to help meet the broad social service, legal, nutritional, and economic needs of older people. Also in 1965, Congress provided a 7 percent across-the-board increase in OASDI benefits, continued benefits to widows age sixty and over and to widowers age sixty-two and over who remarried (whereas previously, benefits stopped when the survivor remarried) and allowed an individual to earn fifteen thousand dollars per year without losing Social Security benefits.

Impact Despite a reduction in the poverty rate from 22.2 percent in 1960 to 11.1 percent in 1973, the role of the federal government and increased reliance on public funding to improve the quality of life for citizens became increasingly less tenuous. High inflation and unemployment in the mid- and late 1970's, advocacy of free enterprise market principles to guide the economy and the anti-big government rhetoric of President Ronald Reagan in the more prosperous 1980's, and the deficit-ridden federal budget that dominated the politics of recession in the early 1990's, all contributed to a change in public philosophy regarding the virtues of the welfare state. In the early 1970's, President Richard M. Nixon sought in vain to federalize public assistance. His Family Assistance Plan would have provided a guaranteed income for all low-income families, thereby doubling the welfare rolls by incorporating an additional eleven million working poor families. With passage of the Personal Responsibility and Work Opportunity Act of 1996, Congress ended the federal mandate of providing income for poor families and turned AFDC over to the states. In the 1970's,

Congress ensured that the living standards of the aging population would keep pace with the economy and passed legislation that provided automatic Cost of Living Adjustments (COLAs) to OASDI beneficiaries. Throughout the 1980's and 1990's, however, the costs of Social Security and Medicare consumed an ever larger share of the federal budget. In 1994, Congress rejected a comprehensive national health care plan proposed by President Bill Clinton. Some advocates of Social Security reform in the 1990's called for privatizing a portion of the program, thereby raising the prospect of further erosion of the idea that increased public expenditures are necessary to ensure the quality of life of the nation's people.

Additional Information Major works on welfare include Edward D. Berkowitz's *America's Welfare State from Roosevelt to Reagan* (1991), Richard K. Caputo's *Welfare and Freedom American Style: The Role of the Federal Government, 1940-1980* (1994), James L. Sundquist's *Politics and Policy: The Eisenhower, Kennedy, and Johnson Years* (1968), and *America's Misunderstood Welfare State* (1990), by Theodore R. Marmor, Jerry L. Mashaw, and Philip L. Harvey.

Richard K. Caputo

See also Aid to Families with Dependent Children (AFDC); Food Stamp Program; Goldwater, Barry; Great Society Programs; Head Start; Job Corps; Johnson, Lyndon B.; Kennedy, John F.; Medicare; Prosperity and Poverty; War on Poverty.

■ *What Ever Happened to Baby Jane?*

Released 1962
Director Robert Aldrich
  (1918-1983)

A stylish gothic horror film with comic overtones. It introduced the Hollywood Grand Guignol tradition wherein aging actresses play psychotic women who shock and horrify audiences with their gruesome and macabre actions.

The Work In *What Ever Happened to Baby Jane?*, two jealous sisters—Jane Hudson (Bette Davis) and Blanche Hudson (Joan Crawford)—live as recluses in a decaying Hollywood mansion. The alcoholic Jane alternates between feelings of rage, because Jane's early fame as a vaudeville child star was eclipsed by Blanche's greater fame in the films, and

guilt, because Jane believes she drunkenly crippled Blanche in a car accident years before, ending Blanche's career, and because Jane is now financially dependent on Blanche. When Jane learns that Blanche plans to sell the mansion and commit her to an asylum, Jane's hatred explodes into violent action. She imprisons Blanche, who uses a wheelchair, in her bedroom, brutalizing her and finally binding and gagging her. Lost in drink and fantasy, Jane plans to revive her Baby Jane act of long ago. She orders costumes and hires pianist Edwin Flagg (Victor Buono), who feigns enthusiasm for Jane's ludicrous performance. When the weekly cleaning lady finds the tortured Blanche, Jane silences her by killing her with a hammer. During another rehearsal, pianist Flagg accidentally discovers the near-to-death Blanche. Horrified, he flees the house, and Jane becomes terrified that he will return with the police. During the early hours, Jane takes the emaciated Blanche to the beach at Malibu, intent on burying her. At dawn, Jane learns from the feeble Blanche that the long-ago accident crippling Blanche was not really caused by Jane but engineered by Blanche herself in a jealous rage.

A crowd gathers to watch the now completely insane Jane cavort on the beach and go through her grotesque Baby Jane routine as two policemen arrest her for murder.

Impact Although many critics in 1962 dismissed the black-and-white film as trashy melodrama, *What Ever Happened to Baby Jane?* became a box-office bonanza, reactivating the careers of both Davis and Crawford. Subsequently, the film has undergone critical reevaluation and is now considered a trendsetter and a superb example of the gothic horror genre. Known in the motion-picture industry as the "menopausal murder story," the film cagily uses aging actresses to play psychotic monsters who kill and commit grotesque acts. Because of the film's financial success, similar ones followed, including *Die, Die My Darling* (1965) and *What Ever Happened to Aunt Alice?* (1969). It exemplifies the well-crafted gothic horror film, depicting decadent Hollywood and the price of fame and its fleeting rewards. Director Robert Aldrich creates an emotional roller coaster that builds with ever-growing force; he relies not on graphic blood and gore but on a dark rush of images and a strong power of suggestion to create suspense, which is heightened by his use of memorable camera angles

Joan Crawford (left) and Bette Davis (right) play aging, once-famous sisters in the 1962 gothic horror film What Ever Happened to Baby Jane? *(Museum of Modern Art/Film Stills Archive)*

and carefully delineated characters. *What Ever Happened to Baby Jane?* is also revered for its nostalgic impact because it uses two veteran actresses (deadly rivals in real life) to play the hate-drenched pair and draws on clips from their early films.

Additional Information For information on the filming of *What Ever Happened to Baby Jane?*, see *The Films and Career of Robert Aldrich* (1986) by Edwin T. Arnold and Eugene L. Miller.

Richard Whitworth

See also Film; Hitchcock Films; *Hush...Hush, Sweet Charlotte*; *Rosemary's Baby*.

■ White Panthers

A political group inspired in equal measures by the radical Left, the drug culture, and rock and roll. The White Panthers manifested a commitment to the total revolution of American society.

Origins and History The White Panther Party formed in 1968 in Ann Arbor, Michigan. The name

expressed solidarity with the Black Panther Party's call for separate revolutionary movements formed by blacks and whites. The White Panthers' manifesto, however, rejected "white honkie culture" in favor of a "program of rock and roll, dope, and f—king in the streets." They proclaimed, "We are LSD-driven total maniacs in the universe."

The Panthers' main public voice was the MC5, a rock group managed by John Sinclair, the party's minister of information. The band spread its revolutionary message at concerts in local high schools, performed in Chicago during the 1968 Democratic National Convention, and released an album, *Kick Out the Jams*, on Elektra Records in 1969. In 1969, Sinclair was sent to prison for possessing two marijuana cigarettes. White Panther Pun Plamondon was later convicted of bombing the Ann Arbor office of the Central Intelligence Agency.

Impact The White Panthers resembled the Yippies in that they made their greatest contribution by creating political theater. Their extreme, whimsical, sometimes profane rhetoric was often quoted by opponents of the counterculture. Like the Weathermen, the White Panthers had a real, but ineffectual, commitment to total revolution.

Subsequent Events   In 1971, following the imprisonment of several members, the White Panthers changed their name to the Rainbow People's Party and thereafter fell into obscurity.

Additional Information   The White Panthers' progress is traced in John Sinclair's 1972 collection, *Guitar Army: Street Writings/Prison Writings.*

Jeremy Mumford

See also   Black Panthers; Counterculture; Democratic National Convention of 1968; LSD; Music; Weathermen; Yippies.

■ Who's Afraid of Virginia Woolf?

Released 1966
Director Mike Nichols (1931-   )

A film that frankly portrayed the battles of a couple whose dreams have died. It contributed to the 1960's trend of treating serious adult content in motion pictures.

The Work   *Who's Afraid of Virginia Woolf?* tells of the desperately unhappy Martha (Elizabeth Taylor) and George (Richard Burton), history professor at the small college where Martha's father is president. Each has sought fulfillment in the approved ways, Martha in romantic love and in social status and George in marital, academic, and artistic success. Martha's father has dashed their hopes by suppress-

Martha (Elizabeth Taylor, center) and husband George (Richard Burton, wearing glasses) play host to Nick (George Segal) and wife Honey (Sandy Dennis) in the 1966 film Who's Afraid of Virginia Woolf?, *one of a number of motion pictures that began to deal with more mature subjects in the 1960's.* (Museum of Modern Art/Film Stills Archive)

ing Martha's first love affair and George's creative writing. In addition, he has not groomed George as successor to his college presidency as Martha had wanted. In middle age, the couple feels trapped, and they blame each other. Martha invites the new biology professor, Nick (George Segal), and his wife, Honey (Sandy Dennis), home after a faculty party. George and Martha force the insecure couple to participate in their mind wars. Martha manipulates the ambitious Nick to provoke George's jealousy. When George refuses to respond as she desires, Martha declares total war and attempts to seduce Nick. Deeply hurt by Martha's actions, George compels Honey to verify that George and Martha's son is dead. Though they are childless, they have consoled themselves by secretly imagining a child. When Martha commits "emotional adultery," George "kills" their son. They are forced to face their future without this comforting illusion.

Impact This adaptation of Edward Albee's first successful full-length play (produced in 1962) was director Mike Nichols's first feature film. Both the play and the film received mixed reviews, with many critics noting the harshness of its humor and tragic emotions and recognizing the work's critique of post-World War II optimism. Partly because it was generally a faithful adaptation, the film reopened reviewers' debates, including whether Albee used George and Martha's marriage as a disguised treatment of a homosexual relationship. The two main censorship boards found the film problematic. For the first time, the National Catholic Office for Motion Pictures (NCOMP) gave an A-4 rating (morally unobjectionable, with reservations) to a film with explicit erotic content and vulgar language. NCOMP judges cited the moral seriousness of the film and the growing contempt of younger educated viewers for the organization's ratings as reasons for its decision. The Motion Picture Association of America (MPAA) believed the film was worthy of Academy Awards, awarding Best Actress to Taylor and Best Supporting Actress to Dennis, but could not give it the organization's seal of approval under its 1930 Motion Picture Production Code. This problem increased the pressure on the industry to modify the code, resulting in the 1968 motion picture rating system.

Additional Information A brief study of the script can be found in *Who's Afraid of Virginia Woolf?* (1990) by Matthew Roudané. The censorship controversy is discussed in "Raw Dialogue Challenges All the Censors," by Thomas Thompson, in the June 10, 1966, issue of *Life* magazine.

Terry Heller

See also Albee, Edward; Censorship; Film; *Graduate, The*; Motion Picture Association Rating System; Theater; Theater of the Absurd.

■ *Wild Bunch, The*

Released 1969
Director Sam Peckinpah (1925-1984)

An elegy for lost causes and nobility gone awry. The film both celebrates and exposes the United States' cherished myths of manhood, frontier, and friendship.

The Work Led by Pike Bishop, a group of outlaws sets out in 1913 to accomplish a heist that will set them for life. The film opens as the Bunch, dressed as soldiers, ride into Starbuck, Texas, to rob a bank. They pass children who are enjoying the spectacle of hundreds of ants doing battle with a scorpion and a temperance meeting. They are also the target of a group of railroad bounty hunters hiding above the false fronts of the town's buildings. The robbery ends in a bloody gun battle in which innocent bystanders as well as robbers and bounty hunters are shot. Several of the Bunch escape only to discover that the loot they managed to get away with is nothing but iron washers. Knowing a posse is after them, they flee to Mexico where they fall in with the anti-revolutionary general Mapache. Mapache hires the Bunch to go back across the border and capture arms from a train carrying munitions for the army. The Bunch—now consisting of Pike, Dutch, Lyle and Tector Gorch, and Angel—accomplish the mission and return to Mapache. Knowing Angel is a Mexican who sympathizes with the revolution, Mapache tortures him. The Bunch decide to rescue their comrade, and a final battle of apocalyptic proportions takes place.

Impact *The Wild Bunch*, at once lyrical and violent, presents an ambivalent vision of redemption. As the 1960's came to an end, the vision of peace and love so ardently held by that generation of young people became difficult to sustain. Old certainties did not hold, and Sam Peckinpah's film expresses both the beauty in the myths of heroism, friendship, and hope associated with the Western frontier as well as the violent implications. The film's heroes are deeply flawed men who claim to live by a code but whose lives are testaments to the failure of that code. Pike Bishop, leader of the Bunch, has on more than one occasion in the past acted with dishonor, selfishness, and rashness. Flashbacks in the film inform us that he failed to keep the woman he loved from death and failed to stick by his friend, Deke Thornton. For Pike, a measure of redemption comes when he leads the Bunch to the square in Agua Verde to rescue their comrade, Angel, from Mapache. The final carnage is futile since Mapache kills Angel and the Bunch cannot achieve victory over Mapache's numerous men. In the battle, however, the Bunch decimate Mapache's forces, thus allowing the Mexican rebels to scavenge guns and materials after the battle ends. In a curious manner, then, the Bunch support a revolutionary movement.

William Holden (right) and Ernest Borgnine exchange a few words in the final shootout in the 1969 film The Wild Bunch, *best known for its violence.* (Museum of Modern Art/Film Stills Archive)

Related Works *Bonnie and Clyde* (1967), directed by Arthur Penn, initiates the aesthetics of violence that Peckinpah perfects. *Butch Cassidy and the Sundance Kid* (1969), directed by George Roy Hill, provides a light-hearted version of a Western elegy.

Additional Information For an eloquent interpretation and defense of *The Wild Bunch*, see Paul Seydor's *Peckinpah: The Western Films, a Reconsideration* (1997).

Roderick McGillis

See also *Bonnie and Clyde*; *Butch Cassidy and the Sundance Kid*; Film.

■ Wilderness Act of 1964

An early piece of environmental legislation reflecting an increasing interest in environmental protection. It provided a legal definition of the wilderness and ensured the preservation of the beauty and solitude of untouched wild areas.

In the first half of the twentieth century, no national policy to guarantee preservation of the wilderness existed. The authority to preserve wild areas rested with either the chief of the U.S. Forest Service or the Secretary of Agriculture. In 1951, the executive director of the Wilderness Society, Howard Zahniser, launched a campaign to support a Sierra Club bill to protect the wilderness. The Wilderness Bill was introduced in Congress on June 7, 1956.

The lines of the debate were drawn roughly between the conservationists and preservationists, who wanted to protect the areas from damaging human influences, and developers, who championed the concept of multiple use. Democratic senator Hubert Humphrey was among those who introduced the bill. Secretary of the Interior Stuart Udall, appointed in 1961, understood and championed the wilderness cause, and at his urging, John F. Kennedy became the first president to support the bill.

Opposition came from many quarters, including the logging and petroleum industries. A spokesman for the Kennecott Copper Corporation argued that the enemy of the free world, the Soviet Union, would delight in a self-imposed limitation on mineral exploration and exploitation in the United States. The New Mexico Wool Growers Association warned that the wilderness was a breeding ground for predators of young livestock. A false rumor that the legislation would expropriate privately owned land spread. Colorado representative Wayne Aspinall, chairman of the House Committee on Interior and Insular Affairs and a spokesperson for mining and ranching interests, thwarted the bill numerous times.

President Lyndon B. Johnson signed the Wilderness Act on September 3, 1964. It created the National Wilderness Preservation System and stipulated that the wilderness be kept free of roads, dams, permanent structures, and logging and land motor vehicles. Hunting and fishing were permitted, subject to regulation. Motor boats and airplanes were allowed where they were already in operation. The bill was somewhat weakened by its granting permission for grazing in wilderness areas and allowing mineral rights to wilderness lands until December 31, 1983.

Impact Upon the signing of the act, fifty-four areas in thirteen states, totaling more than nine million acres, were designated as wilderness. Most of the land was in the West, as areas in the East failed to meet the criterion of being "untrammeled by man" or the five-thousand-acre minimum. Under the Wilderness Act, federal land management agencies—the National Forest Service, the National Park Service, the Fish and Wildlife Service, and the Bureau of Land Management—were requested to review land under their jurisdictions for possible designation as wilderness.

Subsequent Events The wilderness system has grown by millions of acres, much of it in Alaska. Other environment-preserving acts have been passed, including the Eastern Wilderness Act of 1974 and the Alaska National Interest Lands Conservation Act of 1980.

Additional Information The third edition of *Wilderness and the American Mind* (1986), by Roderick Nash, sketches the major concerns and movements of American environmentalists and sets the Wilderness Act of 1964 within its historical context.

Kristen L. Zacharias

See also Environmental Movement.

■ Wolfman Jack

Born January 21, 1938, Brooklyn, New York
Died July 1, 1995, Belvidere, North Carolina

One of the most famous disc jockeys in the history of broadcasting. Through his trademark wolf howls, raspy voice, and unconventional style, Wolfman Jack became a spokesperson for rock and roll in the 1960's.

Early Life Born Robert Weston Smith, Wolfman Jack grew up in one of the toughest neighborhoods of Brooklyn. Despite a tough childhood and some juvenile delinquency, Smith's love of music eventually got him off the streets and out of the gangs. As a teenager, he transformed an old coal bin into a mock studio where he played his radio and spun his records, imitating the daring disc jockeys of the 1950's. Enterprising and persistent, Smith procured odd jobs at the Paramount Theater and at an African American-programmed radio station in New Jersey. After stints as a door-to-door salesperson peddling encyclopedias and Fuller brushes, Smith entered the National Academy of Broadcasting to pursue his dream of becoming a rhythm-and-blues disc jockey.

The 1960's Upon graduation in 1960, Smith secured a job with WYOU in Newport News, Virginia, a radio station that catered predominantly to African American audiences. Creating the character "Daddy Jules," he delivered soul, jazz, and rhythm and blues in vibrant style. In 1961, Smith moved to KCIJ in Shreveport, Louisiana, where he played country music as "Big Smith with the Records," a job that better supported his new family. His big break and first step on the road to stardom came in 1963 when he crossed the border into Mexico and joined the team of XERF radio. After a dramatic takeover involving bold financial scheming, Smith finally obtained the forum to display his alter ego, and Wolfman Jack was born. With XERF's powerful 250,000-watt signal virtually blanketing North America, the Wolfman's howls, guttural voice, and outlandish verbal antics could be heard by a legion of young followers as he promoted his beloved rhythm and blues and soulful rock and roll. In 1966, he moved his base of operations to Los Angeles.

Later Life By 1972, Wolfman Jack had produced the first syndicated rock-and-roll program on the air, eventually broadcasting on twenty-two hundred stations in forty-three countries. In 1973, he played himself in the award-winning film *American Graffiti,* finally revealing the face that matched the voice and catapulting him from cult figure to mainstream celebrity. From 1973 to 1981, the Wolfman hosted the *Midnight Special,* a National Broadcasting Company (NBC) television program that featured live rock-and-roll performances. By 1995, he had amassed countless television and personal appearances, including a live show from Planet Hollywood in Washington, D.C. On July 1, 1995, Wolfman Jack died of a heart attack in his North Carolina home.

Impact At a time when the airwaves were racially segregated, Wolfman Jack was instrumental in providing exposure to African American musicians, thus helping to integrate mainstream, popular music. With the powerful airwaves as his podium, he played a key role in shaping the musical climate of a generation. The Wolfman's dynamic and daring approach to broadcasting has inspired subsequent disc jockeys to emulate his innovative style.

Additional Information In 1995, Wolfman Jack, with coauthor Byron Laursen, published his autobiography, *Have Mercy! Confessions of the Original Rock 'n' Roll Animal.*

Karen L. Gennari

See also Music.

■ Women in the Workforce

Female employees grew in number and type during the 1960's. As the ranks of working women swelled, they began to enter previously male-dominated areas and raise challenges to discriminatory practices in education, hiring, promotion, and salaries.

Women in the lowest social classes had always worked and in much higher proportions than women in the middle and upper classes. Industrialization created new occupations women could fill, and by 1940, women made up 25 percent of the U.S. labor force. Thousands more women joined the assembly lines and other areas of work when they were needed during World War II. Moreover, legislation developed to protect women from long hours, heavy lifting, subminimum wages, and other kinds of abuse by employers that had existed since early in the industrial era.

Appreciation of women as workers, however, declined toward the end of the war when it became apparent that soldiers would need jobs when they returned home. After World War II, government, business, and the media promoted the idea that a woman's place was in the home, caring for children, while a man's place was at work outside the home. This image was accompanied by a tremendous growth in suburbs and child-rearing manuals. Statistics, indeed, reflected the desire of women to marry and to start families at ever younger ages. The birthrate reached its peak in 1957 during the so-called "baby boom."

Stereotypes portrayed women as mechanically inept and as more emotional than task-oriented. The popular media furthered the interests of industrialists and others wanting women kept out of the workforce; advertisements, for example, suggested that working women were not very feminine compared with women who stayed home to nurture children and to be charming housewives. Even some homemakers criticized working wives as selfish and ambitious.

"Women's Work" Even though society seemed to value women only as homemakers, by 1960, two out of five women were in the workforce. Of these, 30 percent were married. Moreover, 19 percent of mothers with children under six were employed outside the home. Most jobs held by women tended to be in the lower-ranking professions or in the lower levels of administrative work, however. Cynthia Fuchs Epstein explained in *Woman's Place* (1970) that women's talents were not being fully utilized. For example, by 1960, only 3.5 percent of lawyers, 6.5 percent of physicians, 2.1 percent of dentists, 2 percent of judges, 1.2 percent of engineers, and 7 percent of scientists were women. Furthermore, the proportion of women going to college and getting doctorates had actually declined since the 1920's.

In 1961, President John F. Kennedy responded to the pleas of Eleanor Roosevelt (the widow of former president Franklin D. Roosevelt) by forming the President's Commission on the Status of Women. The 1963 report of the commission confirmed that discrimination against women in education and employment was pervasive, and women were not provided with adequate support when they wanted to change their lives. Schools and colleges did not encourage girls to develop careers, and the professions often did not grant entry to women. Instead,

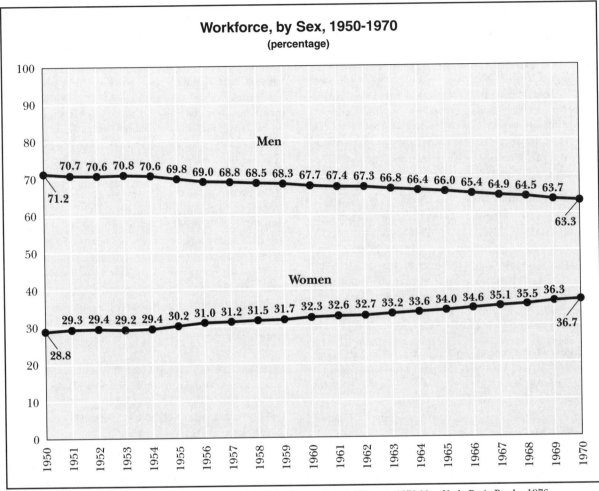

Workforce, by Sex, 1950-1970
(percentage)

Source: U.S. Bureau of the Census. *Historical Statistics of the United States, Colonial Times to 1970.* New York: Basic Books, 1976.

social institutions saw to it that girls from a very early age were encouraged to fill the role that the culture held as ideal for women, that of housewife and mother. Betty Friedan, perhaps the most prominent feminist of the 1960's, criticized both the belief that the truly fulfilled woman was a housewife and the ideology supporting the baby-boom lifestyle as "a conspiracy to trap women in the home" in her book, *The Feminine Mystique* (1963).

When women chose to work, most made occupational choices that were not defined as "men's work." For example, secretarial work, nursing, and elementary school teaching were considered extensions of women's nurturing traits, whereas women in engineering and science careers were seen as threatening to men. Storybooks and elementary schoolbooks depicted women as mothers and not as workers,

even though more than five million children under age twelve had mothers working full-time at the beginning of the 1960's.

The Commission's Findings When women did work, they earned 30 percent to 60 percent less than men, sometimes for the same type of job. Furthermore, many women were denied promotions as a result of sex discrimination. The President's Commission on the Status of Women made specific recommendations to overcome discrimination by schools and employers, including more flexible admission requirements on the part of colleges, government-sponsored day-care centers, adequate job-counseling services for women, and an end to discrimination in hiring and employment practices within the federal government.

Few of the commission's recommendations were followed up by education, industry, and government, and the same commission rejected an Equal Rights Amendment (ERA), because members believed that women's equality was already guaranteed by the Fifth and Fourteenth Amendments. Kennedy was not seen by feminists as being a very active promoter of women's job rights; nonetheless, he asked that department heads of U.S. agencies review their hiring practices, and state welfare agencies were given funds to increase the capacity of their day-care centers. His administration passed the Equal Pay Act of 1963, banning wage discrimination on the basis of sex, although this act did little to address the pay gap between men and women. Watchdog agencies also were formed by the federal government and in several states to investigate the status of women in the workforce.

Legal Aid for Women When Lyndon B. Johnson became president following Kennedy's assassination in 1963, he hired a record number of women to fill high administrative positions. He also increased the number of women on his own staff and the salaries of many female civil servants. Through Title VII of the Civil Rights Act of 1964, Johnson provided women with a legal basis to fight job discrimination. Prohibitions to sex discrimination were extended beyond wages to job classifications, assignments, promotions, and training opportunities. Furthermore, Title VII ordered that affirmative action be used to remedy the results of past discrimination. This meant, for example, that additional recruitment and advertising should be used to attract qualified women (and other protected groups, for example, ethnic minorities), and employment policies should be designed to ensure equal opportunities once women were hired. Title VII also stated that sexual harassment was a form of illegal discrimination.

NOW and Other Organizations Women activists were encouraged by these policy changes, but they did not believe that these approaches were sufficient to address women's employment issues. In 1966, Friedan helped organize the National Organization for Women (NOW). Many of NOW's members had found that their roles as social activists for civil rights and other causes were downplayed by the men who worked with them in these social justice organizations. In developing NOW, members included calls for more educational opportunities for women, for

an end to sex discrimination in employment, and for making women's Social Security payments equal to those of men. They endorsed the Equal Rights Amendment in 1967. Other women's rights organizations, many of which sought the improvement of the status of women as workers, were founded or became active during the 1960's

Two-thirds of all new employees during the 1960's were women. By the end of the decade, almost half of all adult women were in the paid labor force, and women remained in the workforce for longer periods than ever before. However, they continued to hold the lowest paying jobs, and they still earned 30 percent to 60 percent less than men. Affirmative action programs had had little effect in addressing the overall status of women workers. Women of color were more hurt, proportionately, by women's low economic and social status than were American women of European descent.

Impact Home life was very much affected when women joined the workforce. By the end of the 1960's, women with children under six in the workforce had jumped from 19 percent to 30 percent, and more than half of all mothers with school-aged children had jobs. Moreover, the percentage of employed women who were working wives grew from 30 percent to 40 percent. A second income often was necessary to maintain living standards and, in the case of the middle class, to pay for children's college educations. On average, women earned one-quarter of the family's income.

At the same time, women increasingly were becoming single heads of household (one in ten among white families, one in five among black families). In fact, 8 million children under eighteen were being cared for by single women by the end of the decade, and their median family income was $4,000, compared with $11,600 for households headed by men. Furthermore, more than half of all woman-headed American Indian, Mexican American, African American, and Puerto Rican households were below the poverty line by the end of the decade, even as the overall labor force participation rates by women in these groups increased during the 1960's. About one-quarter of white households headed by single women were below the poverty line at the end of the decade.

Sociological studies in the 1960's pointed to the positive impact that working women had on the household. These included reports that a working woman had more influence over family decisions and encouraged more self-reliance in her children than did full-time homemakers. Nonetheless, many women expressed difficulties balancing work and home roles. Instead of feeling newly liberated, many employed women found that they were working a "double day." They did most of the child rearing, cooking, cleaning, and other domestic chores on top of their hours as a paid employee. Studies showed that the average employed wife worked two hours more per day than did the full-time homemaker. Some husbands assumed more of the household chores, although employed wives still did more than half the domestic chores. Another consequence was a decline in the birthrate.

The 1960's brought women's talents and voices to the forefront. More women than ever were educated and employed. The 1960's revived earlier women's movements and brought about a new feminism that included emphases on fulfillment through personal freedom, education, social activism, and work, even as many women also saw that society did not make it easy for the woman worker either at home or at work.

Subsequent Events Women's greater economic independence through paid work has affected women at every stage of life. After the 1960's, most girls and young women came to see their future as involving an occupation outside the home. College enrollment among women surged, and women waited longer to get married. Other women felt freer to leave unhappy marriages, which is one of the reasons for the large increase in the divorce rate after the 1960's. Still others felt that they did not need to get married and could find fulfillment through work, friendships, and hobbies.

Women continued the efforts made in the 1960's to fight discrimination in education, employment, salaries, and promotions. They saw to it that more professions and trades opened the doors to women. Women also more than doubled their representation in unions. Wage differences still loomed large in some professions, however, and jobs traditionally defined as "women's work" still yielded relatively low wages.

Although the conflicts between the demands of work and home affected employed mothers of all social classes, working mothers living below or near the poverty line continued to have special difficulties in taking time off from work to care for children. Working women, feeling the strain of the double day, put pressure on government and business to adopt new social policies affecting them and their families, and they sought broader recognition from society for the work that they did in raising children. Specific demands included affordable day care, paid leave for new parents, paid sick days when children became ill, and shorter workweeks.

Additional Information Teresa Amott and Julie Matthei have written an excellent analysis of the economic history of U.S. women in their book *Race, Gender, and Work* (1996), and just after the 1960's, Cynthia Fuchs Epstein wrote a groundbreaking book called *Woman's Place: Options and Limits in Professional Careers* (1970). Two other books, also supplemented by careful statistical analyses, are *Women, Work, and Fertility, 1900-1986* (1988), by Susan Householder Van Horn, and *Women and the American Experience* (1994), by Nancy Woloch. Angela Davis considered the special challenges confronted by African American women in *Women, Race, and Class* (1983).

Grace Maria Marvin

See also Affirmative Action; Baby Boomers; Civil Rights Act of 1964; Davis, Angela; Equal Pay Act of 1964; Equal Rights Amendment; *Feminine Mystique, The*; Feminist Movement; Friedan, Betty; National Organization for Women (NOW); Women's Identity.

■ Women's Identity

A changing element of women's persona that shaped the way they viewed themselves and their roles in society. At times, women's identity reflected American culture in the 1960's; at other times, the mainstream culture resisted and denied women's perception of themselves.

In the 1960's, women made up a larger section of the workforce and of those receiving higher education than ever before. However, their role in society was still second to that of men, despite the efforts of the equal rights movement during the previous decades. In the early 1960's, 35 percent of women over age sixteen in the United States worked. However, most of the jobs commonly held by women—secretaries, nurses, teachers, factory workers—were service oriented. Marriage remained the greatest aspiration for most women. In 1960, 70 percent of women in the United States married before age twenty-four.

Mainstream culture was replete with images of women engaged in domestic pursuits. Women's magazines such as *McCall's* and *Ladies' Home Journal* were filled with articles related to beauty, homemaking, and child rearing. The suburbanite ideal of the 1950's—woman as homemaker and mother—continued to be portrayed in films and television shows such as *The Adventures of Ozzie and Harriet* (1952-1966) and *Leave It to Beaver* (1957-1963).

The "Happy Housewife" In 1962, a study conducted by the *Saturday Evening Post* reported that "few peo-

ple are as happy as a housewife." After interviewing twenty-three hundred women, the article concluded that most women wanted nothing more than to be a good wife and mother and those who were not married were eager to be wed. Despite the *Post* report, the unhappiness of women became a topic of national debate. Depression was on the rise in women, and many were seeking psychiatric help and regularly using tranquilizers. National newspapers and network television began reporting on the troubles of women, but their reports generally concluded that too much education and not

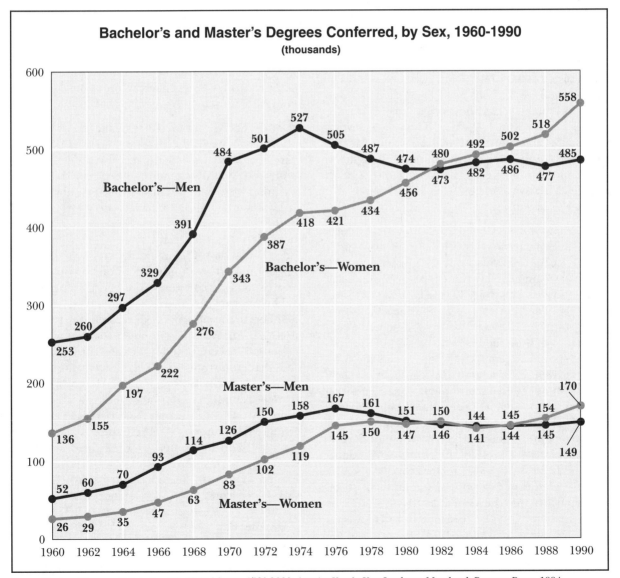

Source: Kurian, George, *Datapedia of the United States, 1790-2000, America Year by Year.* Lanham, Maryland: Bernam Press, 1994.

enough appreciation were the root of the problem.

Betty Friedan addressed women's discontent in _The Feminine Mystique_ (1963), an unprecedented book that described the American housewife's dissatisfactions and the societal problems and pressures contributing to her unhappiness. _The Feminine Mystique_ immediately became a best-seller; this overwhelming response gave credence to Friedan's observations and initiated a change in women's self-perception.

Sex and Women Women's sexual identity was altered in the 1960's. In _Sex and the Single Girl_ (1962), Helen Gurley Brown urged young women to "play the field" and use sex as a weapon in their career ambitions. Film roles for women ranged from the wholesome girls portrayed in the Gidget films to the sexy beauties that populated the James Bond films. The radical findings in William H. Masters and Virginia E. Johnson's book, _Human Sexual Response_ (1966), validated a woman's right to sexual pleasure with or without a male partner. The sexual revolution that erupted in the 1960's fostered women's sexual freedom; however, the commercial objectification and contradictory cultural images of women created confusion as to how women should perceive themselves sexually.

Other Changes The United States in the mid-1960's began to experience strong social upheaval and a resurgence of women's political involvement. Although few women held leadership positions, a large majority of activists involved in the Civil Rights movement, the labor movement, and eventually in protests against the Vietnam War were women.

Women outside the mainstream culture, including older women, minority women, and lesbians, also experienced changes. The conflicting values held by younger and older women created a generation gap that left many older women feeling marginalized and alienated. African American women battled single motherhood and the hardship of poverty wages but were a stronghold of the Civil Rights movement, paving the way for other social causes. By the end of the decade, popular culture featured more positive African American images such as singer Diahann Carroll's lead role in the television situation comedy _Julia_ (1968-1971). In addition, homosexuals gained a greater positive image in the 1960's through films, journals, and the changing social environment. The term "lesbian" developed around 1967 as more women declared their homosexuality and revolted against discriminatory laws.

In 1966, out of the need for a strong political voice, national representation, and the frustrations over the irresolute findings of the President's Commission on the Status of Women (1963), the National Organization for Women (NOW) was formed. By 1969, NOW had fifty chapters in twenty-four states and continuous media attention. The national publicity NOW received helped encourage women's involvement in the fight for equal rights and increase Americans' awareness of women's changing roles in society.

The late 1960's were known for free love, social protest, and lofty ideals, many of which did not match the reality of daily life for most women. In 1969, anthropologist Margaret Mead stated that because of the unrivaled freedoms and choices women had, they could never measure up to the "artificial standards" presented by the national culture.

Impact Throughout the 1960's, American women's self-perceptions were changing, and they began to search for their own identities. The percentage of twenty-four-year-olds never married rose to 35, the declining birth rate put an end to the baby boom, and women demanded that men do a larger share of the housework and child rearing. Television shows depicted single and career women, and the song "D-I-V-O-R-C-E" topped the charts in 1968—a reflection of the rapidly climbing divorce rate. Women made up 40 percent of college enrollment and became engineers and computer programmers, members of the clergy, and syndicated sports columnists. Many universities adopted programs aimed at meeting the needs of older, "second career" women who were returning to college after a number of years as a homemaker and mother. However, pay for women remained comparatively low. By 1967, women were earning only 58.6 percent of men's annual salary, largely because most low-paying jobs were still held by women. Despite the changes in women's identity during the decade, women remained greatly underrepresented in the higher ranks of the workforce and their roles in society were still unclear. Many women found it difficult to live up to the new images and were afraid of being regarded as "unfeminine."

Subsequent Events The collective awareness that women and their roles were changing set the stage for the revolutionary women's movement of the 1970's. Women sought more challenging and satisfying careers, demanded their reproductive rights, and adopted "Ms." in place of "Miss" or "Mrs." in front of their names, symbolizing that their identity was separate from their marital status.

Additional Information Two books that look at women's identity in the 1960's are *American Women in the 1960's: Changing the Future* (1993), by Blanche Linden-Ward and Carol Hurd Green, and *The Woman in America* (1965), by Robert Jay Lifton.

Caralee Hutchinson

See also *Feminine Mystique, The*; Feminist Movement; Women in the Workforce.

■ Woodstock Festival

Date August 15-17, 1969

A three-day concert featuring some of the most popular rock performers of the 1960's. The festival, attended by 450,000 people who endured rain, food shortages, and hopelessly crowded conditions, is remembered for its peaceful, loving atmosphere.

Origins and History John Roberts, heir to a multimillion-dollar trust fund and his friend, Joel Rosenman, in an attempt at venture capitalism, took out an advertisement in *The New York Times* inviting ideas for investment. Eventually, they were introduced to record executive Artie Kornfeld and Michael Lang, producer of the Miami Pop Festival, and the four men hatched the idea for a festival that would attract all the decade's major musical talents.

Originally, the organizers of the Woodstock Music and Art Fair rented land in Wallkill, New York, but the community grew fearful of a massive influx of hippies and thwarted their plans. The producers had already launched a national publicity campaign and had begun securing acts, so with time rapidly evaporating, they found a six-hundred-acre dairy farm in nearby Bethel. Despite some resistance, plans went forward after members of the Hog Farm commune were hired as a quasi-security

force. Michael Wadleigh, a documentary director, was commissioned to film the event. Although the producers had deliberately chosen Woodstock, home of Bob Dylan, as the festival site, they could not convince him to participate.

A week before the event, people began descending on Bethel, eventually clogging highways and disrupting life in the sleepy town. Workers frantically assembled a massive stage, and helicopters were commissioned to ferry performers to the concert site. Early on Friday, August 15, promoters discovered they had not erected ticket booths, and thus, an audience of thousands was admitted free.

The Festival The plan was for folk acts to perform on opening day and for successive days to be filled with rock-and-roll artists, culminating in an extended appearance by Jimi Hendrix. However, the first day's

A concert-goer lies on his muddy motorcycle during the Woodstock Festival in Bethel, New York, August 15-17. Feelings of peace and harmony reigned over the event despite the planners' failure to provide adequate facilities for the attendees. (AP/Wide World Photos)

performances were delayed because of difficulties transporting acts to the site. Richie Havens had to take the stage and play for nearly three hours while the promoters made alternate plans. When Havens finished, Country Joe McDonald—minus his band, the Fish—was pressed into service and roused the crowd with an obscene version of the Fish cheer. John Sebastian, formerly of the Lovin' Spoonful, made an unscheduled appearance. He was followed by the Incredible String Band, Sweetwater, and Tim Hardin. Then Ravi Shankar's performance was interrupted by the first rain of the weekend. The little-known Melanie gave a lovely performance and was followed by the day's star, Joan Baez.

Because of the rain and crowded conditions, the producers realized that the crowd might turn ugly unless the music played continuously. Therefore, Saturday's performances began at noon with Quill, then Keef Hartley, Santana, Mountain, and Canned Heat.

By evening, three acts—Janis Joplin, the Grateful Dead, and the Who—refused to play unless paid in advance, which sent promoters scurrying to secure the necessary funds. Creedence Clearwater Revival was followed by Joplin, and at 1:30 A.M., Sly and the Family Stone provided one of the festival's dynamic highlights. At 3:00 A.M., the Who played songs from the group's rock opera, *Tommy*, and when Yippie leader Abbie Hoffman tried to interrupt the music, the Who's Pete Townsend hit him over the head with his guitar and hurled him from the stage.

Sunday's events began at 8:30 in the morning with the Jefferson Airplane, followed by Joe Cocker and the Grease Band, who gave a stellar performance. A huge storm hit the festival site, and eventually Max Yasgur, owner of the festival site, praised the crowd for remaining calm. Country Joe and the Fish was the next to perform, and that evening, Ten Years After, the Band, Blood, Sweat, and Tears, and Johnny Winter were featured.

At 3:00 A.M., Crosby, Stills, and Nash gave their first public performance, followed by the Paul Butterfield Blues Band and Sha Na Na. The headliner, Jimi Hendrix, took the stage at 8:30 A.M. and launched into a screeching "Star Spangled Banner." He debuted his Gypsy Sun and Rainbows Band, and the performance was an overwhelming success.

After the crowd trailed away, the site was a huge mud pit filled with trash and human waste that cost $100,000 to restore. When all the expenses were tallied, the promoters discovered they were $1.3 million in debt, which the Roberts family eventually paid.

Impact The popular legacy of Woodstock is that a massive group of strangers could meet, enjoy a festival in spite of horrible conditions, and demonstrate the promise of love, peace, and tolerance. The event had all the seeds of a cataclysmic disaster, but unlike the Altamont Music Festival later that year, at which an audience member was murdered in front of the stage, the Woodstock Festival did not turn into a nightmare. However, three people did die in Bethel—one was run over by a tractor—and many were inadvertently exposed to powerful drugs for which there was scant medical treatment.

Many of the bands, representatives of an alternative culture supposedly based on selflessness, were as rapacious as the members of the establishment they criticized. In order to sign acts, Lang doubled performance fees, which ultimately escalated the money the artists could command. A significant aspect of popular music before the festival was the proximity of the audience to the stars; however, the rock icons who appeared at Woodstock were safely ensconced in hotels away from the discomforts of the festival site. After Woodstock, performers grew increasingly remote.

Woodstock encouraged the most popular artists of the day to perform in massive arenas. It was followed by other festivals, including the Isle of Wight festival in Great Britain. In the 1970's, rock promoter Bill Graham pioneered Day on the Green festivals and, in the 1990's, the Lollapalooza extravaganzas. After Woodstock, for musicians, rock music increasingly became a serious industry driven by market conditions rather than something they did for the sheer pleasure of performing.

In 1994 Lang, Roberts, and Rosenman staged an anniversary festival in Saugerties, New York, featuring a few of the original performers and many other popular acts, but the event was widely criticized for its commercial sponsorship and obviously mercantile aspirations. A rival celebration, featuring many of the original groups, took place in Bethel. In 1984, a monument was erected on the original concert site, to which visitors make continual pilgrimages.

Additional Information Jean Young and Lang's *Woodstock Festival Remembered* (1979), Rosenman, Roberts, and Robert Pilpel's *Young Men with Unlimited Capital*

(1974), and Elliot Tiber's *Knock on Woodstock* (1994) are all firsthand accounts by figures intimately connected with the planning and execution of the festival. However, the most exacting and most thoroughly researched account of the festival is John Spitz's *Barefoot in Babylon* (1989), which reveals the genuine chaos and greed that was hidden by the facade of peace and love. Other book-length accounts include Joel Makower's *Woodstock: The Oral History* (1989), Jack Curry's *Woodstock: The Summer of Our Lives* (1989), and Jerry Hopkins's *Festival!—The Book of American Music Celebrations* (1970).

David W. Madden

See also Altamont Music Festival; Baez, Joan; Grateful Dead; Hendrix, Jimi; Hippies; Jefferson Airplane; Joplin, Janis; Monterey Pop Festival; Music; Youth Culture and the Generation Gap.

■ World Health Organization (WHO)

A specialized agency of the United Nations focusing on international cooperation to improve the health conditions of all people. One of the programs it began in the 1960's resulted in the eradication of smallpox.

Origins and History In 1851, nations met at the International Sanitary Conference to discuss health measures to decrease the infiltration of the plague in Europe. Nations soon began to work together to combat other common health threats such as typhus, smallpox, yellow fever, and cholera. The establishment of the Pan American Sanitary Bureau in 1902, the Office International d'Hygiène Publique in 1904, and the Health Organization of the League of Nations in 1919 were all important steps leading to the creation of the World Health Organization (WHO) in 1948.

Activities By the 1960's, the WHO had defined for itself three main functions: information gathering, sponsoring disease control programs, and working with governments to improve health facilities. As a central clearinghouse for information regarding disease throughout the world, the WHO developed a unified system for reporting diseases and causes of death and established international standards for drugs and sanitation. The organization has sponsored campaigns for the control of epidemic and endemic diseases, achieving its aims through vacci-nation programs, instruction in the use of insecticides and antibiotics, assistance in providing pure water supplies, and health education involving sanitation systems. The WHO also works to strengthen already existing national and local health services by cooperating with individual governments.

In the 1960's, worldwide concern developed regarding the shortage of family doctors (general practitioners) in contrast to specialists. In the early 1900's, 80 percent of U.S. physicians were in general practice; however, in the mid-1970's, fewer than 20 percent were in this field. Consequently, in 1963, the WHO published a report stressing the need for the training of doctors in family practice. Residency programs were soon developed to prepare individuals for this field. Also in 1963, the WHO, in cooperation with the Food and Agriculture Organization, established the Codex Alimentarius Commission to develop an international code of food quality standards. These standards involve the definition of foodstuffs and additives, limits on pesticides, and requirements for labeling.

Impact The eradication of smallpox is credited to the WHO vaccination program established in 1967. At that time, more than thirty countries in Africa, Asia, and South America were affected by this viral disease. Vaccination teams were mobilized by the WHO to search, isolate, and vaccinate people with smallpox as well as individuals who had been in contact with them. The number of smallpox-infected countries gradually decreased; consequently, in May, 1980, the WHO formally announced that smallpox had been eradicated.

Subsequent Events Since the 1960's, the WHO has continued to focus on health promotion for all. The elimination of major diseases such as poliomyelitis, guinea-worm disease, leprosy, and river blindness in Africa are focal points of the organization. Coordinating an international effort against acquired immunodeficiency syndrome (AIDS) is another challenge.

Additional Information In 1968, the WHO published the book, *The Second Ten Years of the World Health Organization, 1958-1967*, which is a thorough compilation of activities and accomplishments of the WHO in the 1960's.

Martha M. Henze

See also Medicine.

Golfer Mickey Wright won more than eighty tournaments and dominated the Ladies' Professional Golf Association in the early 1960's. (Ralph W. Miller Golf Library)

■ Wright, Mickey

Born February 14, 1935, San Diego, California

The biggest women's professional golf star of the early 1960's. Wright was one of the greatest woman golfers of all time.

Mary Kathryn "Mickey" Wright started playing golf at age eleven and improved quickly. In 1952, she won the national junior championship. After spending a year at Stanford University, she took a year off from school to play major amateur and open tournaments with much success.

Wright turned professional in 1955 and by 1960 was the top player on the Ladies' Professional Golf Association (LPGA) tour; her peak period mirrors that of Arnold Palmer on the men's tour. In 1965, she reduced her schedule and returned to college at Southern Methodist University, but she remained competitive as a part-time player. Although Wright's full-time professional career was brief, no other player, with the short-term exception of Nancy Lopez in the late 1970's, has rivaled her level of dominance on the LPGA tour.

Wright won more than eighty tournaments and set a number of scoring and money-winning records. She was the longest hitter of her era and often outdrove male professionals. In 1963, she won thirteen times, and during two other years won ten tournaments each. Her major victories included four U.S. Opens (1958, 1959, 1961, 1964) and four LPGA Championships (1958, 1960, 1961, 1963), the only women's majors of the time. She led the money winners four times (1961-1964).

Impact Although arthritis limited her activity after 1965, Wright ranks with Mildred "Babe" Zaharias as one of the two greatest women golfers of all time. The athleticism of recent women golfers traces directly to their mutual example.

Additional Information More detailed information about Wright's life and game can be found in Robert S. Macdonald's *The Great Women Golfers: Classics of Golf* (1998).

Tom Cook

See also Golf; Nicklaus, Jack; Palmer, Arnold; Rawls, Betsy; Sports.

■ Yippies

A protest organization whose purpose was to oppose United States involvement in the Vietnam War. The Yippies were more formally known as the Youth International Party and used extreme methods to attract media attention to the antiwar movement.

Origins and History Abbie Hoffman and Jerry Rubin founded the Youth International Party on January 16, 1968, an organization that quickly became known as the Yippies. Hoffman and Rubin, who were already leading figures in the antiwar movement, created the Yippies to coincide with the 1968 Democratic National Convention in Chicago. The Yippies were not a formal organization with a definite membership but rather a group of people brought together to oppose the policies of the United States government in Vietnam. Unlike more mainstream antiwar protesters, the Yippies believed that the nation's political system itself was corrupt and responsible for continuing the war in Vietnam. Their method of opposing the war was to use outrageous theatrics and stunts to make the U.S. system look absurd. They hoped that by using extreme tactics, they would draw media attention to their cause. In 1968, the Democrats were prepared to nominate Hubert Humphrey for president, and he was widely regarded as a man who would continue President Lyndon B. Johnson's Vietnam policies. Therefore, the Yippies believed that the Democratic National Convention would be the perfect occasion to gain publicity for the antiwar movement.

Activties As the Democratic National Convention approached in August, Hoffman, Rubin, and other Yippie leaders planned what they called a "Festival of Life" in which thousands of young antiwar demonstrators would march and engage in activities designed to disrupt the convention. The Yippies' activities included distributing pamphlets calling for the legalization of drugs, free love, and the abolition of money. They also planned numerous antiwar speeches and marches with the climax being the nomination of a hog named "Pigasus" for president.

Impact Far fewer antiwar demonstrators appeared in Chicago than the Yippies had expected. Nevertheless, the Yippies and other antiwar groups succeeded in turning the convention into a debacle. Mayor Richard Daley mobilized thousands of law enforcement agents against the protesters, and the television networks broadcast images of violence, mayhem, and rioting that were seen by millions of shocked Americans. Memories of the convention severely damaged Humphrey's presidential campaign in the fall. Moreover, the perceived extremism of the Yippies and others caused deep splits in the antiwar movement, as more mainstream protest groups wanted to separate themselves from the Yippies.

Additional Information In 1990, Charles DeBenedetti published *An American Ordeal: The American Antiwar Movement of the Vietnam Era*, which gives a broad overview of the antiwar movement and how the Yippies fit into the context of the times. *Do It! Scenarios of the Revolution*, published in 1970, is a collection of writings by Rubin.

Phillip A. Cantrell II

See also Chicago Seven Trial; Counterculture; Democratic National Convention of 1968; *Do It! Scenarios of the Revolution*; *Medium Cool*; Pentagon, Levitating of the; War Resisters League; Weathermen.

■ Young, Andrew

Born March 12, 1932, New Orleans, Louisiana

One of the nation's most prominent civil rights leaders. Young, an assistant to Martin Luther King, Jr., helped plan and organize many of the most important demonstrations of the 1960's.

Early Life Andrew Jackson Young, who grew up in New Orleans, Louisiana, graduated from Howard University in 1951. He married Jean Childs in 1954, then received a divinity degree from the Hartford Theological Seminary in 1955. For the next two years, Young served as a minister in Thomasville, Georgia. In August, 1957, Young moved to New York

Andrew Young, shown here protesting treatment of participants in the Poor People's March in May, 1968, assisted Martin Luther King, Jr., in the Southern Christian Leadership Conference for much of the 1960's. (AP/Wide World Photos)

City, where he joined the executive staff of the Youth Division of the National Council of the Churches of Christ. He remained in that position until 1961.

The 1960's Young returned to Georgia in September, 1961. There he took control of the Citizenship Education Program, training teachers to go throughout the South and instruct the masses about voting. Young's activities during 1962 increasingly involved him with Martin Luther King, Jr., and the Southern Christian Leadership Conference (SCLC). April, 1963, found Young in Birmingham, Alabama, planning demonstrations against segregation. After the dramatic events of May—involving Chief of Police Eugene "Bull" Conner, his dogs, and courageous young black protesters—Young represented the SCLC in the negotiations with white Birmingham business leaders that ended segregation in the city.

In 1964, Young became King's executive assistant. In May and June, he engineered demonstrations against segregation in St. Augustine, Florida, leading a night march into the old slave market, where members of the Ku Klux Klan knocked him down three times. After being arrested for disturbing the peace, Young conducted negotiations with white leaders of St. Augustine that terminated public segregation. Later in 1964, Young and other SCLC leaders planned a series of demonstrations for Selma, Alabama, which began in January, 1965. When the suppression of a march ignited violence on March 7, Young labored feverishly to stem the unrest. King led another march a few days later, and the publicity from Selma fostered support for voting rights legislation.

Young participated in the SCLC's efforts to improve black housing in Chicago in 1966 and supported King's strong stance against the Vietnam War in 1967. After King's tragic death in April, 1968, Young and other SCLC staffers carried on with the Poor People's Campaign in Washington, D.C. In 1969, Young successfully mediated a hospital workers' strike in Charleston, North Carolina. In 1970, he resigned from his position as SCLC vice president to enter politics.

Later Life Young was elected to Congress in 1972. He served two terms, then became U.S. ambassador to the United Nations during the administration of Jimmy Carter. As ambassador, he contributed to the transition from minority-ruled Southern Rhodesia to majority-ruled Zimbabwe. From 1982 to 1990, he served as mayor of Atlanta. In the 1990's, he became involved in business and was vice chair for the 1996 Olympic Games.

Impact As a leader of the nonviolent campaigns for African American civil rights in the 1960's, Young helped end racial segregation in the South. His efforts contributed to the passage of the Civil Rights Act of 1964 and the Voting Rights Act of 1965. In the 1970's, he carried King's message to the international stage.

Additional Information Young described his civil rights activities in *An Easy Burden*, a memoir published in 1996. Bartlett Jones detailed Young's

United Nations career in *Flawed Triumphs,* published in 1996.

Andy DeRoche

See also Birmingham March; Civil Rights Movement; Southern Christian Leadership Conference (SCLC).

■ Young Americans for Freedom

A conservative youth group. The group was Republican in outlook although formally nonpartisan, and its members took pride in their anticommunism and in their fight against the perceived ascendancy of radical youth groups.

Origins and History Young Americans for Freedom was a militant conservative youth group in an era when many of the nation's young people were active in the Civil Rights and antiwar movements. The organization was founded in September, 1960, with

the help of William F. Buckley, Jr., conservative and founder of the journal *National Review* as well as host of the television show *Firing Line.* Buckley provided the meeting place—his own home in Sharon, Connecticut—for the convention of conservative activists that gave rise to the organization. Young Americans for Freedom members were predominantly white and Christian. Two of its more famous members include former vice president Dan Quayle (during his college years) and Lieutenant Colonel Oliver North, who was implicated in the Iran-Contra Scandal in the 1980's.

Activities Young Americans for Freedom gave strong support to U.S. military intervention in Vietnam, free-market economics, states' rights, and limited government. On September 11, 1960, at Buckley's home, the organization issued what became known as the Sharon Statement, similar to the

In May, 1970, David Keene, national chair of the conservative Young Americans for Freedom, warns that antiwar protesters are planning a violent demonstration at the White House. (AP/Wide World Photos)

Huron Statement issued by the Students for a Democratic Society (SDS) in 1962. The statement called on young people, in what it termed a "time of moral and political crisis," to stand up for their beliefs. The statement said that the most important value is the "individual's use of his God-given free-will," and that political freedom must be accompanied by economic freedom. Young Americans for Freedom also professed a belief in the importance of U.S. national sovereignty and defeating communism rather than maintaining a coexistence with it. In keeping with its counter-SDS stance, during the 1960's, the group organized its own demonstrations whenever the SDS held antiwar protests. Young Americans for Freedom, which had supported Barry Goldwater for the Republican vice presidential nominee in 1960, like Buckley, was active in the Barry Goldwater presidential campaign in 1964. The organization held yearly conventions for conservative youth up to age thirty-nine and their political allies.

Impact Young Americans for Freedom played an active role in moving young Republicans to the right of the political center and acting as a counterpoint to the left-wing student organizations that dominated 1960's campuses. The organization remained active in Republican politics through the 1980's and gave strong support to Ronald Reagan, who served as Honorary National Chairman, and to U.S. intervention in El Salvador. Critics claimed that the the group supported death squads in El Salvador.

Additional Information For a recent study, see John A. Andrews's *The Other Side of the Sixties: Young Americans for Freedom and the Rise of Conservative Politics* (1997).

Susan A. Stussy

See also Buckley, William F., Jr.; Conservatism in Politics; Goldwater, Barry; Students for a Democratic Society (SDS).

■ Young Lords

A Puerto Rican revolutionary organization formed to fight racial, cultural, and language discrimination and economic exploitation. It established chapters in several U.S. cities.

Origins and History The first Young Lords Organization (YLO) was formed in Chicago and worked with local Black Panthers and a white revolutionary group in a so-called "Rainbow Coalition." A group of young Puerto Ricans in New York City read an article about the Chicago YLO in the June 7, 1969, issue of the Black Panther newspaper, and a month later obtained permission to start their own chapter. In addition to Puerto Ricans, the membership included Dominicans, African Americans, Cubans, and Latinos. The group's admiration for the Black Panther Party can be seen in its thirteen-point political program, paramilitary style, and the brown berets that members wore. In May, 1970, the East Coast YLO became the Young Lords Party and published a bilingual newspaper, *Palante* (literally "forward in struggle"). Chapters formed in Hoboken, Newark, and Jersey City, New Jersey; Bridgeport and New Haven, Connecticut; Boston, Massachusetts; and Philadelphia, Pennsylvania.

Activities New York City's chapter was the most active, with early actions focused on improving living conditions in the barrio. When a church refused to give them space to run a free breakfast program, the Young Lords occupied it for eleven days. When neighborhood cleanups were met with hostility from the sanitation department, the Young Lords turned them into "garbage protests" in which the streets of East Harlem were blockaded with trash until the city picked it up. Later, the Young Lords used direct action to improve community health care by hijacking a medical truck to service the community, starting drug treatment programs, and occupying a hospital in the South Bronx to demand better services. Support of Puerto Rican independence and prison struggles were other major areas of activity.

Impact The Young Lords gave voice to an increasing militancy in the Latino community. Internal debates about sexism and homophobia resulted in advances for women and gays within the organization and also served to educate the community about the dangers of "machismo." In part by embracing an Afro-Indio-Latino multiculturalism, the Young Lords facilitated connections between activists of differing racial and cultural backgrounds.

Subsequent Events The Federal Bureau of Investigation's COINTELPRO (Counterintelligence Program), which targeted Puerto Rican independence activists, many of whom were also active in the Young Lords, took a toll on the organization. In January,

1971, the group split over whether to open chapters in Puerto Rico or continue working only in U.S. communities. Two island chapters were started but did not survive long. In July, 1972, the Young Lords Party changed its name to the Puerto Rican Revolutionary Workers Organization and shifted to labor organizing. By 1976, it had dissolved.

Additional Information The Young Lords Party published its own account, *Palante* (1971), which includes essays by members as well as an extensive photographic essay by Michael Abramson. *Palante, Siempre Palante* (1996), a video by Iris Morales, is a critical history of the organization and its demise.

Vanessa Tait

See also Black Panthers; Brown Berets; Chicano Movement.

■ Youth Culture and the Generation Gap

The emergence of youth as a distinct political and cultural force. Political activism by college students, the popularity of youth-generated styles, and perceptions of a "generation gap" contributed to the idea that age might become as important an indicator of social identity as race, class, or gender.

The concept of "youth" is a social product made possible, even necessary, by those changes that have been variously called the industrialization, modernization, or rationalization of American life. Advanced educational opportunities, career choices, sexual anxieties, marriage decisions, political and social self-definition are all modern problems that have come to be associated with a hybrid stage of life

The Young Lords, a militant Puerto Rican group in New York, worked to improve conditions in Latino areas of the city. Members are shown guarding the casket of a member who died in prison in October, 1970. (AP/Wide World Photos)

between family protection and adult autonomy, often called adolescence but much better expressed in the elastic term "youth."

Youth did not simply spring up because the need for it existed. It developed because American society gave it room to grow as institutions were reshaped to modern dimensions. As the family retreated to the private arena of emotion, two institutions—the school and the peer group—came to define the social world of middle-class youth. Neither was new in the 1960's, but each became more significant in the context of changes in the family and the larger society. Together these institutions effected the transition from the family, where personal identity was formed, to the society, where social identity was expressed. Between the two, a youth culture took shape and took hold.

The College Campus In the mid-1960's, the creation and maintenance of a self-conscious and multifaceted youth culture took place most effectively on American college campuses, where students were gathered. Of course, what was happening to college youth was only one subset of youth experiences; indeed, in high schools, at work, and on the streets, peers were helping to lead individual youths into social maturity. Nevertheless, peer life on college campuses, in its density, its isolation, and its rootedness in the values of the white middle class, provided a unique environment in which to nurture a cult of youth.

The generation in college in the 1960's replaced a neatly combed and respectful generation that had been nurtured on McCarthyism and social orthodoxy. By 1963 McCarthyism was fading into an embarrassing memory, and African American students were engaged in a movement for their civil rights, presenting white students with a model for attacking their own ancestral structure. Young people, united by age and their college experience, began acquiring a special sense of themselves and of their potential to challenge societal norms. The principles for this self-recognition, and the means for its dissemination were found within the structure of higher education and in popular culture. The desire to throw off familiar and societal mores spurred the demand for relevant and unprescribed education. This led to the establishment on some college campuses of "free universities"—educational experiments that included open registration and courses

ranging from traditional academic offerings or political study groups to transcendental meditation and macrobiotic cooking.

Underground newspapers, made possible by technical progress in inexpensive offset printing, appeared on every major university campus. These papers carried an assortment of forums: political analysis and polemics, music reviews, discussions of experimental ways of living, inventive graphic art work, and excursions into mysticism, Asian religion, and the effects of drugs such as LSD (lysergic acid diethylamide), hashish, and mescaline, which were believed to be mind-expanding.

The association of these psychedelic drugs with rock music produced a cultural style different from that of some early-1960's performers, most notably Phil Ochs, Joan Baez, and Bob Dylan, who had combined their musical talents with political commentary. The new sound, softer than hard rock and haunting in tone, was acid (LSD) or psychedelic rock, the special province of San Francisco-based groups such as the Grateful Dead and Jefferson Airplane. San Francisco's Haight-Ashbury district became the site of 1967's Summer of Love; thousands of youths swarmed in from across the country for free concerts in Golden Gate Park, drawn by images of the summer that appeared in theaters and on televisions.

Youth Leaves the Campus The 1960's generation was the first to be raised on a steady diet of television viewing. The emerging technology played a crucial role in shaping the images of a youth culture and in portraying them to society. The appearance of Elvis Presley and the Beatles on *The Ed Sullivan Show,* for example, purveyed the message that youthful tastes in fashion and grooming should be socially acceptable. Individual and collective identities began to surround longer hair and more revealing and brighter clothing, formulating a challenge to the physical and social mores instituted by previous generations. Through shows such as *American Bandstand,* television ultimately served to expand this developing message of the cult of youth beyond the college campuses to society at large.

By the late 1960's, young people nationwide were beginning to establish residences in small groups; such living arrangements were popularly referred to as communes. An era of sexual tolerance and freedom encouraged by oral contraceptives helped make such gatherings more common and acceptable. Groups of unmarried men and women could live openly under the same roof. Nevertheless, the great majority of communes were probably not experimental or utopian, rather they were merely practical arrangements among young people for sharing expenses. However, even in these communes (just as among college youth), something new was being attempted, the creation of a free yet family-like association that could be a model for the rest of society. To this extent, the 1960's youth culture would prove to be the organizing basis for many of the era's movements for political and social change; many of the decade's most active organizations for social change drew membership from radicalized youth.

However, the radical nature of the youth culture's organizational principles and tactics would also serve as a wedge between parent and child, dividing them along lines of conservative and radical beliefs, values, and cognition. This ideological division would become known as the "generation gap." Many of the differences that arose between parents and children in the decade can be linked to a difference of opinion about the nature of American society. Dissent from and criticism of the social order by rebellious youth, as well as challenges to order and authority did not fit well with adult values in the 1960's. Having lived through periods of uncertainty because of war and economic depression, parents in the 1960's found it unacceptable when their children issued challenges to their views on life. Protesting against the Vietnam War, dropping out of college to wander around the country, and voicing social visionary opinions had no place in the practical world of parents. For their part, members of the youth culture found their parents' interest in making money and securing materialistic comforts to be socially unacceptable. Generational anxieties were intensified by the decade's cultural transformations. The generation gap exacerbated the cultural division between the two camps, making it difficult to resolve the contradictions inherent in the culture. Still, attitudes toward life were not the same after the 1960's. Social criticism once again was a part of the nation's political battleground.

Impact A tangle of work and play, career preparation, and mating games, the practice of youth became in the 1960's a fully-structured, directed, and effective social act. Youth incorporated the changes

that were vividly ushering in a new era. In the post-World War II United States, the shape of political and cultural life was in flux. After the Great Depression of the 1930's and the market scarcities of the war years, the majority of Americans had achieved by the early 1960's a level of unprecedented material comfort. Such affluence had created a "happiness explosion" that offered nearly unlimited opportunity for people to find novel ways of enjoying themselves. For the young, this happiness translated into participation in many of the social movements of the era.

The cultural radicalism of youth, unlike some other forms of political radicalism that were born in the 1960's, insisted on the toleration and acceptance of varieties of personal behavior and contributed to a significant modification in the treatment of many social groups. Women's rights groups, gay and lesbian action committees, racial and ethnic rights coalitions, labor leagues, and several environmental action groups gained organizational and tactical impetus from the student movement. In short, youth culture aided many of the democratizing processes that characterized the 1960's by providing both an ideological foundation and membership.

However, youth culture also contained aspects that impeded the democratization of American society and ensured youths' isolation from other age groups. Its emphasis on happiness, freedom, and the cultivation of personal experience often encouraged a turn away from community into privacy. By the beginning of the 1970's, many in the youth culture were adopting faddish philosophies that advocated one method or another of self-cultivation to the near exclusion of politics or social concerns. The wildly eccentric tastes in fashion, grooming, and music adopted by the young generation served to differentiate and alienate them from previous generations. Indeed, sociologists have characterized the United States of the 1960's as a mass society of "other-directed" individuals dependent upon peer approval, in contrast with earlier generations of "inner-directed" individuals who were self-motivated and independent.

Additional Information Sources of information on the youth culture during the 1960's include David Farber's *The 1960's: From Memory to History* (1994); *Social Movements of the Sixties and Seventies* (1983), edited by Jo Freeman; *The Revolution Wasn't Televised:*

Sixties Television and Social Conflict (1997), by Lynn Speigel and Michael Curtin; Milton Viorst's *Fire in the Streets: America in the 1960's* (1979); and Nicholas Von Hoffman's *We Are the People Our Parents Warned Us Against* (1968).

Thomas J. Edward Walker
Cynthia Gwynne Yaudes

See also Baby Boomers; Baez, Joan; Beatles, The; Civil Rights Movement; Communes; Demographics of the United States; Dylan, Bob; Education; Environmental Movement; Fashions and Clothing; Feminist Movement; Folk Music; Free Love; Grateful Dead; Jefferson Airplane; Hairstyles; San Francisco as Cultural Mecca; Summer of Love; Underground Newspapers.

Z

■ Zappa, Frank

Born December 21, 1940, Baltimore, Maryland
Died December 4, 1993, Los Angeles, California

A unique figure in the history of rock music. Acclaimed as a composer and musician, Zappa provided scathing commentary on the establishment as well as the counterculture during the 1960's.

Early Life Frank Vincent Zappa's father was a government scientist who played guitar for fun. Zappa inherited his father's love of music, playing in various school bands and choosing the electric guitar as his primary instrument. When he was ten, Zappa's family moved to the Los Angeles area, a hotbed of pop music. Zappa collected rhythm-and-blues and rock-and-roll recordings. He also listened avidly to modern classical music, particularly the works of Edgard Varèse. In high school, Zappa started a band called the Blackouts. He studied music theory at Chaffey College in 1959, dropping out after six months.

The 1960's In 1964, Zappa joined the Soul Giants, which, under his tutelage, would become the Muthers, then the Mothers, and, finally, the Mothers of Invention. The band's first album, *Freak Out!* (1966), parodied pop music with tunes such as "Go Cry on Somebody Else's Shoulder" and "You Didn't Try to Call Me" and included political fare such as "Who Are the Brain Police?" and "Trouble Every Day." Musically impeccable, the album emphasized off-center humor and was commercially disappointing. The band's

next album, *Absolutely Free* (1967), included a song entitled "Plastic People," which illustrates Zappa's philosophical perspective. Plasticity (or phoniness) applies to the establishment, counterculture, listeners, and even Zappa himself. *We're Only in It for the Money* (1967) lampooned police, flower children, and even the Beatles. *Lumpy Gravy* (1967) was Zappa's first experiment with orchestral arrangements. *Cruisin' with Ruben and the Jets* (1968) offered

Frank Zappa, musician and inventive composer, and the mastermind behind the Mothers of Invention, combined rock, pop, jazz, and classic music in compositions that often scoffed at convention and conformity. (Archive Photos)

an inspired parody of doo-wop. In 1969, the band released two more albums, *Mothermania* and *Uncle Meat*, which combined dialogue from a movie in progress with strikingly original instrumental music. The band had by this time moved to the East Coast, playing a lengthy gig at Greenwich Village's Garrick Theater. This exposure, along with the band's recordings, made Zappa and the Mothers of Invention nationally notorious icons of the 1960's.

Later Life Zappa moved the band back to Los Angeles and continued to produce distinctive music until his death from prostate cancer in 1993. Sometimes with the Mothers of Invention (whose membership fluctuated), sometimes flying solo, Zappa recorded more than fifty albums, made a feature film (*200 Motels*) in 1971, and played countless live performances. He saw his serious compositions recorded by world-renowned orchestras, had his live guitar solos anthologized, and won a 1988 Grammy Award. Zappa remained an unwavering proponent of free expression, opposing censorship in testimony before the U.S. Congress.

Impact Zappa helped expand the technical and intellectual limits of rock music, artfully combining low and high culture. He crossed barriers between musical forms, taking fans along as he navigated between rock, classical music, and jazz. Zappa's lyrics fostered a healthy skepticism about political machinations along all wings of the ideological spectrum. His unconditional defense of free expression demonstrates that there are still principles worth honoring. Along with Lenny Bruce, Zappa helped stretch the parameters of socially acceptable public expression.

Additional Information In 1989, Zappa combined with Peter Occiogrosso to write an autobiography entitled *The Real Frank Zappa Book*.

Ira Smolensky

See also Bruce, Lenny; Censorship; Counterculture; Flower Children; Greenwich Village; Music; Social Satires.

■ Drama

Major Films

1960

The Alamo. United Artists. Director: John Wayne. Wayne himself plays Davy Crockett, Richard Widmark plays Jim Bowie, and Laurence Harvey plays William Travis in this pious account of how a small band of brave volunteers became martyrs to the cause of Texas freedom in 1836.

The Apartment. United Artists. Director: Billy Wilder. A mordant blend of slapstick and pathos driven by contemporary corporate culture. Jack Lemmon is C. C. Baxter, a lonely, ambitious clerk in a large insurance company in New York who lets his philandering boss Jeff D. Sheldrake (Fred MacMurray) borrow his apartment for illicit trysts but opposes his designs on Miss Kubelik (Shirley MacLaine).

Butterfield Eight. Metro-Goldwyn-Mayer. Director: Daniel Mann. Elizabeth Taylor stars as a society call girl in a tepid drama, based on a John O'Hara novel and co-starring Laurence Harvey and Eddie Fisher, that was considered quite shocking when originally released.

Elmer Gantry. United Artists. Director: Richard Brooks. Burt Lancaster plays the eponymous preacher, a charlatan evangelist, in this adaptation of a Sinclair Lewis novel set in the 1920's Midwest. Jean Simmons plays his accomplice, Shirley Jones a victim, and Arthur Kennedy a journalist intent on exposing the religious scam.

Exodus. United Artists. Director: Otto Preminger. In this story, based on a popular novel by Leon Uris, of the modern Jewish struggle for an independent homeland, Paul Newman, as Ari Ben-Kanaan, became the handsome incarnation of Israeli heroism. The film reflected and strengthened American support for Zionism.

Inherit the Wind. United Artists. Director: Stanley Kramer. Spencer Tracy, playing a figure based on Clarence Darrow, and Fredric March, playing a version of William Jennings Bryan, face off in this fictionalization of the notorious 1925 Scopes "monkey trial," in which a high school biology teacher was convicted of teaching evolution.

The Little Shop of Horrors. Allied Artists Television Corporation. Director: Roger Corman. A quirky, hastily assembled "B" movie that declares its independence from Hollywood standards of beauty and gravity, this cult favorite is the story of a man-eating plant inadvertently created by the meek employee (Jonathan Haze) of a florist shop and of the oafish humans who blunder into its vicinity.

The Magnificent Seven. United Artists. Director: John Sturges. A transposition of the Japanese director Akira Kurosawa's *Seven Samurai* to the violent frontier West. Yul Brynner, Steve McQueen, Robert Vaughn, James Coburn, Charles Bronson, Horst Buchholz, and Eli Wallach play American gunmen hired by a Mexican village to provide protection against bandits.

Psycho. Shamley Productions. Director: Alfred Hitchcock. Legendary for a scene in which Janet Leigh's character is stabbed to death while taking a shower, this Hitchcock shocker stars Anthony Perkins as the mentally deranged manager of a secluded motel who maintains an unhealthy relationship with his deceased mother.

Spartacus. Universal. Director: Stanley Kubrick. Based on a novel by Howard Fast and a screenplay by black-listed leftist Dalton Trumbo, this epic about a slave revolt in ancient Rome celebrates proletarian resistance to tyranny. The cast includes Kirk Douglas, Laurence Olivier, Charles Laughton, Tony Curtis, Jean Simmons, and Peter Ustinov.

1961

Breakfast at Tiffany's. Paramount. Director: Blake Edwards. Audrey Hepburn plays Holly Golightly, a sweetly daft New York call girl befriended by George Peppard, in this gentle, sexless adaptation of a novella by Truman Capote. The signature song "Moon River," by Henry Mancini, became a hit.

Flower Drum Song. U-I. Director: Henry Koster. A screen adaptation of the Broadway musical by Richard Rodgers and Oscar Hammerstein notable for its rare attention to the lives of Asian Americans. Nancy Kwan, James Shigeta, and Juanita Hall star in a cloyingly cute melodrama about the romantic tribulations of immigrants living in San Francisco's Chinatown.

The Guns of Navarone. Columbia. Director: J. Lee Thompson. Carl Foreman's script blends a World War II adventure thriller with ponderous ethical argument. In 1942, Gregory Peck, David Niven, and Anthony Quinn are sent on a mission to a Mediterranean island to destroy German batteries that threaten Allied troop transports.

The Hustler. Twentieth Century Fox. Director: Robert Rossen. Veteran con man Jackie Gleason serves as the mentor to young Paul Newman, whose career as a pool hall hustler is ruined when he falls in love with Piper Laurie. A portrait of blighted talent that excels in tone and atmospherics.

Judgment at Nuremberg. United Artists. Director: Stanley Kramer. A long and somewhat long-winded drama starring Spencer Tracy, Marlene Dietrich, Burt Lancaster, Richard Widmark, and Maximilian Schell. A high-minded, expository fictionalization of the 1948 trial of Nazi German leaders for crimes against humanity.

The Misfits. United Artists. Director: John Huston. Final film appearances by both Marilyn Monroe and Clark Gable, in a strained melodrama by Arthur Miller about cowboys who gather in the Nevada desert to round up wild mustangs.

One-Eyed Jacks. Paramount. Director: Marlon Brando. Midway through production, Brando took over direction from Stanley Kubrick. He also stars in a violent, self-conscious Western about an outlaw who pursues revenge against a deceitful former partner (Karl Malden).

One, Two, Three. United Artists. Director: Billy Wilder. A frenetic Cold War comedy set in divided Berlin. James Cagney plays a Coca Cola executive who is trying to sell the American soft drink to the Russians while preventing his boss's daughter from marrying a Communist.

Splendor in the Grass. Warner Bros. Director: Elia Kazan. Set in 1920's Kansas, William Inge's drama of tortured, sensual adolescent love between Warren Beatty and Nathalie Wood portrays adults as obtuse, selfish, and destructive.

West Side Story. United Artists. Directors: Jerome Robbins and Robert Wise. Bold adaptation, by Arthur Laurents, Leonard Bernstein, and Stephen Sondheim, of William Shakespeare's *Romeo and Juliet* to the musical stage translated to the screen. A powerful portrait of urban disorder and of the rifts between generations and ethnic groups.

1962

Birdman of Alcatraz. United Artists. Director: John Frankenheimer. Burt Lancaster portrays Robert Stroud, a convict who became famous as an ornithologist while serving almost sixty years, for murder, in the infamous California prison.

Cape Fear. U-I. Director: J. Lee Thompson. Based on the novel *The Executioners* by John D. MacDonald, this classic of film noir stars Gregory Peck and Polly Bergen as a lawyer and his wife who are menaced by ex-convict Robert Mitchum, who blames Peck for the prison sentence he had to serve.

Days of Wine and Roses. Warner Bros. Director: Blake Edwards. Shattering drama of middle-class self-destruction. Jack Lemmon plays a public relations man who is consumed by alcoholism and then recovers. Lee Remick is the wife who does not.

Lawrence of Arabia. Columbia. Director: David Lean. Spectacular four-hour epic, written by Robert Bolt, about the life of T. E. Lawrence, an English adventurer who led the Arabs in military exploits against the Turks. Peter O'Toole plays Lawrence, and the supporting cast includes Omar Sharif, Arthur Kennedy, Jack Hawkins, and Anthony Quayle.

Lolita. Metro-Goldwyn-Mayer. Director: Stanley Kubrick. Vladimir Nabokov's subtle novel about a middle-aged European scholar who falls in love with a twelve-year-old American vamp became a national sensation after it was banned. The film adaptation, starring James Mason, Sue Lyon, Shelley Winters, and Peter Sellers, offers moments of manic mugging but lacks the richness and the impact of the book.

Lonely Are the Brave. U-I. Director: David Miller. Kirk Douglas plays a superannuated cowboy struggling to maintain his way of life in an urban, industrialized world transformed by jeeps and helicopters. A kind of elegy to the Western genre.

The Man Who Shot Liberty Valance. Paramount. Director: John Ford. A valedictory work by the aging Ford and a self-conscious reworking of Western conventions, starring John Wayne, James Stewart, and Lee Marvin. A young tough becomes famous for gunning down a notorious outlaw, though in truth the shot is fired by his friend.

The Manchurian Candidate. United Artists. Director: John Frankenheimer. A Cold War spy thriller that hilariously mocks its own conventions. Laurence Harvey plays a military hero who returns from the Korean War brainwashed with orders to assassinate a liberal politician. Angela Lansbury is his grotesquely ambitious mother.

The Miracle Worker. United Artists. Director: Arthur Penn. Patty Duke plays Helen Keller and Anne Brancroft is her teacher, Annie Sullivan, in this renowned adaptation of William Gibson's stage play about Sullivan's struggle to overcome the stubbornness and isolation of her blind, deaf, and dumb pupil.

The Music Man. Warner Bros. Director: Morton da Costa. In his signature role, Robert Preston plays an itinerant con man who fleeces the gullible inhabitants of a small town and wins the unsuspecting heart of a timorous local librarian (Shirley Jones). Spirited book and music by Meredith Willson.

1963

The Birds. Universal. Director: Alfred Hitchcock. Hitchcock appears to be parodying his own penchant for shock in this fascinatingly silly thriller, starring Rod Taylor and Tippi Hedren. A flock of birds attacks and kills human beings along the coast of Northern California.

Bye Bye Birdie. Columbia. Director: George Sidney. A genial musical comedy about a rock star (Bobby Rydell) whose final appearance in a small town before induction into the army wreaks havoc among Janet Leigh, Dick Van Dyke, and Ann-Margret.

Cleopatra. Twentieth Century Fox. Director: Joseph L. Mankiewicz. This story of the love affair between the ancient Egyptian queen and the Roman emperor Julius Caesar is an expensive dud, but the off-screen, adulterous romance of Elizabeth Taylor and Richard Burton made it one of the most highly publicized productions in film history.

Dr. Strangelove: Or, How I Learned to Stop Worrying and Love the Bomb. Columbia. Director: Stanley Kubrick. A cautionary black comedy about the dangers of militarism in the nuclear age. Sterling Hayden plays a deranged Air Force general who launches an attack against Russia, and Peter Sellers takes on three roles: the president of the United States, a Royal Air Force captain, and a mad German American physicist.

The Great Escape. United Artists. Director: John Sturges. A long but exciting drama about the efforts of Allied prisoners of war James Garner, Steve

McQueen, Richard Attenborough, and Charles Bronson to break out of a special German military prison.

How the West Was Won. Metro-Goldwyn-Mayer. Directors: Henry Hathaway, John Ford, and George Marshall. A spectacular, epic encyclopedia of Western conventions and clichés, this composite film, made by three directors for showing in Cinerama theaters, follows the fortunes of a pioneering family from 1830 to late in the century. Spencer Tracy is the narrator, and the large cast of Western veterans includes John Wayne, James Stewart, Henry Fonda, Gregory Peck, Walter Brennan, Richard Widmark, and Eli Wallach.

Hud. Paramount. Director: Martin Ritt. Paul Newman stars as an arrogant young wastrel who disappoints his father (Melvyn Douglas), and pursues the family housekeeper (Patricia Neal). An incisive character study set on an arid Texas ranch. Adapted from a novel by Larry McMurtry.

Irma la Douce. United Artists. Director: Billy Wilder. In adapting a ribald stage musical to the screen, Wilder excised the songs but not the scurrilous humor. A Paris policeman (Jack Lemmon) falls in love with a prostitute (Shirley MacLaine).

It's a Mad Mad Mad Mad World. United Artists. Director: Stanley Kramer. A large-scale wacky comedy made for Cinerama with a glittering cast that includes Jimmy Durante, Milton Berle, Jonathan Winters, Buddy Hackett, Sid Caesar, Mickey Rooney, and Phil Silvers. The convoluted, zany plot has Spencer Tracy as a police captain monitoring the attempts of money-demented citizens to find the hiding place of stolen loot.

Lilies of the Field. United Artists. Director: Ralph Nelson. An uplifting, sentimental comedy about the efforts of a black handyman to build a chapel in New Mexico for a group of German nuns. The film, which radiates racial benevolence, earned Sidney Poitier an Oscar and further esteem among white audiences of good will.

1964

The Americanization of Emily. Metro-Goldwyn-Mayer. Director: Arthur Hiller. A bizarre black comedy of eccentric characters set in World War II on the eve of D-Day. Julie Andrews plays an English war widow who falls for a cowardly American commander (James Garner).

Fail-Safe. Columbia. Director: Sidney Lumet. An earnest Cold War drama with a title that entered the common language as a byword for foolproof security against nuclear blundering. After an American aircraft is mistakenly dispatched to drop an atomic bomb on Russia, the president of the United States (Henry Fonda) is compelled to avert global catastrophe by destroying New York as a demonstration of good will.

Hush . . . Hush, Sweet Charlotte. Twentieth Century Fox. Director: Robert Aldrich. An exercise in Southern gothic horror, starring Bette Davis and Olivia de Havilland. An aging, reclusive belle, tormented for thirty-seven years by nightmares about murdering her fiancé, learns that she was innocent after all.

Marnie. Universal. Director: Alfred Hitchcock. After a rich man (Sean Connery) marries a kleptomaniac (Tippi Hedren), he becomes determined to discover the truth about her sexual frigidity. A bizarre late Hitchchock psychodrama with notable music by Bernard Herrmann.

Mary Poppins. Walt Disney. Director: Robert Stevenson. To socially conscious rebels, this popular musical film about a charming nanny (Julie Andrews) in Edwardian London was the epitome of sanguine froth.

My Fair Lady. CBS/Warner. Director: George Cuckor. The musical adaptation, by Alan Jay Lerner and Frederick Loewe, of George Bernard Shaw's *Pygmalion* was a huge hit on Broadway. Although Rex Harrison reprised his stage role as Professor Henry Higgins, who transforms Audrey Hepburn's Cockney Liza Doolittle into a suave aristocrat, the film was not as successful.

The Night of the Iguana. Metro-Goldwyn-Mayer. Director: John Huston. Based on a campy play by Tennessee Williams. A former clergyman, Richard Burton, is a travel courier in Mexico and the sexual prey of a libidinous adolescent (Sue Lyon), a middle-aged hotel keeper (Ava Gardner), and a frustrated artist (Deborah Kerr)

Seven Days in May. Seven Arts. Director: John Frankenheimer. A gripping Cold War political thriller about the attempt to avert a military coup against the president of the United States (Frederic March), who is scorned by a rebellious general for being a pacifist. The cast also includes Kirk Douglas, Burt Lancaster, and Ava Gardner.

A Shot in the Dark. United Artists. Director: Blake Edwards. Reprising the role of *The Pink Panther*'s inept Inspector Clouseau, Peter Sellers is a master of slapstick as he examines the possibilities of whether a woman (Elke Sommers) murdered her lover.

The Unsinkable Molly Brown. Metro-Goldwyn-Mayer. Director: Charles Walters. A buoyant, genial musical starring Debbie Reynolds as an orphan who grows up determined to be accepted by Denver society. Based on the true story of a spunky woman who survived the sinking of the Titanic.

1965

Cat Ballou. Columbia. Director: Eliot Silverstein. An uneven musical spoof of Westerns, about a young woman (Jane Fonda) who turns outlaw after her father is shot dead by a vicious gunman. Lee Marvin stands out as both the gunman and the inept drunk Cat hired to protect her father.

The Collector. Columbia. Director: William Wyler. A fitfully chilling adaptation of a subtle novel by John Fowles, this is is the disturbing study of a timorous, deranged butterfly collector (Terence Stamp) who kidnaps a beautiful young woman (Samantha Eggar) and waits for her to fall in love with him.

Dr. Zhivago. Metro-Goldwyn-Mayer. Director: David Lean. Adapted from Boris Pasternak's novel, this is the epic story of a Moscow physician and poet (Omar Sharif) who loses his true love (Julie Christie) during the upheavals of the Russian Revolution.

In Harm's Way. Paramount. Director: Otto Preminger. An awkward blend of military spectacle and personal romance, starring John Wayne, Kirk Douglas, Patricia Neal, Tom Tryon, and Paul Prentiss, about the U.S. Navy's response to the Japanese attack on Pearl Harbor.

The Loved One. Metro-Goldwyn-Mayer. Director: Tony Richardson. A manic, giddy satire, based on an Evelyn Waugh novel, of American funereal customs. Robert Morse plays a young English poet who gets a job at an exclusive California cemetery.

A Patch of Blue. Metro-Goldwyn-Mayer. Director: Guy Green. A sentimental fantasy about racial reconciliation that earned Shelley Winters an Academy Award for supporting actress. Because she is blind, Elizabeth Hartman falls in love with Sidney Poitier without realizing that he is black.

The Pawnbroker. Landau Company. Director: Sidney Lumet. One of the first mainstream films to treat the Holocaust, two decades after the fact, this tells the story of a survivor (Rod Steiger) trying to repress the violent nightmare of his personal history while running a pawnshop in Harlem.

The Sound of Music. Twentieth Century Fox. Director: Robert Wise. One of the most popular movies ever made. An adaptation of the Rodgers and Hammerstein musical about governess Julie Andrews and the escape of the Trapp family from Nazi Austria.

A Thousand Clowns. United Artists. Director: Fred Coe. An adaptation of the stage play by Herb Gardner, starring Jason Robards as a cheerful, talented nonconformist whose efforts to raise his nephew (Barry Gordon) are not appreciated by the bureaucracies of the welfare system and the school board.

The Train. United Artists. Director: John Frankenheimer. A suspense thriller, starring Burt Lancaster and Paul Scofield, about the efforts of the French resistance to prevent a train carrying art looted by the Nazis from delivering its cargo to Germany.

1966

The Chase. Columbia. Director: Arthur Penn. A small Texas town ruled by a masochistic sheriff (Marlon Brando) is plunged into turmoil when an escaped convict (Robert Redford, in an early leading role) returns. Convoluted script adapted by Lillian Hellman from a novel by Horton Foote.

The Flight of the Phoenix. Twentieth Century Fox. Director: Robert Aldrich. A plane carrying James Stewart, Richard Attenborough, Peter Finch, Ernest Borgnine, and others crashes in the Sahara desert, and the tension builds over whether they will survive to rebuild the aircraft and fly it to safety.

The Fortune Cookie. United Artists. Director: Billy Wilder. Walter Matthau won an Oscar for his first pairing with Jack Lemmon, as a larcenous lawyer who persuades his brother-in-law to sue for a million dollars after being slightly injured at a football game. A pointed but only intermittently funny comedy.

The Group. United Artists. Director: Sidney Lumet. An adaptation of the novel by Mary McCarthy, this film is woven out of the subsequent love lives of a group of women (Joanna Pettet, Candice Bergen, Jessica Walter, Joan Hackett, Elizabeth Hartman, Mary Robin-Redd, Kathleen Widdoes) who graduate from Vassar in 1933.

Harper. Warner Bros. Director: Jack Smight. Paul Newman plays the eponymous Los Angeles private eye who is hired by a wealthy woman to find her husband. Genre entertainment based on a novel by Ross Macdonald and distinguished by a supporting cast that includes Lauren Bacall, Shelley Winters, Arthur Hill, Julie Harris, and Janet Leigh.

How to Steal a Million. Twentieth Century Fox. Director: William Wyler. Bland but elegant romantic comedy starring Audrey Hepburn as the daughter of an art forger (Charles Boyer) who mistakenly involves a private detective (Peter O'Toole) in a robbery.

The Professionals. Columbia. Director: Richard Brooks. Burt Lancaster, Lee Marvin, Robert Ryan, and Woody Strode are the professionals hired by a tycoon (Ralph Bellamy) to bring back his wife (Claudia Cardinale) kidnapped by a Mexican bandit (Jack Palance). Writer-director Brooks creates effective suspense in this adventure film.

The Russians Are Coming! The Russians Are Coming! United Artists. Director: Norman Jewison. A large cast of manic notables including Carl Reiner, Alan Arkin, and Jonthan Winters does not save this Cold War comedy from tediousness. When the crew of a disabled Russian submarine is forced to go ashore on a Connecticut island, the result is mirthful panic.

What Did You Do in the War, Daddy? United Artists. Director: Blake Edwards. A giddy antiwar comedy, starring James Coburn and Dick Shawn, set in 1943, when an Italian town surrenders to the American army on condition that it be permitted to stage its wine festival and a football match.

Who's Afraid of Virginia Woolf?. Warner Bros. Director: Mike Nichols. A very successful adaptation of Edward Albee's stage play, the drama is a mordant dissection of the illusions that tenuously sustain the marriages of academic couples Richard Burton and Elizabeth Taylor and George Segal and Sandy Dennis. A breakthrough in the use of offensive language.

1967

Barefoot in the Park. Paramount. Director: Gene Saks. An adaptation of a Neil Simon stage comedy, in

which Robert Redford and Jane Fonda play new-
lyweds who move into a cold-water flat in Manhattan and plot to marry the bride's mother to an
eccentric neighbor.

Bonnie and Clyde. Warner Seven Arts. Director: Arthur Penn. The sorry escapades of actual 1930's
bank robbers are transformed, through superb
filmmaking, into the violent and romantic saga
of youthful rebels against authority. Faye Duna-
way and Warren Beatty are brilliant as the title
characters, as is a supporting cast that includes
Gene Hackman, Estelle Parson, and Michael J.
Pollard.

Camelot. Warner Bros. Director: Joshua Logan. This
work by Lerner and Loewe not only contributed
"Camelot" and "If Ever I Would Leave You" to
musical culture but also popularized the use of
King Arthur's court as a metaphor for the vanished glamour of the John F. Kennedy administration. Richard Harris plays Arthur, Vanessa
Redgrave plays Guinevere, and Franco Nero plays
her illicit lover Lancelot.

Cool Hand Luke. Warner Bros. Director: Stuart
Rosenberg. Paul Newman plays a Christ-like convict who is sentenced to two years of hard labor
on a Southern chain gang and is shot during an
attempted escape. George Kennedy won an Oscar
for his supporting role as a prisoner.

The Dirty Dozen. Metro-Goldwyn-Mayer. Director:
Robert Aldrich. The very violent but both funny
and suspenseful story of twelve hardened criminals (Lee Marvin, Ernest Borgnine, Robert Ryan,
Charles Bronson, Jim Brown, and others) who
during World War II are released from prison to
undertake a suicide commando mission behind
German lines.

*Fearless Vampire Killers: Or, Pardon Me, Your Teeth Are in
My Neck.* Metro-Goldwyn-Mayer. Director: Roman
Polanski. A clever send-up of the Dracula genre,
starring Polanski, Jack McGowran, Alfie Bass, and
Polanski's ill-fated wife Sharon Tate, about a professor and his assistant who track down a Transyl-
vanian vampire.

The Graduate. United Artists. Director: Mike Nichols.
A rallying point for youthful alienation from a
culture of vapid materialism, it made a star of
Dustin Hoffman, as Benjamin Braddock, a listless
young man who drifts from an affair with Mrs.
Robinson (Anne Brancroft), the wife of his father's friend, to true love with her daughter

Elaine (Katharine Ross). Innovative use of popular music, by Simon and Garfunkel.

Guess Who's Coming to Dinner. Columbia. Director:
Stanley Kramer. A high-minded drama of racial
reconciliation, about a wealthy young San Francisco white woman (Katharine Houghton) who
introduces her wary parents (Spencer Tracy and
Katharine Hepburn) to the black man she intends to marry (Sidney Poitier).

In Cold Blood. Director: Richard Brooks. A brutal
adaptation of Truman Capote's acclaimed nonfiction novel about the wanton murders of a
prominent Kansas farming family by two drifters
(Robert Blake and Scott Wilson). Shot in black
and white to simulate a documentary, this disturbing film follows the case through to the capture
and execution of the killers.

In the Heat of the Night. United Artists. Director:
Norman Jewison. A tense, racially charged murder mystery, released during a time of violent
polarization between blacks and whites in America. A bigoted white Southern sheriff (Rod
Steiger) and a black Northern detective (Sidney
Poitier) reluctantly team up to solve a crime.

1968

Bullitt. Warner Bros. Director: Peter Yates. A crime
thriller in which Steve McQueen plays a San Francisco detective who determines to track down the
killers when a witness in his charge mysteriously
dies. Includes a spectacular car chase in the pic-
turesque California city that was becoming the
capital of the 1960's.

Charly. Selmur. Director: Ralph Nelson. Cliff Robertson won an Oscar for his performance as a mentally retarded man transformed, through surgery,
into a genius, but only temporarily. A sentimental
drama about the inherent dignity of even the
most humble human being.

Funny Girl. Columbia. Director: William Wyler. A star
was born in Barbra Streisand, as Fanny Brice, the
homely Jewish girl who became a Broadway star
but lost her husband (Omar Sharif). Streisand
won an Oscar for her boisterous performance in
this glossy, platitudinous adaptation of a stage
musical.

Night of the Living Dead. Image Ten. Director: George
Romero. Low-budget cult favorite about revenant
corpses, activated by radiation from a space
rocket, intent on devouring the living. Reflects

the self-destructive tumults and violence of a society torn by assassinations, riots, and war.

The Odd Couple. Paramount. Director: Gene Saks. The title of playwright Neil Simon's comedy became a common figure of speech to refer to unlikely human pairings. The film version yokes Jack Lemmon's fastidious Felix with Walter Matthau's sloppy Oscar in the New York apartment that they attempt to share.

Planet of the Apes. Twentieth Century Fox. Director: Franklin Schaffner. A popular and thoughtful science-fiction cult film that generated several sequels and two television series, one live-action and one animated. Four American astronauts, including Charlton Heston, land on a distant planet (which turns out to be a future version of Earth) where apes are the dominant species and humans are beasts.

The Producers. Avco/Springtime/Metro-Goldwyn-Mayer/Crossbow. Director: Mel Brooks. Reveling in the hilarity of bad taste, writer-director Brooks constructs a frantic comedy about a theatrical producer (Zero Mostel) who attempts to fleece elderly widows by selling them shares in a Broadway musical he intends as a flop. Though utterly inept and offensive, the musical, *Springtime for Hitler*, turns out to be a hit, as does the film that showcases it.

Rosemary's Baby. Paramount. Director: Roman Polanski. Mia Farrow plays a woman who is impregnated by the devil in a baroque melodrama about satanic possession that opened up the subject of the occult to popular movies. Ruth Gordon received an Oscar for her performance as a peculiar neighbor.

The Subject Was Roses. Metro-Goldwyn-Mayer. Director: Ulu Grosbard. Adaptation of a stage play by Frank D. Gilroy that concerns the gap in communication between a young war veteran (Martin Sheen) and his parents (Jack Albertson, in an Oscar-winning performance, and Patricia Neal, who also received an Oscar nomination).

2001: A Space Odyssey. Metro-Goldwyn-Mayer. Director: Stanley Kubrick. Ambitious, pioneering attempt at serious science fiction, a spectacular allegory, written by Arthur C. Clarke, of human evolution from primitive hominid to sophisticated space traveler vying with the even more sophisticated technology that turns on its creators.

1969

Butch Cassidy and the Sundance Kid. Twentieth Century Fox. Director: George Roy Hill. A popular celebration of male camaraderie and of the vanished frontier. Paul Newman and Robert Redford are exuberant in the title roles as train robbers who end up in Bolivia. The Burt Bacharach song "Raindrops Keep Fallin' on My Head" became a hit.

Cactus Flower. Columbia. Director: Gene Saks. This comedy marks Goldie Hawn's Oscar-winning screen debut as the batty girlfriend of dentist Walter Matthau, who is actually in love with his prim nurse Ingrid Bergman, whom he tries to pass off as his wife.

Easy Rider. Columbia/Pando/Raybert. Director: Dennis Hopper. A landmark success in independent, low-budget filmmaking and a popular embodiment of the era's spirit of youthful freedom and mobility. Peter Fonda and Dennis Hopper encounter bigotry and violence as they motorcycle across America. They also encounter Jack Nicholson as a tipsy but lovable lawyer, a role that propelled him to stardom.

Medium Cool. Paramount. Director: Haskell Wexler. Set in Chicago during the tumultuous 1968 Democratic National Convention, writer-director-cinematographer Wexler's story about a television news cameraman is a meditation on contemporary intolerance and violence and on the role of the mass media in shaping public perceptions.

Midnight Cowboy. United Artists. Director: John Schlesinger. John Voight plays Joe Buck, an ingenuous Texan who comes to New York to hustle as a stud to rich women but ends up being outhustled by everyone else and bonding with the tubercular, sleazy con man Ratso (Dustin Hoffman). Remarkable for its frankness in portraying the brutalities of contemporary urban life.

Paint Your Wagon. Paramount. Director: Joshua Logan. A listless adaptation of the Alan Jay Lerner and Frederick Loewe musical about two partners (Clint Eastwood and Lee Marvin) during the California gold rush who share everything, including their mail-order bride (Jean Seberg).

Take the Money and Run. Palomar. Director: Woody Allen. Allen's first feature as writer-director. He also stars in this absurd comedy, a profusion of sight gags and verbal jokes. Presented as if a documentary, the film reviews a social misfit's inept career in crime.

They Shoot Horses, Don't They? ABC/Palomar. Director: Sydney Pollack. A harrowing drama set in the dismal 1930's during four days of a dance marathon that tests the desperate contestants' ability to endure. Powerful performances by Gig Young, Jane Fonda, Susannah York, and Michael Sarrazin.

True Grit. Paramount. Director: Henry Hathaway. John Wayne acts his age in this playful Western about a paunchy, bibulous old marshal, Rooster Cogburn, who comes to the reluctant aid of a girl (Kim Darby) who seeks revenge against the men (led by Robert Duvall) who murdered her father.

The Wild Bunch. Warner Seven Arts. Director: Sam Peckinpah. William Holden, Ernest Borgnine, Robert Ryan, and Edmond O'Brien are among the Texas bandits who in 1914 make a bloody last stand against a vicious Mexican revolutionary (Jack Palance). Peckinpah's intelligent film stylizes its exaggerated, graphic violence.

Steven G. Kellman

Major Broadway Plays and Theatrical Awards

1959/1960 Season

The Andersonville Trial

The Best Man
　Tony Award: Best Actor (Drama), Melvyn
　　Douglas

Caligula

The Deadly Game

Destry Rides Again

Duel of Angels

The Fighting Cock
　Tony Award: Best Supporting Actor (Drama),
　　Roddy McDowall

Fiorello!
　Pulitzer Prize: Jerome Weidman, George
　　Abbott, Sheldon Harnick, Jerry Bock
　New York Drama Critics Circle Award: Best
　　Musical
　Tony Awards: Best Director, George Abbott;
　　Best Supporting Actor, Tom Bosley

Five Finger Exercise
　New York Drama Critics Circle Award: Best
　　Foreign Play

Greenwillow

Gypsy

The Miracle Worker
　Tony Awards: Best Play, William Gibson; Best
　　Director, Arthur Penn; Best Actress (Drama),
　　Anne Bancroft

Once upon a Mattress

The Sound of Music
　Tony Awards: Best Musical, Howard Lindsay,
　　Russel Crouse, Oscar Hammerstein II,
　　Richard Rodgers; Best Actress, Mary Martin;
　　Best Supporting Actress, Patricia Neway

Sweet Bird of Youth

Take Me Along
　Tony Award: Best Actor (Musical), Jackie Gleason

The Tenth Man

A Thurber Carnival
　Tony Special Citation Award

Toys in the Attic
　New York Drama Critics Circle Award: Best
　　American Play
　Tony Award: Best Supporting Actress (Drama),
　　Anne Revere

1960/1961 Season

All the Way Home
　Pulitzer Prize: Tad Mosel
　New York Drama Critics Circle Award: Best
　　American Play
　Tony Award: Best Supporting Actress (Drama),
　　Colleen Dewhurst

Bye, Bye Birdie
　Tony Awards: Best Musical, Michael Stewart,
　　Charles Strouse, Lee Adams; Best Director,
　　Gower Champion; Best Supporting Actor
　　(Musical), Dick Van Dyke

Becket
　Tony Award: Best Play (Drama), Jean Anouilh

Big Fish, Little Fish
　Tony Award: Best Director (Drama), Sir John
　　Gielgud; Best Supporting Actor, Martin Gabel

Camelot
　Tony Award: Best Actor (Musical), Richard
　　Burton

The Devil's Advocate

Do Re Mi

A Far Country

The Hostage

Invitation to a March

Irma la Douce
　Tony Award: Best Actress (Musical) Elizabeth
　　Seal

Mary, Mary

Period of Adjustment

Rhinoceros
　Tony Award: Best Actor (Drama), Zero Mostel

A Taste of Honey
　New York Drama Critics Circle Award: Best
　　Foreign Play
　Tony Award: Best Actress (Drama), Joan Plowright

Tenderloin

The Unsinkable Molly Brown
　Tony Award: Best Supporting Actress (Musical),
　　Tammy Grimes

1961/1962 Season

The Caretaker

Carnival
　New York Drama Critics Circle Award: Best
　　Musical

Tony Award: Best Actress (Musical), Anna Maria
　Alberghetti

The Complaisant Lover
The Egg
The Gay Life
Gideon
Great Day in the Morning
How to Succeed in Business Without Really Trying
   Pulitzer Prize: Abe Burrows, Willie Gilbert, Jack
      Weinstock, Frank Loesser
   New York Drama Critics Circle Award: Best
      Musical
   Tony Awards: Best Director (Musical), Abe
      Burrows; Best Actor, Robert Morse; Best
      Featured Actor, Charles Nelson Reilly
I Can Get It for You Wholesale
Kean
A Man for All Seasons
   New York Drama Critics Circle Award: Best
      Foreign Play
   Tony Awards: Best Play, Robert Bolt; Best
      Director (Drama), Noel Willman; Best Actor,
      Paul Scofield
Milk and Honey
The Night of the Iguana
   New York Drama Critics Circle Award: Best
      American Play
   Tony Award: Best Actress (Drama), Margaret
      Leighton
No Strings
   Tony Award: Best Actress (Musical), Diahann
      Carroll
*Oh Dad, Poor Dad, Mamma's Hung You in the Closet and
   I'm Feelin' So Sad*
A Shot in the Dark
   Tony Award: Best Supporting Actor (Drama),
      Walter Matthau
Stone and Star
Subways Are for Sleeping
   Tony Award: Best Supporting Actress (Musical),
      Phyllis Newman
Take Her, She's Mine
   Tony Award: Best Supporting Actress (Drama),
      Elizabeth Ashley

1962/1963 Season
Andorra
Beyond the Fringe
   New York Drama Critics Circle Special Citation
      Award
Brigadoon
The Collection

Enter Laughing
   Tony Award: Best Supporting Actor (Drama),
      Alan Arkin
A Funny Thing Happened on the Way to the Forum
   Tony Awards: Best Musical, Burt Shevelove,
      Larry Gelbart, Stephen Sondheim; Best
      Director, George Abbott; Best Actor, Zero
      Mostel; Best Supporting Actor, David Burns
Little Me
The Milk Train Doesn't Stop Here Anymore
Mother Courage and Her Children
Never too Late
Oliver!
P.S. 193
Rattle of a Simple Man
She Loves Me
Stop the World—I Want to Get Off
   Tony Award: Best Actress (Musical), Anna
      Quayle
Tchin-tchin
A Thousand Clowns
   Tony Award: Best Supporting Actress (Drama),
      Sandy Dennis
Tovarich
   Tony Award: Best Actress (Musical), Vivien
      Leigh
Who's Afraid of Virginia Woolf?
   New York Drama Critics Circle Award: Best Play
   Tony Awards: Best Play, Edward Albee; Best
      Director (Drama), Alan Schneider; Best
      Actor, Arthur Hill; Best Actress, Uta Hagen

1963/1964 Season
Any Wednesday
   Tony Award: Best Actress (Drama), Sandy
      Dennis
After the Fall
   Tony Award: Best Supporting Actress (Drama),
      Barbara Loden
Arturo Ui
The Ballad of the Sad Cafe
Barefoot in the Park
   Tony Award: Best Director (Drama), Mike
      Nichols
Blues for Mister Charlie
Chips with Everything
The Deputy
Dylan
   Tony Award: Best Actor (Drama), Alec
      Guinness

Foxy
  Tony Award: Best Actor (Musical), Bert Lahr
Funny Girl
The Girl Who Came to Supper
  Tony Award: Best Supporting Actress (Musical),
    Tessie O'Shea
Hamlet
  Tony Award: Best Supporting Actor (Drama),
    Hume Cronyn
Hello, Dolly!
  New York Drama Critics Circle Award: Best
    Musical
  Tony Awards: Best Musical, Michael Stewart;
    Best Actress, Carol Canning; Best Director,
    Gower Champion
High Spirits
Luther
  New York Drama Critics Circle Award: Best Play,
    John Osborne
Next Time I'll Sing to You
110 in the Shade
The Passion of Josef D.
The Rehearsal
She Loves Me
  Tony Award: Best Supporting Actor (Musical),
    Jack Cassidy
The Trojan Women
  New York Drama Critics Circle Special Citation
    Award
What Makes Sammy Run?

1964/1965 Season
The Amen Corner
Baker Street
Ben Franklin in Paris
Do I Hear a Waltz?
Fiddler on the Roof
  New York Drama Critics Circle Award: Best
    Musical
  Tony Awards: Best Play, Joseph Stein, Jerry
    Bock, Sheldon Harnick; Best Director,
    Jerome Robbins; Best Actor, Zero Mostel;
    Best Supporting Actress, Maria Karnilova
Flora the Red Menace
  Tony Award: Best Actress (Musical), Liza Minelli
Half a Sixpence
Incident at Vichy
Luv
  Tony Award: Best Director (Drama), Mike
    Nichols (also for *The Odd Couple*)

The Odd Couple
  Tony Awards: Best Director (Drama) Mike
    Nichols; Best Actor, Walter Matthau
Oh What a Lovely War
  Tony Award: Best Supporting Actor (Musical),
    Victor Spinetti
The Owl and the Pussycat
The Physicists
Poor Bitos
The Roar of the Greasepaint—the Smell of the Crowd
The Sign in Sidney Brustein's Window
  Tony Award: Best Supporting Actress (Drama),
    Alice Ghostley
Slow Dance on the Killing Ground
The Subject Was Roses
  Pulitzer Prize: Frank D. Gilroy
  New York Drama Critics Circle Award: Best Play
  Tony Awards: Best Play; Best Supporting Actor
    (Drama), Jack Albertson
Tartuffe
Tiny Alice
  Tony Award: Best Actress (Drama), Irene
    Worth
The Toilet

1965/1966 Season
Cactus Flower
Generation
Hogan's Goat
Inadmissable Evidence
It's a Bird, It's a Plane, It's Superman
The Lion in Winter
  Tony Award: Best Actress (Drama), Rosemary
    Harris
Mame
  Tony Awards: Best Actress (Musical), Angela
    Lansbury; Best Supporting Actress, Beatrice
    Arthur; Best Supporting Actor, Frankie
    Michaels
Man of La Mancha
  New York Drama Critics Circle Award: Best
    Musical
  Tony Awards: Best Musical, Dale Wasserman,
    Mitch Lee, Joe Darion; Best Actor, Richard
    Kiley; Best Director, Herbert Marre
Mark Twain Tonight
  Tony Award: Best Actor (Drama), Hal
    Holbrook
On a Clear Day You Can See Forever
Pickwick

The Persecution and Assassination of Jean-Paul Marat As Performed by the Inmates of the Asylum at Charenton Under the Direction of the Marquis de Sade
New York Drama Critics Circle Award: Best Play
Tony Awards: Best Play, Peter Weiss/English version Geoffrey Skelton; Best Director (Drama), Peter Brook; Best Supporting Actor, Patrick Magee

Philadelphia, Here I Come!
The Right Honourable Gentleman
The Royal Hunt of the Sun
Skyscraper
Slapstick Tragedy
Tony Award: Best Supporting Actress (Drama), Zoe Caldwell

Sweet Charity
You Can't Take It with You

1966/1967 Season
America Hurrah
The Apple Tree
Tony Award: Best Actress (Musical), Barbara Harris

Black Comedy
Cabaret
New York Drama Critics Circle Award: Best Musical
Tony Awards: Best Musical Joe Masterhoff, John Kander, Fred Ebb; Best Supporting Actor, Joel Grey; Best Supporting Actress, Peg Murray; Best Director, Harold Prince

A Delicate Balance
Pulitzer Prize: Edward Albee
Tony Award: Best Supporting Actress (Drama), Marian Seldes

Hamp
The Homecoming
New York Drama Critics Circle Award: Best Play
Tony Awards: Best Play (Drama), Harold Pinter; Best Actor, Paul Rogers; Best Supporting Actor, Ian Holm; Best Director, Peter Hall

I Do, I Do!
Tony Award: Best Actor (Musical), Robert Preston

The Killing of Sister George
Tony Award: Best Actress (Drama), Beryl Reid

Walking Happy
You're a Good Man, Charlie Brown

1967/1968 Season
After the Rain

The Birthday Party
Tony Award: Best Supporting Actor (Drama), James Patterson

The Boys in the Band
Darling of the Day
Tony Award: Best Actress (Musical), Patricia Routledge

A Day in the Death of Joe Egg
Tony Awards: Best Actor (Drama), Albert Finney; Best Supporting Actress, Zena Walker

Golden Rainbow
Hallelujah, Baby
Tony Awards: Best Musical, Arthur Laurents, Jule Styne, Betty Comden, Adolph Green; Best Actress (Musical), Leslie Uggams; Best Supporting Actress, Lillian Hayman

The Happy Time
Tony Awards: Best Director (Musical), Gower Champion; Best Actor, Robert Goulet

Henry, Sweet Henry
How Now, Dow Jones
Tony Award: Best Supporting Actor (Musical), Hiram Sherman

I Never Sang for My Father
Ilya, Darling
Plaza Suite
Tony Award: Best Director, Mike Nichols

The Price
Tony Award: Best Supporting Actor (Drama), Harold Gary

The Prime of Miss Jean Brodie
Tony Award: Best Actress (Drama), Zoe Caldwell

R & G and Loot
Rosencrantz and Guildenstern Are Dead
New York Drama Critics Circle Award: Best Play
Tony Award: Best Play (Drama), Tom Stoppard

Scuba Duba
Spofford
Staircase
You Know I Can't Hear You When the Water's Running
Tony Award: Best Actor (Drama), Martin Balsam

Your Own Thing
New York Drama Critics Circle Award: Best Musical

1968/1969 Season
Adaptation/Next
Canterbury Tales
Celebration

Dear World
   Tony Award: Best Actress (Musical), Angela
      Lansbury
Does a Tiger Wear a Necktie?
   Tony Award: Best Supporting Actor (Drama),
      Al Pacino
Forty Carats
   Tony Award: Best Actress, Julie Harris
George M!
The Great White Hope
   Pulitzer Prize: Howard Sackler
   New York Drama Critics Circle Award: Best Play
   Tony Awards: Best Play (Drama); Best Actor,
      James Earl Jones; Best Supporting Actress;
      Jane Alexander
Hadrian VII
   Tony Award: Best Director (Drama), Peter Dews
Hair
In the Matter of J. Robert Oppenheimer
Lovers and Other Strangers
The Man in the Glass Booth
No Place to Be Somebody
Play It Again Sam
Promises, Promises
   Tony Awards: Best Actor (Musical) Jerry
      Ohrbach; Best Supporting Actress, Marian
      Mercer
1776
   New York Drama Critics Circle Award: Best
      Musical
   Tony Awards: Best Musical, Peter Stone,
      Sherman Edwards; Best Director, Peter
      Hunt; Best Supporting Actor, Ronald Holgate
Zorba

1969/70 Season
Applause
   Tony Awards: Best Musical, Betty Comden,
      Adolph Green, Charles Strouse, Lee Adams;
      Best Director, Ron Field; Best Actress,
      Lauren Bacall
Borstal Boy
   Tony Award: Best Play (Drama), Frank
      McMahon
Butterflies Are Free
   Tony Award: Best Supporting Actress, Blythe
      Danner
Child's Play
   Tony Awards: Best Director (Drama), Joseph
      Hardy; Best Actor, Fritz Weaver; Best
      Supporting Actor, Ken Howard
Coco
   Tony Award: Best Supporting Actor, Rene
      Auberjonois
Company
Georgy
Indians
The Last of the Red-Hot Lovers
A Patriot for Me
Private Lives
   Tony Award: Best Actress (Drama), Tammy
      Grimes
Purlie Victorious
   Tony Awards: Best Actor (Musical), Cleavon
      Little; Best Supporting Actress, Melba Moore
The Serpent
What the Butler Saw
The White House Murder Case

Jo Manning

Most-Watched U.S. Television Shows

1960-1961 season
1. Gunsmoke
2. Wagon Train
3. Have Gun Will Travel
4. The Andy Griffith Show
5. The Real McCoys
6. Rawhide
7. Candid Camera
8. The Untouchables
9. The Price Is Right
10. The Jack Benny Program

1961-1962 season
1. Wagon Train
2. Bonanza
3. Gunsmoke
4. Hazel
5. Perry Mason
6. The Red Skelton Show
7. The Andy Griffith Show
8. The Danny Thomas Show
9. Dr. Kildare
10. Candid Camera

1962-1963 season
1. The Beverly Hillbillies
2. Candid Camera
3. The Red Skelton Show
4. Bonanza
5. The Lucy Show
6. The Andy Griffith Show
7. Ben Casey
8. The Danny Thomas Show
9. The Dick Van Dyke Show
10. Gunsmoke

1963-1964 season
1. The Beverly Hillbillies
2. Bonanza
3. The Dick Van Dyke Show
4. Petticoat Junction
5. The Andy Griffith Show
6. The Lucy Show

7. Candid Camera
8. The Ed Sullivan Show
9. The Danny Thomas Show
10. My Favorite Martian

1964-1965 season
1. Bonanza
2. Bewitched
3. Gomer Pyle, U.S.M.C.
4. The Andy Griffith Show
5. The Fugitive
6. The Red Skelton Hour
7. The Dick Van Dyke Show
8. The Lucy Show
9. Peyton Place
10. Combat

1965-1966 season
1. Bonanza
2. Gomer Pyle, U.S.M.C.
3. The Lucy Show
4. The Red Skelton Hour
5. Batman
6. The Andy Griffith Show
7. Bewitched
8. The Beverly Hillbillies
9. Hogan's Heroes
10. Green Acres

1966-1967 season
1. Bonanza
2. The Red Skelton Hour
3. The Andy Griffith Show
4. The Lucy Show
5. The Jackie Gleason Show
6. Green Acres
7. Daktari
8. Bewitched
9. The Beverly Hillbillies
10. Gomer Pyle, U.S.M.C.

1967-1968 season
1. The Andy Griffith Show
2. The Lucy Show
3. Gomer Pyle, U.S.M.C.
4. Gunsmoke
5. Family Affair

  6. Bonanza
  7. The Red Skelton Hour
  8. The Dean Martin Show
  9. The Jackie Gleason Show
 10. Saturday Night at the Movies

1968-1969 season
  1. Rowan and Martin's Laugh-In
  2. Gomer Pyle, U.S.M.C.
  3. Bonanza
  4. Mayberry, R.F.D.
  5. Family Affair
  6. Gunsmoke
  7. Julia
  8. The Dean Martin Show

  9. Here's Lucy
 10. The Beverly Hillbillies

1969-1970 season
  1. Rowan and Martin's Laugh-In
  2. Gunsmoke
  3. Bonanza
  4. Mayberry, R.F.D.
  5. Family Affair
  6. Here's Lucy
  7. The Red Skelton Hour
  8. Marcus Welby, M.D.
  9. The Wonderful World of Disney
 10. The Doris Day Show

Robert L. Patterson

Major U.S. Legislation

Year	Legislation	Significance
1960	Civil Rights Act	Included provisions that made it a federal offense to attempt flight in order to evade prosecution for bombings and for interference with any court order that touched upon the desegregation of schools. A loophole in the law prevented its implementation until the Justice Department had put forward specific cases proving that complainants had been denied rights because of their race or color.
1960	Federal Highway Act	Set aside an appropriation of $1,025,000,000 for the construction, improvement and upkeep of U.S. roads.
1960	Public Debt and Tax Extension Act	Authorized a temporary increase of $285,000,000,000 in the national debt ceiling and extended prior temporary increases in excise and corporate income taxes.
1960	Mutual Security Act	Authorized the appropriation of $1,366,200,000 for military, economic, and technical assistance to designated foreign states.
1960	Department of Defense Appropriations Act	Set aside $39,996,608,000 for the U.S. Armed Forces during the 1960-1961 fiscal year.
1960	Latin American Aid Act	Provided $500,000,000 in economic assistance to Latin American states. An additional $100,000,000 was allocated for Chile for relief in the aftermath of severe earthquakes.
1960	Social Security Act Amendment	Established a new federal assistance program to provide medical and hospital services for the elderly poor.
1960	Act for Regulation of Bank Mergers	Set up standard rules and procedures governing bank merger applications.
1960	Foreign Tax Credit Act	Permitted taxpaying U.S. citizens and residents with income from foreign sources the option of either a per-country credit or an overall credit for purposes of computing federal income tax; also required U.S. corporations to file an annual report regarding foreign subsidiaries.
1960	Sugar Act Extension	Extended the provisions of the Sugar Act and authorized the president to adjust quotas on Cuban sugar.
1961	Peace Corps Act	Gave the Corps, which had already been established through executive order, a permanent status and an authorized appropriation of $40,000,000 for the fiscal year 1962.
1961	Foreign Assistance Act	Authorized appropriations of up to $1,200,000,000 in developmental loans for foreign assistance.
1961	Agricultural Act	An omnibus farm bill that included, among its more important provisions, extentions of both the feed grains program and the wheat grains program.
1961	Federal Highway Act	Allowed for an additional $9,000,000,000 for highway revenues through the year 1972; continued federal taxes on diesel, gasoline, and special motor fuels; and increased taxes on certain major automotive items.

Year	Legislation	Significance
1961	Arms Control and Disarmament Act	Set up the U.S. Arms Control and Disarmament Agency to carry out studies and to conduct negotiations on matters of disarmament.
1961	International Travel Act	Set up the U.S. Travel Service Bureau within the Commerce Department, allocating to the Bureau a sum of $3,000,000 for fiscal 1962 and $4,700,000 per annum thereafter.
1961	Crimes Aboard Aircraft in Air Act	Made the hijacking of aircraft a felony under federal law, punishable by death or imprisonment. Additional penalties were established for other crimes committed aboard aircraft.
1961	Fair Labor Standards Amendments	Raised the minimum wage from $1.00 to $1.25 per hour, and extended coverage to include more than three million workers in the retail and service trades. Increases were implemented in two stages: to $1.15 per hour in September, 1964, and $1.25 in September, 1965.
1961	Call Up of Armed Forces Ready Reserve	Authorized the president to call up reserve units and individuals serving in the reserves to active duty for a period of twelve months.
1961	Identification Number Act	Required taxpayers to use a taxpayer identification number when filing federal income tax returns; corporations and institutions paying out interest and dividends were required to file information returns for each individual receiving payments.
1962	Migration and Refugee Assistance Act	Authorized appropriations to be used for the aid and relief of refugees and provided that up to $10,000,000 in foreign aid might be set aside for coping with emergency refugee situations.
1962	Revenue Act	Allowed businesses tax deductions for entertainment and lobbying expenses; provided income tax credits for business investments; and ended tax deferments for income that U.S. corporations placed into foreign subsidiaries.
1962	Trade Expansion Act	Gave the president authority to reduce or remove duties on certain categories of goods; allowed trade concessions to be withdrawn for nations restricting U.S. exports.
1962	Congressional Resolution on Cuba	Authorized the president to use military force against Cuba; included a statement of U.S. intent to resist Communist expansion into any part of the Americas.
1962	Self-Employed Individuals Tax Retirement Act	Permitted owner-employees to make yearly deposits into retirement funds and to take deductions on federal income taxes.
1962	Federal-Aid Highway Act	Authorized funds for highways, forest roads, and trails, including $32,000,000 for the Inter-American Highway and $850,000 for an Alaska Highway study.
1962	Drug Amendments	Authorized the FDA to set manufacturing practices standards and placed the burden of proof regarding drug-safety standards on manufacturers.
1962	Communications Satellite Act	Authorized the incorporation of a Communications Satellite Corporation to develop a satellite system and to monitor its international services.

Year	Legislation	Significance
1962	Manpower Training and Development Act	Provided for the retraining of workers with obsolete skills, the assessment of employment trends, and the reintegration of workers into the job market.
1962	Public Welfare Amendments	Provided for federal participation in community work and training programs for unemployed men whose families were supported under the Aid to Dependent Children Program.
1963	Health Professions Education Assistance Act	Established a program of federal matching grants for the construction and repair of medical professional schools and loan programs for medical students.
1963	Clean Air Act	Established an expanded national air-pollution program with $95,000,000 in matching grants to state and local authorities.
1963	Higher Education Facilities	Provided federal grants and loans for construction and improvement of higher-education facilities.
1963	Extension of the National Defense Education Act	Provided for an increased allocation of federal student loans.
1963	Mental Retardation Facilities Construction Act	Allocated $26,000,000 for the construction and maintenance of research centers, clinical facilities, and other buildings.
1963	Maternal and Child Health and Mental Retardation Planning Amendments	Provided funds for maternal and child-care services and prenatal care programs for low-income and at-risk mothers.
1963	Extension of the Civil Rights Commission	Continued the commission's mandate for an additional year, to September 30, 1964.
1963	Extension of the Military Draft	Authorized a four-year extension of the induction provisions of the Military Training and Selective Service Act of 1951.
1963	Atomic Test Ban Treaty	Congress approved an international agreement to halt nuclear tests in the atmosphere, underwater, or in outer space, thereby limiting such testing to underground explosions.
1963	Equal Pay Act	Forbade discrimination in the payment of wages for jobs on the basis of an employee's gender. Employers were barred from achieving compliance by cutting wages, and unions were prohibited from urging employers to discriminate on the basis of gender.
1964	Civil Rights Act	Forbade discrimination in businesses that catered to the public in food, gasoline, lodging, or entertainment; disallowed discrimination by employers and labor unions in promotion, dismissal, hiring, or job referrals; permitted federal agencies to withhold funds from programs practicing discrimination; gave the attorney-general authority to compel desegregation of public schools, playgrounds, libraries, parks, recreational areas, and swimming pools; nullified literacy tests as voting requirements.
1964	Internal Revenue Act	Reduced personal and corporate income-tax rates over a three-year period.

Year	Legislation	Significance
1964	Economic Opportunity Act	Provided for the creation of the Jobs Corps to offer youth job-training and employment; of community-action programs to combat poverty at the neighborhood level; of a domestic Peace Corps; of local work-training programs; and of adult-education programs.
1964	Amendments to the National Defense Education Act	Extended the program for three extra years, increased its budget to provide low-interest student loans, and authorized the creation of teacher-training institutes and the addition of fellowships.
1964	Urban Mass Transportation Act	Set aside federal grants for the development of urban mass transportation through both the public and private sectors.
1964	National Aeronautics and Space Administration Budget	Provided $5,200,000,000 in funds, some of which were specially allocated for a lunar landing.
1964	Wilderness Act	Authorized the establishment of a National Wildlife Preservation system and declared that claims under the 1872 Mining Act would expire on December 31, 1983.
1964	Public Land Review Act	Created the Public Land Review Commission to initiate studies on public land laws and make recommendations to Congress.
1964	Automation and Technological Progress Act	Created the National Commission to initiate studies of technological change and make recommendations on possible effects on the job market.
1964	Tonkin Gulf Resolution	Gave the president virtually unlimited authority to commit military forces to South Vietnam and to provide military assistance to any member or "protocol state' of the SEATO Treaty.
1965	Voting Rights Act	Banned educational voting requirements in areas where discrimination was suspected; authorized the assignment of federal voting registrars; required the federal district court in Washington, D.C., to approve any changes in voting procedure in areas with a history of discrimination.
1965	Elementary and Secondary Education Act	Authorized federal grants to school districts with above-average percentages of impoverished children and provided funds for the purchase of textbooks and library materials by school districts.
1965	Higher Education Act	Appropriated scholarship funds for needy students; assumed interest costs on loans for low-income students; and transferred the Work-Study Program from the Office of Economic Opportunity to the Office of Education.
1965	National Foundation for the Arts and Humanities Grant	Authorized by Congress for scholarship and research loans in the humanities and for assistance to eligible individuals and groups engaged in the arts.
1965	Housing and Urban Development Act	Authorized a low-income rent supplement, insurance for land-development loans, and the extension of the Home Mortgage Program.
1965	Highway Beautification Act	Set regulations and guidelines for billboard advertisements and junkyards along interstate, federal, and primary road systems; authorized funds for highway landscaping and maintainence of rest and recreation areas.

Year	Legislation	Significance
1965	Coinage Act	The first radical change in U.S. coinage system in the century; eliminated the silver content of dimes and quarters and reduced it in silver dollars; provided penalties for counterfeiters
1965	Economic Development Act	Enacted to foster economic development in depressed areas by providing grants for public works and economic growth projects; giving technical assistance to economically deprived localities; and setting up regional economic planning commissions.
1965	Appalachia Regional Development Act	Set aside $1,092,400,000 in development appropriations for the multi-state Appalachia area. Money was reserved for cleaning up derelict mines, erosion management, and health facilities construction.
1965	Excise Tax Reduction	Reduced excise taxes by a total of $4,700,000,000 over the 1965-1969 period. Affected items included automobiles, televisions, jewelry, firearms, liquor, tobacco, gasoline, and air transportation.
1966	Foreign Investors—Xmas Tree Act	Included a potpourri of measures: Closed tax loopholes previously enjoyed by U.S. investors abroad and offered incentives to foreign investors to buy U.S. stocks and bonds; allowed senior citizens full tax deductions on medical expenses; and introduced a campaign-funds component to federal tax forms.
1966	Transportation Act	Established the Department of Transportation as a Cabinet-level agency, in charge of formulating and carrying out national transportation policy and its various programs.
1966	Clean Waters Restoration Act	Allocated $3,550,000,000 to be used in building and upgrading sewage-treatment plants; conducting reseach on industrial wastes; and constructing and maintaining water-purification plants.
1966	Demonstration Cities and Metropolitan Development Act	Launched a three-year, $1,200,000,000 program for the rehabilitation of decayed urban areas by selecting "demonstration cities" to receive funds.
1966	Manpower Development and Training Act	Encompassed a series of training programs that would concentrate on skills for which there was a workers' shortage.
1966	Teacher Corps	Given its first appropriation through act of Congress; the amount was set at $9,500,000 for the 1966 fiscal year, and $7,500,000 for 1967. A restrictive clause was added stating that schools that requested assistance from the corps must first secure the approval of their state education agency.
1966	Birth Control Amendments	Tacked onto the Economic Opportunity Act; the authority to determine the eligibility of unmarried women to receive family-planning information was taken from the Federal Anti-Poverty Office and vested in local action agencies. $61,000,000 was allocated for neighborhood health centers that could incorporate family-planning units.

Year	Legislation	Significance
1966	Truth-in-Packaging Act	Set weight and quality standards for commercial packaging and prohibited the use of deceptively shaped containers or containers with misleading labels or pictures.
1966	Veterans Readjustment Benefits Act	Authorized funds for full-time instructional training for veterans and alloted them monthly allowances.
1966	Minimum Wage Act	Extended coverage to 9,100,000 additional nonprofessional workers and authorized minimum-wage increases to $1.40 per hour (1967) and $1.60 (1968).
1967	Social Security Amendments	Approved a 13 percent across-the-board increase in benefits, with additional cash benefits going to some 100,000 younger workers who had been disabled before the age of thirty-one; the minimum monthly benefit was raised from $44 to $55 per month.
1967	Model Cities Act	Expanded the provisions of the Demonstration Cities and Metropolitan Development Act (1966); "demonstration cities" were relabelled "model cities."
1967	Public Broadcasting Act	Authorized the formation of the Corporation for Public Broadcasting to assist in the development of public, noncommercial radio and television.
1967	Air Quality Control Act	Authorized expanded grants to states and localities to plan and implement air-quality standards. The secretary of health, education, and welfare was empowered to define atmospheric quality regions, recommend pollution-control measures, and take alleged violators to court.
1967	Equal Opportunity Act Amendments	Authorized appropriations of $1,980,000,000 (1968) and $2,180,000,000 (1969); and stated that control of local community-action funds would be transferred from private organizations to public officials.
1967	Postal Revenue Act	Raised rates on all classes of mail; extended free mailing privileges for all material posted to the blind and visually handicapped; and banned all mail solicitations that might misleadingly convey the impression that they were bills for goods or services already delivered.
1967	Military Selective Service Act	Extended the draft for a further four years; specified that nineteen-year-olds would be called up before older inductees; directed the Justice Department to prosecute draft resisters; and prohibited the president from ending student deferments.
1967	Wholesome Meat Act	Updated federal meat-inspection standards, provided for assistance to states in their own efforts at upgrading, and made pre-slaughtering inspections mandatory.
1967	Veterans Pension and Readjustment Act	Authorized a cost-of-living increase, larger educational allowances, expanded training programs, and more sweeping medical benefits.
1967	Pay Increases for Federal Civilian Workers	Increases of 4.5 percent were approved, with automatic pay increases occurring annually without the necessity of congressional approval. Pay commissions were to be named to recommend rates of increase for officials in the executive, legislative, and judicial branches of government.

Year	Legislation	Significance
1968	Civil Rights Act	Banned discrimination in the sale or rental of property; set criminal penalties for interference with persons attempting to vote, attend educational institutions, serve on juries, or use public facilities. An anti-riot provision set criminal penalties for using interstate commerce facilities to incite or take part in a riot.
1968	Jury Selection and Service Act	Provided for impartial, random selection of jurors from official voting lists and banned discrimination in jury selection on the basis of race, color, economic status, national origin, religion, or sex.
1968	Omnibus Crime Control and Safe Streets Act	Authorized appropriations to upgrade state and local police forces; banned handgun sales to persons under the age of twenty-one; allowed confessions to be admitted as evidence regardless of whether suspects had been advised of their rights; and permitted wiretapping in certain state and federal cases.
1968	Gun Control Act	Prohibited mail order or interstate shipment of firearms to persons not residing in the dealer's state; banned rifle, shotgun, and ammunition sales to persons under the age of eighteen and handgun and handgun ammunition sales to those under twenty-one.
1968	Juvenile Delinquency Prevention and Control Act	Set aside $150,000,000 for a program of block grants to states to plan and implement projects to prevent juvenile delinquency and rehabilitate offenders.
1968	Housing and Urban Development Act	Enlarged the rent-supplements authorization to $5,3000,000,000 over a three-year span and provided funds for 1,700,000 new housing units.
1968	Truth-in-Lending Act	Required that all buyers be informed of the cost of loans and installment purchase plans in terms of annual rate calculations; the federal Reserve Board was empowered to draft the specifics of the law.
1968	Gas Pipeline Safety Act	Authorized the secretary of transportation to set both interim and permanent standards regarding safety factors for 760,000 miles of transmission and distribution lines.
1968	Wholesome Poultry Products Act	Mandated inspection of poultry both before and after slaughter; required the regular inspection of poultry facilities and their personnel; and extended the authority of federal agencies to inspect poultry production in states where federal-level programs had not been established.
1968	Radiation Control Act	Empowered the Department of Health, Education, and Welfare to prescribe radiation emission standards for electronic products.
1969	Selective Service Act Revision	Gave the president authority to implement a draft lottery and reduced the period of draft eligibility from seven years to one.
1969	Mine Safety Act	Set payments to disabled victims of "black lung" disease over the span 1969-1972. The Interior Department was directed to set mine-safety standards and oversee a minimum of four yearly mine inspections for each mine.

Year	Legislation	Significance
1969	Air Quality Control Act Amendments	Authorized an additional $45,000,000 for research on pollution resulting from internal fuel combustion in diesel- and gasoline-powered vehicles.
1969	National Environmental Policy Act	Established the Council on Environmental Quality to advise Congress and the president on environmental matters. Federal agencies were directed to factor in the probable environmental impact of all proposed programs and to include environmental analyses in their recommendations.
1969	Children Protection and Toy Safety Act	Stated that childrens' toys that were determined to present accident or health hazards could be designated as hazardous substances and taken off the market by the secretary of health, education, and welfare.
1969	Defense Appropriations Act	Included controversial appropriations for maintaining an Anti-Ballistic Missiles (ABM) defense system against nuclear attack.
1969	National Commitments Resolution	Adopted largely as a result of the conflicts in Southeast Asia; affirmed the right of Congress to be consulted by the president regarding the commitment of U.S. troops abroad.
1969	Tax Reform Act	Provided a 15 percent increase in Social Security benefits, extended income-tax surcharges, and increased personal and standard exemptions.
1969	National Commission on Product Safety Extension	The commisssion's mandate was extended to June 30, 1970, to enable it to complete its study on hazardous merchandise and to report its findings to Congress.
1969	Nuclear Non-Proliferation Treaty	Approved by Congress; major provisions contained an international agreement to halt the spread of nuclear weapons and to permit nondiscriminatory access to peacetime use of nuclear energy.

Raymond Pierre Hylton

The U.S. Supreme Court

Supreme Court Justices

Hugo Black (1937-1971)
William O. Douglas (1939-1975)
Felix Frankfurter (1939-1962)
Tom Clark (1949-1967)
Earl Warren (chief justice, 1953-1969)
John M. Harlan (1955-1971)

William Brennan (1956-1990)
Charles Whittaker (1957-1962)
Potter Stewart (1958-1981)
Arthur Goldberg (1962-1965)
Abe Fortas (1962-1969)
Byron White (1962-1993)
Thurgood Marshall (1967-1991)

Notable Decisions

Year	Case	Significance
1960	*Shelton v. Tucker*	As part of the Court's gradual reversal of anticommunist legislation, five justices ruled that an Arkansas law mandating that public school teachers file affidavits giving the names and addresses of all organizations to which they belonged or contributed was overbroad and unconstitutionally violated the teachers' First Amendment associational rights.
1961	*Times Film Corp. v. Chicago*	A five-member majority, over strong dissents by Warren, Black, Brennan, and Douglas that the law was an unlawful prior restraint, upheld the right of city officials to mandate a review of films prior to their being shown.
1961	*Communist Party v. Subversive Activities Control Board*	A five-member majority, again over dissents of Warren, Black, Brennan, and Douglas, upheld the 1950's Internal Security Act requiring the Communist Party to register and file financial statements with the Justice Department.
1961	*Scales v. United States*	The five more conservative justices, over dissents of the more liberal Warren, Black, Brennan, and Douglas, upheld the conviction of an "active" member of the Communist Party for party membership alone, even absent evidence of any immediate threat.
1961	*Mapp v. Ohio*	Over three conservative dissents, this Fourteenth Amendment incorporation case applied the Fourth Amendment's prohibition against unreasonable searches and seizures to the states, requiring state courts to exclude any unlawfully gathered materials from evidence as required in the federal courts.
1961	*Hoyt v. Florida*	In the Warren Court's only sex discrimination case, the justices unanimously upheld the conviction of a woman for murdering her husband, even though she claimed that an all-male jury had denied her a fair trial.
1962	*Baker v. Carr*	Seven justices, ignoring warnings from Frankfurter that they were entering a political thicket, overturned *Colegrove v. Green* and ruled that the federal courts had jurisdiction to hear legislative reapportionment cases in states; some states such as Tennessee had not been reapportioned in more than sixty years.

Year	Case	Significance
1962	*Engel v. Vitale*	By an eight-to-one vote, the Court declared that a twenty-two-word nondenominational prayer composed by New York's educational authority was an unconstitutional establishment of religion.
1962	*Glidden Company v. Zdanok*	A seven-vote majority ruled against congressional efforts to create two special jurisdiction courts, since neither court provided life tenure for judges.
1963	*Bantam Books, Inc. v. Sullivan*	With only conservative Justice Harlan dissenting, the Court threw out a plan by which a state could compile a list of books objectionable to minors and prosecute their distributors.
1963	*Edwards v. South Carolina*	An incorporation case in which an eight-member majority applied the First Amendment's protection of peaceable assembly to the states, refusing to let them bar demonstrations of unpopular views in traditional forums.
1963	*Gideon v. Wainwright*	A landmark case in which the Court, applying the Sixth Amendment to the states through the principal of incorporation, unanimously reversed earlier decisions that allowed states to fail to provide counsel to indigents accused of serious crimes.
1963	*School District of Abington Township v. Schempp*	Having stricken state-composed prayers previously, another eight-member majority forbade the reading of the Lord's Prayer or other biblical passages as a part of public school exercises.
1964	*Wesberry v. Sanders*	Following *Baker v. Carr*, a six-to-three majority struck down Georgia's unequal congressional redistricting, arguing that districts should be as nearly equal in population as practical.
1964	*Katzenbach v. McClung*	The Court unanimously upheld the application of the 1964 Civil Rights Acts public accommodations section to a family-owned restaurant without interstate patrons because much of the food served there had moved in interstate commerce.
1964	*New York Times v. Sullivan*	This unanimously decided landmark case gave vastly greater protection to the news media from libel suits brought on the basis of technical factual errors. Henceforth, plaintiffs in libel suits were required to prove that such errors had been disseminated with actual malice or a reckless disregard for the truth.
1964	*Schneider v. Rusk*	Writing for a six-vote majority, Justice Douglas invalidated an immigration law that deprived naturalized citizens of their citizenship if they lived three years in their native lands, arguing that the statute made them second-class citizens.
1964	*Reynolds v. Sims*	With only Justice Harlan dissenting, the Court ruled that the "one person, one vote" principal should apply to both houses of state legislatures, thereby prompting an unsuccessful effort to amend the U.S Constitution.

Year	Case	Significance
1964	*Malloy v. Hogan*	A five-vote liberal majority reversed the contempt citation of a man who had declined to testify in a state court, thereby applying the Fifth Amendment's protection against self-incrimination to the states under the incorporation doctrine.
1964	*Escobedo v. Illinois*	A five-vote majority ruled that neither federal nor state courts could admit into evidence statements taken by police from a defendant who had not been told of the right to remain silent and allowed to talk to a lawyer.
1964	*Aptheker v. Secretary of State*	A six-vote liberal majority finally had enough votes to void part of the Subversive Activities Control Act. The act had denied the right to travel abroad to "subversive" organization members, without regard to the purpose of their travel or whether or not they were active or even conscious members of the organization.
1964	*Jacobellis v. Ohio*	A six-vote majority decided that a French film either was not obscene by national standards or else could not be banned, whether obscene or not, without violating freedom of expression.
1964	*Garrison v. Louisiana*	The Court unanimously reversed the conviction of Louisiana attorney general Jim Garrison, who had criticized eight Louisiana judges who had in turn won a criminal libel conviction against him. The Court held that such a conviction for criticism of elected officials would require a showing of actual malice or a reckless disregard for the truth in order to be valid.
1964	*Heart of Atlanta Motel v. United States*	The Justices unanimously upheld the validity of the public accommodations section of the 1964 Civil Rights Act against a motel owner who advertised and rented extensively to interstate travelers, holding that the services rendered to those travelers were a part of interstate commerce.
1965	*Cox v. Louisiana*	A seven-to-two majority overturned the conviction of civil rights demonstrators for blocking traffic, since the state had allowed other approved groups to block traffic in similar ways.
1965	*Pointer v. Texas*	The Court ruled that the Sixth Amendment's guarantee of a defendant's right to confront witnesses applied to the states under the Fourteenth Amendment's due process clause.
1965	*Zemel v. Rusk*	A six-to-three majority upheld the right of Congress to grant the executive branch the power to deny passports to American citizens who wished to travel to Cuba.
1965	*Lamont v. Postmaster General*	The justices unanimously struck down a post office regulation that required the intended recipient of unsealed international mail determined to be communist propaganda to sign a card requesting the material.

Year	Case	Significance
1965	*Griswold v. Connecticut*	A seven-to-two majority overturned a statute under which two Connecticut citizens had been convicted of providing birth-control information to a married couple. In this landmark case, Justice Douglas found a right to privacy as a penumbra that extended from other specific rights listed in the First, Third, Fourth, and Fifth Amendments and from an unenumerated right found in the Ninth Amendment. All were applied to the states under the Fourteenth Amendment. This case became the basis for the 1971 *Roe v. Wade* abortion decision.
1965	*Estes v. Texas*	A five-to-four majority reversed the conviction of accused swindler Billie Sol Estes because the trial court had allowed television cameras in the courtroom, thereby depriving the defendant of a fair trial.
1965	*Albertson v. Subversive Activities Control Bd.*	The Court unanimously ruled that the failure of the Communist Party to register with the government in the wake of the decision in *Communist Party v. Subversive Activities Control Board* could not be prosecuted because registration would involve self-incrimination in violation of the Fifth Amendment. This decision rendered inoperative several sections of the 1950 Internal Security Act.
1966	*Brown v. Louisiana*	A five-vote majority reversed the conviction of several African American youths who had entered a segregated library and refused to leave after a sheriff ordered them to do so.
1966	*South Carolina v. Katzenbach*	The Court, unanimous except for a partial dissent from Justice Black, upheld the constitutionality of the 1965 Voting Rights Act, which mandated federal voting registrars in states with a history of voting discrimination.
1966	*Memoirs v. Massachusetts*	Writing for a six-vote majority, Justice Brennan ruled that each of the three elements of the national obscenity test announced in *Roth* had to be met independently for a book to be declared obscene. Since the book in question did not meet all three tests, it could not be banned.
1966	*Ginzburg v. United States*	Writing for a five-vote majority, Justice Brennan ruled that a book need not be deemed obscene in itself to be banned from the U.S. mail if the promoter engaged in pandering.
1966	*Kent v. United States*	Writing for a five-vote majority, Justice Fortas held that the District of Columbia had acted unconstitutionally by trying a juvenile without protections normally given to adults and then transferring the case to an adult court, where the sentences were more severe.
1966	*Harper v. Virginia Board of Elections*	A six-vote majority outlawed all poll taxes, which had been banned in federal elections by the Twenty-fourth Amendment but allowed in state elections.
1966	*Sheppard v. Maxwell*	An eight-member majority voided the conviction of Sam Sheppard for the murder of his wife on grounds that the trial judge had allowed excessive pretrial and trial publicity to create a circus atmosphere.

Year	Case	Significance
1966	*Miranda v. Arizona*	This landmark case followed the logic of *Escobedo v. Illinois* in overturning the conviction of a defendant who had not been informed of his rights to counsel and to remain silent. A six-member majority then spelled out in some detail the proper requirements, over the objections of three other justices and the partial dissent of another.
1966	*Adderley v. Florida*	Justice Black, writing for a five-member majority, upheld the conviction of civil rights protesters who had demonstrated on special jail grounds. Using a literal reading of the First Amendment, Black found that the demonstration did not meet the "peaceable assembly" standard and could be banned.
1966	*Bond v. Floyd*	The justices unanimously ruled the Georgia legislature had violated African American leader Julian Bond's free speech by denying him a seat in the legislature because of his criticism of the Vietnam War.
1967	*Time v. Hill*	Justice Brennan, writing for a six-member majority, held that *Time* magazine was not liable for a libel judgment because the plaintiff had failed to prove that the magazine had acted out of actual malice or a reckless disregard of the truth.
1967	*Keyishian v. Board of Regents*	In a five-to-four decision, the justices held that a New York law that required teachers to take a loyalty oath was unconstitutionally vague and deprived teachers of free speech.
1967	*In re Gault*	Justice Fortas, writing for an eight-vote majority, upheld a habeas corpus petition for a fifteen-year old boy who had been sent to a juvenile detention center without notice to his parents. The Court ruled that juveniles had to be accorded the same rights of notice, legal counsel, privilege against self-incrimination, and cross-examination as were accorded to adults.
1967	*Afroyim v. Rusk*	Justice Black, writing for a five-member majority, held that the government had no right to deny citizenship to a man simply because he had voted in another country's election.
1967	*Reitman v. Mulkey*	A critical decision in support of open nondiscriminatory housing. Justice White, writing for a five-member majority, ruled unconstitutional a provision in the California state constitution that prohibited the state from denying absolute discretion in the renting, lease, or sale of property.
1967	*Loving v. Virginia*	The Court unanimously declared unconstitutional all laws forbidding interracial marriage as both a denial of the Fourteenth Amendment's equal-protection law and as a denial of liberty.
1967	*Katz v. United States*	The eight-member majority overturned the earlier *Olmstead v. United States* decision, which had exempted electronic surveillance from the provisions of the Fourth Amendment.
1968	*Harris v. United States*	This unanimous ruling affirmed that a court was allowed to introduce into evidence an automobile registration card that a police officer had found in plain view in a suspect's car, even though the officer had no search warrant.

Year	Case	Significance
1968	*Ginsberg v. New York*	Justice Brennan, writing for a six-member majority, upheld a New York statute and conviction for selling obscene magazines to minors, reasoning that materials sold to adults may be prohibited from sale to minors.
1968	*Duncan v. Louisiana*	Justice White, writing for a seven-member majority, held that jury trials are mandatory in a state court for offenses that would entitle a defendant to a jury trial in federal court.
1968	*United States v. O'Brien*	The chief justice wrote for a nearly unanimous Court that the government has a substantial interest in continuing the selective service system, thereby upholding a defendant's conviction for burning his draft card. The Court thus ruled the government's right outweighed the incidental limitation on free speech; Justice Douglas dissented.
1968	*Green v. County School Board*	A unanimous Court ruled that the time granted in the 1954 *Brown v. Board of Education* case for school desegregation with "all deliberate speed" had run out. The Court ruled "intolerable" a Virginia county "freedom of choice" plan in which no white student chose to attend a formerly all-black public school.
1968	*Rabeck v. New York*	In contrast to the ruling in *Ginsberg v. New York*, the Court ruled that a New York statute was unconstitutionally vague because it forbade the sale to minors of materials that might appeal to their curiosity about sex or the anatomical differences between the sexes. Justice Harlan alone dissented.
1968	*Witherspoon v. Illinois*	Writing for a six-member majority, Justice Stewart overturned a death sentence because potential jury members had been excluded for expressing general or conscientious objections to the death penalty.
1968	*Terry v. Ohio*	An eight-member majority upheld the right of police to frisk suspects for concealed weapons without probable cause.
1968	*Flast v. Cohen*	An eight-member majority allowed taxpayer suits on the constitutionality of federal expenditures under certain circumstances.
1968	*Maryland v. Wirtz*	Justice Harlan, writing for a seven-vote majority, upheld the constitutionality of 1961 and 1966 Fair Labor Standards Acts that applied wage and hour legislation to enterprise concept entities in state governments.
1968	*Jones v. Alfred H. Mayer Company*	Justice Stewart, writing for a seven-to-two majority, upheld an 1866 statute that banned racial discrimination in the sale or rental of housing.
1968	*Epperson v. Arkansas*	The Court unanimously overturned an Arkansas Supreme Court ruling that upheld statutes banning the teaching of evolution, holding that the laws violated the freedom of religion mandate of the First Amendment.

Year	Case	Significance
1969	*Tinker v. Des Moines*	A seven-member majority voided a school ban on the wearing of black arm bands by students protesting the Vietnam War absent any other behavior which might be subject to discipline. The Court found no relation between the regulation and school discipline and stated that student opinions could not be confined to those officially approved.
1969	*Kirkpatrick v. Preisler*	Justice Brennan, writing for a seven-member majority, held that all voting districts must be as nearly equal in population as possible, thereby ending a series of arguments over legislative redistricting.
1969	*Stanley v. Georgia*	A unanimous Court held that a state could not convict an adult for the mere possession of obscene materials.
1969	*Shapiro v. Thompson*	Justice Brennan, writing for a six-member majority, struck down state statutes that set a one-year residency requirement for the receipt of welfare assistance, ruling that the limit was too long and invidiously discriminated against recipients.
1969	*Street v. New York*	A five-vote majority threw out the conviction of an African American who had burned a flag and said "we don't need no damn flag" in the wake of the shooting of Martin Luther King, Jr.; the Court ruled that the defendant had been convicted for the constitutionally protected words he uttered.
1969	*Brandenberg v. Ohio*	A unanimous Court overturned an earlier ruling permitting states to punish the mere advocacy of the overthrow of the U.S. government.
1969	*Powell v. McCormick*	Chief Justice Warren, writing for an eight-to-one majority, ruled that the House of Representatives could not add to the constitutional qualifications of their members and could expel a member only by a two thirds vote. Congress had sought to block Adam Clayton Powell from taking his seat by alleging that he had filed improper expense reports.
1969	*Benton v. Maryland*	A seven-to-two majority voided the conviction in a second trial of a defendant who had been previously acquitted of a crime, thus applying the double jeopardy provisions of the Fifth Amendment to the states through the incorporation doctrine of the Fourteenth Amendment.

Richard L. Wilson

U.S. Best-Sellers and Pulitzer Prize Winners

1960

Best-Sellers

Fiction
1. *Advise and Consent*, Allen Drury
2. *Hawaii*, James A. Michener
3. *The Leopard*, Giuseppe di Lampedusa
4. *The Chapman Report*, Irving Wallace
5. *Ourselves to Know*, John O'Hara

Nonfiction
1. *Folk Medicine*, D. C. Jarvis
2. *Better Homes and Gardens First Aid for Your Family*
3. *The General Foods Kitchens Cookbook*
4. *May This House Be Safe from Tigers*, Alexander King
5. *Better Homes and Gardens Dessert Book*

Pulitzer Prizes

Fiction	*Advise and Consent*, Allen Drury
Drama	*Fiorello!*, Jerome Weidman and George Abbott
History	*In the Days of McKinley*, Margaret Leech
Biography	*John Paul Jones*, Samuel Eliot Morison
Poetry	*Heart's Needle*, W. D. Snodgrass

1961

Best-Sellers

Fiction
1. *The Agony and the Ecstasy*, Irving Stone
2. *Franny and Zooey*, J. D. Salinger
3. *To Kill a Mockingbird*, Harper Lee
4. *Mila 18*, Leon Uris
5. *The Carpetbaggers*, Harold Robbins

Nonfiction
1. *The New English Bible: The New Testament*
2. *The Rise and Fall of the Third Reich*, William Shirer
3. *Better Homes and Gardens Sewing Book*
4. *Casserole Cook Book*
5. *A Nation of Sheep*, William Lederer

Pulitzer Prizes

Fiction	*To Kill a Mockingbird*, Harper Lee
Drama	*All the Way Home*, Tad Mosel
History	*Between War and Peace: The Potsdam Conference*, Herbert Feis
Biography	*Charles Sumner and the Coming of the Civil War*, David Donald
Poetry	*Times Three: Selected Verse from Three Decades*, Phyllis McGinley

1962

Best-Sellers

Fiction
1. *Ship of Fools*, Katherine Anne Porter
2. *Dearly Beloved*, Anne Morrow Lindbergh
3. *A Shade of Difference*, Allen Drury
4. *Youngblood Hawke*, Herman Wouk
5. *Franny and Zooey*, J. D. Salinger

Nonfiction
1. *Calories Don't Count*, Dr. Herman Taller
2. *The New English Bible: The New Testament*
3. *Better Homes and Gardens Cook Book: New Edition*
4. *O Ye Jigs and Juleps!*, Virginia Cary Hudson
5. *Happiness Is a Warm Puppy*, Charles M. Schulz

Pulitzer Prizes

Fiction	*The Edge of Sadness*, Edwin O'Connor
Drama	*How to Succeed in Business Without Really Trying*, Frank Loesser and Abe Burrows
History	*The Triumphant Empire: Thunder-Clouds Gather in the West*, Lawrence H. Gipson
Biography	No award
Poetry	*Poems*, Alan Dugan

1963

Best-Sellers

Fiction
1. *The Shoes of the Fisherman*, Morris L. West
2. *Raise High the Roof Beam, Carpenters, and Seymour—An Introduction*, J. D. Salinger
3. *Caravans*, James A. Michener
4. *Elizabeth Appleton*, John O'Hara
5. *Grandmother and the Priests*, Taylor Caldwell

Nonfiction
1. *Happiness Is a Warm Puppy*, Charles M. Schulz
2. *J. F. K.: The Man and the Myth*, Victor Lasky
3. *Profiles in Courage*, John F. Kennedy
4. *O Ye Jigs and Juleps!*, Virginia Clay Hudson
5. *Better Homes and Gardens Bread Cook Book*

Pulitzer Prizes

Fiction	*The Reivers*, William Faulkner
Drama	No award
History	*Washington, Village and Capital, 1800-1878*, Constance McLaughlin Green
Biography	*Henry James*, Leon Edel
Poetry	*Pictures from Breughel*, William Carlos Williams

1964

Best-Sellers

Fiction
1. *The Spy Who Came in from the Cold*, John Le Carré
2. *Candy*, Terry Southern
3. *Herzog*, Saul Bellow
4. *Armageddon*, Leon Uris
5. *The Man*, Irving Wallace

Nonfiction
1. *Four Days*, American Heritage and United Press International
2. *I Need All the Friends I Can Get*, Charles M. Schulz
3. *Profiles in Courage*, John F. Kennedy
4. *In His Own Write*, John Lennon
5. *Christmas Is Together-time*, Charles M. Schulz

Pulitzer Prizes

Fiction	No award
Drama	No award
History	*Puritan Village: The Formation of a New England Town*, Sumner Chilton Powell
Biography	*John Keats*, Walter Jackson Bate
Poetry	*At the End of the Open Road*, Louis Simpson

1965

Best-Sellers

Fiction
1. *The Source*, James Michener
2. *Up the Down Staircase*, Bel Kaufman
3. *Herzog*, Saul Bellow
4. *The Looking Glass War*, John Le Carré
5. *The Green Berets*, Robin Moore

Nonfiction
1. *How to Be a Jewish Mother*, Dan Greenburg
2. *A Gift of Prophecy*, Ruth Montgomery
3. *Games People Play*, Eric Berne
4. *World Aflame*, Billy Graham
5. *Happiness Is a Dry Martini*, Johnny Carson

Pulitzer Prizes

Fiction	*The Keepers of the House*, Shirley Ann Grau
Drama	*The Subject Was Roses*, Frank D. Gilroy
History	*The Greenback Era*, Irwin Unger
Biography	*Henry Adams*, Ernest Samuels
Poetry	*Seventy-seven Dream Songs*, John Berryman

1966

Best-Sellers

Fiction
1. *Valley of the Dolls*, Jacqueline Susann
2. *The Adventurers*, Harold Robbins
3. *The Secret of Santa Vittoria*, Robert Crichton
4. *Capable of Honor*, Allen Drury
5. *The Double Image*, Helen MacInnes

Nonfiction
1. *How to Avoid Probate*, Norman Dacey
2. *Human Sexual Response*, Masters and Johnson
3. *In Cold Blood*, Truman Capote
4. *Games People Play*, Eric Berne
5. *A Thousand Days*, Arthur Schlesinger, Jr.

Pulitzer Prizes

Fiction	*The Collected Stories of Katherine Anne Porter*, Katherine Anne Porter
Drama	No award
History	The Life of the Mind in America: From the Revolution to the Civil War, Perry Miller
Biography	*A Thousand Days: John F. Kennedy in the White House*, Arthur M. Schlesinger, Jr.
Poetry	*Selected Poems, 1930-1965*, Richard Eberhart

1967

Best-Sellers

Fiction

1. *The Arrangement*, Elia Kazan
2. *The Confessions of Nat Turner*, William Styron
3. *The Chosen*, Chaim Potok
4. *Topaz*, Leon Uris
5. *Christy*, Catherine Marshall

Nonfiction

1. *Death of a President*, William Manchester
2. *Misery Is a Blind Date*, Johnny Carson
3. *Games People Play*, Eric Berne
4. *Stanyan Street and Other Sorrows*, Rod McKuen
5. *A Modern Priest Looks at His Outdated Church*, Father James Kavanaugh

Pulitzer Prizes

Fiction	*The Fixer*, Bernard Malamud
Drama	*A Delicate Balance*, Edward Albee
History	*Exploration and Empire*, William H. Goetzmann
Biography	*Mr. Clemens and Mark Twain*, Justin Kaplan
Poetry	*Live or Die*, Anne Sexton

1968

Best-Sellers

Fiction

1. *Airport*, Arthur Hailey
2. *Couples*, John Updike
3. *The Salzburg Connection*, Helen MacInnes
4. *A Small Town in Germany*, John Le Carré
5. *Testimony of Two Men*, Taylor Caldwell

Nonfiction

1. *Better Homes and Gardens New Cook Book*
2. *The Random House Dictionary of the English Language: College Edition*
3. *Listen to the Warm*, Rod McKuen
4. *Between Parent and Child*, Haim Ginott
5. *Lonesome Cities*, Rod McKuen

Pulitzer Prizes

Fiction	*The Confessions of Nat Turner*, William Styron
Drama	No award
History	*The Ideological Origins of the American Revolution*, Bernard Bailyn
Biography	*Memoirs, 1925-1950*, George F. Kennan
Poetry	*The Hard Hours*, Anthony Hecht

1969

Best-Sellers

Fiction

1. *Portnoy's Complaint*, Philip Roth
2. *The Godfather*, Mario Puzo
3. *The Love Machine*, Jacqueline Susann
4. *The Inheritors*, Harold Robbins
5. *The Andromeda Strain*, Michael Crichton

Nonfiction

1. *American Heritage Dictionary of the English Language*
2. *In Someone's Shadow*, Rod McKuen
3. *The Peter Principle*, Laurence Peter and Raymond Hull
4. *Between Parent and Teenager*, Haim Ginott
5. *The Graham Kerr Cook Book*, Graham Kerr, the Galloping Gourmet

Pulitzer Prizes

Fiction	*House Made of Dawn*, N. Scott Momaday
Drama	*The Great White Hope*, Howard Sackler
History	*The Origins of the Fifth Amendment*, Leonard W. Levy
Biography	*The Man from New York: John Quinn and His Friends*, B. L. Reid
Poetry	*Of Being Numerous*, George Oppen

Victoria Price

Popular Musicians

Act	Members	Notable 1960's Songs	Notable Facts
The Angels	Barbara Allbut, Peggy Santiglia McGannon, Phyllis "Jiggs" Allbut Meister	"My Boyfriend's Back"	The band drew the name Blue Angels out of a hat, then dropped the "Blue."
The Animals	Eric Burdon, Bryan Chandler, Alan Price, Dave Rowberry, John Steel, Hilton Valentine	"The House of the Rising Sun," "Don't Let Me Be Misunderstood," "We Gotta Get Out of This Place"	After several personnel shifts, The Animals became known as Eric Burdon and the New Animals in 1966.
The Association	Jules Alexander, Ted Buechel Jr., Brian Cole, Russ Giguere, Terry Kirkman, Jim Yester	"Windy," "Cherish," "Along Comes Mary"	The song "Along Comes Mary" was believed by many to be about marijuana.
The Band	Rick Danko, Levon Helm, Garth Hudson, Richard Manuel, Robbie Robertson	"The Weight," "Up on Cripple Creek," "The Night They Drove Old Dixie Down"	Originally known as the Hawks, the Band first came to prominence as Bob Dylan's backing band.
The Beach Boys	Al Jardine, Bruce Johnston, Mike Love, David Marks, Brian Wilson, Carl Wilson, Dennis Wilson	"I Get Around," "Good Vibrations," "California Girls"	In 1966, group leader Brian Wilson deliberately destroyed the tapes for the nearly completed album *Smile.*
The Beatles	George Harrison, John Lennon, Paul McCartney, Ringo Starr	"I Want To Hold Your Hand," "Yesterday," "Hey Jude"	Ringo Starr replaced the group's original drummer, Pete Best, in 1962.
The Jeff Beck Group	Jeff Beck, Rod Stewart, Mickey Waller, Ron Wood	"Ol' Man River," "Blues Deluxe"	In 1965, Jeff Beck replaced Eric Clapton in the Yardbirds.
The Bee Gees	Barry Gibb, Maurice Gibb, Robin Gibb	"I Started a Joke," "I've Got to Get a Message to You"	The Bee Gees later defined mid-1970's dance music.
Brook Benton	born: Benjamin Franklin Peay	"The Boll Weevil Song," "Rainy Night in Georgia"	Brook Benton's early hits included two duets with Dinah Washington.
Big Brother and the Holding Company	Peter Albin, Sam Andrews, David Getz, James Gurley, Janis Joplin	"Piece of My Heart"	At the end of 1968, Janis Joplin left Big Brother and the Holding Company for a solo career.

Act	Members	Notable 1960's Songs	Notable Facts
Bobby "Blue" Bland		"Turn on Your Love Light"	Bland was a member of the Beale Streeters, a Memphis-based group of blues musicians.
Blind Faith	Ginger Baker, Eric Clapton, Rick Grech, Steve Winwood	"Can't Find My Way Home"	Blind Faith's superstar lineup lasted only long enough for one album and one tour.
Blood, Sweat and Tears	Bobby Colomby, Jim Fielder, Dick Halligan, Jerry Hyman, Steve Katz, Al Kooper, Fred Lipsius, Lew Soloff, David Clayton-Thomas, Chuck Winfield	"You've Made Me So Very Happy," "Spinning Wheel," "And When I Die"	Founder Al Kooper left the band after the release of its first album, *Child Is Father to the Man.*
Booker T. and the MGs	Steve Cropper, Donald "Duck" Dunn, Al Jackson, Booker T. Jones, Lewis Steinberg	"Green Onions," "Time Is Tight"	Booker T. and the MGs were the rhythm section of the Stax Records house band, backing such artists as Otis Redding, Sam and Dave, and Wilson Pickett.
The Box Tops	Rick Allen, Tom Boggs, Alex Chilton, Bill Cunningham, Gary Talley	"The Letter," "Cry Like a Baby"	Two band members quit at the height of the group's success to return to college.
James Brown		"Papa's Got A Brand New Bag," "I Got You," "It's A Man's Man's Man's World"	Jimi Hendrix was once a member of James Brown's band.
The Buckinghams	Nick Fortune, Carl Giammerse, Marty Grebb, John Poulos, Denny Tufano	"Kind of a Drag"	The entire band was arrested on drug charges in 1968.
Solomon Burke		"Got to Get You Off My Mind"	Solomon Burke was one of Mick Jagger's main influences.
The Buffalo Springfied	Richie Furay, Dewey Martin, Bruce Palmer, Stephen Stills, Neil Young	"For What It's Worth," "Broken Arrow"	The band was named after a brand of steamroller.
The Byrds	Gene Clark, Michael Clarke, David Crosby, Chris Hillman, Kevin Kelley, Roger McGuinn	"Mr. Tambourine Man," "Turn! Turn! Turn!," "Eight Miles High"	"Turn! Turn! Turn!," based on the biblical Ecclesiastes, was set to music by Pete Seeger.

Act	Members	Notable 1960's Songs	Notable Facts
Glen Campbell		"By the Time I Get to Phoenix," "Gentle on My Mind," "Wichita Lineman"	Campbell was briefly a member of the Beach Boys.
Canned Heat	Frank Cook, Bob "Bear" Hite, Larry Taylor, Henry Vestine, Alan Wilson	"Goin' Up the Country," "Let's Work Together"	Canned Heat broke through with an appearance at the renowned 1967 Monterey Pop Festival.
Johnny Cash		"Ring of Fire," "A Boy Named Sue"	Cash's daughter Rosanne became a country star in the 1980's.
Gene Chandler	born: Eugene Dixon	"Duke of Earl"	"Duke of Earl" sold one million copies in the first month after its release.
Ray Charles		"I Can't Stop Loving You," "Hit the Road, Jack," "Georgia on My Mind"	Ray Charles studied composition at the St. Augustine School for the Blind.
Chubby Checker	born: Ernest Evans	"The Twist"	Ernest Evans was dubbed "Chubby Checker" by Dick Clark's wife.
The Chiffons	Patricia Bennet, Judy Craig, Barbara Lee, Sylvia Peterson	"He's So Fine," "One Fine Day," "Sweet Talkin' Guy"	George Harrison was found guilty of plagiarizing "He's So Fine" for his 1970 hit "My Sweet Lord."
The Dave Clark Five	Dave Clark, Lenny Davidson, Richard Huxley, Dennis Payton, Mike Smith	"Glad All Over," "Catch Us if You Can"	The band originally formed to raise money for Dave Clark's soccer team.
Petula Clark		"Downtown," "Don't Sleep in the Subway," "I Know a Place"	Petula Clark had a successful European singing career for nearly a decade before reaching the U.S. market with "Downtown" in 1965.
Judy Collins		"Both Sides Now," "Suzanne"	The Crosby, Stills, Nash, and Young song "Suite: Judy Blue Eyes," was written for Collins.
The Contours	Joe Billingslea, Huey Davis, Billy Gordon, Billy Hoggs, Hubert Johnson, Sylvester Potts	"Do You Love Me?"	"Do You Love Me" was covered by the Dave Clark Five.

Act	Members	Notable 1960's Songs	Notable Facts
Sam Cooke		"Chain Gang," "Another Saturday Night," "Wonderful World"	Sam Cooke owned his own record label, music publishing business, and management firm.
Cream	Ginger Baker, Jack Bruce, Eric Clapton	"Sunshine of Your Love," "White Room"	With only guitars, bass, and drums, Cream came to be regarded as the archetypal "power trio."
Creedence Clearwater Revival	Doug Clifford, Stu Cook, John Fogerty, Tom Fogerty	"Proud Mary," "Green River," "Bad Moon Rising"	Early names for Creedence Clearwater Revival include the Blue Velvets and the Golliwogs.
Crosby, Stills, Nash, and Young	David Crosby, Graham Nash, Stephen Stills, Neil Young	"Marrakesh Express," "Suite: Judy Blue Eyes,"	All four members had previously belonged to successful 1960's bands.
The Crystals	Barbara Alston, Dolores Brooks, Dee Dee Kennibrew, Mary Thomas, Pat Wright	"He's a Rebel," "Da Doo Ron Ron"	The groups only number-one hit, "He's a Rebel," was actually recorded by a group of session singers.
The Spencer Davis Group	Spencer Davis, Muff Winwood, Steve Windwood, Pete York	"Gimmie Some Lovin'"	Steve Winwood left The Spencer Davis Group in 1967 to form Traffic.
Joey Dee and the Starlighters	David Brigati, Willie Davis, Joseph "Joey Dee" Dinicola, Carlton Latimor, Larry Vernieri	"The Peppermint Twist"	Joey Dee and the Starlighters were the house band at New York City's Peppermint Lounge.
Deep Purple	Ritchie Blackmore, Rod Evans, Ian Gillan, Roger Glover, Jon Lord, Ian Paice, Nick Semper	"Hush"	Deep Purple was once listed in the *Guinness Book of World Records* as the world's loudest rock band.
Jackie DeShannon		"What the World Needs Now Is Love," "Put a Little Love in Your Heart"	Jackie DeShannon and Jimmy Page cowrote several songs for Marianne Faithfull.
Neil Diamond		"Cherry Cherry," "Sweet Caroline," "Song Sung Blue"	Diamond wrote the Monkees' hit "I'm a Believer."

Act	Members	Notable 1960's Songs	Notable Facts
Dion	born: Dion DiMucci	"Runaround Sue," "The Wanderer," "Abraham, Martin, and John"	Dion followed the success of "Abraham, Martin and John" with an unsuccessful cover of Jimi Hendrix's "Purple Haze."
The Dixie Cups	Barbara Ann Hawkins, Rosa Lee Hawkins, Joan Marie Johnson	Chapel of Love	Phil Spector originally wrote "Chapel of Love" for his wife Ronnie's band, the Ronettes.
Donovan	born: Donovan Leitch	"Sunshine Superman," "Mellow Yellow," "Hurdy Gurdy Man"	At eighteen, Donovan was a regular on the British television show "Ready Steady Go."
The Doors	John Densmore, Robby Krieger, Ray Manzarek, Jim Morrison	"Light My Fire," "Touch Me," "Break on Through (to the Other Side)"	"The Doors" is a reference to Aldous Huxley's book about mescaline, *The Doors of Perception*.
The Drifters	Ben E. King, Rudy Lewis, Billy Pinkney, Andrew Thrasher, Gerhart Thrasher	"This Magic Moment," "Save the Last Dance for Me," "Up on the Roof"	The group's original lead singer was Clyde McPhatter.
Bob Dylan	born: Robert Allen Zimmerman	"Blowin' in the Wind," "Like a Rolling Stone"	Dylan reportedly introduced the Beatles to marijuana.
The Everly Brothers	Don Everly, Phil Everly	"Cathy's Clown," "Bye Bye Love," "Wake Up Little Susie"	The Everly Brothers starred in a short-lived CBS television series.
The Fifth Dimension	Billy Davis, Jr., Florence LaRue Gordon, Marilyn McCoo, LaMonte McLemore, Ron Townson	"Up, Up, and Away," "Stoned Soul Picnic," "Aquarius/Let the Sunshine In"	The group was originally known as "The Versatiles."
The Four Seasons	Tommy DeVito, Bob Gaudio, Joey Long, Nick Massi, Frankie Valli	"Sherry," "Big Girls Don't Cry," "Walk Like a Man"	The Four Seasons recorded a cover of Bob Dylan's "Don't Think Twice" as the Wonder Who.
The Four Tops	Renaldo Benson, Abdul Fakir, Lawrence Payton, Levi Stubbs	"I Can't Help Myself," "Reach Out I'll Be There," "Standing in the Shadows of Love"	Unlike many 1960's supergroups, The Four Tops' retained their original lineup for nearly thirty years.

Act	Members	Notable 1960's Songs	Notable Facts
Connie Francis	born: Concetta Franconero	"Everybody's Somebody's Fool," "My Heart Has a Mind of Its Own," "Don't Break the Heart That Loves You"	Connie Francis also appeared in the films *Where the Boys Are* and *When the Boys Meet the Girls.*
Aretha Franklin		"Baby I Love You," "Respect," "Chain of Fools"	Aretha Franklin is known throughout the United States and Europe as "Lady Soul."
Marvin Gaye		"Stubborn Kind Of Fellow," "Can I Get A Witness," "I Heard It Through the Grapevine"	Marvin Gaye's first job at Motown was as a session drummer.
Bobby Gentry	born: Bobbie Lee Street	"Ode to Billie Joe"	Bobbie Gentry's only hit, "Ode to Billie Joe," won three Grammy awards and was the basis for a 1976 movie of the same name.
Jimmy Gilmer and the Fireballs	Eric Budd, Jimmy Gilmer, Stan Lark, George Tomsco	"Sugar Shack"	In the 1960's, Jimmy Gilmer split with Fireballs, who later charted with "Bottle of Wine."
Leslie Gore		"It's My Party," "Judy's Turn To Cry"	Leslie Gore was discovered by Quincy Jones.
The Grateful Dead	Jerry Garcia, Mickey Hart, Bill Kreutzmann, Phil Lesh, Ron "Pigpen" McKernan, Bob Weir	"Dark Star"	Originally known as the Warlocks, the Grateful Dead inspired legions of fans, or "Deadheads," to follow them on tour.
The Guess Who	Randy Bachman, Burton Cummings, Jim Kale, Garry Peterson	"These Eyes," "Laughing"	The Canadian-based group's first hit was a cover of Johnny and the Pirates' "Shakin' All Over."
Arlo Guthrie		"Alice's Restaurant"	Arlo Guthrie is the son of folk legend Woody Guthrie.
Merle Haggard		"Okie from Muskogee," "The Bottle Let Me Down," "Today I Started Loving You Again"	Haggard spent three years in California's San Quentin prison before the start of his musical career.

Act	Members	Notable 1960's Songs	Notable Facts
Jimi Hendrix		"Purple Haze," "All Along the Watchtower," "Foxy Lady"	Since his death in 1970, virtually every song ever recorded by Hendrix has been released, resulting in an estimated 100 albums.
Herman's Hermits	Karl Greene, Keith Hopwood, Derek Leckenby, Peter "Herman" Noone, Barry Whitham	"Mrs. Brown You've Got a Lovely Daughter," "I'm Henry VIII I Am," "I'm into Something Good"	The original version of "I'm Henry VIII I Am" dates back to 1911 and was written for a Cockney comedian.
The Hollies	Bernard Calvert, Allan Clarke, Robert Elliot, Eric Heydock, Anthony Hicks, Graham Nash, Terry Sylvester	"Bus Stop," "Stop Stop Stop"	When Graham Nash left the band in 1968, the band advertised for his replacement in the British trade papers.
Janis Ian	born: Janis Eddy Fink	"Society's Child"	Written about an interracial romance, "Society's Child" was banned by many radio stations.
The Iron Butterfly	Eric Braunn, Ron Bushy, Daryl DeLoach, Lee Dorman, Doug Ingle, Jerry Penrod, Danny Weiss	"In-A-Gadda-Da-Vida"	"In-A-Gadda-Da-Vida" is seventeen minutes long and features a two-and-a-half-minute drum solo.
The Isley Brothers	Everett Collins, Ernie Isley, Marvin Isley, O'Kelly Isley, Ronald Isley, Rudolph Isley, Chris Jasper	"Shout," "Twist and Shout," "This Old Heart of Mine"	Jimi Hendrix was once a member of the Isley Brothers' backing band.
Tommy James and the Shondells	Tommy James, Joseph Kessler, George Magura, Vincent Pietropaoli, Ronald Rosman, Michael Vale	"Hanky Panky," "Crimson and Clover," "Crystal Blue Persuasion"	Tommy James and the Shondells are considered by many to be the first "bubble gum" rock group.
Jan and Dean	Jan Berry, Dean Torrence	"Surf City," "The Little Old Lady (from Pasadena)," "Dead Man's Curve"	Jan Berry's near-fatal automobile accident in 1966 effectively ended the group's career.
Jefferson Airplane	Signe Anderson, Marty Balin, Jack Casady, Spencer Dryden, Paul Kantner, Jorma Kaukonen, Grace Slick, Skip Spence	"Somebody to Love," "White Rabbit"	Grace Slick's trademark vocals were her imitation of the sound of the lead guitar.

Act	Members	Notable 1960's Songs	Notable Facts
B. B. King	born: Riley B. King	"Why I Sing the Blues," "The Thrill Is Gone"	B. B. King's original nickname was "Beale Street Blues Boy," which later became simply "B. B."
Ben E. King	born: Benjamin Earl Soloman	"Spanish Harlem," "Stand by Me"	King was also a lead vocalist for the Drifters.
The Kingsmen	Gary Abbot, Lynn Easton, Don Gallucci, Mike Mitchell, Norman Sundholm	"Louie Louie"	"Louie Louie" is one of the most notorious songs of the 1960's; though the lyrics are indecipherable, many radio stations banned it for obscenity.
The Kinks	Mick Avory, Dave Davies, Ray Davies, Pete Quaife	"You Really Got Me," "All Day and All of the Night," "Dedicated Follower of Fashion"	Problems with the American Federation of Musicians prevented The Kinks from touring in the United States during most of the late 1960's.
Gladys Knight and the Pips	William Guest, Gladys Knight, Merald Knight, Edward Patten	"I Heard It Through the Grapevine"	Marvin Gaye recorded the original version of "I Heard It Through the Grapevine."
Led Zeppelin	John Bonham, John Paul Jones, Jimmy Page, Robert Plant	"Communication Breakdown," "Whole Lotta Love"	The band was originally known as the New Yardbirds.
Brenda Lee	born: Brenda Mae Tarpley	"I'm Sorry," "I Want to Be Wanted," "Sweet Nothing"	Brenda Lee's recorded her first hit, "Rockin' Around the Christmas Tree," in 1956 at the age of eleven
John Lennon and Yoko Ono		"Give Peace a Chance," "Cold Turkey"	Background chanters on "Give Peace a Chance" include Timothy Leary and Tommy Smothers.
Bobby Lewis		"Tossin' and Turnin'," "One Track Mind"	Bobby Lewis grew up in an orphanage and by age five had learned to play the piano.
Gary Lewis and the Playboys	David Costell, Gary Lewis, Al Ramsey, David Walkes, John R. West	"This Diamond Ring," "Save Your Heart for Me," "Count Me In"	Gary Lewis is the son of comedian Jerry Lewis.

Act	Members	Notable 1960's Songs	Notable Facts
Little Eva	born: Eva Narcissus Boyd	"The Loco-Motion"	Eva Boyd was discovered by Carole King and Gerry Goffin; at the time, she was their babysitter.
The Lovin' Spoonful	Steve Boone, Joe Butler, John Sebastian, Zal Yanovsky, Jerry Yester	"Summer in the City," "Do You Believe in Magic," "Daydream"	In the late 1960's, the Lovin' Spoonful provided soundtracks for movies by Francis Ford Coppola and Woody Allen.
Lulu	born: Marie McDonald McLaughlin Lawrie	"To Sir with Love"	Lulu was once married to the Bee Gees' Maurice Gibb.
The Mamas and the Papas	Dennis Doherty, Cass Elliot, John Phillips, Michelle Phillips	"Monday, Monday," "California Dreamin'"	The original "Papas" reunited for a tour in the early eighties with Elaine "Spanky" McFarlane and John Phillips's actress daughter, Mackenzie.
Martha and the Vandellas	Rosalind Ashford, Betty Kelly, Martha Reeves	"Heat Wave," "Dancing in the Streets," "Jimmy Mack"	The Vandellas took their name from a combination of Detroit's Van Dyke Street and Martha Reeve's favorite singer, Della Reese.
The Marvelettes	Katherine Anderson, Juanita Cowart, Georgeanna Dobbins, Gladys Horton, Wanda Young	"Please Mr. Postman," "Beechwood 4-5789"	The Marvelettes turned down a chance to record "Baby Love," which became one of the Supremes' biggest hits.
The MC5	Michael Davis, Wayne Kramer, Fred "Sonic" Smith, Dennis Thompson, Rob Tyner	"Kick out the Jams"	Controversy over the lyrics to "Kick out the Jams" kept the single off the airwaves and ended the band's relationship with its record label.
Barry McGuire		"Eve of Destruction"	The pessimistic lyrics of "Eve of Destruction" inspired an answer record, "Dawn of Correction."

Act	Members	Notable 1960's Songs	Notable Facts
The Monkees	Mickey Dolenz, David Jones, Michael Nesmith, Peter Tork	"I'm a Believer," "Daydream Believer," "Last Train to Clarksville"	Known as the "Prefab Four," The Monkees successfully fought for the right to play on their own records—a move that did not affect the band's hit-making abilities.
Moody Blues	Graeme Edge, Justin Hayward, Denny Laine, John Lodge, Mike Pinder, Ray Thomas, Clint Warwick	"Go Now," "Nights in White Satin"	Though the orchestral rock album *Days of Future Passed* was released in 1967, it continued to appear on the charts well into the early 1970's.
Van Morrison		"Brown Eyed Girl"	Prior to his successful solo career, Morrison was the leader of the Irish rock band Them.
Rick Nelson	born: Eric Hilliard Nelson	"Travelin' Man," "Hello Mary Lou"	After "Hello Mary Lou" in 1961, Nelson did not have another hit until 1972's "Garden Party."
Harry Nilsson	born: Harry Edward Nelson III	"Everybody's Talkin'"	Nilsson never performed a public concert.
1910 Fruitgum Company	Mark Gutkowski, Frank Jeckell, Pat Karwan, Joey Levine, Floyd Marcus, Rusty Oppenheimer, Larry Ripley, Bruce Shay, Chuck Travis	"Simon Says," "1, 2, 3 Red Light"	Joey Levine was also the lead singer for the equally anonymous studio band Ohio Express.
The Ohio Express	Tim Corwin, Doug Grassel, Dean Kastran, Joey Levine, Jim Pfayler, Dale Powers	"Yummy Yummy Yummy"	With the 1910 Fruitgum Company, Ohio Express defined late-1960's "bubblegum" rock.
Roy Orbison		"Oh, Pretty Woman," "Running Scared," "Only the Lonely"	Orbison wrote the Everly Brothers' hit "Claudette," which was named for his late wife.
Paul and Paula	Ray Hildebrand, Jill Jackson	"Hey Paula"	Novelty artist Tiny Tim later covered "Hey Paula," performing both voices.

Act	Members	Notable 1960's Songs	Notable Facts
Peter, Paul, and Mary	Paul Stookey, Mary Travers, Peter Yarrow	"Blowin' in the Wind," "Puff the Magic Dragon," "Leavin' on a Jet Plane"	Their 1962 recording of "Blowin' in the Wind" was the first commercially successful version of a Bob Dylan song.
Wilson Pickett		"Land of 1,000 Dances," "In the Midnight Hour," "Mustang Sally"	Prior to his successful solo career, Wilson Pickett recorded with the Falcons.
Gene Pitney		"Town Without Pity," "Only Love Can Break a Heart," "(The Man Who Shot) Liberty Valance"	Gene Pitney wrote "Hello Mary Lou" for Rick Nelson and "He's a Rebel" for the Crystals.
Elvis Presley		"Are You Lonesome Tonight," "It's Now or Never," "Can't Help Falling in Love"	After an unprecedented string of hit records in the 1950's, Presley spent most of the 1960's making B movies.
Procol Harum	Gary Brooker, Matthew Fisher, Dave Knights, Robin Trower, B. J. Wilson	"A Whiter Shade of Pale"	The organ line in "A Whiter Shade of Pale" is taken from Johann Sebastian Bach's Suite No. 3.
Gary Puckett and the Union Gap	Dwight Bement, Kerry Chater, Gary Puckett, Paul Wheatbread, Mutha Withem	"Woman, Woman," "Young Girl," "Lady Willpower"	The Union Gap performed in replica blue-and-gold Civil War uniforms.
Otis Redding		"(Sittin' on) The Dock of the Bay," "I've Been Loving You Too Long," "Try a Little Tenderness"	Otis Redding and four members of his backing band the Bar-Kays died in a plane crash in 1967.
The Righteous Brothers	Bobby Hatfield, Bill Medley	"You've Lost That Lovin' Feeling," "(You're My) Soul and Inspiration," "Unchained Melody"	In 1974, Medley and Hatfield had another hit with "Rock and Roll Heaven," a tribute to dead rock stars.
Jeannie C. Riley		"Harper Valley PTA"	Riley was working as a secretary when "Harper Valley PTA" reached number one on both the pop and country charts.

Act	Members	Notable 1960's Songs	Notable Facts
Johnny Rivers	born: John Ramistella	"Memphis," "Poor Side of Town," "Secret Agent Man"	Rivers is credited with discovering the Fifth Dimension and Jimmy Webb.
Smokey Robinson and the Miracles	Pete Moore, Claudette Rogers Robinson, William "Smokey" Robinson, Bobby Rogers, Ronnie White	"You've Really Got a Hold on Me," "I Second That Emotion," "The Tracks of My Tears"	Robinson also wrote hit songs for many other Motown acts, including the Marvelettes, Marvin Gaye, Mary Wells, and the Temptations.
The Rolling Stones	Mick Jagger, Brian Jones, Keith Richards, Mick Taylor, Charlie Watts, Bill Wyman	"(I Can't Get No) Satisfaction," "Paint It, Black," "Honky Tonk Woman"	For a 1967 appearance on *The Ed Sullivan Show*, the lyrics to "Let's Spend the Night Together" were changed to "Let's Spend Some Time Together."
The Ronettes	Estelle Bennett, Veronica "Ronnie" Bennett, Nedra Talley	"Be My Baby," "Baby I Love You"	In 1968, Ronnie Bennett married super-producer Phil Spector.
Mitch Ryder and the Detroit Wheels	John Badanjek, Joseph Cubert, Earl Elliot, James McCarty, Mitch Ryder	"Jenny Take a Ride/C. C. Rider," "Devil with a Blue Dress/Good Golly Miss Molly"	The Detroit Wheels were originally known as the Rivieras.
Sam and Dave	Samuel Moore, David Prater	"Soul Man," "Hold On! I'm Comin'"	In 1979, Sam and Dave enjoyed a brief return to the limelight with the success of the Blues Brothers' cover of "Soul Man."
Sam the Sham and the Pharoahs	Butch Gibson, Dave Martin, Jerry Patterson, Ray Stinnet, Domingo "Sam the Sham" Samudio	"Wooly Bully," "Li'l Red Riding Hood"	After the band disbanded in 1967, Sam the Sham went solo under his given name, Domingo Samudio.
The Searchers	Frank Allen, John Blunt, Chris Curtis, Tony Jackson, John McNally, Mike Pender	"Needles and Pins," "Love Potion Number 9"	The Searchers were named after a John Ford/John Wayne movie of the same name.
Neil Sedaka		"Calendar Girl," "Breaking Up Is Hard to Do"	Sedaka came back with several more hits in the mid-1970's.

Act	Members	Notable 1960's Songs	Notable Facts
Del Shannon	born: Charles Westover	"Runaway"	Shannon was the first American to cover a Beatles tune, "From Me to You."
The Shirelles	Shirley Owens Alston, Micki Harris, Doris Coley Kenner, Beverly Lee	"Will You Love Me Tomorrow?," "Soldier Boy"	The Shirelles were one of the few girl groups to write some of their own hits.
Simon and Garfunkel	Art Garfunkel, Paul Simon	"Sounds of Silence," "Mrs. Robinson," "Bridge over Troubled Water"	Simon and Garfunkel originally performed as "Tom and Jerry."
Percy Sledge		"When a Man Loves a Woman"	"When a Man Loves a Woman" was once recorded by Mae West.
Sly and the Family Stone	Greg Errico, Larry Graham, Jr., Jerry Martini, Cynthia Robinson, Sylvester "Sly" Stewart, Freddie Stone, Rosie Stone	"Everyday People," "Dance to the Music," "I Want to Take You Higher"	Sly and the Family Stone were considered to be the first "pyschedelic soul" group.
Sonny and Cher	Salvatore Bono, Cherilyn Sarkasian LaPier	"I Got You Babe," "The Beat Goes On"	Cher later became an Academy Award-winning actress, Sonny a U.S. Congressman.
The Staples	Cleo Staples, Mavis Staples, Pervis Staples, Roebuck "Pop" Staples, Yvonne Staples	"Respect Yourself," "I'll Take You There"	The Staples began as a gospel group.
Steppenwolf	Jerry Edmonton, John Kay, Goldy McJohn, Michael Monarch, John Russell Morgan	"Born to Be Wild," "Magic Carpet Ride"	"Born to Be Wild" was featured in the film *Easy Rider*.
The Strawberry Alarm Clock	George Bunnel, Lee Freeman, Ed King, Gary Lovetro, Randy Seol, Mark Weitz	"Incense and Peppermints"	The Strawberry Alarm Clock embodied late-1960's psychedelic pop.
The Supremes	Florence Ballard, Cindy Birdsong, Diana Ross, Mary Wilson	"Baby Love," "Stop! In the Name of Love," "Where Did Our Love Go?" "Someday We'll Be Together"	The 1980's hit Broadway musical *Dreamgirls* was based on the Supremes' career.
The Surfaris	Bob Berryhill, Pat Connolly, Jim Fuller, Jim Pash, Ron Wilson	"Wipeout"	"Wipeout" reached the pop charts in 1963 and again in 1966.

Act	Members	Notable 1960's Songs	Notable Facts
The Temptations	Dennis Edwards, Melvin Franklin, Eddie Kendricks, David Ruffin, Otis Williams, Paul Williams	"My Girl," "I Can't Get Next to You"	The Temptations recorded fifteen top-ten singles.
Three Dog Night	Mike Allsup, Jimmy Greenspoon, Danny Hutton, Chuck Negron, Joe Schermie, Floyd Sneed, Cory Wells	"Easy to Be Hard," "Eli's Coming"	The band's version of "Lady Samantha" was the first U.S. hit for songwriters Elton John and Bernie Taupin.
The Tokens	Mitchel Margo, Phil Margo, Hank Medress, Jay Siegel, Joseph Venneri	"The Lion Sleeps Tonight"	"The Lion Sleeps Tonight" is based on a Zulu folk melody.
The Tornadoes	George Bellamy, Heinz Burt, Alan Caddy, Clem Cattini, Roger Laverne Jackson	"Telstar"	"Telstar" was the name of the first U.S. communications satellite.
Traffic	Jim Capaldi, Dave Mason, Steve Winwood, Chris Wood	"Feelin' Alright"	Steve Winwood left the Spencer Davis Group to form Traffic in 1967.
The Troggs	Ronnie Bond, Chris Britton, Reg Presley, Peter Staples	"Wild Thing," "Love Is All Around"	The group's name was taken from the word "troglodyte."
The Turtles	Howard Kaylan, Donalr Ray Murray, Al Nichol, Chuck Portz, Mark Volman	"Happy Together," "She'd Rather Be with Me"	Mark Volman and Howard Kaylan also performed as the duo Flo and Eddie.
Bobby Vee	born: Robert Velline	"Take Good Care of My Baby," "The Night Has a Thousand Eyes"	Vee's first big break came in 1959, when he filled a concert bill left open by Buddy Holly's death.
The Velvet Underground	John Cale, Sterling Morrison, Christa Päffgen (Nico), Lou Reed, Maureen Tucker, Doug Yule	"Heroin," "Femme Fatale"	The band's debut album featured cover art by Andy Warhol.
Junior Walker and the All-Stars	James Graves, Vic Thomas, Junior Walker, Willie Woods	"Shotgun," "What Does It Take (To Win Your Love)"	Walker played tenor sax on Foreigner's 1981 hit "Urgent."
Dionne Warwick		"Walk on By," "I Say a Little Prayer for You," "Do You Know the Way to San Jose?"	Many of Warwick's hits were written by the team of Burt Bacharach and Hal David.

Act	Members	Notable 1960's Songs	Notable Facts
Mary Wells		"My Guy," "Two Lovers," "You Beat Me to the Punch"	Many of Wells' hits were written by Smokey Robinson.
The Who	Roger Daltrey, John Entwistle, Keith Moon, Pete Townshend	"My Generation," "I Can See for Miles," "Pinball Wizard"	The Who's 1969 *Tommy* pioneered the rock opera and was made into a popular 1975 film.
Jackie Wilson		"Baby Workout," "(Your Love Keeps Lifting Me) Higher and Higher"	Wilson suffered an on-stage heart attack during a 1975 performance.
Stevie Wonder	born: Steveland Morris	"Fingertips (Part 2)," "For Once in My Life," "My Cherie Amour"	As "Little" Stevie Wonder, he recorded his first hit, "Fingertips (Part 2)," at age thirteen.
The Yardbirds	Jeff Beck, Eric Clapton, Chris Dreja, Jim McCarty, Jimmy Page, Keith Relf, Paul Samwell-Smith	"Heart Full of Soul," "For Your Love"	In Beck, Page, and Clapton, the Yardbirds boasted three of the leading guitarists in rock history.
The Young Rascals	Eddie Brigati, Gene Cornish, Felix Cavaliere, Dino Danelli	"Good Lovin'," "Groovin'," "A Beautiful Morning"	In an effort to be taken more seriously, the group dropped the "Young" from its name in 1967.

P. S. Ramsey

Top-Selling U.S. Recordings

1960

Top 20 Singles

1. "The Theme from *A Summer Place*" — Percy Faith
2. "Are You Lonesome Tonight?" — Elvis Presley
3. "It's Now or Never" — Elvis Presley
4. "Cathy's Clown" — The Everly Brothers
5. "Stuck on You" — Elvis Presley
6. "I'm Sorry" — Brenda Lee
7. "Running Bear" — Johnny Preston
8. "Save the Last Dance for Me" — The Drifters
9. "Teen Angel" — Mark Dinning
10. "My Heart Has a Mind of Its Own" — Connie Francis
11. "El Paso" — Marty Robbins
12. "Everybody's Somebody's Fool" — Connie Francis
13. "The Twist" — Chubby Checker
14. "Itsy Bitsy Teenie Weenie Yellow Polka Dot Bikini" — Brian Hyland
15. "Alley-Oop" — Hollywood Argyles
16. "Mr. Custer" — Larry Verne
17. "I Want to Be Wanted" — Brenda Lee
18. "Stay" — Maurice Williams and the Zodiacs
19. "Georgia on My Mind" — Ray Charles
20. "Last Date" — Floyd Cramer

Top 10 Albums

1. *The Sound of Music* — Original Cast
2. *Inside Shelley Berman* — Shelley Berman
3. *The Button-Down Mind of Bob Newhart* — Bob Newhart
4. *Sixty Years of Music America Loves Best, Vol. I* — Various Artists
5. *Here We Go Again* — Kingston Trio
6. *Sold Out* — Kingston Trio
7. *Heavenly* — Johnny Mathis
8. *South Pacific* — Soundtrack
9. *Faithfully* — Johnny Mathis
10. *Outside Shelley Berman* — Shelley Berman

1961

Top 20 Singles

1. "Tossin' and Turnin'" — Bobby Lewis
2. "Big Bad John" — Jimmy Dean
3. "Runaway" — Del Shannon
4. "Wonderland By Night" — Bert Kaempfert
5. "Pony Time" — Chubby Checker
6. "The Lion Sleeps Tonight" — The Tokens
7. "Blue Moon" — The Marcels
8. "Take Good Care of My Baby" — Bobby Vee
9. "Calcutta" — Lawrence Welk
10. "Runaround Sue" — Dion
11. "Michael" — The Highwaymen
12. "Travelin' Man" — Ricky Nelson
13. "Quarter to Three" — Gary U.S. Bonds
14. "Hit the Road Jack" — Ray Charles
15. "Surrender" — Elvis Presley
16. "Will You Love Me Tomorrow?" — The Shirelles
17. "Mother-in-Law" — Ernie K-Doe
18. "Please Mr. Postman" — The Marvelettes
19. "Wooden Heart" — Joe Dowell
20. "Moody River" — Pat Boone

In 1961 and 1962, changing technology led Billboard to compile separate charts for monaural and stereo albums.

Top 10 Monaural Albums

1. *Camelot* — Original Cast
2. *Great Motion Picture Themes* — Various Artists
3. *Never on Sunday* — Soundtrack
4. *The Sound of Music* — Original Cast
5. *Exodus* — Soundtrack
6. *Knockers Up* — Rusty Warren
7. *G.I. Blues* — Elvis Presley
8. *Sing Along with Mitch* — Mitch Miller
9. *Calcutta* — Lawrence Welk
10. *Tonight in Person* — Limeliters

Top 10 Stereo Albums

1. *The Sound of Music* — Original Cast
2. *Calcutta* — Lawrence Welk
3. *Exodus* — Soundtrack
4. *Camelot* — Original Cast
5. *Great Motion Picture Themes* — Various Artists
6. *Music from "Exodus" and Other Great Themes* — Mantovani

7. *Belafonte at Carnegie Hall*	Harry Belafonte
8. *Sing Along with Mitch*	Mitch Miller
9. *Persuasive Percussion*	Terry Snyder and the All Stars
10. *Provocative Percussion*	Enoch Light and the Light Brigade

1962

Top 20 Singles

1. "I Can't Stop Loving You"	Ray Charles
2. "Big Girls Don't Cry"	The Four Seasons
3. "Sherry"	The Four Seasons
4. "Roses Are Red (My Love)"	Bobby Vinton
5. "The Peppermint Twist"	Joey Dee and the Starliters
6. "Telstar"	The Tornadoes
7. "Soldier Boy"	The Shirelles
8. "Hey! Baby"	Bruce Channel
9. "Duke of Earl"	Gene Chandler
10. "The Twist"	Chubby Checker
11. "Johnny Angel"	Shelley Fabares
12. "He's a Rebel"	The Crystals
13. "Breaking Up Is Hard to Do"	Neil Sedaka
14. "Monster Mash"	Bobby "Boris" Pickett and the Crypt-Kickers
15. "Good Luck Charm"	Elvis Presley
16. "Sheila"	Tommy Roe
17. "Stranger on the Shore"	Mr. Acker Bilk
18. "The Stripper"	David Rose
19. "The Loco-Motion"	Little Eva
20. "Don't Break the Heart That Loves You"	Connie Francis

Top 10 Monaural Albums

1. *West Side Story*	Soundtrack
2. *Breakfast at Tiffany's*	Henry Mancini
3. *Blue Hawaii*	Elvis Presley
4. *West Side Story*	Original Cast
5. *The Sound of Music*	Original Cast
6. *Time Out*	Dave Brubeck
7. *Camelot*	Original Cast
8. *Your Twist Party*	Chubby Checker
9. *Knockers Up*	Rusty Warren
10. *Judy at Carnegie Hall*	Judy Garland

Top 10 Stereo Albums

1. *West Side Story*	Soundtrack
2. *Breakfast at Tiffany's*	Henry Mancini
3. *Stereo 35MM*	Enoch Light and His Orchestra
4. *Camelot*	Original Cast
5. *The Sound of Music*	Original Cast
6. *Blue Hawaii*	Elvis Presley
7. *Judy at Carnegie Hall*	Judy Garland
8. *West Side Story*	Original Cast
9. *Time Out*	Dave Brubeck
10. *Moon River*	Lawrence Welk

1963

Top 20 Singles

1. "Sugar Shack"	Jimmy Gilmer and the Fireballs
2. "He's So Fine"	The Chiffons
3. "Dominique"	The Singing Nun
4. "Hey Paula"	Paul and Paula
5. "My Boyfriend's Back"	The Angels
6. "Blue Velvet"	Bobby Vinton
7. "Sukiyaki"	Kyu Sakamoto
8. "I Will Follow Him"	Little Peggy March
9. "Fingertips (Part 2)"	Little Stevie Wonder
10. "Walk Like a Man"	The Four Seasons
11. "Go Away Little Girl"	Steve Lawrence
12. "I'm Leaving It up to You"	Dale and Grace
13. "Surf City"	Jan and Dean
14. "It's My Party"	Lesley Gore
15. "Walk Right In"	The Rooftop Singers
16. "Easier Said Than Done"	The Essex
17. "If You Wanna Be Happy"	Jimmy Soul
18. "So Much in Love"	The Tymes
19. "Deep Purple"	Nino Tempo and April Stevens
20. "Our Day Will Come"	Ruby and the Romantics

Top 10 Albums

1. *West Side Story*	Soundtrack
2. *Peter, Paul and Mary*	Peter, Paul and Mary
3. *Moving*	Peter, Paul and Mary
4. *Joan Baez in Concert*	Joan Baez
5. *I Left My Heart in San Francisco*	Tony Bennett

6. *Moon River and Other Great Movie Themes* — Andy Williams
7. *Lawrence of Arabia* — Soundtrack
8. *Days of Wine and Roses* — Andy Williams
9. *Oliver* — Original Cast
10. *Modern Sounds in Country and Western Music, Vol. 2* — Ray Charles

1964

Top 20 Singles

1. "I Want to Hold Your Hand" — The Beatles
2. "Can't Buy Me Love" — The Beatles
3. "There! I've Said It Again" — Bobby Vinton
4. "Baby Love" — The Supremes
5. "Oh, Pretty Woman" — Roy Orbison
6. "The House of the Rising Sun" — The Animals
7. "Chapel of Love" — The Dixie Cups
8. "I Feel Fine" — The Beatles
9. "She Loves You" — The Beatles
10. "I Get Around" — The Beach Boys
11. "Come See About Me" — The Supremes
12. "Where Did Our Love Go?" — The Supremes
13. "Do Wah Diddy Diddy" — Manfred Mann
14. "My Guy" — Mary Wells
15. "A Hard Day's Night" — The Beatles
16. "Rag Doll" — The Four Seasons
17. "Hello, Dolly!" — Louis Armstrong
18. "Mr. Lonely" — Bobby Vinton
19. "Everybody Loves Somebody" — Dean Martin
20. "A World Without Love" — Peter and Gordon

Top 10 Albums

1. *Hello, Dolly!* — Original Cast
2. *In the Wind* — Peter, Paul and Mary
3. *Honey in the Horn* — Al Hirt
4. *The Barbra Streisand Album* — Barbra Streisand
5. *West Side Story* — Soundtrack
6. *Peter, Paul and Mary* — Peter, Paul and Mary
7. *The Second Barbra Streisand Album* — Barbra Streisand
8. *Meet the Beatles* — The Beatles
9. *The Third Barbra Streisand Album* — Barbra Streisand

10. *Moon River and Other Great Movie Themes* — Andy Williams

1965

Top 20 Singles

1. "(I Can't Get No) Satisfaction" — The Rolling Stones
2. "Yesterday" — The Beatles
3. "Turn! Turn! Turn!" — The Byrds
4. "Mrs. Brown You've Got a Lovely Daughter" — Herman's Hermits
5. "I Got You Babe" — Sonny and Cher
6. "Help!" — The Beatles
7. "I Can't Help Myself" — The Four Tops
8. "You've Lost That Lovin' Feelin'" — The Righteous Brothers
9. "Downtown" — Petula Clark
10. "This Diamond Ring" — Gary Lewis and the Playboys
11. "Stop! In the Name of Love" — The Supremes
12. "Help Me, Rhonda" — The Beach Boys
13. "Get off My Cloud" — The Rolling Stones
14. "I Hear a Symphony" — The Supremes
15. "I'm Telling You Now" — Freddie and the Dreamers
16. "Eight Days a Week" — The Beatles
17. "My Girl" — The Temptations
18. "Hang on Sloopy" — The McCoys
19. "Mr. Tambourine Man" — The Byrds
20. "Eve of Destruction" — Barry McGuire

Top 10 Albums

1. *Mary Poppins* — Soundtrack
2. *Beatles '65* — The Beatles
3. *The Sound of Music* — Soundtrack
4. *My Fair Lady* — Soundtrack
5. *Fiddler on the Roof* — Original Cast
6. *Goldfinger* — Soundtrack
7. *Hello, Dolly!* — Original Cast
8. *Dear Heart* — Andy Williams
9. *Introducing Herman's Hermits* — Herman's Hermits
10. *Beatles VI* — The Beatles

1966

Top 20 Singles

1. "I'm a Believer" — The Monkees
2. "The Ballad of the Green Berets" — Barry Sadler

3. "Winchester Cathedral"	The New Vaudeville Band
4. "(You're My) Soul and Inspiration"	The Righteous Brothers
5. "Monday, Monday"	The Mamas and the Papas
6. "We Can Work It Out"	The Beatles
7. "Summer in the City"	The Lovin' Spoonful
8. "Cherish"	The Association
9. "You Can't Hurry Love"	The Supremes
10. "Wild Thing"	The Troggs
11. "Reach Out I'll Be There"	Four Tops
12. "Paint It, Black"	The Rolling Stones
13. "When a Man Loves a Woman"	Percy Sledge
14. "You Keep Me Hangin' On"	The Supremes
15. "Hanky Panky"	Tommy James and the Shondells
16. "My Love"	Petula Clark
17. "The Sounds of Silence"	Simon and Garfunkel
18. "Paperback Writer"	The Beatles
19. "96 Tears"	? and the Mysterians
20. "Last Train to Clarksville"	The Monkees

Top 10 Albums

1. *Whipped Cream and Other Delights*	Herb Alpert's Tijuana Brass
2. *The Sound of Music*	Soundtrack
3. *Going Places*	Herb Alpert and the Tijuana Brass
4. *Rubber Soul*	The Beatles
5. *What Now My Love*	Herb Alpert and the Tijuana Brass
6. *If You Can Believe Your Eyes and Ears*	The Mamas and the Papas
7. *Dr. Zhivago*	Soundtrack
8. *Revolver*	The Beatles
9. *Color Me Barbra*	Barbra Streisand
10. *Ballad of the Green Berets*	Barry Sadler

1967

Top 20 Singles

1. "To Sir with Love"	Lulu
2. "Daydream Believer"	The Monkees
3. "Windy"	The Association
4. "Ode to Billie Joe"	Bobbie Gentry
5. "Somethin' Stupid"	Nancy Sinatra and Frank Sinatra
6. "Groovin'"	The Young Rascals
7. "The Letter"	The Box Tops
8. "Light My Fire"	The Doors
9. "Happy Together"	The Turtles
10. "Hello Goodbye"	The Beatles
11. "Respect"	Aretha Franklin
12. "Kind of a Drag"	The Buckinghams
13. "Incense and Peppermints"	The Strawberry Alarm Clock
14. "Love Is Here and Now You're Gone"	The Supremes
15. "Ruby Tuesday"	The Rolling Stones
16. "All You Need Is Love"	The Beatles
17. "The Happening"	The Supremes
18. "Penny Lane"	The Beatles
19. "I Heard It Through the Grapevine"	Gladys Knight and the Pips
20. "Soul Man"	Sam and Dave

Top 10 Albums

1. *More of the Monkees*	The Monkees
2. *The Monkees*	The Monkees
3. *Dr. Zhivago*	Soundtrack
4. *The Sound of Music*	Soundtrack
5. *The Temptations' Greatest Hits*	The Temptations
6. *A Man and a Woman*	Soundtrack
7. *S.R.O.*	Herb Alpert and the Tijuana Brass
8. *Whipped Cream and Other Delights*	Herb Alpert and the Tijuana Brass
9. *Going Places*	Herb Alpert and the Tijuana Brass
10. *Sgt. Pepper's Lonely Hearts Club Band*	The Beatles

1968

Top 20 Singles

1. "Hey Jude"	The Beatles
2. "I Heard It Through the Grapevine"	Marvin Gaye
3. "Love Is Blue"	Paul Mauriat
4. "Honey"	Bobby Goldsboro

5. "People Got to Be Free" The Rascals
6. "(Sittin' on) The Dock of the Bay" Otis Redding
7. "This Guy's in Love with You" Herb Alpert
8. "Mrs. Robinson" Simon and Garfunkel
9. "Love Child" Diana Ross and the Supremes
10. "Tighten Up" Archie Bell and the Drells
11. "Hello, I Love You" The Doors
12. "Judy in Disguise (with Glasses)" John Fred and His Playboy Band
13. "Grazing in the Grass" Hugh Masekela
14. "Harper Valley P.T.A." Jeannie C. Riley
15. "Green Tambourine" The Lemon Pipers
16. "(Theme from) Valley of the Dolls" Dionne Warwick
17. "Young Girl" Gary Puckett and the Union Gap
18. "Those Were the Days" Mary Hopkin
19. "The Horse" Cliff Nobles and Company
20. "Born to Be Wild" Steppenwolf

Top 10 Albums

1. *Are You Experienced?* The Jimi Hendrix Experience
2. *The Graduate* Simon and Garfunkel
3. *Disraeli Gears* Cream
4. *Magical Mystery Tour* The Beatles
5. *Diana Ross and the Supremes' Greatest Hits* Diana Ross and the Supremes
6. *Sgt. Pepper's Lonely Hearts Club Band* The Beatles
7. *Doors* Doors
8. *Parsley, Sage, Rosemary, and Thyme* Simon and Garfunkel
9. *Vanilla Fudge* The Vanilla Fudge
10. *Blooming Hits* Paul Mauriat and His Orchestra

1969

Top 20 Singles

1. "Aquarius/Let the Sunshine In" The Fifth Dimension
2. "In the Year 2525" Zager and Evans
3. "Get Back" The Beatles
4. "Sugar, Sugar" The Archies
5. "Honky Tonk Woman" The Rolling Stones
6. "Everyday People" Sly and the Family Stone
7. "Dizzy" Tommy Roe
8. "Wedding Bell Blues" The Fifth Dimension
9. "I Can't Get Next to You" The Temptations
10. "Crimson and Clover" Tommy James and the Shondells
11. "Na Na Hey Hey Kiss Him Goodbye" Steam
12. "Love Theme from *Romeo and Juliet*" Henry Mancini
13. "Leaving on a Jet Plane" Peter, Paul and Mary
14. "Come Together" The Beatles
15. "Someday We'll Be Together" Diana Ross and the Supremes
16. "Suspicious Minds" Elvis Presley
17. "Crystal Blue Persuasion" Tommy James and the Shondells
18. "Proud Mary" Creedence Clearwater Revival
19. "Spinning Wheel" Blood, Sweat, and Tears
20. "A Boy Named Sue" Johnny Cash

Top 10 Albums

1. *In-A-Gadda-Da-Vida* Iron Butterfly
2. *Hair* Original Cast
3. *Blood, Sweat, and Tears* Blood, Sweat, and Tears
4. *Bayou Country* Creedence Clearwater Revival
5. *Led Zeppelin* Led Zeppelin
6. *Johnny Cash at Folsom Prison* Johnny Cash
7. *Funny Girl* Soundtrack
8. *The Beatles* The Beatles
9. *Donovan's Greatest Hits* Donovan
10. *The Association's Greatest Hits* The Association

J. P. Piskulich

Time Line

1960	Anthropology	Mary Leakey and Louis S. B. Leakey discover fossils of an ancestor of modern humans that will later be designated as *Homo habilis*. *Homo habilis* is considered to be the earliest member of the genus Homo, the genus to which the modern human (*Homo sapiens*) and its closest ancestors belong.
1960	Astronomy	Frank Drake directs Project Ozma, an unsuccessful attempt to detect radio signals from extraterrestrial life forms, at the National Radio Astronomy Observatory in Green Bank, West Virginia.
1960	Astronomy	Allan Sandage discovers 3C48, the first starlike object that emits powerful radio waves. Over the next several years, more of these objects would be found. Eventually, they will be named quasi-stellar objects, or quasars.
1960	Biology	James Frederick Bonner discovers that chromosomes synthesize ribonucleic acid (RNA).
1960	Biology	Lyman Creighton Craig purifies the active hormone parathormone (PTH) from the parathyroid gland.
1960	Biology	Kenneth Norris and John Prescott establish that dolphins use echolocation, similar to sonar, to locate underwater objects.
1960	Biology	Christian B. Anfinsen, Stanford Moore, and William Howard Stein determine the exact sequence of the 124 amino acids that make up the pancreatic enzyme ribonuclease.
1960	Biology	Jacques Monod and Francois Jacob announce the discovery of messenger-RNA, which carries the genetic information from deoxyribonucleic acid (DNA) to transfer-RNA within the nucleus of somatic cells.
1960	Biology	Max Ferdinand Perutz and John Cowdery Kendrew determine the three-dimensional structures of the proteins hemoglobin (found in human blood) and myoglobin (found in muscles).
1960	Biology	Earl Wilbur Sutherland, Jr., determines the three-dimensional structure of adenosine monophosphate (cyclic-AMP), a molecule critical to animal cell metabolism.
1960	Chemistry	K. H. Hofmann chemically synthesizes the hormone found in the pituitary gland.
1960	Chemistry	Robert Burns Woodward chemically synthesizes chlorophyll, the compound responsible for photosynthesis in plants.
1960	Computer Science	The first integrated circuits, thin pieces of a semiconducting material etched with numerous small transistor circuits, are developed.
1960	Geology	Geothermal power, or power using the energy of the earth's internal heat, is produced for the first time in the United States at a site of natural geyser activity near San Francisco, California.
1960	Geology	Harry H. Hess develops the theory of sea-floor spreading to explain the movement of continents: The expansion of the bottom of the Atlantic Ocean causes continental drift.
1960	Medicine	The first cardiac pacemakers, designed to regulate the heartbeat, are developed.

1960	Medicine	G. N. Robinson discovers the antibiotic methicillin, a substance similar to penicillin.
1960	Oceanography	Jacques Piccard and Don Walsh explore the Challenger Deep, a trench more than 10,000 meters below the surface of the Pacific Ocean, in the bathyscaphe *Trieste*.
1960	Oceanography	The nuclear submarine *Triton* completes the first underwater circumnavigation of the earth.
1960	Physics	The International Bureau of Weights and Measures defines the meter as equal to 1,650,763.73 times the wavelength of the orange-red line in the spectrum of the element Krypton-86.
1960	Physics	Luis Walter Alvarez discovers extremely short-lived subatomic particles known as resonance particles.
1960	Physics	The Mössbauer effect, a method of producing gamma rays of a single wavelength developed by Rudolf Ludwig Mössbauer, is used to prove that gravity increases the wavelength of electromagnetic radiation (light), supporting the theory of relativity.
1960	Space Exploration	Tiros 1, the world's first weather satellite, is launched on April 1 by the United States.
1960	Space Exploration	Echo 1, the world's first communications satellite, is launched on August 12 by the United States.
1960	Technology	Theodore Harold Maiman produces the world's first light amplification by stimulated emission of radiation (laser).
1961	Astronomy	C. Roger Lynds detects radio waves coming from planetary nebulae (clouds of glowing gas surrounding very hot stars) at the National Radio Astronomy observatory.
1961	Astronomy	Microwaves are reflected off the planet Venus, allowing its distance from Earth to be determined with great accuracy.
1961	Astronomy	M. Ryle uses evidence from radio astronomy observations to conclude that the universe changes over time.
1961	Biology	Howard M. Dintis establishes that transfer-RNA brings amino acids together to build proteins within somatic cells.
1961	Biology	Francis Crick and S. Brenner prove that each "letter" in the genetic code consists of a group of three nucleotide bases (chemical groups connected to DNA and RNA molecules within the cell's chromosomes).
1961	Biology	Robert William Holley produces purified samples of three different varieties of transfer-RNA.
1961	Biology	In a widely publicized report that is later discredited, James V. McConnell announces that flatworms that eat other flatworms that have learned simple mazes go on to learn how to follow those same mazes more quickly.
1961	Biology	Jacques Monod and Francois Jacob postulate the existence of gene regulators, substances that slow down or speed up the activities of particular genes.
1961	Biology	Marshall Warren Nirenberg begins deciphering the genetic code by producing messenger-RNA containing uracil as the only nucleotide base, thus proving that the nucleotide sequence UUU is the code for the production of the amino acid phenylalanine.

1961	Chemistry	A team of scientists at the University of California, Berkeley, led by Albert Ghiorso, creates the artificial element 103 by bombarding the element californium (atomic number 98) with boron (atomic number 5) within a nuclear accelerator. The element is named lawrencium after the American physicist Ernest Orlando Lawrence.
1961	Computer Science	Atlas, the world's largest computer, is put into operation for use in atomic research and weather forecasting.
1961	Computer Science	The silicon chip, a type of integrated circuit, is patented by Texas Instruments.
1961	Computer Science	Edward N. Lorenz begins the study of chaotic systems while working on computer models of atmospheric behavior. Chaotic systems are models of activity in which small changes magnify over time to produce unpredictably complex results.
1961	Geology	The Cuss I, a converted oil-drilling rig, is used at a depth of 3.5 kilometers below the surface of the ocean to drill through the sediment on the ocean floor. After nearly two hundred meters, the hard surface of the ocean floor is reached.
1961	Medicine	The Barnet Ventilation electric lung pump is invented.
1961	Medicine	Judah Folkman suggests that tumors release a substance that promotes the growth of blood vessels into the tumor, thus providing it with the extra nutrition that it needs to grow.
1961	Medicine	F. L. Horsfall suggests that all forms of cancer are caused by mutations in cell DNA.
1961	Medicine	Jack Lippes develops an inert plastic intrauterine device (IUD) for use in birth control.
1961	Physics	Robert Hofstadter discovers that protons and neutrons consist of a central positive core surrounded by two shells of particles known as mesons. A proton, a positive nuclear particle, has two positive mesons in its makeup, while a neutron, a neutral nuclear particle, has one negative meson and one positive meson.
1961	Physics	Murray Gell-Mann classifies subatomic particles (protons and neutrons) using a system known as the eightfold way and postulates that they are made up of smaller particles known as quarks.
1961	Space Exploration	Yuri Gagarin of the Soviet Union becomes the first human being in space and orbits Earth one time in Vostok 1, which was launched on April 21.
1961	Space Exploration	Alan B. Shepard, Jr., becomes the first American in space in *Freedom 7*, which was launched on May 5.
1961	Space Exploration	Virgil I. "Gus" Grissom becomes the second American in space in *Liberty Bell 7*, which was launched on July 21.
1961	Space Exploration	Gherman Titov becomes the second Soviet citizen in space and orbits Earth seventeen times in Vostok 2, which was launched on August 6.
1961	Space Exploration	Marcel Nicolet uses changes in the orbit of Echo 1 to determine that Earth's atmosphere contains a region about 300 to 1000 kilometers above the surface that consists mostly of small amounts of helium.
1961	Technology	Electronic watches using electric tuning forks in place of mechanical springs become available.

1962	Astronomy	The first radar contact with the planet Mercury is made. The Sugar Grove project, an attempt to build a fully steerable radio telescope nearly two hundred meters wide, is abandoned after the expenditure of ninety-six million dollars.
1962	Astronomy	Roland L. Carpenter and Richard M. Goldstein use microwaves reflected from the surface of Venus to determine that the planet has a period of rotation of about 250 days in a direction opposite to that of the other planets.
1962	Astronomy	Riccardo Giacconi, H. Gursky, F. R. Paolini, and Bruno B. Rossi discover the first known source of X rays outside the solar system.
1962	Astronomy	Peter van de Kamp detects a periodic wobble in the motion of Barnard's star, suggesting that it is orbited by a planet.
1962	Biology	The publication of *Silent Spring* by Rachel Carson alerts the public to the dangers of environmental pollution.
1962	Biology	Jacques F. A. P. Miller demonstrates that the thymus gland is involved in the immune system by removing it from newborn mice, which fail to develop white blood cells and lymph nodes.
1962	Biology	Emile Zuckerkandl and Linus Pauling suggest that changes in genetic material over time could be used to determine how long ago different species separated from each other during the course of evolution.
1962	Chemistry	Neil Bartlett produces xenon platinum hexafluoride, the first compound made with one of the noble gas elements, formerly thought to be completely inert.
1962	Computer Science	The Aviation Supply Office in Philadelphia, Pennsylvania, introduces computer time-sharing, in which several peripheral terminals interact with a central processing unit.
1962	Computer Science	Tibor Rado produces an example of a mathematical function that is not computable, demonstrating the mathematical limitations of computers.
1962	Geology	Harry H. Hess suggests that sea-floor spreading is caused by convection currents in the molten rock in Earth's mantle.
1962	Medicine	Lasers are used in eye surgery for the first time.
1962	Medicine	L. Harrington develops a surgical treatment for scoliosis (curvature of the spine).
1962	Medicine	Thomas Huckle Weller develops a vaccine for rubella (German measles).
1962	Physics	Researchers at the Brookhaven National Laboratory in Upton, New York, discover two types of neutrinos, the electron neutrino and the muon neutrino.
1962	Physics	Brian David Josephson discovers the Josephson effect, the ability of electrons to pass through an insulating layer between two superconductors.
1962	Physics	Heinz London uses a new cooling technique involving a mixture of isotopes of helium to reach extremely low temperatures.
1962	Space Exploration	John Glenn, Jr., becomes the first American to orbit the Earth in *Friendship 7*, launched February 20.
1962	Space Exploration	Malcolm Scott Carpenter orbits the Earth three times in *Aurora 7*, launched June 24.
1962	Space Exploration	Telstar 1, the first communications satellite capable of amplifying signals rather than simply reflecting them, is launched on July 10.

1962	Space Exploration	Mariner 2, the first successful planetary probe, is launched on August 27 and makes its closest approach to Venus on December 14.
1962	Space Exploration	Walter M. Schirra, Jr., orbits the Earth six times in *Sigma 7*, launched October 3.
1962	Technology	The light-emitting diode (LED), a semiconductor that produces visible light, is introduced.
1962	Technology	The Unimation company markets the world's first industrial robot.
1962	Technology	The *Savannah*, an experimental nuclear-powered merchant ship, begins sea trials in March.
1962	Technology	F. Trombe directs the construction of a solar-powered furnace in the French Pyrenees.
1963	Anthropology	Ice Age skeletons found in a cave near Cosenza, Italy, include that of a dwarf, indicating that individuals unable to survive on their own were supported by the community.
1963	Anthropology	The prehistoric paintings in the Lascaux cave in France are closed to the public to prevent damage caused by the humidity of human breath.
1963	Astronomy	Hydroxyl groups, each containing one oxygen atom and one hydrogen atom, are detected in interplanetary space.
1963	Astronomy	The largest radio telescope in the world, three hundred meters in diameter, goes into operation near Arecibo, Puerto Rico.
1963	Astronomy	Herbert Friedman and colleagues at the United States Naval Research Laboratory in Washington, D.C., detect Scorpius X-1, the strongest X-ray source ever discovered.
1963	Astronomy	Allan Sandage discovers that the galaxy M82 has been undergoing a massive explosion at its center for 1.5 million years.
1963	Astronomy	Maarten Schmidt determines that the spectrum of the quasar 3C273 has a very large red-shift, indicating that it is extremely far away and that therefore it must contain an enormous amount of energy to be detectable from Earth.
1963	Biology	Alan Hodgkin and John Eccles investigate the chemical mechanisms involved in the transmission of nerve impulses.
1963	Biology	Carl Sagan detects adenosine triphosphate (ATP), a molecule used to store energy in living cells, in a mixture of chemicals designed to reproduce conditions before life arose on Earth.
1963	Geology	F. J. Vine and D. H. Matthews show that the bottom of the Atlantic Ocean contains strips of sediment with alternating directions of magnetic orientation, providing evidence for both sea-floor spreading and the periodic reversal of Earth's magnetic field.
1963	Medicine	The tranquilizer Valium (diazepam) is introduced.
1963	Medicine	Allan MacLeod Cormack and Godfrey Newbold Hounsfield develop computerized axial tomography (the CAT scan), a method of obtaining detailed X-ray images.
1963	Medicine	Michael Ellis De Bakey uses an artificial heart during cardiac surgery.
1963	Medicine	F. D. Moore and T. D. Starzl perform the first liver transplant.
1963	Physics	The anti-xi-zero particle, a fundamental particle of antimatter, is discovered.

1963	Physics	Nicola Cabibbo develops a theory of the interaction known as the weak force, leading indirectly to the electroweak theory, which explains both the weak force and the electromagnetic force.
1963	Space Exploration	Syncom 2, the first satellite in a geosynchronous orbit, is launched on February 14.
1963	Space Exploration	Leroy Gordon Cooper, Jr., orbits the Earth twenty-two times in *Faith 7*, launched May 14.
1963	Space Exploration	Valentina Tereshkova becomes the first woman in space and orbits the Earth forty-eight times in Vostok 6, launched June 16.
1963	Technology	Cassette tapes are introduced.
1963	Technology	Semiconductor diodes using electron tunneling, in which electrons pass through solid barriers, are marketed.
1963	Technology	Carbon fiber materials are developed.
1963	Technology	Friction welding, a method of bonding two objects together using the heat of friction produced when one rotates against the other, is invented.
1963	Technology	The Spyder, the first automobile to use a Wankel rotary engine, is produced.
1964	Astronomy	The 213-centimeter reflecting telescope at Kitt Peak, Arizona, goes into operation.
1964	Astronomy	Herbert Friedman and coworkers at the U.S. Naval Research Laboratory detect X rays from the Crab Nebula.
1964	Astronomy	Arno Allan Penzias and Robert Woodrow Wilson detect microwave radiation coming from all directions of the universe equally; this cosmic background radiation provides strong evidence that the universe began in an enormous explosion known as the big bang.
1964	Biology	The International Rice Research Institute begins the "green revolution" with the development of improved varieties of rice.
1964	Biology	The publication of W. D. Hamilton's *The Genetic Evolution of Social Behavior*, a study of the behavior of social insects, contributes to the newly emerging field of sociobiology.
1964	Biology	Robert William Holley determines the structure of one form of transfer-RNA.
1964	Chemistry	The artificial element 104 is produced and named rutherfordium after the British physicist Ernest Rutherford.
1964	Computer Science	The first word processor is introduced by IBM.
1964	Geology	Project Mohole, an attempt to reach the Mohorovicic discontinuity that separates the crust of Earth from the mantle, is begun; it is later abandoned without success.
1964	Medicine	Home kidney dialysis treatments are introduced.
1964	Medicine	The U.S. Surgeon General issues *Smoking and Health*, a report linking smoking and lung cancer.
1964	Medicine	Baruch Samuel Blumberg discovers a human antigen to hepatitis B, which later leads to the development of a vaccine.
1964	Physics	The omega-minus particle is discovered and is shown to have properties that provide strong evidence for the theory of quarks.

1964	Physics	Raymond Y. Chiao, Boris P. Stoicheff, and Charles H. Townes discover stimulated Brillouin scattering, an effect named for French physicist Leon Brillouin, in which dim light passes through a transparent substance but bright light is reflected from it.
1964	Physics	James Watson Cronin and Val Logsden Fitch discover that the neutral K-meson violates the combined conservation of the properties known as charge conjugation and parity (CP conservation); instead, the property known as time reversal is involved to produce CPT conservation.
1964	Space Exploration	Ranger 7 obtains close-range photographs of the Moon on July 31.
1964	Space Exploration	Voskhod 1, the first spacecraft to carry more than one person, is launched on October 12 with three Soviet cosmonauts aboard.
1964	Technology	Container ships (ships designed to carry standardized containers of cargo) are introduced.
1964	Technology	Permanent press clothing is marketed.
1964	Technology	The Verrazano-Narrows Bridge, the largest suspension bridge in the world until 1981, is opened to traffic in New York City.
1965	Anthropology	In the book *Stonehenge Decoded*, Gerald Stanley Hawkins argues that Stonehenge was an ancient astronomical observatory.
1965	Astronomy	Cosmic masers, regions of interstellar gas that produce coherent microwave radiation, are discovered.
1965	Astronomy	Astronomers learn that Venus rotates in a direction opposite that of the other planets.
1965	Astronomy	Rolf Buchanan Dyce and Gordon H. Pettengill use microwaves reflected from the surface of Mercury to show that the planet has a period of rotation of about fifty-nine days.
1965	Astronomy	Frederick Reines and J. P. F. Sellshop detect neutrinos from cosmic rays using detectors deep inside a South African gold mine.
1965	Astronomy	Allan Sandage discovers quasars that do not emit radio waves.
1965	Biology	Alec D. Bangham forms closed spheres in water from two layers of phospholipids, similar to the way that cell membranes are formed.
1965	Biology	Elso Sterrenberg Barghoorn discovers microscopic fossils in rocks 3.5 billion years old.
1965	Biology	Melvin Calvin and coworkers discover breakdown products of chlorophyll in rocks nearly 3 billion years old.
1965	Biology	William J. Dreyer and J. Claude Bennet suggest that a single antibody can match numerous antigens because the antibody has variable genes.
1965	Biology	Harry Harlow demonstrates that monkeys reared in isolation have severe emotional impairment.
1965	Biology	W. A. Jones, Morton Beroza, and Martin Jacobson develop artificial insect pheromones.
1965	Biology	Hans Ris and Walter Plaut discover that the chloroplasts in algae cells have their own DNA.
1965	Biology	Sol Spiegelman synthesizes a self-reproducing virus.
1965	Chemistry	Mixtures of rare earth elements are separated by gas chromatography.
1965	Chemistry	Robert Bruce Merrifield chemically synthesizes insulin.

1965	Chemistry	David Phillips chemically synthesizes the enzyme lysozome.
1965	Computer Science	A computer is used to solve a mathematical problem first proposed by Archimedes more than two thousand years ago.
1965	Computer Science	John Kemeny and Thomas Kurtz develop the computer language BASIC (beginners all-purpose symbolic instruction code), used by owners of personal computers.
1965	Geology	J. Tuzo Wilson suggests that faults perpendicular to mid-ocean rifts develop during sea-floor spreading.
1965	Medicine	A measles vaccine is developed.
1965	Medicine	Soft contact lenses are invented.
1965	Medicine	Researchers discover that injections of synthetic progesterone and estrogen can prevent ovulation for a full month.
1965	Medicine	Morris E. Davis reports that estrogen can help prevent atherosclerosis and osteoporosis in postmenopausal women.
1965	Medicine	J. Ochsner uses plastic mesh to correct large defects in body tissue.
1965	Oceanography	A team of aquanauts under the direction of Jacques-Yves Cousteau spend twenty-three days at a depth of one hundred meters beneath the surface of the Mediterranean Sea.
1965	Oceanography	The U.S. Navy completes the Sealab II project, with a team of aquanauts living forty-five days at a depth of sixty-two meters beneath the surface of the Pacific Ocean.
1965	Physics	The Stanford Linear Accelerator Center (SLAC) goes into operation.
1965	Physics	Moo-Young Han and Yoichiro Nambu introduce the concept of a property of quarks that is later known as "color."
1965	Space Exploration	A Soviet space probe becomes the first human-made object to reach another planet when it strikes the surface of Venus.
1965	Space Exploration	The Gemini program begins, carrying two American astronauts on each mission.
1965	Space Exploration	Aleksei Leonov makes the first spacewalk when he leaves the spacecraft Voskhod 2 for twenty minutes on March 18.
1965	Space Exploration	Early Bird, the first commercial communications satellite, is launched on April 6.
1965	Space Exploration	Edward Higgins White II makes the first American spacewalk from Gemini 4 on June 3.
1965	Space Exploration	Mariner 4 photographs the surface of Mars on July 14.
1965	Space Exploration	Gemini 7 approaches Gemini 6 in the first space rendezvous on December 15.
1965	Technology	Joseph Giordmaine and Robert Miller develop the continuously tunable laser.
1965	Technology	Emmet N. Leith and Juris Upatnieks use lasers to produce the first holograms.
1966	Anthropology	Clifford Evans and Betty J. Maggers suggest that South American pottery from five thousand years ago is essentially the same as pottery of the same age from Japan.
1966	Astronomy	Herbert Friedman, Edward T. Byram, and Talbot A. Chubb discover a powerful X-ray source in the galaxy Cygnus-A.

1966	Astronomy	Martin Rees discovers quasars with components that appear to be moving faster than the speed of light; this is later shown to be an optical illusion.
1966	Biology	Human aggression is discussed in scientific terms with the publication of *The Territorial Imperative* by Robert Ardrey and *On Aggression* by Konrad Lorenz.
1966	Biology	Sol Spiegelman and Iciro Haruna discover an enzyme that allows RNA molecules to reproduce themselves.
1966	Geology	Richard G. Doell, G. Brent Dalrymple, and Allan Cox establish the fact that Earth's magnetic field periodically reverses its north and south poles.
1966	Medicine	The French Academy of Medicine establishes brain inactivity as the clinical definition of death.
1966	Medicine	The first radioimmunoassay tests, which use radioactivity to detect very small amounts of medically important substances, are performed.
1966	Medicine	Daniel Carleton Gajdusek infects chimpanzees with Kuru, the first time a viral disease of the central nervous system has been transferred from humans to another species.
1966	Medicine	Harry M. Meyer, Jr., and Paul D. Parman develop a live-virus vaccine for rubella.
1966	Physics	The U.S. Atomic Energy Commission announces that it will build a 200-billion-electron-volt particle accelerator near Chicago, Illinois.
1966	Space Exploration	The United States launches ESSA I, the first weather satellite capable of viewing the entire Earth.
1966	Space Exploration	The Soviet Union launches Luna 9 to see it make the first soft landing (not a crash) on the Moon on February 3. On April 3, the Soviet probe Luna 10 becomes the first probe to orbit the Moon. The United States achieves landing on the Moon with Surveyor 1 on June 2; a series of American probes later orbit the Moon and map its entire surface.
1966	Space Exploration	Neil Armstrong and David R. Scott, aboard Gemini 8, link their vessel with an orbiting Agena rocket in the first successful space docking.
1966	Technology	Fuel-injected automobile engines are developed.
1967	Anthropology	J. R. Cann, J. E. Dixon, and Colin Renfew use studies of prehistoric obsidian tools to establish that complex trade routes existed in the Mediterranean region nearly ten thousand years ago.
1967	Anthropology	Elwyn L. Simons discovers a fossil skull thirty million years old belonging to a primate he names *Aegyptopithecus*, the earliest known direct ancestor of humans.
1967	Astronomy	A bright nova visible without a telescope appears in the constellation Delphinus.
1967	Astronomy	Graduate student Jocelyn Bell discovers a star that produces short, regular bursts of microwaves, the first of what will later be known as pulsars.
1967	Astronomy	Raymond Davis, Jr., uses a large tank of carbon tetrachloride buried deep in a gold mine to detect neutrinos from the sun; fewer than expected are found, creating a mystery for astronomers.
1967	Biology	Charles T. Caskey, Richard E. Marshall, and Marshall W. Nirenberg find evidence that the genetic code is identical in all species.
1967	Biology	H. Green forms hybrid cells containing both mouse and human chromosomes, raising the possibility of genetic engineering.

1967	Biology	John B. Gurden clones a frog, the first time this has been done in a vertebrate.
1967	Biology	Arthur Kornberg uses a single strand of natural DNA to synthesize biologically active DNA.
1967	Biology	Alf E. Porsild and Charles R. Arington grow living plants from seeds frozen in the Arctic for ten thousand years.
1967	Biology	Charles Yanofsky and coworkers prove definitely that the genetic code determines the sequence of amino acids in proteins, as biologists has previously assumed.
1967	Biology	Ecologists R. H. MacArthur and Edward O. Wilson begin the study of equilibrium biogeography, or the study of stable ecosystems.
1967	Biology	S. Manabe and R. T. Wetherald announce that human activities that increase the amount of carbon dioxide in the atmosphere promote global warming.
1967	Chemistry	The artificial element 105 is created and named "hahnium" after the German chemist Otto Hahn.
1967	Computer Science	Keyboards to enter data into computers are introduced.
1967	Computer Science	Gene Amdahl develops the idea of parallel processing, in which a computer undergoes several operations at the same time.
1967	Geology	Angelos Galanopoulos suggests that the volcanic explosion that nearly destroyed the Mediterranean island of Thera in ancient times gave rise to the myth of Atlantis.
1967	Geology	Researchers discover that a large portion of the sediment at the bottom of the Atlantic consists of dust blown from Africa and Europe.
1967	Geology	The theory of plate tectonics, which explains the movement of continents, is developed.
1967	Medicine	The microorganism that causes leprosy is grown in the laboratory for the first time.
1967	Medicine	Long-term studies prove that fluoridated water reduces dental cavities.
1967	Medicine	Mammographies for detecting breast cancer are developed.
1967	Medicine	Christiaan Barnard performs the first human heart transplant.
1967	Medicine	Albert M. Cohen reports that lysergic acid diethylamide (LSD) can cause genetic damage.
1967	Medicine	I. S. Cooper uses cryosurgery (surgery using supercold instruments) to treat Parkinson's disease.
1967	Medicine	Rene Favaloro develops the coronary bypass operation to treat heart disease.
1967	Medicine	Michael S. Gazzinga reports that in patients in which the tissue that links the two halves of the brain has been severed the two sides function independently.
1967	Physics	The International Bureau of Weights and Measures defines the second as the time in which the microwaves from hot cesium vibrate 9,192,631,770 times.
1967	Physics	The electroweak unification theory is fully developed.
1967	Physics	V. M. Lobashov shows that the strong force, like the weak force, violates CP conservation.
1967	Physics	Bern Matthias develops an alloy of niobium, aluminum, and germanium that demonstrates superconducting properties at a higher temperature than other substances.

1967	Space Exploration	The Apollo program begins, carrying three American astronauts on each mission, with the goal of reaching the Moon.
1967	Space Exploration	Soviet and American probes prove that Venus has an extremely dense atmosphere of carbon dioxide, resulting in a very high surface temperature.
1967	Space Exploration	On January 27, American astronauts Virgil I. "Gus" Grissom, Edward H. White, and Roger B. Chaffee die in a fire during a ground test of an Apollo vehicle.
1967	Space Exploration	On April 19, the U.S. spaceprobe Surveyor 3 lands on the Moon. It digs small trenches in the lunar surface and photographs it, sending the photographs back to Earth. The data is used to determine that it will be safe for astronauts to walk on the Moon.
1967	Space Exploration	On April 24, Soviet cosmonaut Vladimir M. Komarov dies during the descent of Soyuz 1 when the vehicle becomes entangled in its parachute lines.
1967	Technology	The U.S. Department of Agriculture tests using radiation to kill insects in food.
1967	Technology	Direct-dialing telephone calls across the Atlantic are introduced.
1967	Technology	R. M. Dolby develops the Dolby noise-reduction system to reduce background sound in audio recordings.
1968	Astronomy	Molecules of water and ammonia are discovered in interstellar space, beginning the study of astrochemistry.
1968	Astronomy	Gamma rays and infrared radiation are detected coming from the center of the galaxy.
1968	Astronomy	A pulsar is discovered at the center of the Crab Nebula, a remnant of a supernova observed in the year 1054.
1968	Astronomy	Astronomers at Cornell University use radar to map part of the surface of Venus.
1968	Astronomy	Thomas Gold suggests that pulsars are rapidly rotating neutron stars, extremely dense collapsed stars consisting entirely of neutrons.
1968	Biology	The U.S. House of Representatives reports that Lake Erie is so polluted that it would take five hundred years for it to recover.
1968	Biology	Strains of wheat from New Mexico introduced to India increase yields by 50 percent.
1968	Biology	Werner Arber discovers bacterial enzymes that cut viral DNA; these "restriction" enzymes will later be used in genetic engineering.
1968	Biology	Elso S. Banghoorn discovers amino acids in rocks three billion years old.
1968	Medicine	Tooth decay is shown to be caused by normal oral streptococcal bacteria that metabolize sugar.
1968	Medicine	Oral contraceptives are shown to increase the risk of blood clots in some women.
1968	Medicine	Fertility drugs result in the birth of sextuplets.
1968	Medicine	The drug thalidomide is shown to cause severe birth defects when given to pregnant women.
1968	Medicine	M. Arnstein develops a vaccine against meningitis.
1968	Medicine	Roger Guillemin and Andrew Victor Schally discover substances in the brain that control the hormones produced by the pituitary gland.

1968	Oceanography	The Deep Sea Drilling Project begins taking samples of the ocean floor.
1968	Physics	Scientists at Bell Labs use pulses from a laser to measure picoseconds, the smallest unit of time ever measured.
1968	Space Exploration	The Soviet space probe Zond 5 is the first human-made object to orbit the Moon.
1968	Space Exploration	Aboard Apollo 8, Frank Bowman, James A. Lovell, Jr., and William A. Anders orbit the Moon ten times and return safely to Earth.
1968	Technology	Regular hovercraft service across the English Channel begins.
1968	Technology	The first supertankers for shipping petroleum are put into service.
1968	Technology	The Nuclear Materials Equipment Corporation begins sterilizing food with radiation.
1968	Technology	The U.S. Air Force begins using radar to detect changes in weather.
1968	Technology	The world's first supersonic passenger airliner, the Soviet Tupolev TU-144, is demonstrated.
1968	Technology	A power station using the energy of the tides begins operating in France.
1969	Astronomy	The pulsar at the center of the Crab Nebula is seen to give off pulses of visible light; this is the first optical pulsar.
1969	Astronomy	The Antarctic ice cap is discovered to be a rich source of meteorites.
1969	Biology	Exercise is shown to cause an allergic response in certain people.
1969	Biology	Jonathan Beckwith isolates a single gene involved in sugar metabolism in a particular species of bacterium.
1969	Biology	Gerald Maurice Edelman determines the structure of a gamma globulin, a type of protein involved in antibody formation.
1969	Biology	Dorothy Crowfoot Hodgkin determines the three-dimensional structure of insulin.
1969	Biology	M. Perutz determines the structure of hemoglobin, a protein found in red blood cells.
1969	Biology	In a highly controversial report, Arthur R. Jensen claims that genetic factors cause African Americans to score lower on standardized tests than white Americans.
1969	Biology	David Zipser discovers the function of the genetic codon UGA (uracil-guanine-adenine).
1969	Chemistry	C. H. Li chemically synthesizes the enzyme ribonuclease, the first enzyme to be synthesized.
1969	Computer Science	Bubble memory, which retains information when a computer is turned off, is developed.
1969	Medicine	The U.S. government bans cyclamates and limits the use of monosodium glutamate when these food additives are linked to cancer in animal experiments.
1969	Medicine	Dento Cooley and Domongo Liotta implant the first artificial heart.
1969	Physics	After years of development, the scanning electron microscope becomes available for scientific use.
1969	Physics	The Fermi National Accelerator Laboratory (Fermilab) is founded in Batavia, Illinois.

1969	Space Exploration	The first movement of human beings between linked spacecraft occurs between the Soviet vehicles Soyuz 4 and Soyuz 5 on January 14.
1969	Space Exploration	Apollo 11 reaches the Moon, and Neil A. Armstrong becomes the first human to step on its surface.
1969	Technology	The French/British supersonic passenger airliner Concorde makes its first flight.

Rose Secrest

■ Sports

Winners of Major Events

Major League Baseball

World Series
1960 Pittsburgh Pirates (NL) 4, New York Yankees (AL) 3
1961 New York Yankees (AL) 4, Cincinnati Reds (NL) 1
1962 New York Yankees (AL) 4, San Francisco Giants (NL) 3
1963 Los Angeles Dodgers (NL) 4, New York Yankees (AL) 0
1964 St. Louis Cardinals (NL) 4, New York Yankees (AL) 3
1965 Los Angeles Dodgers (NL) 4, Minnesota Twins (AL) 3
1966 Baltimore Orioles (AL) 4, Los Angeles Dodgers (NL) 0
1967 St. Louis Cardinals (NL) 4, Boston Red Sox (AL) 3
1968 Detroit Tigers (AL) 4, St. Louis Cardinals (NL) 3
1969 New York Mets (NL) 4, Baltimore Orioles (AL) 1

All-Star Games
1960 National League 5, American League 3
1960 National League 6, American League 0
1961 National League 5, American League 4 (10 innings)
1961 American League 1, National League 1 (9 innings, rain)
1962 National League 3, American League 1
1962 American League 9, National League 4
1963 National League 5, American League 3
1964 National League 7, American League 4
1965 National League 6, American League 5
1966 National League 2, American League 1 (10 innings)
1967 National League 2, American League 1 (15 innings)
1968 National League 1, American League 0
1969 National League 9, American League 3

Most Valuable Players

	American League	*National League*
1960	Roger Maris, New York	Dick Groat, Pittsburgh
1961	Roger Maris, New York	Frank Robinson, Cincinnati
1962	Mickey Mantle, New York	Maury Wills, Los Angeles
1963	Elston Howard, New York	Sandy Koufax, Los Angeles
1964	Brooks Robinson, Baltimore	Ken Boyer, St. Louis
1965	Zoilo Versalles, Minnesota	Willie Mays, San Francisco
1966	Frank Robinson, Baltimore	Roberto Clemente, Pittsburgh
1967	Carl Yastrzemski, Boston	Orlando Cepeda, St. Louis
1968	Denny McClain, Detroit	Bob Gibson, St. Louis
1969	Harmon Killebrew, Minnesota	Willie McCovey, San Francisco

Basketball

National Basketball Association (NBA) Championship
1960 Boston Celtics 4, St. Louis Hawks 3
1961 Boston Celtics 4, St. Louis Hawks 1

1962   Boston Celtics 4, Los Angeles Lakers 2
1963   Boston Celtics 4, Los Angeles Lakers 1
1964   Boston Celtics 4, San Francisco Warriors 1
1965   Boston Celtics 4, Los Angeles Lakers 1
1966   Boston Celtics 4, Los Angeles Lakers 3
1967   Philadelphia 76ers 4, San Francisco Warriors 2
1968   Boston Celtics 4, Los Angeles Lakers 2
1969   Boston Celtics 4, Los Angeles Lakers 3

NBA Most Valuable Players
1960   Wilt Chamberlain, Philadelphia
1961   Bill Russell, Boston
1962   Bill Russell, Boston
1963   Bill Russell, Boston
1964   Oscar Robertson, Cincinnati
1965   Bill Russell, Boston
1966   Wilt Chamberlain, Philadelphia
1967   Wilt Chamberlain, Philadelphia
1968   Wilt Chamberlain, Philadelphia
1969   Wes Unseld, Baltimore

American Basketball Association (ABA) Championship
1968   Pittsburgh 4, New Orleans 2
1969   Oakland 4, Indiana 1

ABA Most Valuable Players
1968   Connie Hawkins, Pittsburgh
1969   Mel Daniels, Indiana

National Collegiate Athletic Association (NCAA) Championship
1960   Ohio State 75, California 55
1961   Cincinnati 70, Ohio State 65
1962   Cincinnati 71, Ohio State 59
1963   Loyola-Illinois 60, Cincinnati 58
1964   UCLA 98, Duke 83
1965   UCLA 91, Michican 80
1966   Texas Western 72, Kentucky 65
1967   UCLA 79, Dayton 64
1968   UCLA 78, North Carolina 55
1969   UCLA 92, Purdue 72

Football

The Super Bowl
1967   Green Bay (NFL) 35, Kansas City (AFL) 21
1968   Green Bay (NFL) 33, Oakland (AFL) 14
1969   New York (AFL) 16, Baltimore (NFL) 7

National Football League (NFL) Championship
1960   Philadelphia 17, Green Bay 13
1961   Green Bay 37, New York 0
1962   Green Bay 16, New York 7

1963 Chicago 14, New York 10
1964 Cleveland 27, Baltimore 0
1965 Green Bay 23, Cleveland 12
1966 Green Bay 34, Dallas 27
1967 Green Bay 21, Dallas 17
1968 Baltimore 34, Cleveland 0
1969 Minnesota 27, Cleveland 7

American Football League (AFL) Championship

1960 Houston 24, Los Angeles 16
1961 Houston 10, San Diego 3
1962 Dallas 20, Houston 17
1963 San Diego 51, Boston 10
1964 Buffalo 20, San Diego 7
1965 Buffalo 23, San Diego 0
1966 Kansas City 31, Buffalo 7
1967 Oakland 40, Houston 7
1968 New York 27, Oakland 23
1969 Kansas City 17, Oakland 7

National Hockey League (NHL)

Stanley Cup

1960 Montreal 4, Toronto 0
1961 Chicago 4, Detroit 2
1962 Toronto 4, Chicago 2
1963 Toronto 4, Detroit 1
1964 Toronto 4, Detroit 3
1965 Montreal 4, Chicago 3
1966 Montreal 4, Detroit 2
1967 Toronto 4, Montreal 2
1968 Montreal 4, St. Louis 0
1969 Montreal 4, St. Louis 0

Tennis

Major Tournament Champions

Men

	Australian Open	*French Open*	*U.S. Championship*	*Wimbledon*
1960	Rod Laver	Nicola Pietrangeli	Neale Fraser	Neale Fraser
1961	Roy Emerson	Manuel Santana	Roy Emerson	Rod Laver
1962	Rod Laver	Rod Laver	Rod Laver	Rod Laver
1963	Roy Emerson	Roy Emerson	Rafael Osuna	Chuck McKinley
1964	Roy Emerson	Manuel Santana	Roy Emerson	Roy Emerson
1965	Roy Emerson	Fred Stolle	Manuel Santana	Roy Emerson
1966	Roy Emerson	Tony Roche	Fred Stolle	Manuel Santana
1967	Roy Emerson	Roy Emerson	John Newcombe	John Newcombe
1968	Bill Bowery	Ken Rosewall	Arthur Ashe	Rod Laver
1969	Rod Laver	Rod Laver	Rod Laver	Rod Laver

Women

	Australian Open	French Open	U.S. Championship	Wimbledon
1960	Margaret Smith	Darlene Hard	Darlene Hard	Maria Bueno
1961	Margaret Smith	Ann Hayden	Darlene Hard	Angela Mortimer
1962	Margaret Smith	Margaret Smith	Margaret Smith	Karen Susman
1963	Margaret Smith	Lesley Turner	Maria Bueno	Margaret Smith
1964	Margaret Smith	Margaret Smith	Maria Bueno	Maria Bueno
1965	Margaret Smith	Lesley Turner	Margaret Smith	Margaret Smith
1966	Margaret Smith	Ann Jones	Maria Bueno	Billie Jean King
1967	Nancy Richey	Françoise Durr	Billie Jean King	Billie Jean King
1968	Billie Jean King	Nancy Richey	Virginia Wade	Billie Jean King
1969	Margaret Court	Margaret Court	Margaret Court	Ann Jones

Golf

Major Tournament Champions

Men

	British Open	Masters	PGA Championship	U.S. Open
1960	Kel Nagle	Arnold Palmer	Jay Hebert	Arnold Palmer
1961	Arnold Palmer	Gary Player	Jerry Barber	Gene Littler
1962	Arnold Palmer	Arnold Palmer	Gary Player	Jack Nicklaus
1963	Bob Charles	Jack Nicklaus	Jack Nicklaus	Julius Boros
1964	Tony Lema	Arnold Palmer	Bobby Nichols	Ken Venturi
1965	Peter Thomson	Jack Nicklaus	Dave Marr	Gary Player
1966	Jack Nicklaus	Jack Nicklaus	Al Geiberger	Billy Casper
1967	Roberto de Vincenz	Gary Brewer	Don January	Jack Nicklaus
1968	Gary Player	Bob Goalby	Julius Boros	Lee Trevino
1969	Tony Jacklin	George Archer	Raymond Floyd	Orville Moody

Women

	LPGA Championship	Titleholders Championship	U.S. Women's Open	Western Open
1960	Mickey Wright	Faye Crocker	Betsy Rawls	Joyce Ziske
1961	Mickey Wright	Mickey Wright	Mickey Wright	Mary Lena Faulk
1962	Judy Kimball	Mickey Wright	Murle Lindstrom	Mickey Wright
1963	Mickey Wright	Marilynn Smith	Mary Mills	Mickey Wright
1964	Mary Mills	Marilynn Smith	Mickey Wright	Carol Mann
1965	Sandra Haynie	Kathy Whitworth	Carol Mann	Susie Maxwell
1966	Gloria Ehret	Kathy Whitworth	Sandra Spuzich	Mickey Wright
1967	Kathy Whitworth	Not held	Catherine Lacoste	Kathy Whitworth
1968	Sandra Post	Not held	Susie M. Berning	Not held
1969	Betsy Rawls	Not held	Donna Caponi	Not held

Boxing

World Heavyweight Champions

1959-1960	Ingemar Johannson
1960-1962	Floyd Patterson
1962-1964	Sonny Liston
1964-1967	Muhammad Ali*
1968-1969	Joe Frazier, Jimmy Ellis

*Ali was known as Cassius Clay when he won the title; in 1967, he was stripped of his title for refusing induction into the U.S. military. Frazier and Ellis were subsequently each recognized as champions until Frazier defeated Ellis in February, 1970.

Auto Racing

Indianapolis 500 Winners
1960 Jim Rathmann
1961 A. J. Foyt
1962 Rodger Ward
1963 Parnelli Jones
1964 A. J. Foyt
1965 Jim Clark
1966 Graham Hill
1967 A. J. Foyt
1968 Bobby Unser
1969 Mario Andretti

Horse Racing

	Belmont Stakes	*Kentucky Derby Winners*	*Preakness Stakes*
1960	Celtic Ash	Venetian Way	Bally Ache
1961	Sherluck	Carry Back	Carry Back
1962	Jaipur	Decidedly	Greek Money
1963	Chateaugay	Chateaugay	Candy Spots
1964	Quadrangle	Northern Dancer	Northern Dancer
1965	Hail to All	Lucky Debonair	Tom Rolfe
1966	Amberoid	Kauai King	Kauai King
1967	Damascus	Proud Clarion	Damascus
1968	Stage Door Johnny	Forward Pass	Foward Pass
1969	Arts and Letters	Majestic Prince	Majestic Prince

David L. Porter

■ Statistical Look at the United States

The following charts and graphs provide a snapshot of the major demographic trends in the United States during the 1960's.

U.S. Population, 1950-1970

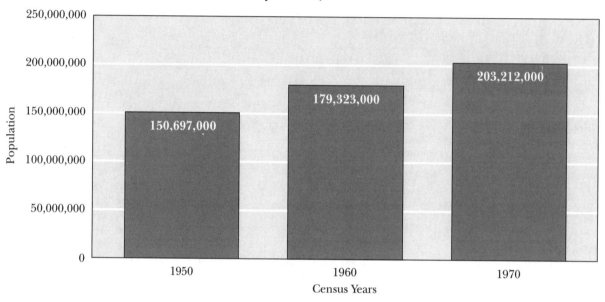

Source: U.S. Bureau of the Census.

U.S. Population by Race, 1960 and 1970

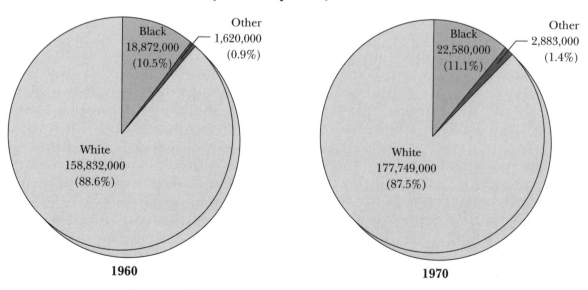

Source: U.S. Bureau of the Census.

U.S. Population by Sex, 1960 and 1970

Male
88,331,000
(49.3%)

Female
90,992,000
(50.7%)

1960

Male
98,912,000
(48.7%)

Female
104,300,000
(51.3%)

1970

Source: U.S. Bureau of the Census.

U.S. Birth and Death Rates, 1960-1970

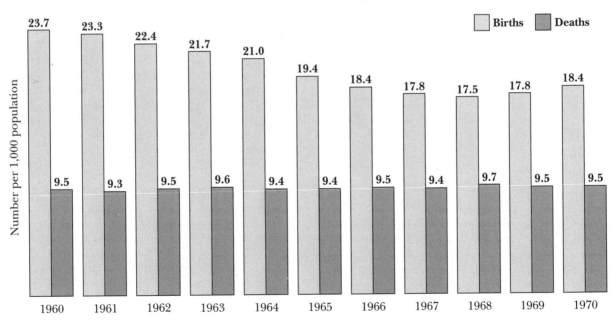

□ **Births**   ■ **Deaths**

Number per 1,000 population

Year	Births	Deaths
1960	23.7	9.5
1961	23.3	9.3
1962	22.4	9.5
1963	21.7	9.6
1964	21.0	9.4
1965	19.4	9.4
1966	18.4	9.5
1967	17.8	9.4
1968	17.5	9.7
1969	17.8	9.5
1970	18.4	9.5

Source: U.S. Department of Commerce, *Historical Statistics of the United States, Colonial Times to 1970, Bicentennial Edition, Part 1.* Washington, D.C.: U.S. Government Printing Office, 1975.

U.S. Life Expectancy by Sex, 1960-1970

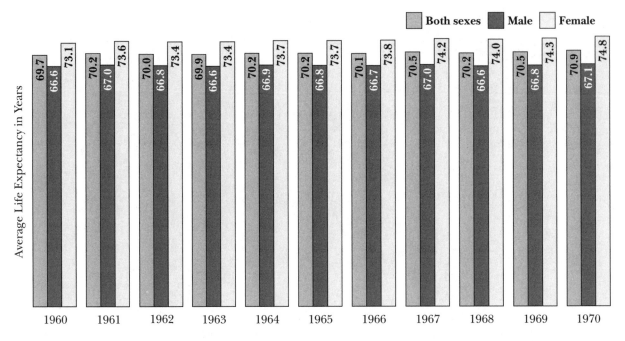

Source: U.S. Department of Commerce, *Historical Statistics of the United States, Colonial Times to 1970, Bicentennial Edition, Part 1.* Washington, D.C.: U.S. Government Printing Office, 1975.

U.S. Life Expectancy by Race, 1960-1970

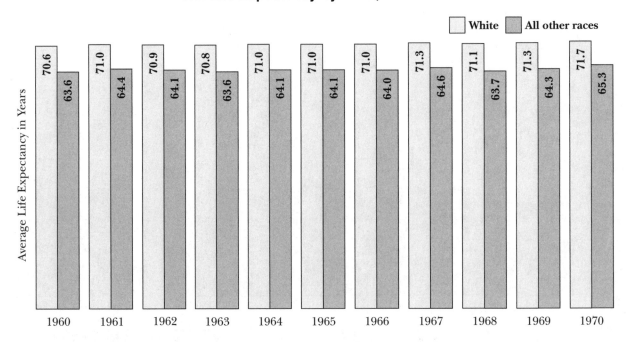

Source: Kurian, George, *Datapedia of the United States, 1790-2000, America Year by Year.* Lanham, Maryland: Bernam Press, 1994.

Crime in the United States, 1960-1969

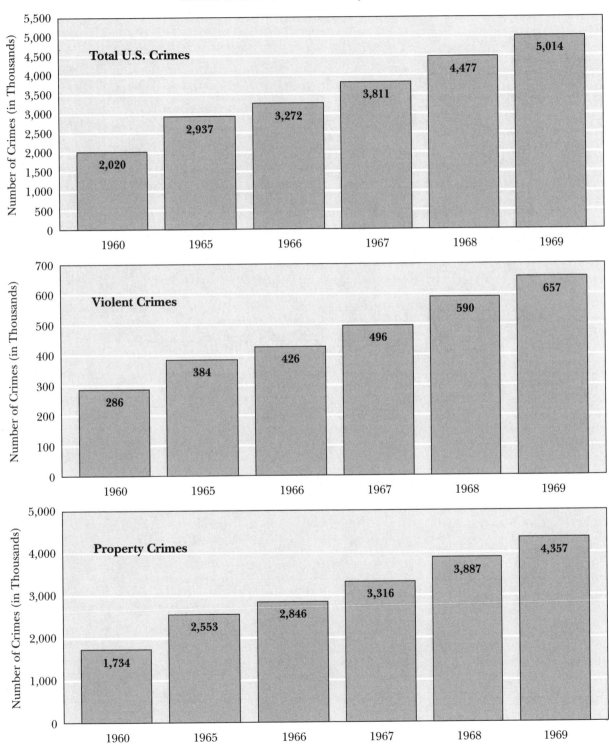

Source: Federal Bureau of Investigation.

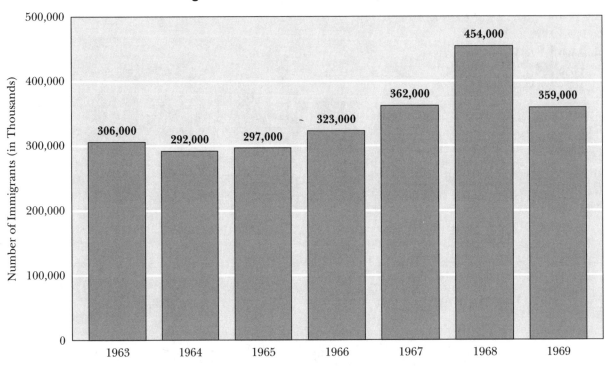

Immigration to the United States, 1963-1969

Source: U.S. Immigration and Naturalization Service.

Robert McClenaghan

■ Time Line

Subject Key

AMM	Arts, Music, Media	**ST**	Science and Technology
BDE	Business, Demographics, Environment	**SRG**	Social Revolution, Gender
CR	Civil Rights	**SP**	Sports
HGP	History, Government, Politics	**VW**	Vietnam War

1960

Date	Subject	Event
January 4	CR	The Atlanta School Board speeds school desegregation in compliance with U.S. District Court rulings.
January 23	ST	The bathyscope *Trieste* dives to the deepest point on the ocean floor, the Mariana Trench in the Pacific Ocean.
February 1	CR	Four African American college students stage a sit-in in a Greensboro, North Carolina, restaurant.
February 20	BDE	The U.S. Census Bureau reports a significant decline in the farm population.
February 23	CR	U.S. Supreme Court overturns conviction of two Arkansas women who refused to name members of the National Association for the Advancement of Colored People (NAACP) to Little Rock city officials.
February 28	CR	Independent Klans from seventeen southern states form the Knights of the Ku Klux Klan.
March 3	SP	Carol Heiss wins the ladies' world figure skating title.
April 17	CR	Julian Bond and other civil rights activists form the Student Nonviolent Coordinating Committee (SNCC) in Raleigh, North Carolina.
May	AMM	Folksingers Joan Baez and Pete Seeger perform at the Newport Folk Festival.
May 1	HGP	The Soviet Union shoots down an American U-2 spy plane over its territory.
May 2	HGP	Death Row prisoner Caryl Chessman is executed in California, setting off a national debate on capital punishment.
May 6	CR	The Civil Rights Act of 1960 becomes law.
May 10	ST	The USS *Triton* becomes the first submarine to circumnavigate the planet underwater.
August 9	SRG	Harvard professor Timothy Leary tries psilocybin mushrooms.
August 31	CR	When new housing measures do not pass the Senate, Congress uses a stopgap to extend existing legislation.
September	HGP	William F. Buckley, Jr., and others found the Young Americans for Freedom, a conservative young people's group.
September 3	SP	Carolyn Schuler wins a gold medal in swimming in the Summer Olympics.
September 11	SP	The Summer Olympics conclude in Rome: Soviets win forty-three gold medals—Americans win thirty-four.
September 26	HGP	The first of four televised debates between presidential candidates John F. Kennedy and Richard M. Nixon takes place.

October 3	CR	The Southern Christian Leadership Conference (SCLC) organizes protests against discriminatory voter registration practices.
October 12	HGP	Soviet premier Nikita Khrushchev bangs his shoe on a desk during his speech at United Nations.
October 19	CR	Civil rights activist Martin Luther King, Jr., and thirty-five student protesters are jailed in Atlanta, Georgia, after a sit-in.
November	HGP	President Dwight D. Eisenhower warns against the "military-industrial complex."
December	SRG	Birth control pills go on sale in the United States.

1961

January	AMM	Singer-songwriter Bob Dylan arrives in Greenwich Village and begins to perform in local clubs.
January 10	CR	Hamilton Holmes and Charlayne Hunter become the first African Americans to attend the University of Georgia.
March 6	CR	President John F. Kennedy issues an executive order requiring companies doing business with federal government to "take affirmative action" in hiring minorities.
April 12	ST	Soviet Yuri Gagarin becomes the first human in space.
April 17	HGP	A group of Cuban refugees opposed to Fidel Castro's regime invade their native land at the Bay of Pigs; by April 20, the Cuban troops have completely defeated the rebel force.
May 4	CR	Civil rights activist James Farmer and the Congress of Racial Equality (CORE) begin the Freedom Rides.
May 10	CR	Two Freedom Riders (one black, one white) are arrested in Winnsboro, South Carolina, at a segregated restaurant.
May 25	ST	President John F. Kennedy announces that the United States will send a man to the Moon by the end of the decade.
May 25	ST	Alan B. Shepard, Jr., becomes first American in space.
June	HGP	President John F. Kennedy and Soviet premier Nikita Khrushchev meet in Vienna for a summit.
August	CR	Native American college students found the National Indian Youth Council (NIYC) in Gallup, New Mexico.
August 13	HGP	East German troops close off checkpoints between East and West Germany and create the Berlin Wall.
September	CR	Civil rights activist Andrew Young assumes leadership of the Citizenship Education Program in Georgia and begins a drive for African American voter registration.
September 10	SP	Darlene Hard wins the national women's tennis championship.
September 11	BDE	The United Automobile Workers (UAW) begins a major strike against General Motors.
October 3	BDE	The United Automobile Workers (UAW) begins a major strike against Ford Motor Company.
December 11	VW	The first U.S. helicopter units arrive in Vietnam.

| December 14 | SRG | President John F. Kennedy establishes the President's Committee on the Status of Women, headed by Eleanor Roosevelt, to study ways of eliminating sex discrimination in the nation. |
| December 18 | SP | The Associated Press names track and field star Wilma Rudolph female athlete of the year for the second time. |

1962

February 7	HGP	SANE (National Committee for a Sane Nuclear Policy) holds its first antinuclear march on Washington, D.C.
February 20	ST	John Glenn becomes the first American to orbit Earth.
March	SRG	Comedian Lenny Bruce is tried on obscenity charges in San Francisco.
May 8	VW	Buddhist priests in Vietnam protest against President Ngo Dinh Diem.
May 31	HGP	German Nazi Adolph Eichmann is executed in Israel for crimes he committed during World War II.
June 12	SRG	The Students for a Democratic Society (SDS) releases the Port Huron Statement, a position paper for the liberal student group.
June 25	HGP	The Supreme Court rules against prayer in public schools in *Engel v. Vitale*.
July 19	ST	The Telstar satellite sends the first transatlantic television pictures.
July 22	ST	The first Mariner spacecraft is launched.
August 4	AMM	Actress Marilyn Monroe dies of an apparent drug overdose.
August 10	ST	The Soviet Ministry of Health announces the development of an abortion device capable of removing a fetus by vacuum in a nearly painless one-minute operation.
September 25	SP	Sonny Liston knocks out Floyd Patterson to become the world heavyweight boxing champion.
September 30	CR	James H. Meredith arrives in Oxford, Mississippi, to become first African American enrolled at the University of Mississippi.
October	SRG	President John F. Kennedy signs legislation to regulate LSD (lysergic acid diethylamide), a hallucinogenic drug.
October 22	HGP	President John F. Kennedy announces the imposition of a naval blockade against Cuba based on firm evidence that the Soviet Union has begun constructing offensive ballistic missiles in Cuba.
October 28	HGP	Soviet premier Nikita Khrushchev announces the withdrawal of all Soviet missiles from Cuba.
December 8	SP	Emile Griffith retains the world welterweight title by defeating Jorge Fernandez.

1963

January 14	CR	Alabama governor George Wallace gives a speech in which he vows to maintain "segregation forever."
February 20	SP	Willie Mays becomes the highest-paid baseball player in the nation's history.
March 19	SP	Wilt Chamberlain's field goal percentage (.528) sets a new National Basketball Association (NBA) record.
April 4-May 7	CR	Birmingham march against segregation occurs in Alabama.
April 10	ST	The USS *Thresher*, a nuclear-powered submarine, sinks in the North Atlantic.

April 12	CR	Martin Luther King, Jr., is among those arrested in a Birmingham, Alabama, march.
May 3	CR	Birmingham police commissioner Eugene "Bull" Connor orders fire hoses to be used against civil rights marchers in Alabama.
May 16	CR	Nearly two hundred civil rights protests occur in the South.
June 11	CR	African Americans Vivian Malone and James Hood confront Alabama governor George Wallace as they desegregate the University of Alabama.
June 12	CR	Civil rights activist Medgar Evers is shot dead in Jackson, Mississippi, in front of his home.
June 17	HGP	The Supreme Court rules that schools cannot require students to pray in *Murray v. Curlett.*
June 23	SP	Golf pro Julius Boros defeats Arnold Palmer to win the U.S. Open.
July	AMM	Nearly forty thousand people attend the Newport Folk Festival.
August 5	HGP	The United States, Soviet Union, and the United Kingdom sign a treaty severly limiting the testing of nuclear weapons.
August 28	CR	More than two hundred thousand people gather in Washington, D.C., for a nonviolent demonstration that culminates in a speech by civil rights activist Martin Luther King, Jr.
August 28	SRG	Two young working women are brutally murdered in New York City; the "Career Girl Murders" serve to highlight defendant's rights issues.
September 15	CR	The Sixteenth Street Baptist Church is bombed in Birmingham, Alabama; four young African American girls are killed.
October 7	HGP	Bobby Baker resigns from his position as secretary of Senate Majority Leader Lyndon B. Johnson amid charges of financial impropriety.
November 22	HGP	President John F. Kennedy is assassinated in Dallas, Texas.
November 24	HGP	Jack Ruby shoots Lee Harvey Oswald, the suspected killer of President John F. Kennedy, in Dallas, Texas.
1964		
January 4	SP	The Associated Press designates golfer Mickey Wright as the 1963 female athlete of the year.
January 11	ST	The Surgeon General issues a warning about the dangers of cigarette smoking.
January 11	SP	Peggy Fleming wins a title in ladies' figure skating.
January 20	SP	Baseball player Sandy Koufax is designated athlete of the year and receives the Hickok Award.
February 9	AMM	The Beatles, an extremely popular British rock-and-roll group, appear on *The Ed Sullivan Show.*
February 9	SP	The Winter Olympics conclude in Innsbruck: The Soviets win twenty-five medals to the Americans' six.
February 25	SP	Cassius Clay (later Muhammad Ali) knocks out Sonny Liston to become world heavyweight boxing champion.
March 9	HGP	The Supreme Court rules that awards for damages for libel violate the right to freedom of speech in *New York Times Company v. Sullivan.*

March 13	SRG	Kitty Genovese is murdered outside her apartment in New York City as her neighbors watch; their failure to help her becomes known as bystander apathy.
March 16	BDE	President Lyndon B. Johnson declares a War on Poverty.
March 27	BDE	An earthquake measuring 8.4 on the Richter scale devastates southern Alaska, causing sixty-six deaths.
June 5	SP	Jim Ryun becomes the first high school student to run a sub-four-minute mile with a time of three minutes, fifty-nine seconds.
June 10	BDE	The Equal Pay Act of 1963 goes into effect.
June 21	CR	Three civil rights workers, two white, one black, are murdered by the Ku Klux Klan in Mississippi.
June 22	SRG	The Supreme Court rules that Nico Jacobellis is not guilty of obscenity charges in *Jacobellis v. Ohio*.
July 2	CR	The Civil Rights Act of 1964 becomes law.
July 22	CR	Four nights of rioting start in New York City.
August 2	HGP	North Vietnam allegedly attacks a U.S. destroyer outside Vietnam's territorial waters in the Gulf of Tonkin.
August 20	HGP	President Lyndon B. Johnson signs a bill that launches the War on Poverty.
September 3	BDE	President Lyndon B. Johnson signs the Wilderness Act of 1964.
September 27	HGP	The Warren Commission makes public its report on the assassination of President John F. Kennedy, which concludes that the killing was committed by Lee Harvey Oswald acting alone.
October	SRG	The Free Speech movement begins at the University of California, Berkeley.
October 14	HGP	Soviet premier Nikita Khrushchev is ousted from office and replaced by Leonid Brezhnev.
October 24	SP	The Summer Olympics conclude in Tokyo: The Soviets win ninety-six medals to the Americans' ninety.
November	SRG	Comedian Lenny Bruce is convicted of obscenity charges in New York.
November 24	BDE	R. Sargent Shriver, director of the Office of Economic Development, unveils several new programs designed to help the economically disadvantaged: Job Corps, VISTA, and Neighborhood Youth Corps.
December 10	CR	Civil rights activist Martin Luther King, Jr., is awarded the Nobel Peace Prize.
December 14	CR	The Supreme Court rules that businesses open for interstate commerce must serve customers of any race in *Katzenbach v. McClung*.
1965		
February 21	CR	African American leader Malcolm X is murdered in New York City.
March 7-25	CR	Martin Luther King, Jr., and other civil rights leaders conduct the March on Selma.
March 23	ST	Virgil I "Gus" Grissom and John W. Young orbit Earth three times in the Gemini 3 flight.
March 24	VW	The Students for a Democratic Society (SDS) conducts its first antiwar teach-in at the University of Michigan.
April and May	HGP	President Lyndon B. Johnson orders federal troops to occupy and control the Dominican Republic.

April 9	SP	The Astrodome, a domed sports facility, opens in Houston, Texas.
June 3	ST	Edward H. White becomes first American to walk in space during the Gemini 4 flight.
July 30	HGP	President Lyndon B. Johnson signs legislation creating Medicare and Medicaid, designed to provide medical insurance for the elderly and indigent.
August 6	CR	President Lyndon B. Johnson signs the Voting Rights Act.
August 11	CR	Rioting erupts in Watts, a predominately African American neighborhood in Los Angeles, California.
September 16	CR	Grape workers go on strike in Delano, California.
October 9	HGP	Two-day power failure in New York City and Northeast begins; it is the largest power failure in U.S. history.
October 20	BDE	President Lyndon B. Johnson signs the Motor Vehicle Air Pollution Act.
October 22	BDE	The Highway Beautification Act becomes law.
December 5	SRG	The Vatican II concludes meetings in Rome and subsequently publishes new guidelines for the world's Roman Catholics.
December 15	ST	Gemini flights 6 and 7 rendezvous in space.
1966		
January 1	ST	Cigarette packages begin to carry health warning labels.
January 15	HGP	Coup attempt sets off Biafran War.
January 17	AMM	Truman Capote's *In Cold Blood*, a nonfiction novel about the murders of a family in rural Kansas, is published.
January 21-23	AMM	The Trips Festival, a rock concert and multimedia celebration, is held in San Francisco.
April 18	SRG	William H. Masters and Virginia E. Johnson publish *Human Sexual Response*, the first study in which researchers directly observed people engaging in sexual acts.
June 6	CR	James H. Meredith is shot while marching alone through Mississippi; other activists carry on the march as the injured Meredith recovers.
June 13	HGP	The Supreme Court rules that individuals being arrested must be informed of their rights in *Miranda v. Arizona*.
June 23	AMM	A film version of Edward Albee's *Who's Afraid of Virginia Woolf?* is released.
July 13	SRG	Richard Speck murders eight student nurses in Chicago.
August 1	SRG	Charles Whitman climbs the tower on the University of Texas campus in Austin, Texas, and goes on a killing spree.
September 15	ST	Gemini 11 shoots the first pictures of Earth's surface from space.
September 18	SRG	Valerie Percy, daughter of Illinois senator Charles Percy, is murdered.
October 29	SRG	Betty Friedan, the author of *The Feminine Mystique*, and other feminists form the National Organization for Women.
November	CR	The Black Panthers are formed in North Oakland, California.
November 8	CR	The first African American is elected to the U.S. Senate since Reconstruction.
November 16	SRG	Prominent doctor Sam Sheppard (the apparent basis for the television show *The Fugitive*) is found not guilty of killing his wife.

December	SRG	The Johns Hopkins Gender Clinic announces it has performed its first sex-change operation.
1967		
January	AMM	The Rolling Stones sing "Let's Spend the Night Together" on *The Ed Sullivan Show*, provoking controversy over the song's lyrics and furthering the group's bad-boy image.
January 15	SP	The Green Bay Packers and the Kansas City Chiefs play the first Super Bowl in Los Angeles.
January 18	HGP	In Massachusetts, Albert DeSalvo, the man believed to be the Boston Strangler, is convicted of armed robbery and rape charges but is not charged with the murders of eleven Boston-area women.
January 27	HGP	More than sixty nations sign the Outer Space Treaty prohibiting the use of space for military purposes.
January 27	ST	Astronauts Virgil I. "Gus" Grissom, Edward H. White, and Roger B. Chaffee die in a fire aboard the Apollo 1 space capsule during a simulated space flight.
February 5	AMM	The first episode of *The Smothers Brothers Comedy Hour*, a variety show featuring satire and political humor, is broadcast on national television.
April 5	SRG	A council made up of representatives of various counterculture groups in the San Francisco area meets to organize the Summer of Love.
April 13	AMM	Random House publishes Ira Levin's *Rosemary's Baby*, a dark tale of Satan worship.
April 19	CR	Demonstrators are arrested at Chicago's draft induction center.
May	HGP	Arab-Israeli tensions erupt in the Six-Day War.
May 12	CR	The Supreme Court strikes down a Virginia law prohibiting interracial marriage.
June 2	AMM	The Beatles' *Sgt. Pepper's Lonely Hearts Club Band* album goes on sale in the United States.
June 16-18	AMM	The Monterey International Pop Festival, a multiday concert in Monterey, California, initiates the Summer of Love.
June 20	SP	Boxer Muhammad Ali is convicted of violating Selective Service laws.
June 21	ST	The American Medical Association goes on record as favoring the liberalization of U.S. abortion laws.
July 12-17	CR	Racial riots erupt in Newark, New Jersey.
July 23-28	CR	One of the nation's worst urban race riots occurs in Detroit, Michigan.
September 9	CR	Random House publishes William Styron's *The Confessions of Nat Turner*, the best-seller provokes different reactions from black Americans than white Americans.
October	VW	Five days of antiwar and antidraft protests occur in Oakland, California; these demonstrations become known as the Oakland riots.
October 2	CR	Thurgood Marshall becomes the first African American on the Supreme Court.
October 6	SRG	Hippies in San Francisco stage the Death of Hippie event in response to commercialization, overcrowding, and other negative changes in the Haight-Ashbury scene.

October 9	SRG	The first edition of *Rolling Stone* magazine, a countercultural rock-and-roll magazine, goes on sale.
October 9	HGP	Che Guevara, Cuban revolutionary and military leader, is killed in Bolivia.
October 21	VW	Thousands of antiwar demonstrators march on the Pentagon to "exorcise" it.
November	CR	Oakland, California, police are involved in a shootout with Black Panther Huey P. Newton; demonstrations ensue.
November	CR	Mexican American college students form the Brown Berets.
November 28	ST	Graduate student Jocelyn Bell discovers and records pulsating radio waves, known as pulsars.
December 2	AMM	*Hair*, a rock-and-roll musical based on countercultural ideas and concepts, premiers on Broadway.
December 3	ST	Cardiologist Christiaan Bernard performs the first human heart transplant in South Africa.

1968

January 16	VW	Abbie Hoffman and Jerry Rubin found the Youth International Party, usually known as the Yippies.
January 23	HGP	The *Pueblo*, a U.S. intelligence-gathering ship, is captured by the North Koreans.
January 30-March 31	VW	Tet Offensive surprises American and South Vietnamese troops in Vietnam; this military victory becomes a psychological defeat for the United States.
February 1	ST	McGraw-Hill publishes Desmond Morris's *The Naked Ape*, which looks at humans as members of the ape family.
February 28	HGP	Kerner Commission Report on urban violence is published; it blames white racism for the riots that occurred in the nation's cities.
March 12	VW	Democrat Eugene McCarthy, a staunch opponent of the Vietnam War, wins 42 percent of the New Hampshire presidential primary vote.
March 31	HGP	President Lyndon B. Johnson announces he will not seek a second term.
April	VW	A chapter of the Students for a Democratic Society (SDS) occupies several buildings at Columbia University.
April 3	AMM	MGM releases Stanley Kubrick's *2001: A Space Odyssey*, a science-fiction cinematic marvel, in New York.
April 4	CR	Civil rights activist Martin Luther King, Jr., is assassinated in Memphis, Tennessee.
April 11	CR	The Civil Rights Act of 1968 becomes law.
April 11	CR	American Indian Civil Rights Act is signed into law
May 2	CR	Mule trains from across the country head for Resurrection City on the mall in Washington, D.C., as part of the Poor People's March.
May 12	VW	The United States and North Vietnam meet in the first of the Paris Peace Talks, designed to bring about an end to the Vietnam War.
May 17	VW	Roman Catholic priests Philip Berrigan and Daniel Berrigan and others raid the Selective Service office in Catonsville, Maryland.
May 20-June 14	VW	The Boston Five, pediatrician Benjamin Spock and four other antiwar activists, are tried for conspiracy to aid draft resisters.
May 22	ST	The USS *Scorpion* nuclear submarine sinks in the eastern Atlantic Ocean.

June 3	AMM	Pop artist Andy Warhol is shot by radical feminist Valerie Solanas.
June 4	HGP	Senator Robert F. Kennedy is shot and killed in Los Angeles after winning the California primary.
June 8	CR	American James Earl Ray is arrested in London and charged with killing Martin Luther King, Jr.
June 10	HGP	The Supreme Court establishes a taxpayer's right to sue the federal government with its ruling in *Flast v. Cohen.*
July 1	HGP	Sixty nations sign the Nuclear Non-Proliferation Treaty.
August 19	AMM	Farrar, Straus, and Giroux publishes Tom Wolfe's *The Electric Kool-Aid Acid Test*, an nonfiction novel describing Ken Kesey and the Merry Prankster's 1964 trip across the United States.
August 20	HGP	The Soviets invade Czechoslovakia.
August 26-29	HGP	The Democratic National Convention in Chicago is marred by violent, televised antiwar protests.
September	CR	The American Indian Movement is formed to defend the rights and further the welfare of Native Americans.
September 7	SRG	Radical feminists protest the Miss America Pageant in Atlantic City, New Jersey.
October 31	VW	President Lyndon B. Johnson orders a halt to all bombing in Vietnam.
November 5	HGP	Republican Richard M. Nixon defeats Democrat Hubert Humphrey in the presidential election.
November 5	CR	Democrat Shirley Chisholm of New York becomes the first African American woman elected to Congress.
December 3	AMM	Early rock star Elvis Presley appears in a well-received television concert after years of appearing mostly in music films.
December 21-27	ST	Apollo 8, with three astronauts aboard, circles the Moon ten times and photographs Earth.
1969		
January 12	SP	The New York Jets and the Baltimore Colts compete in the first Super Bowl in Miami.
March 1	AMM	Jim Morrison of the Doors is arrested on obscenity charges after the group's concert in Miami.
March 31	AMM	The Delacorte Press publishes Kurt Vonnegut, Jr.'s *Slaughterhouse-Five*, an antiwar novel.
April	SRG	Student protesters build the People's Park in Berkeley, California.
May 12	HGP	Supreme Court associate justice Abe Fortas resigns under threat of impeachment.
May 19	BDE	Random House publishes Jane Jacob's *The Economy of Cities*, a work critical of urban planners.
May 21	HGP	President Richard M. Nixon appoints conservative Warren Burger Chief Justice of the Supreme Court.
May 25	AMM	United Artists releases John Schlesinger's film *Midnight Cowboy*, which deals with the underside of city life.
June	CR	The League of Revolutionary Black Workers, a radical labor organization formed to fight racism within the United Automobile Workers, is formed.

June 28-July 2	SRG	A police raid on homosexuals at the Stonewall Inn in New York City results in rioting that ignites the gay liberation movement.
July 11	AMM	Harper Lee's *To Kill a Mockingbird*, a novel condemning racism in the South, is published.
July 18	HGP	A car driven by Senator Edward "Ted" Kennedy runs off the bridge on Chappaquiddick Island, Massachusetts, and plunges into the water, killing a female passenger.
July 20	ST	American Neil A. Armstrong becomes the first person to walk on the Moon.
August 9	SRG	The Charles Manson "family" murders Sharon Tate and several others.
August 15	AMM	Three hundred thousand youths attend the Woodstock Festival, a three-day rock festival in Bethel, New York.
August 17	BDE	Hurricane Camille strikes the coast of Mississippi and moves inland.
September	VW	The trial of the Chicago Seven, people involved in protests during the Democratic National Convention of 1968, begins.
September 3	VW	Ho Chi Minh, vital North Vietnamese leader, dies.
October 8-11	VW	Weathermen and other groups stage Days of Rage protests against the Vietnam War in Chicago.
October 30	CR	The Supreme Court rules that the nation should desegregate immediately.
November 13-15	VW	Antiwar protesters conduct the March Against Death in Washington, D.C.
November 20	CR	Members of the American Indian Movement begin a nineteen-month occupation of Alcatraz Island in the San Francisco Bay.
November 24	ST	The Apollo 12 flight puts Americans on the Moon for the second time.
November 24	VN	Lieutenant William L. Calley, Jr., is charged with the massacre of South Vietnamese civilians in My Lai in March, 1968.
December	ST	The U.S. Air Force shuts down Project Blue Book, an official investigation of unidentified flying objects (UFOs).
December 1	VW	The first national military draft lottery occurs.
December 4	CR	Black Panther members Fred Hampton and Mark Clark are killed by Illinois police.
December 6	AMM	The Rolling Stones perform at Altamont music festival; violence ensues and one concert-goer dies.
December 18	BDE	President Richard M. Nixon announces he will veto antipoverty funds allocated by Congress.
December 21	SRG	The Gay Activists Alliance is organized.

Compiled by Carl Singleton

■ Bibliography and Mediagraphy

This bibliography and mediagraphy presents books, audiovisual resources, and web sites that contain information about various aspects of the 1960's. The bibliography presents books and other publications broken into twelve subject categories: arts, music and media; business and the economy; civil rights; gender issues; government and politics; histories and studies; media; reference works and photograph collections; science and technology; social revolution; sports; and the Vietnam War. The mediagraphy is divided into three sections: electronic materials, videocassettes, and web sites, listed alphabetically by title or name.

Bibliography

Arts, Music, and Media

Adams, Hugh. *Art of the Sixties.* New York: E. P. Dutton, 1978. An excellent short survey of art, artists, and art movements in Europe and the United States during the 1960's. More than sixty photographs complement the discussion, and a short, useful bibliography is included.

Amaya, Mario. *Pop Art . . . and After.* New York: Viking Press, 1966. A rather popularly oriented discussion of every aspect of 1960's pop art. In early chapters, Amaya defines and explains the advent of pop art during the decade; in later chapters, he provides sections on particular artists such as Roy Lichtenstein, George Segal, and Andy Warhol. Photographs of works, an index, and a bibliography are included.

Budds, Michael J. *Jazz in the Sixties: The Expansion of Musical Resources and Techniques.* Iowa City: University of Iowa Press, 1978. A complete study of the various developments in jazz during the decade. Chapters are devoted to instruments, melody, meter and rhythm, influences, and legacy. This scholarly study contains chapter notations, a bibliography, and index.

Harris, Norman. *Connecting Times: The Sixties in Afro-American Fiction.* Jackson: University Press of Mississippi, 1988. A study in literary criticism. Discussions of the literature are organized topically to include the role of African Americans in the Vietnam War and the Civil Rights movement. Norman's thesis is that the fiction reveals that African Americans' goals in bringing about social change were not achieved. He examines six works, including Alice Walker's *Meridian* and George Davis's *Coming Home.* Cited references serve as a bibliography.

Hewison, Robert. *Too Much: Art and Society in the Sixties, 1960-75.* New York: Oxford University Press, 1987. A general discussion of the arts in the 1960's, with focus on the decade in Britain. Written by a university professor, the work attempts to relate various developments in all important aspects of 1960's culture; topics include pop art, theater of the absurd, theater of cruelty, and the role of the underground. Hewison pays particular attention to identifying and explaining "cultural politics," relating art movements to the political setting. The notes on sources serves as a bibliography.

Marowitz, Charles, Tom Milne, and Owen Hale, eds. *New Theater Voices of the Fifties and Sixties.* London, England: Eyre Methuen, 1981. A collection of several dozen articles, reviews, essays, and memoirs that discuss various dramatists and their works. All were previously published in *Encore,* an English theater magazine. Although most of the entries are about European plays and playwrights, the critical writings contains entries on American theater. Collectively, the essays give an overview of various movements in theater during the decade. The text is indexed.

Quinn, Edward, and Paul J. Dolan, eds. *The Sense of the '60's.* New York: Free Press, 1968. A collection of essays, stories, articles, speeches, and other writings. When published, the book was designed to be a reader in college classes. It serves as an amalgam of intellectual thought from some of the best writers, artists, journalists, and politicians active in the decade.

Tuchman, Maurice. *American Sculpture of the Sixties.* Los Angeles: Los Angeles County Museum of Art, 1967. A collection of photographs of and short essays about sculptures in the 1960's. These items, displayed at the Los Angeles County Museum of Art in 1967, represent the works of numerous important sculptors of the time. The essays are critical evaluations of the works and collectively serve as an explanation of American sculpture in the decade. The book contains a general bibliography on the subject; short biographies of the sculptors are given.

Business and the Economy

Berry, Brian J. L. *Growth Centers in the American Urban System, Volumes I and II.* Cambridge, Massachusetts: Ballinger, 1973. An academic study of growth centers in the United States during the 1960's. This work compiles endless facts and statistics about the nation's growth, including information on population, business, and industry. Maps, charts, diagrams, tables, lists, and graphs appear throughout.

Consumers Guide. Automobiles of the '60's. Lincolnwood, Illinois: Publications International, 1997. An informative study of some thirty popular automobiles produced in the United States in the 1960's. This book contains numerous photographs as well as short histories of the cars, information about sales, and problems and successes involving the various models.

Cunningham, James V. *Urban Leadership in the Sixties.* Waltham, Massachusetts: Brandeis University, 1970. A study of urban problems in the 1960's. The introduction, "A Disappointing Decade," sets out to show that failures in city governments and leadership far outweighed successes. Individual chapters are given to Cleveland, Chicago, Pittsburgh, and New Haven. The book attempts to show that lack of leadership was a common problem in many American cities during the decade. Copious, scholarly notes are included in the text.

Dobrow, Larry. *When Advertising Tried Harder: The Sixties, the Golden Age of American Advertising.* New York: Friendly Press, 1984. A record of important people and events in advertising during the 1960's. The author, a professor who worked for an advertising agency during the 1960's, explains important developments in advertising, particularly as television became more important. A short index is included.

Fairfield, Roy P., ed. *Humanizing the Workplace.* Buffalo, New York: Prometheus Books, 1974. Essays discussing various workforce issues from the 1950's through the early 1970's. Covered issues include the problems caused by affluence and poverty, the role of government, unions and strikes, women, child care, and technology.

Frank, Thomas. *The Conquest of Cool: Business Culture, Counterculture, and the Rise of Hip Consumerism.* Chicago: University of Chicago Press, 1997. A sociological study concerned with the effects of culture on business—and vice versa. The study looks at culture and business as manifested in politics, advertising, creativity, the stock market, and fashion. The appendix includes numerous charts and tables that supplement various aspects of the study. Photographs are included.

Hamm, Bobby L. *Theoretical Controversy and Macroeconomic Policies: 1960's and 1970's.* Ruston: Louisiana Technical University, 1974. A scholarly study of economic problems facing the United States in the 1960's and early 1970's. The author focuses on policies of the Richard M. Nixon administration, inflation, and what he calls the "behavior of money." His treatment is highly theoretical; however, his conclusions are supported by facts and figures. Equations, charts, and diagrams are included.

Hansen, Alvin Harvey. *Economic Issues of the 1960's.* New York: McGraw-Hill, 1960. A study of the nation's economy by an expert on the subject. The book attempts to identify problems in the economy and to shape their resolution. The author is greatly concerned with the prospect of an economic depression. The book looks at what might have happened to the nation's business and economy if the Civil Rights movement and Vietnam had never taken place. Appendices focus on urbanization, economic cycles, and the public debt.

Jameson, Kenneth, and Roger Skurski, eds. *U.S. Trade in the Sixties and Seventies.* Lexington, Massachusetts: Lexington Books, 1974. A collection of nine chapter-length essays examining various aspects of U.S. trade during the 1960's and early 1970's. The introduction and the overview present the attitudes and opinions of experts on American trade at the time. Subsequent chapters usually are devoted to particular and potential trading partners such as Japan, the Soviet Union, and China. Individual writers have contributed numerous tables, charts, and lists.

Levitan, Sar A., and Garth L. Mangum. *Federal Training Programs and Work Programs in the Sixties.* Ann Arbor, Michigan: Institute of Labor and Industrial Relations, 1969. A study focusing on the role of the federal government in labor training to eliminate unemployment. The book is organized into sections that describe various federal laws and their implementations, successes, and failures. Particularly valuable are discussions of the Job Corps and Neighborhood Youth Corps. Numerous charts and tables complement the study.

Schussheim, Morton J. *Toward a New Housing Policy: The Legacy of the Sixties*. New York: Committee for Economic Development, 1969. A study that examines federal housing policy from the 1940's through 1969. The author's primary concern is housing for low-income groups; he criticizes governmental legislation and bureaucracy and finds the government's efforts to be inadequate. Perhaps his main contention is that a new housing policy should have been implemented in the late 1960's.

Tompkins, Dorothy Campbell. *Poverty in the United States During the Sixties: A Bibliography*. Berkeley: University of California, 1970. An extensive bibliography covering every aspect of poverty in the United States during the decade. The entries are organized into six main topics (such as "Where Do the Poor Live?" and "Aspects of Life of the Poor") and then into subtopics. Contains a bibliography and index.

Civil Rights

Berman, Ronald. *America in the Sixties: An Intellectual History*. New York: Free Press, 1968. A study that focuses on the ideas and involvement of intellectuals and academics in the Civil Rights movement. The author argues that such people perceive a minority race as a "cultural object." He also discusses the emerging New Left in light of civil rights and other issues. Chapters are organized into topics such as religion, ideology, and activism.

Chalmers, David. *And the Crooked Places Made Straight: The Struggle for Social Change in the 1960's*. Baltimore, Maryland: The Johns Hopkins University Press, 1996. A history of the Civil Rights movement that gives a special interpretation to its significance. The work's overall purpose is to demonstrate that the Civil Rights movement was the model and catalyst for other important developments in the decade including the antiwar and antipoverty movements.

Donato, Ruben. *The Other Struggle for Equal Schools: Mexican Americans During the Civil Rights Era*. Albany: State University of New York Press, 1997. A study of the Mexican American struggle for civil rights during the 1960's and early 1970's with special emphasis given to the desegregation of public schools. A chapter is devoted to the issue of bilingual education. Most of the study focuses on Mexican Americans in California. Scholarly notes and a bibliography are included.

Horne, Gerald. *Fire This Time: The Watts Uprising and the 1960's*. Charlottesville: University Press of Virginia, 1995. A study that attempts to explain the causes of urban riots in the 1960's. Although the book focuses on events in the Watts area of Los Angeles, racial violence in other major cities is discussed. The author explains the various uprisings not only in terms of race but also with regard to such factors as economics, communism, police and government agencies, welfare, radicals and intellectuals, and the roles of various leaders. Black-and-white photographs and lengthy scholarly notes are included.

McEvoy, James, and Abraham Miller, eds. *Black Power and Student Rebellion: Conflict on the American Campus*. Belmont, California: Wadsworth, 1969. Most of the essays in the collection were written by college professors. Collectively, their purpose is to detail the role of African American students in the social revolution, with particular emphasis on higher education.

Sanger, Kerran L. *"When the Spirit Says Sing!" The Role of Freedom Songs in the Civil Rights Movement*. New York: Garland, 1995. A study of the "implicit rhetorical theory" of civil rights activists and an analysis of the lyrics of various freedom songs during the 1960's. Sanger shows how civil rights leaders used song to communicate their messages and motivate others. Much information is also given about the origins and traditions of African American music. The appendix contains the lyrics of dozens of the songs.

Nelsen, Hart M., and Anne Kusener Nelsen. *Black Churches in the Sixties*. Lexington: University Press of Kentucky, 1975. A sociological study of black churches, with particular emphasis on their role in the Civil Rights movement. Early chapters provide a history of black religion in the United States; later chapters explain various aspects of the churches' importance in the movement. Of particular interest are the two chapters that explore the connection between "religiosity" and "militancy." Scholarly notes, which also serve as a bibliography, accompany each chapter.

Stern, Mark. *Calculating Visions: Kennedy, Johnson, and Civil Rights*. New Brunswick, New Jersey: Rutgers University Press, 1992. A bittersweet interpretation of the contributions of Presidents John F. Kennedy and Lyndon B. Johnson to the Civil Rights movement. Historian Stern finds that these presidents often shaped events and gave them direction; however, they were sometimes hampered in their efforts because of immobility, politics, or lack of resolve. Kennedy is called the "Reluctant Hero" of the Civil Rights movement; Johnson is termed the "Coincident Hero of the Second Black Revolution." Appendices include an epilogue, scholarly notes, a bibliography, and an index.

Young, Andrew. *An Easy Burden: The Civil Rights Movement and the Transformation of America.* New York: HarperCollins, 1996. A history of the civil rights struggle in the United States from 1932 until 1972. The best section of the book is that devoted to the early 1960's. Written by an important leader who has an insider's insight, the work is informative and detailed in perspective and content. Black-and-white photographs of important events are included.

Gender Issues

Burwell, Jennifer. *Notes on Nowhere: Feminism, Utopian Logic, and Social Transformation.* Minneapolis: University of Minnesota Press, 1997. A general study of idealism and the perception of utopia in feminist thought. Burwell focuses on the second wave of the movement in the 1960's and 1970's and often touches on Marxism, radical feminism, and lesbianism. Scholarly notes and a lengthy list of cited works are included.

Costain, Anne N. *Writing Women's Rebellion: A Political Process Interpretation of the Women's Movement.* Baltimore, Maryland: The Johns Hopkins University Press, 1992. This analysis focuses on the politics (lobbying, funding, campaigning, and advertising) of passing legislation espoused by women's groups. Much of the author's information comes from personal interviews. The second chapter of the book describes the origins of the movement in the early 1960's. Appendices contain tables and charts to delineate the movement's successes in the political arena.

Davis, Flora. *Moving the Mountain: The Women's Movement in America Since 1960.* New York: Simon & Schuster, 1991. A comprehensive account of the women's movement in the United States from 1960 until 1990. Written by a journalism professor with a bent for social criticism, this balanced and factual chronicle provides details about the people, politics, and events important to the move-

ment and its accomplishments. Copious scholarly notes and a bibliography are provided.

Didion, Joan. "The Women's Movement." In *The White Album.* New York: Farrar, Straus & Giroux, 1979. An essay, synopsis, and interpretation of the women's movement. Didion concludes that the "women's movement is no longer a cause but a symptom."

Friedan, Betty. *"It Changed My Life": Writings on the Women's Movement.* New York: Laurel Books, 1991. A collection of Friedan's writings from 1963 to 1990. These various articles, addresses, and lectures encapsulate the important aspects of the women's movement: the beginning of the movement, the formation of the National Organization for Women, the fight for abortion rights, and the entry of women into politics. The author's lengthy introduction is especially noteworthy.

Linden-Ward, Blanche, and Carol Hurd Green. *American Women in the 1960's: Changing the Future.* New York: Twayne, 1993. A scholarly study designed as a comprehensive, interdisciplinary survey. Chapters take up the role of women in such matters as civil rights, education, work, culture, and the arts. A lengthy bibliography is included.

Sommers, Christina Hoff. *Who Stole Feminism? How Women Have Betrayed Women.* New York: Simon & Schuster, 1994. An analysis of the feminist movement and its leaders that criticizes "errors and excesses." The author points out factual errors in leading feminist books and documents. For example, Sommers uses the National Center for Health Statistics and other sources to show that Gloria Steinem's published claim that one hundred fifty thousand American women die of anorexia each year is wrong; the number is probably fewer than one hundred. Similarly, she undermines the validity of other feminist claims in issues such as academics, employment, rape, and self-esteem. Includes scholarly notes and an index.

Umansky, Lauri. *Motherhood Reconceived: Feminism and the Legacies of the Sixties.* New York: New York University Press, 1996. A book that differs from other histories of feminism and the women's movement in the 1960's because it focuses on motherhood. The author sees motherhood as the most pivotal, yet defining, issue confronting women; it is a metaphor for all other important issues. A lengthy bibliography is paired with scholarly notes.

Government and Politics

Andrew, John A., III. *The Other Side of the Sixties: Young Americans for Freedom and the Rise of Conservative Politics.* New Brunswick, New Jersey: Rutgers University Press, 1997. A history of the conservative movement in American politics in the 1960's. The author argues that, ultimately, the conservatives achieved their goals and defeated their liberal counterparts. Includes substantial scholarly notes and an index.

Burner, David. *Making Peace with the '60's.* Princeton, New Jersey: Princeton University Press, 1996. An examination of the ways that politics affected society and culture during the decade. Burner claims that division occurred on several fronts where there should have been unity; specifically, in civil rights, antiwar protests, and liberal politics. The extensive bibliography, organized topically, is integrated into contextual discussion and comments.

Ginsburgh, Robert N. *U.S. Military Strategy in the Sixties.* New York: W. W. Norton, 1965. A scholarly book that describes U.S. military strategy of the decade (although not concerning the Vietnam War). The author discusses the role of the executive and legislative branches of government in defining strategy and includes a chapter comparing the strategies of the United States and the Soviet Union.

Lasch, Christopher. *The Agony of the American Left.* New York: Alfred A. Knopf, 1969. Five extended essay-lectures about various matters confronting the Left in the 1960's. The author discusses what he calls a "crisis of radicalism" brought on by populism, socialism, and black nationalism. The work is as political as it is scholarly; Lasch argues that the goals of radicals can be achieved through understanding and correcting past failures.

Lee, Marvin A., and Bruce Shlain. *Acid Dreams: The CIA, LSD, and the Sixties Rebellion.* New York: Grove Press, 1985. An exploration of the effects of the 1960's rebellion on domestic and international politics. The author uses the "LSD story" to explain what he finds central to the various movements of the era. The book presents a history of LSD from its discovery in 1943 through the early 1980's and a discussion of the failure and collapse of the youth movement. It contains a rather extensive bibliography and an index.

Lyons, Paul. *New Left, New Right, and the Legacy of the Sixties.* Philadelphia, Pennsylvania: Temple University Press, 1996. A scholarly study of the two main currents of political thought and action during the decade, the Vietnam War and race relations. The author demonstrates that a significant and undying legacy from both the left and right survive in the nation's politics.

O'Neill, William L. *Coming Apart: An Informal History of America in the 1960's.* Chicago: Quadrangle Books, 1971. A twelve-chapter study of the most important historical movements of the 1960's. Both extremely readable and meticulously detailed, the overview of the decade provided by O'Neill focuses on changes in the nation's identity and culture. Each chapter concludes with a profile of one particularly significant topic. Black-and-white photographs are included, and the notes on sources also serves as a bibliography.

Thompson, Robert Smith. *The Missiles of October: The Declassified Story of John F. Kennedy and the Cuban Missile Crisis.* New York: Simon & Schuster, 1992. The most authoritative account of the Cuban Missile Crisis. The author provides clear and documented evidence that Kennedy did intend an invasion of Cuba and made major concessions in resolving the crisis with the Soviet Union. The scholarship includes an excellent bibliography.

Histories and Studies

Gitlin, Todd. *The Sixties: Years of Hope, Days of Rage.* New York: Bantam, 1987. A history of the cultural revolution in the 1960's. The author, a professor of sociology at the University of California, Berkeley, manages to coalesce such topics as civil rights, the Vietnam War, gender issues, and student rights into a single social study. The work is at once scholarly and readable. Gitlin attempts to explain the failures of 1960's activists and finds much hypocrisy in their actions.

Goldstein, Toby. *Waking from the Dream: America in the Sixties.* New York: Julian Messner, 1988. This study includes chapters on such important topics as American attitudes, the Vietnam War, civil rights, the underground culture, students and women, and politics and space. The highly readable text adopts the premise that the visionaries of the day were well-intentioned dreamers who should be applauded, perhaps, for their idealism. The book, which contains several dozen photographs, provides a quick, reasoned study of the 1960's without scholarly citations and explanations.

Haskins, James, and Kathleen Benson. *The 60's Reader.* New York: Viking Kestrel, 1988. The ten chapters in this historical overview examine the most readily identifiable trends and events of the decade, including civil rights, the Vietnam War, and the drug culture. This easy-to-read book is a worthy study of the period.

Inglis, Fred. *The Cruel Peace: Everyday Life in the Cold War.* New York: HarperCollins, 1991. This book chronicles the major events of the Cold War and attempts to explain their effect on the lives of common citizens on both sides of the Iron Curtain and in the United States. The author covers Cold War leaders, events, literature, films, spies, and other related topics and demonstrates the pervasive influence of the Cold War in defining the way people lived. A lengthy bibliography is provided.

Joseph, Peter. *Good Times: An Oral History of America in the Nineteen Sixties.* New York: Charterhouse, 1973. A collection of one hundred and twenty-five brief pieces compiled from tape-recorded interviews. The interviews, conducted toward the end of the decade, examine a wide variety of topics and issues. Among those interviewed are Tom Wolfe, Margaret Mead, Dean Rusk, Julian Bond, and Ken Kesey. The author also includes interviews with ordinary people (for example, people living on welfare in an apartment in Chicago). The optimism indicated by the title is evident in many interviews although not all.

Kunz, Diane B. *Butter and Guns: America's Cold War Economic Diplomacy.* New York: Free Press, 1997. A study of the Cold War from the 1940's until its end in 1989. Three chapters focus on events in the 1960's. Much of the author's attention is given to the role of global economics. A major aim of the author is to show that "guns and butter are not mutually exclusive." Several tables and figures are included.

Matusow, Allen J. *The Unraveling of America: A History of Liberalism in the 1960's.* New York: Harper & Row, 1984. A comprehensive history of the decade explaining major movements and events against the backdrop of liberal politics. The three major sections are on business and the economy, politics and government, and the counterculture. Although the author clearly sympathizes with liberal causes and programs, he believes liberal leaders, particularly John F. Kennedy and Lyndon B.

Johnson, ultimately failed to achieve all the goals they set.

Viorst, Milton. *Fire in the Streets: America in the 1960's.* New York: Simon & Schuster, 1979. A collection of lengthy interviews with fourteen prominent 1960's figures, including James Farmer, Tom Hayden, Stokely Carmichael, and Jerry Rubin. This study aims to make sense of the 1960's rather than to provide a history of the decade. The interviews not only are engaging reading but also provide insight into how the perspectives of famous people change over time. A bibliography and index are provided.

Media

Allen, Mary. *The Necessary Blankness: Women in Major American Fiction of the Sixties.* Urbana: University of Illinois Press, 1976. A general interpretation of the role of women in major fiction of the decade. Allen finds women typically depicted as "dreadfully bleak characters" and identifies around a dozen common portrayals—women who are destined to fail at motherhood, extremely materialistic, or on the border between sanity and insanity—that are responsible for this image. Works discussed include those of Thomas Pynchon, Ken Kesey, Philip Roth, John Updike, Joyce Carol Oates, and Sylvia Plath.

Glessing, Robert J. *The Underground Press in America.* Bloomington: Indiana University Press, 1970. A study providing a general overview of the underground press in the United States and focusing on the 1960's. Fourteen chapters examine various aspects of these newspapers and problems surrounding their publication. Particularly of interest is the discussion of how underground presses were used by radical groups. The appendix lists about two hundred underground papers.

Houston, Penelope. *The Contemporary Cinema.* Baltimore, Maryland: Penguin Books, 1966. Written by an international film critic and published in the middle of the decade, this book provides an insightful, contemporaneous perspective on major films, themes, actors and actresses, and directors. A list of films and directors and a bibliography round out the volume.

James, David E. *Allegories of Cinema: American Film in the Sixties.* Princeton, New Jersey: Princeton University Press, 1989. A serious look at American films made during the decade that fall outside the popular domain. Chapters discuss underground, political, pure, and women's films. Black-and-white photographs are included; the substantial list of cited works doubles as a bibliography.

Leff, Leonard J., and Jerold L. Simmons. *The Dame in the Kimono: Hollywood, Censorship, and the Production Code from the 1920's to the 1960's.* New York: Grove Weidenfeld, 1990. This survey of censorship of films in the United States focuses on changes in morality that are reflected in the films and existing codes. Films discussed include *Lolita* and *Who's Afraid of Virginia Woolf?*.

Lloyd, Ann, ed. *Movies of the Sixties.* London: Orbis, 1983. This book covers important films of the decade that were made internationally, although most of the entries are about films made in the United States or that were popular there. More than sixty writers discuss nearly as many films, although some of the entries are about important actors and actresses. Two or three photographs are on each page of text.

Peck, Abe. *Uncovering the Sixties: The Life and Times of the Underground Press.* New York: Pantheon Books, 1985. Written by a journalist who worked for the underground press during the 1960's, this book clearly demonstrates that such presses were part of the counterculture. The author takes specific historical events (such as the 1968 Democratic National Convention in Chicago and the Stonewall Inn riots) and examines how each was covered in underground newspapers. He provides copious citations and a useful bibliography.

Schwartz, Richard A. *Cold War Culture: Media and the Arts, 1945-1990.* New York: Facts on File, 1998. An encyclopedic reference work that examines the changes and influences at work in American culture as evidenced in art, literature, television, films, and the lives of prominent individuals.

Reference Works and Photograph Collections

Keylin, Arleen, and Laurie Barnett. *The Sixties as Reported by The New York Times.* New York: Arno Press, 1980. An oversized volume that presents headlines, news stories, and photographs from the decade as they were reported in the nation's leading newspaper. The text's usefulness is hindered by the absence of an index. Contents are arranged chronologically.

Layman, Richard, ed. *American Decades 1960-1969.* New York: Gale Research, 1995. An omnibus reference text organized into thirteen chapters on topics such as education, religion, and sports. Each chapter contains an overview and sections that cover major news stories. Generally, topics within chapters are arranged chronologically. Photographs appear on nearly every page, and a general bibliography with hundreds of entries is included.

Maxwell, Nigel. *Marketing the Sixties: A Bibliography.* Southhampton, England: Hampshire Technical Research Industrial Commercial Service, 1968. A bibliography of books and articles about international marketing in the 1960's. The entries are not annotated.

O'Neil, Doris C., ed. *Life: The '60's.* Boston, Massachusetts: Bullfinch Press, 1989. A collection of more than two hundred photographs documenting people and events from the decade, including the Cold War, the space race, the social revolution, and rock musicians. Each photograph is accompanied by paragraph-length comments. The introduction is by journalist Tom Brokaw.

Sann, Paul. *The Angry Decade: The Sixties.* New York: Crown, 1979. Perhaps the most readily available, comprehensive collection of photographs from the decade. More than four hundred black-and-white photographs are presented in chronological order with brief captions. The photographs complement and explain the author's running commentary. The index is thorough.

Workman, Brooke. *Teaching the Sixties: An In-Depth, Interactive, Interdisciplinary Approach.* Urbana, Illinois: National Council of Teachers of English, 1992. This classroom text focuses on the culture of the 1960's. Chapter topics include culture, history, architecture and painting, poetry, and dancing and music. The appendices include a bibliography organized according to chapter topics.

Science and Technology

Arm, David L. *Science in the Sixties.* Albuquerque, New Mexico: Air Force Office of Scientific Research Scientific Seminars, 1965. A general discussion of science in the 1960's intended for non-specialists. Its twenty-five essays cover such diverse subjects as physics, chemistry, psychology, and biology; some of the topics are more social in nature, such as one on science and technology in emerging nations. Most of the articles include charts and tables; a few contain photographs.

Bordley, James, and A. McGehee Harvey. *Two Centuries of American Medicine: 1776-1976.* Philadelphia, Pennsylvania: W. B. Saunders, 1976. A chronicle of developments in medicine in the United States written for general readers. The last third of the text covers the period from 1946 through 1976. Chapters are devoted to topics such as medical education, the federal government's role in medicine and health care, drugs, and specific treatments and breakthroughs in heart disease, genetics, immunology, virology, and cancer research. Scholarly references are included.

Butler, S. T., and H. Messel, eds. *Apollo and the Universe: Selected Lectures on the U.S. Manned Space Flight Program and Selected Fields of Modern Physics and Cosmology.* New York: Pergamon Press, 1968. A collection of essays written in the mid-1960's that discuss technical and historical aspects of the race to the Moon. Intended for non-specialists, the essays reveal an optimism about the eventual success of a manned lunar landing and the importance of such an event in history.

Evans, Christopher Riche. *The Making of the Micro: A History of the Computer.* New York: Van Nostrand Reinhold, 1981. A study that traces the development of computers and shows their importance in an overall scientific context. The book is organized chronologically, and later chapters relate progress in the 1960's and 1970's. Evans also discusses the role of computers in the space race and Cold War.

Holton, Gerald, ed. *The Twentieth-Century Sciences: Studies in the Biography of Ideas.* New York: W. W. Norton, 1972. A collection of fifteen essays focusing on the nontechnical aspects of developments in science during the twentieth century. Although the essays are only incidentally concerned with the 1960's, large sections of the discussion cover this time period. Topics include ecology, education, and DNA.

Lukoff, Herman. *From Dits to Bits: A Personal History of the Electronic Computer.* Portland, Oregon: Robotics Press, 1979. A history of computers from the end of World War II through the 1970's. Lukoff discusses the particulars of their development, the significance of their use and application, and the computer industry. Chapters examine specific kinds of computers and their functions. A short bibliography is included.

National Museum of History and Technology. *Technology and the Frontiers of Knowledge: The First Frank Nelson Doubleday Lectures, 1972-73.* Garden City, New York: Doubleday, 1975. A series of five lectures that explore technology as understood by important figures from arts and letters. Written and presented in the early 1970's, these lectures examine technology throughout history but most often discuss developments from the previous decade. Of particular note are Saul Bellow's "Literature in the Age of Technology" and Arthur C. Clarke's "Technology and the Limits of Knowledge."

Portugal, Franklin E. *A Century of DNA: A History of the Discovery of the Structure and Function of the Genetic Substance.* Cambridge, Massachusetts: MIT Press, 1977. A complete history of DNA from its discovery in 1869 through the mid-1970's. Although the book is technical and was written with the specialist in mind, much of it is readable for general audiences. The author presents detailed information about every aspect of DNA, particularly the unraveling of the genetic code in the 1960's. The lengthy scholarly notes serve as a bibliography.

Reiser, Stanley Joel. *Medicine and the Reign of Technology.* Cambridge, Massachusetts: Cambridge University Press, 1978. A general history of technology in medicine from the seventeenth century to the 1970's. Later sections focus on developments in the 1960's and 1970's. Topics include the advent of specialists, the shortcomings of technology, and automation. A substantial bibliography is included.

Shepard, Alan, and Deke Slayton. *Moon Shot: The Inside Story of America's Race to the Moon.* Atlanta, Georgia: Turner Publishing, 1994. A detailed personal account by two astronauts of the race to the Moon and the first visit there. The book reveals much information not available in the 1960's because of the role of the space race in the Cold War. The brief introduction by Neil A. Armstrong succeeds in emphasizing the importance of the mission to the nation.

Worster, Donald. *Nature's Economy: A History of Ecological Ideas.* Cambridge, Massachusetts: Cambridge University Press, 1994. A history of ecology and the environment from the eighteenth century to the 1990's. In the final section of the study, Worster examines the post-World War II period in which concern for the environment produced a political movement. Many of the chapters consider moral and ethical problems. A glossary and extensive bibliography are included.

Social Revolution

Archer, Jules. *The Incredible Sixties: The Stormy Years that Changed America.* New York: Harcourt Brace Jovanovich, 1986. A guide to the 1960's that presents major events and interprets them. The author provides a social criticism that delineates the decade's changes in culture.

Collier, Peter, and David Horowitz, eds. *Second Thoughts: Former Radicals Look Back at the Sixties.* New York: Madison Books, 1988. A collection of essays in which three dozen radicals (including Barry Rubin, P. J. O'Rourke, and Julius Lester) look back at their activities, achievements, and failures from a perspective of twenty years. This book is an excellent source for information on the impact of the 1960's on later decades.

Connikie, Yvonne. *Fashions of a Decade: The 1960's.* New York: Facts on File, 1990. A study of clothing fashions in the 1960's with several photographs on every page. The text is divided into eight parts that examine the impact of beatniks, music, space, flower children, and various trends and topics on fashions.

Gerzon, Mark. *The Whole World Is Watching: A Young Man Looks at Youth's Dissent.* New York: Viking Press, 1970. A study that focuses on the generation gap between baby boomers and their parents from the World War II generation. Gerzon attempts to explain social rebellion among the boomers coming of age during the 1960's and discusses the military draft, the media, attitudes toward sex, nuclear weapons, and various other topics. Although something of a self-appointed spokesperson, Gerzon gives a worthy explanation if not a provocative analysis.

Hartley, Ruth E. "American Core Culture: Changes and Continuities." In *Sex Roles in Changing Society,* edited by Georgene H. Seward and Robert C. Williamson. New York: Random House, 1970. An essay that identifies sex roles in American society at the end of the 1960's and attempts to explain changes in terms of overall patterns within the society. The article covers issues such as role-culture interaction, patriarchy, women and work, and equalitarianism. A bibliography is provided.

Levitt, Cyril. *Children of Privilege: Student Revolt in the Sixties.* Toronto, Canada: University of Toronto Press, 1984. The author details major aspects of student revolt, including social issues such as the Vietnam War, the military draft, and civil rights and problems in education such as student enrollment, campus life, and government research. The author discusses the student movement not only in the United States but also in Canada and West Germany. A rather extensive bibliography is provided.

Reynolds, Simon, and Joy Press. *The Sex Revolts: Gender, Rebellion, and Rock 'n' Roll.* Cambridge, Massachusetts: Harvard University Press, 1995. An examination of rock music and the sex revolt "through the lens of gender." The authors' overall point is that apparent freedom can mask the beginnings of domination. The book traces developments in the 1960's through the mid-1990's, examining their effects and repercussions. Dozens of rock figures and groups are analyzed.

Tipton, Steven T. *Getting Saved from the Sixties: Moral Meaning in Conversion and Cultural Change.* Berkeley: University of California Press, 1982. A social study of the period that focuses on religious aspects of the cultural revolution. Tipton is particularly concerned with how mainstream youth became involved with religions outside the mainstream, particularly Buddhism. The chapters "Culture and Counterculture" and "Communal Love and Order" further examine the matter.

Sports

Brock, Ted, and Larry Eldridge, Jr. *Twenty-five Years: The NFL Since 1960.* New York: Simon & Schuster, 1985. A book detailing the history of the National Football League from 1960 through 1984. Part I gives a year-by-year chronology of highlights; Part II describes all-star teams for each of these years; Part III (the bulk of the book) describes the most outstanding game from each year; Part IV presents famous quotations and interchanges from players, coaches, and sportscasters. The book has photographs on nearly every page.

Dolin, Nick, et al. *Basketball Stars: The Greatest Players in the History of the Game.* New York: Black Dog and Leventhal, 1997. A look at fifty important basketball players. A two-page spread (including profiles, statistics, and photographs) is devoted to each athlete. Several basketball stars from the

1960's are highlighted, including Kareem Abdul-Jabbar.

Gilbert, Tom. *Baseball and the Color Line.* New York: Franklin Watts, 1995. An historical study of racism, racial politics, and the ultimate downfall of segregation in baseball. The history gives details about major events and figures in the conflict from the origins of baseball as the national pastime through the mid-1990's. Chapter VIII ("They Never Had It Made") focuses on the period 1947-1994 and examines the controversy as it unfolded in the 1960's. A useful bibliography is included.

Gruver, Ed. *The American Football League: A Year-by-Year History, 1960-1969.* Jefferson, North Carolina: McFarland, 1997. A chronological history of the American Football League during the 1960's, with separate chapters devoted to each Super Bowl during the decade. The book-length study examines the role of television in defining the game, and early chapters focus on Lamar Hunt's leadership in organizing the league. The author also discusses important players and teams. The appendix contains statistical information.

Mead, William B. *The Explosive Sixties: Baseball's Decade of Expansion.* New Berlin, Wisconsin: Redefinition, 1989. A multipurpose omnibus collection detailing every aspect of baseball in the 1960's. The book's eleven chapters focus on important teams, major players, baseball's expansion, the Astrodome, and related topics. The book attempts to identify every important event, player, coach, and development in the game during the decade. The appendix contains statistical information, and photographs appear on nearly every page.

Radar, Benjamin J. *American Sports: From the Age of Folk Games to the Age of Spectators.* Englewood Cliffs, New Jersey: Prentice-Hall, 1983. A survey of American sports from the colonial period through the early 1980's. Chapters devoted to issues and developments important in the 1960's emphasize the significance of spectators and their effect on various games, including college sports and the Olympics. Particular topics include African Americans, women, and the status of professional athletes.

Roberts, Randy, and James S. Olson. *Winning Is the Only Thing: Sports in America Since 1945.* Baltimore, Maryland: The Johns Hopkins University Press,

1989. A general discussion of developments in American sports after World War II. Topics covered in the ten chapters include integration of teams, scandals, the media, mass culture, and economics. Black-and-white photographs are included. The bibliography is written as an essay.

Sage, George Harvey, ed. *Sports and American Society: Selected Readings.* Reading, Massachusetts: Addison-Wesley, 1974. A study dealing with the social aspects of sports in the United States. The book contains essays by various writers and major chapters on the history of sports in the United States, women and sports, race and sports, and sports in the school.

Staudohar, Paul D. *The Sports Industry and Collective Bargaining.* Ithaca, New York: ILR Press, 1986. A history of collective bargaining in American sports with chapters devoted to baseball, football, basketball, and hockey. The introductory chapter and the prologue identify similar and contrasting developments in these four major sports. Information pertaining to the 1960's can be readily located in the chronologically organized chapters, and the book has both name and subject indexes.

Wiggins, David K., ed. *Sport in America: From Wicked Amusement to National Obsession.* Champaign, Illinois: Human Kinetics, 1995. A history of sports in the United States spanning four centuries. The final section contains five essays dealing with sports and the Cold War, the Roone Revolution, steroids, roles of men and women, and the cultural significance of prizefighting. Index included.

Vietnam War

DeBenedetti, Charles, and Charles Chatfield. *An American Ordeal: The Antiwar Movement of the Vietnam Era.* Syracuse, New York: Syracuse University Press, 1990. A study that argues that the Vietnam War was both won and lost at home in the United States. The authors study the failures and successes of the antiwar movement and delineate the movement's effects on other aspects of life in the United States. Photographs of major antiwar events are included.

Hallin, David C. *The "Uncensored War": The Media and Vietnam.* New York: Oxford University Press, 1986. A study that ultimately argues that the media did not cause the United States to lose the Vietnam

War nor was it responsible for the withdrawal of American troops. Hallin focuses primarily on television coverage of the war but includes discussion of other media.

Karnow, Stanley. *Vietnam: A History.* New York: Viking Press, 1983. The best available study on the Vietnam War in its entirety, this book presents a comprehensive account of events both in Vietnam and the United States. Karnow manages to present an authoritative and objective history of the war, both in Asia and in the United States. It is well-researched, clearly written, and detailed. He also includes a general chronology of events, a cast of principal characters, notes, and photographs.

Moser, Richard R. *The New Winter Soldiers: GI and Veteran Dissent During the Vietnam War.* New Brunswick, New Jersey: Rutgers University Press, 1996. The author argues that opposition to the Vietnam War among soldiers and veterans was much more pronounced than it was thought to be. This history of the antiwar movement shows that veteran dissent was present and important from the beginning of U.S. involvement.

Powers, Thomas. *The War at Home: Vietnam and the American People, 1964-1968.* New York: Grossman, 1973. A study of the Vietnam War and its relation to other issues such as campus unrest, the youth rebellion, assassinations, and civil rights. The author concludes that the eventual withdrawal of American troops before victory was not the result of the peace movement.

Sanders, Jacquin. *The Draft and the Vietnam War.* New York: Walker and Company, 1966. A book providing information to potential draft evaders. The work contains information about draft laws and tests; it is openly political in its purpose.

Wells, Tom. *The War Within: America's Battle over Vietnam.* Berkeley: University of California Press, 1994. A history that chronicles with great detail the leaders, movements, activities, successes, and failures of those against the Vietnam War and those for it. Although the book is thorough and scholarly, the author has a noticeable bias against the activities of the government in its attempt to quell protest.

Zaroulis, Nancy, and Gerald Sullivan. *Who Spoke Up? American Protest Against the War in Vietnam 1963-1975.* Garden City, New York: Doubleday, 1984. A comprehensive study of domestic protest against the war in Vietnam. Events in Vietnam are presented in chronological order and described in a way that permits the reader to focus on their endless repercussions within the United States. Scholarly and documented, the work clearly believes in the morality of the protests and supports the end of the war.

Mediagraphy

Electronic Materials

Apollo NASA PPMI: "Lessons Learned." National Aeronautics and Space Administration, 1997. Two laser optical discs. A collection of videos covering the various Apollo missions and providing many details about the flights and major astronauts.

Black American History: Slavery to Civil Rights. Queve, 1994. Computer laser optical disc. A rather extensive multimedia presentation covering the history of African Americans from the colonial period to the late twentieth century. The 1960's are represented in topics such as the Kerner Commission Report, various civil rights protests and leaders, and Supreme Court cases. The disc is indexed.

Chicano! History of the Mexican American Civil Rights Movement. Produced by National Latino Communications Center. NLCC Educational Media, 1998. Computer laser optical disc. A documentary video series originally produced for television. The material covers events, organizations, and political movements of Mexican Americans from the U.S.-Mexican War of 1846-1848 through the later decades of the twentieth century. Much of the information focuses on events in labor, education, and politics from 1965 until 1975. Provides photographs, maps, and more than 250 biographies of important Mexican Americans.

Conflict in Vietnam. MicroProse Simulation Software, 1986. Computer disc. An educational computer game. Players learn the history of the Vietnam War from 1954 through 1972 while testing their skills on the digital battlefield.

Classified Top Secret. Infobusiness, 1996. Computer laser optical disc. A collection of Central Intelligence Agency documents declassified during the 1990's. Documents include those from the Office of Research and Estimates (1946-1950) and the National Intelligence Estimates (1950-1983).

Decisions, Decisions: The Cold War. Tom Snyder Productions, 1998. Computer optical disc. Primarily for use in history classrooms. This disc recalls and simulates conditions and events of the Cold War, raising the issues involved.

The Encyclopedia of the JFK Assassination. Zane Publishing, 1996. Computer laser optical disc. A multimedia reference work covering every aspect of the assassination of John F. Kennedy. The disc contains the home movie made by a bystander, more than three hundred photographs, twenty essays, and the Warren Commission Report.

Haight-Ashbury in the Sixties! Produced by Rockument. Compton's NewsMedia, 1995. Two laser optical discs. A documentary focusing on San Francisco in the late 1960's. The discs contain specific information about underground newspapers and art movements and give a history of the place and time.

The History of Rock 'n' Roll. Produced by Quincy Jones, Bob Metrowitz, and David Salzman. Time-Life Video & Television, 1995. Five laser discs. A series of laser discs for the hearing impaired. Content is arranged both chronologically and thematically, with such titles as "Rock 'n' Roll Explodes" and "Britain Invades, America Fights Back."

Investigating Twentieth Century Art. Produced by Tate Gallery (Oxford, England). ATTICA Cybernetics, 1994. Computer optical disc. A survey of twentieth century art that focuses on collections in the Tate Gallery. The disc attempts to show how art and culture are connected. One section provides information about pop art artists and their works.

Life Story. Produced by Kristina Hooper Woolsey and Marge Cappo. Wings for Learning, 1993. Computer optical disc. A history of the discovery of DNA and the scientists who unraveled the genetic code. The treatment of the subject is at once historical, biographical, and scientific. Segments of interviews are included, as well as articles devoted to specific aspects of the subject.

Martin Luther King, Jr. Optical Data Corporation, 1989. Thirteen computer discs. Part of the series "Instant Replay of History." These discs focus on the life of Martin Luther King, Jr., and his role in the Civil Rights movement.

NASA—The Twenty-fifth Year. Troika Multimedia, 1991. Computer laser optical disc. A history of NASA from the first Mercury flight through the first space shuttle. Contents focus on NASA's accomplishments. Much of the information is about early flight testing and research programs conducted in the 1960's.

Rock Expedition: The 1960's. Compton's NewMedia, 1995. Two computer optical discs. A collection of hit records from the 1960's. Users can watch rock groups perform some of their most popular songs and see interviews with the musicians and singers.

The Sixties: America 1960-70, A Multimedia History on CD-ROM. Produced by Marc J. Schulman and Awet I. Andemicael. MultiEducator, 1997. Two CD-ROMs. Primarily a collection of important photographs from the decade. The discs also contain one hour of video that narrates the most memorable of the decade's events.

Soul Expedition: The 1960's. Compton's NewMedia, 1995. Two computer optical discs. A collection of hit records from the 1960's. The discs contain interviews with the musicians and clips of soul groups performing their most famous songs.

Vietnam: A Visual Investigation. Medio Multimedia, 1994. Computer laser optical disc. Contains the full text of *America's Longest War* (1986) by George C. Herring. Additionally, this multimedia collection has excerpts from American Broadcast Company News coverage of the war in Vietnam and of protests at home and sections from the Pentagon papers.

The War in Vietnam: A Multimedia Chronicle. Macmillan Digital USA, 1995. Computer disc. Primarily a collection of articles from *The New York Times* and of clippings from broadcasts made by Columbia Broadcasting Service News. Also included are essays, photographs, and a searchable database listing Americans who died in the war.

Videocassettes

Apollo: Missions to the Moon. Produced by NASA. 203 min. Entertainment Distributing, 1995. Seven videocassettes. A series of documentary films about Apollo space missions 10 through 17 (excluding 12). The focus is on NASA's accomplishments; where appropriate, information is given about the space program of the Soviet Union and its corresponding efforts, failures, and achievements.

Chopper Wars. 57 min. Video Treasures, 1987. Videocassette. A collection of stories about U.S. helicopter pilots fighting in Vietnam. The video documents the daily activities and heroism of several pilots.

Cold War: Confrontation. Produced by the British Broadcasting Company. 20 min. Films, Inc.,

Video, 1981. Videocassette. A brief outline of the Cold War. The video focuses on two major events: the Korean War and the Berlin air lift. The production is part of the Twentieth Century History series.

Eyes on the Prize. Produced by Blackside. 360 min. Public Broadcasting Service Video, 1986. Six videocassettes. The definitive documentary on the Civil Rights movement in the United States. Comprehensive in scope, the videos cover major events and figures from the mid-1950's through 1965. Of the six tapes, five are devoted to the 1960's.

Eyes on the Prize 2: America at the Racial Crossroads (1965-1985). Produced by Blackside. 480 min. Public Broadcasting Service Video, 1987. Four videocassettes. A continuation of the original *Eyes on the Prize* series. These tapes document events from 1965 through the mid-1980's.

The Fabulous Sixties: The Decade that Changed Us All. Produced by American Broadcasting Company News and narrated by Peter Jennings. 550 min. MPI Home Video, 1990. Eleven videocassettes. A multipart documentary that focuses on news events in the 1960's. The first ten tapes each cover a year of the decade; the eleventh presents an overview.

Fields of Fire: Sports in the '60's. 58 min. HBO Home Video, 1995. Videocassette. A film that examines sports in the 1960's, setting major events against the backdrop of the decade.

Greatest Moments of the U.S. Open. Produced by Brad Turkel and narrated by Dan Hicks. 50 min. United States Golf Association, 1996. Videocassette. A documentary of American golf covering four decades. The section of the tape devoted to the 1960's pays special attention to Arnold Palmer and Jack Nicklaus.

In Remembrance of Martin. Produced by Public Broadcasting Service. 60 min. PBS Video, 1986. Videocassette. A documentary featuring newsreel footage of important events from the life of Martin Luther King, Jr. and interviews with family members and friends.

Jackie Onassis: An Intimate Portrait. Produced by Ellen M. Krass, Henry Schleiff, and Myrna Blyth. 46 min. Ellen M. Krass Productions, 1993. Videocassette. A film biography of the life of Jacqueline Bouvier Kennedy Onassis. The film was updated in 1994 to include coverage of her funeral.

John Lennon/Yoko Ono: Then and Now. Produced by Barbara Graustark. 56 min. Media Home Entertainment, 1984. Comments from Yoko Ono about her life with John Lennon. Music selections by both Lennon and Ono are included.

LBJ: A Biography. Produced by Public Broadcasting Service and written by David Grubin. 240 min. PBS Video, 1991. Four videocassettes. A political documentary detailing the life and presidency of Lyndon B. Johnson. The third tape of the series, entitled "We Shall Overcome," focuses on the Great Society and the war in Vietnam.

Mafia: The Definitive History of the Mob in America. Produced by David Osterland and narrated by Bill Curtis. 400 min. A&E Home Video, 1993. Four videocassettes. A history of the Mafia in major cities of the United States from Prohibition to the 1990's. Mob figures from the 1960's are discussed in detail, particularly their arrests and convictions.

The Nixon Interviews with David Frost. Produced by David Frost and directed by Jorn Wintehr. 371 min. MCA Home Video, 1992. Three videocassettes. A series of three television interviews with Richard M. Nixon. The second of these, entitled "War at Home and Abroad," focuses on Nixon's involvement in the Vietnam War.

The Official History of Baseball. Narrated by Warner Fusselle. 156 min. Major League Baseball Productions, 1994. Two videocassettes. An official history of the sport. The videos present the highlights of baseball during the 1960's, set in the context of the sport's overall history.

The Sensational Sixties. Narrated by John Facenda. 30 min. NFL Films and Video, 1980. Videocassette. A collection of National Football League football highlights from the decade. The video covers famous players, important games, and noteworthy plays.

The Sixties. 300 min. Columbia River Entertainment Group, 1997. Four videocassettes. A series of video tapes covering 1960 through 1964. The focus is on politics, life, and sports; producers relied heavily on newsreels.

The Sixties: 1965-1969. Narrated by Larry Lewman. 60 min. Barr Films, 1992. Videocassette. Part of a series entitled Focus on the Last Hundred Years. This film collection covers many important events of the decade; assassinations and riots are given particular attention. (The film originally appeared in 1982 under the title *The Angry Years.*)

Timothy Leary's Last Trip. 56 min. WinStar Home Entertainment, 1997. Videocassette. A film biography of Timothy Leary. This video features Ken Kesey and includes music by the Grateful Dead.

Vietnam: A Television History. Produced by Judith Vecchione, et al. 780 min. WGBH Boston Video, 1996. Seven videocassettes. The standard film documentary about the Vietnam War. The series of videos is organized chronologically into thirteen programs. Its coverage of the war provides balance between events in Asia and their effects at home. The series originally appeared in 1983.

Web Sites

Black Power Points
http://www.keele.ac.uk/depts/as/tebogo.html
A link site to dozens of other Internet sources such as the National Civil Rights Museum, the Martin Luther King, Jr., Memorial Anthology, and the Black Film Centre Archive. These links refer users to information on African American art, culture, history, and music.

Counterculture: 1960-1975
gopher://gopher.well.sf.ca.us/00/Community/60sTimeline/list60-75.nrf
A time line of hundreds of events from 1960 through 1975. Time line listings concentrate on the counterculture—people, organizations, events, and legal matters.

Documents from the Women's Liberation Movement: An On-line Archival Collection
http://scriptorium.lib.duke.edu/wlm
This collection of documents chronicles the women's movement in the 1960's and early 1970's. Subject categories such as "Medicine and Reproductive Rights," "Organizations and Activism," "Socialist Feminism," and "Women's Work and Roles" refer users to specific material.

John F. Kennedy Library
http://www.nara.gov.70/1/inform/library/jfk/
The homepage of the John F. Kennedy Library. Substantial information is provided about every aspect of Kennedy's life and presidency. The site features archives and manuscripts, audiovisuals, printed materials, and oral history interviews.

Lorraine's Sixties Page
http://www.geocities.com/SoHo/5317/sixties.html

A home page serving as a link to several dozen additional 1960's web sites. "Visit the Sixties" and "Flashbacks" are among the more interesting connections.

Music Festival Home Page
http://www.geocities.com/SunsetStrip/3869/
A collection of photographs and songs from three popular 1960's music festivals, those at Woodstock, Monterey, and Big Sur. Related information is provided, and links to other sites are listed.

National Civil Rights Museum
http://www.mecca.org/~crights/cyber.html
General material about the Civil Rights movement in the United States. Most of the information is about events from the 1960's, including marches, sit-ins, and other demonstrations. The cyber tour is arranged chronologically.

Oldies Music
http://www.oldiesmusic.com/open.htm
An attempt to collect all important information about popular rock songs and groups in the 1950's, 1960's, and 1970's. Lists of number-one songs, an "oldies calendar," and a section called "oldies news" are provided. Visitors can also log on to a chat line and check the bulletin board.

People's Park
http://www.dnai.com/~hi_there/people's_park.html
A site of interest to those seeking information and photographs about events in People's Park (Berkeley, California) in 1969. The site is something of nostalgic indulgence; yet most of the information here pertains to current issues in and around San Francisco.

Popular Culture in the 1960's: Influences in Film
http://www.d.umn.edu/cla/faculty/tbacing/hmcl3270/films.html
An on-line collection of information about movies, actors, and directors important to the decade. Reviews, comments, and discussion are provided.

Rock and Roll Hall of Fame and Museum
http://rockhall.com/induct/clardick.html
Home page hosted by Dick Clark from the *American Bandstand* television show. The site gives a cyberspace tour of the Rock and Roll Hall of Fame while providing information about its inductees. Other features are also provided.

Route 66

http://route66.netvision.be/

A web site featuring Route 66 as it was before the interstate highway system was built. Visitors can find information about the highway on any stretch of the road, which passed through eight states.

The '60's

http://www.hippy.com/60s.htm

An Internet link connecting to other 1960's sites. Photographs, terms, art, and music from the decade can be located by using links listed here.

The Sixties

http://home.ptd.net/~nikki/sixties.htm

An Internet link site connecting to dozens of additional 1960's sites. Although most of these are for musical groups, sites devoted to Vietnam, civil rights, and other important topics from the decade can be accessed.

The Sixties

http://www.slip.net/~scmetro/sixties.htm

A major Internet link site for dozens of connections to topics from the 1960's. Link lists are organized for easy access; topics are numerous and varied.

SIXTIES-L

http://lists.village.edu/sixties/HTML_docs/
SIXTIES-

A 1960's web site for researchers and scholars in any discipline. Visitors can register to receive daily postings (queries, comments, and book reviews). The site also maintains an archive section.

The Sixties Project and Viet Nam Generation, Inc.

http://jefferson.village.virginia.edu/sixties

Contains thousands of pages of documents. The site is organized into sections that refer users to the "Book Catalog," the "Viet Nam Generation," "References, Bibliographies, and Historical Documents," and "Personal Narratives Project."

Vietnam Veterans Home Page

http://grunt.space.swri.edu

"An interactive, on-line forum for Vietnam veterans and their families and friends." The site provides an omnibus of information about the Vietnam War; however, its main purpose is to help veterans locate other veterans and to provide a means of discussing the war. The "Post Exchange" lists publications about the war.

The Wild Bohemian Home Page

http://www.helcyon.com/colinp/bohemian.htm

A web site catering to decadent baby boomers. Visitors here will find information about hippies, the Beat generation, and the Grateful Dead, as well as a "Hip Dictionary."

Compiled by Carl Singleton

The Sixties in America

■ List of Entries by Category

Subject Headings Used in List

Arts
Asian Americans
Business and the Economy
Civil Rights
Crimes and Scandals
Drug Culture
Environment and Demographics
Film
Gender Issues
Government and Politics
Health and Medicine

Hippies and the Counterculture
International Affairs
Latinos
Laws and Acts
Literature
Media
Music
Native Americans
Organizations and Institutions
Science and Technology
Sexual Revolution

Social Revolution
Social Welfare
Space
Sports
Supreme Court Cases
Theater
Vietnam War
Visual Arts
Women's Issues

Arts

Albee, Edward
Arbus, Diane
Architecture
Art Movements
Baldwin, James
Brautigan, Richard
Brooks, Gwendolyn
Catch-22
Cat's Cradle
Cheever, John
Chicano: Twenty-five Pieces of a Chicano Mind
City of Night
Confessions of Nat Turner, The
Dances, Popular
Death of a President, The
Didion, Joan
Eat a Bowl of Tea
Federal Aid to the Arts Bill
Ferlinghetti, Lawrence
Ginsberg, Allen
Giovanni, Nikki
Hansberry, Lorraine
Hesse, Eva
House Made of Dawn
Indians
Lichtenstein, Roy
Literature
Lucky Come Hawaii
McKuen, Rod
Max, Peter

Merriam, Eve
Metafiction
Midnight Cowboy
Mountain of Gold
Oates, Joyce Carol
Oh, Calcutta!
One Flew over the Cuckoo's Nest
Op Art
Photography
Piercy, Marge
Poetry
Pop Art
Roth, Phillip
Sanchez, Sonia
Silko, Leslie Marmon
Simon, Neil
Slaughterhouse-Five
Social Satires
Stranger in a Strange Land
Susann, Jacqueline
Teachings of Don Juan, The
Teatro Campesino, El
Terry, Megan
Theater
Theater of the Absurd
To Kill a Mockingbird
2001: A Space Odyssey
Tyler, Anne
Updike, John
Warhol, Andy
Way to Rainy Mountain, The
Who's Afraid of Virginia Woolf?

Asian Americans

Eat a Bowl of Tea
Immigration
Lucky Come Hawaii
Mountain of Gold

Business and the Economy

Agriculture
Automobiles and Auto Manufacturing
Branch Banks
Business and the Economy
Corporate Liberalism
Credit and Debt
Economic Oppportunity Act of 1964
Economy of Cities, The
Gross National Product (GNP)
Inflation
International Trade
Japanese Imports
Motor Vehicle Air Pollution Act of 1965
Office of Minority Business Enterprise (OMBE)
Prosperity and Poverty
Unemployment
Unions and Collective Bargaining
Urban Renewal
War on Poverty

McGovern, George
McNamara, Robert
Marshall, Thurgood
Medicare
Memoirs v. Massachusetts
Miranda v. Arizona
Mississippi Freedom Democratic
    Party (MFDP)
Muskie, Edmund
My Lai Incident
National States Rights Party
Nixon, Pat
Nixon, Richard M.
Nuclear Test Ban Treaties
Nureyev Defection
Paris Peace Talks
Peace Corps
Powell, Adam Clayton, Jr.
Presidential Election of 1960
Presidential Election of 1964
Presidential Election of 1968
Pueblo Incident
Radio Free Europe
Reapportionment Revolution
Rockefeller, Nelson A.
Rusk, Dean
Six-Day War
Smith, Margaret Chase
Supreme Court Decisions
Tet Offensive
Vietnam War
Wallace, George
War on Poverty
Warren, Earl
Warren Report

Health and Medicine
Abortion
Agent Orange Controversy
Birth Control
Cancer
Cyclamates
Genetics
Heart Transplants
Human Sexual Response
Kidney Transplants
Lasers
Medicare
Medicine
Pill, The

Sex-Change Operations
Sexual Revolution
Silicone Injections
Thalidomide
Weight Watchers
World Health Organization
    (WHO)

Hippies and the Counterculture
Alice's Restaurant
Altamont Music Festival
Be-ins and Love-ins
Beat Generation
Communes
Counterculture
Cults
Death of Hippie
Drug Culture
East Village
Easy Rider
Electric Kool-Aid Acid Test, The
Fashions and Clothing
Fitzpatrick Drug Death
Flower Children
Free Love
Ginsberg, Allen
Grateful Dead
Greenwich Village
Haight-Ashbury
Hair
Hairstyles
Happenings
Hippies
Jefferson Airplane
Joplin, Janis
Leary, Timothy
LSD
Marijuana
Manson Murders
Monterey Pop Festival
San Francisco as Cultural Mecca
*Sgt. Pepper's Lonely Hearts Club
    Band*
Summer of Love
Teachings of Don Juan, The
Trips Festival
Underground Newspapers
Woodstock Festival
Youth Culture and the
    Generation Gap

International Affairs
Arms Race
Bay of Pigs Invasion
Berlin Wall
Biafran War
Castro, Fidel
Central Intelligence Agency
    (CIA)
Cold War
Cuban Missile Crisis
Czechoslovakia, Soviet Invasion
    of
Dominican Republic, Invasion of
Gulf of Tonkin Incident
International Trade
Japanese Imports
Liberty Incident
My Lai Incident
New York World's Fair
Nuclear Test Ban Treaties
Nureyev Defection
Paris Peace Talks
Peace Corps
Pueblo Incident
Radio Free Europe
Seattle World's Fair
Six-Day War
Space Race
Tet Offensive
Vietnam War
World Health Organization
    (WHO)

Latinos
Brown Berets
Chávez, César
Chicano Movement
*Chicano: Twenty-five Pieces of a
    Chicano Mind*
Grape Workers' Strike
Plum Plum Pickers, The
Teatro Campesino, El
United Mexican American
    Students (UMAS)
Young Lords

Laws and Acts
American Indian Civil Rights Act
    of 1968
Bilingual Education Act
Civil Rights Act of 1960

Civil Rights Act of 1964
Civil Rights Act of 1968
Economic Opportunity Act of 1964
Equal Pay Act of 1963
Equal Rights Amendment
Federal Aid to the Arts Bill
Higher Education Act
Housing Laws, Federal
Interracial Marriage Laws
Motor Vehicle Air Pollution Act of 1965
Voting Rights Legislation
Wilderness Act of 1964

Literature
Baldwin, James
Bell Jar, The
Brautigan, Richard
Brooks, Gwendolyn
Catch-22
Cat's Cradle
Cheever, John
Chicano: Twenty-five Pieces of a Chicano Mind
City of Night
Confessions of Nat Turner, The
Eat a Bowl of Tea
Electric Kool-Aid Acid Test, The
Ferlinghetti, Lawrence
Ginsberg, Allen
Giovanni, Nikki
House Made of Dawn
In Cold Blood
Literature
Lord of the Rings, The
Lucky Come Hawaii
McKuen, Rod
MAD Magazine
Merriam, Eve
Metafiction
Mountain of Gold
Oates, Joyce Carol
One Flew over the Cuckoo's Nest
Piercy, Marge
Poetry
Plum Plum Pickers, The
Roth, Phillip
Sanchez, Sonia
Silko, Leslie Marmon

Slaughterhouse-Five
Steppenwolf
Stranger in a Strange Land
Susann, Jacqueline
Teachings of Don Juan, The
Thompson, Hunter S.
To Kill a Mockingbird
Tyler, Anne
Updike, John
Way to Rainy Mountain, The

Media
Advertising
Allen, Woody
American Bandstand
Beach Films
Blow-up
Bruce, Lenny
Buckley, William F., Jr.
Butch Cassidy and the Sundance Kid
Censorship
Charlie Brown
Communications
Cronkite, Walter
Didion, Joan
Dr. Strangelove
Ed Sullivan Show, The
Farrow, Mia
Film
Flintstones, The
Gidget Films
Graduate, The
Gregory, Dick
Guess Who's Coming to Dinner
Hitchcock Films
Hughes, Howard
Hush . . . Hush Sweet Charlotte
In Cold Blood
James Bond Films
Jetsons, The
McLuhan, Marshall
Mailer, Norman
Media
Medium Cool
Motion Picture Association of America Rating System
New York Times Company v. Sullivan
Planet of the Apes
Rosemary's Baby

Sheppard, Sam
Smothers Brothers Comedy Hour, The
Sontag, Susan
Sound of Music, The
Taylor, Elizabeth
Telecommunications Satellites
Television
Thompson, Hunter S.
Tonight Show, The
Underground Newspapers
Weather Satellites
What Ever Happened to Baby Jane?
Wild Bunch, The

Music
Altamont Music Festival
Baez, Joan
Beach Boys, The
Beatles, The
Bernstein, Leonard
British Invasion
Brown, James
Doors
Dylan, Bob
Faithfull, Marianne
Folk Music
Grateful Dead
Hendrix, Jimi
Jagger, Mick
Jefferson Airplane
Joplin, Janis
McKuen, Rod
Minimalism
Monkees
Monterey Pop Festival
Motown
Music
Newport Folk Festivals
Ono, Yoko
Presley, Elvis
Price, Leontyne
Protest Songs
Rock Operas
Rolling Stones
Rubinstein, Arthur
Sgt. Pepper's Lonely Hearts Club Band
Simon and Garfunkel
Sonny and Cher
Streisand, Barbra

Supremes
Switched-on Bach
Thomson, Virgil
Tiny Tim
Tommy
Trips Festival
Twist
Wolfman Jack
Woodstock Festival
Zappa, Frank

Native Americans
Alcatraz Island Occupation
American Indian Civil Rights
  Act of 1968
American Indian Movement
  (AIM)
House Made of Dawn
Mills, Billy
National Indian Youth Council
  (NIYC)
Native American Fishing
  Rights
Silko, Leslie Marmon
Teachings of Don Juan, The
Wauneka, Annie Dodge
Way to Rainy Mountain, The

Organizations and Institutions
American Indian Movement
  (AIM)
American Nazi Party
Black Liberation Front
Black Panthers
Black United Students
Brown Berets
Central Intelligence Agency
  (CIA)
Congress of Racial Equality
  (CORE)
Hare Krishnas
Hell's Angels
Job Corps
John Birch Society
Ku Klux Klan (KKK)
League of Revolutionary Black
  Workers
Minutemen
Mississippi Freedom Democratic
  Party (MFDP)
Nation of Islam

National Association for the
  Advancement of Colored
  People (NAACP)
National Commission on the
  Causes and Prevention of
  Violence
National Indian Youth Council
  (NIYC)
National Mobilization
  Committee to End the War in
  Vietnam (MOBE)
National Organization for
  Women (NOW)
National States Rights Party
Office of Minority Business
  Enterprise (OMBE)
Radio Free Europe
SANE (National Committee for
  a Sane Nuclear Policy)
Southern Christian Leadership
  Conference (SCLC)
Student Nonviolent Coordi-
  nating Committee (SNCC)
Students for a Democratic
  Society (SDS)
United Mexican American
  Students (UMAS)
War Resisters League
Weathermen
Weight Watchers
White Panthers
World Health Organization
  (WHO)
Yippies
Young Americans for Freedom
Young Lords

Science and Technology
Air Pollution
Apollo 1 Disaster
Apollo Space Program
Arms Race
Birth Control
Cancer
Communications
Computers
Concorde
Condon Report
Cyclamates
Environmental Movement

Gemini Space Program
Genetics
Geodesic Domes
Heart Transplants
Kidney Transplants
Lasers
Mariner Space Program
Medicine
Mercury Space Program
Microwave Ovens
Moon Landing
Naked Ape, The
New York World's Fair
Nobel Prizes
Nuclear Reactors
Photocopying
Pill, The
Power Failure of 1965
Pulsating Radio Waves
Quasars, Discovery of
SANE (National Committee for
  a Sane Nuclear Policy)
Science and Technology
Scorpion Disappearance
Sealab
Seattle World's Fair
Sex-Change Operations
Silicone Injections
Space Race
Supersonic Jets
Telecommunications Satellites
Thalidomide
Thresher Disaster
Travel
Trieste Dive
Triton Submarine
2001: A Space Odyssey
Unidentified Flying Objects
VCRs
Water Pollution
Weather Satellites
World Health Organization
  (WHO)

Sexual Revolution
Abortion
Birth Control
Censorship
City of Night
Counterculture

■ Personage Index

Page numbers in boldface type indicate full articles devoted to the topic.

■ Index

Page numbers in boldface type indicate full articles devoted to the topic.